BiTTER SWEET TRUTH

An Autobiography

Esther Mary Lyons

BITTER SWEET TRUTH
Esther Mary Lyons
An Autobiography
A revised and added version of 'Unwanted'

Book produced by
Parker Pattinson Publishing
Suite 2, 211 Forest Road, Hurstville NSW 2220
Phone/Fax: (02) 9570 1923

Cover design: BEE ART

Typeset in Palatino 10.5/13

National Library of Australia
Cataloguing-in-Publication Data

Lyons, Esther M. (Esther Mary), 1940–
Bitter sweet truth : an autobiography.

Rev. ed.
ISBN 1 876409 14 2.

1. Lyons, Esther M. (Esther Mary), 1940–. 2. Women – Australia – Biography. 3. Anglo-Indians – Biography. 4. Women – India – Biography. 5. Lyons, Michael, 1901–1974 – Family. 6. Lyons family. I. Lyons, Esther M. (Esther Mary), 1940– Unwanted. II. Title

920. 720994

DEDICATION

This book is dedicated to my beloved mother,
Agnes Julius Shah (Sister Cecilia),
who struggled to bring us up throughout her lifetime.
To Late Dr Wallace Arthur Suchting,
retired Reader of Philosophy, Sydney University, Australia,
who inspired, encouraged and edited my work throughout.
Without his help it would never have been possible.
To Natalia Rai and Edward Wright,
who made it possible for us to live in a stable family,
giving us a home and opportunity for good education.
And to my father, Rev. Michael DeLisle Lyons, SJ.,
whom I loved dearly throughout my childhood,
but could never claim.

ACKNOWLEDGEMENT

I thank Jeff McQueen, the grandnephew of Father Michael Delisle Lyons, the Jesuit priest who supplied archive information, Christian Soulard a relative in Paris France, and Gail Moreau, the editor of the Michigan Habitant Heritage magazine.

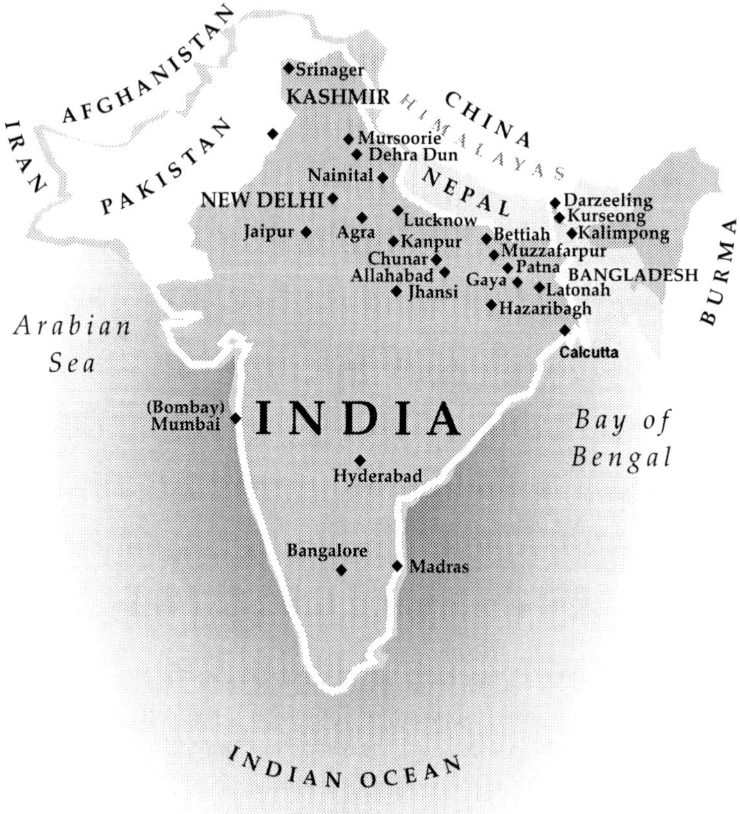
AFGHANISTAN
IRAN
PAKISTAN
Srinager
KASHMIR
CHINA
HIMALAYAS
Mursoorie
Dehra Dun
Nainital
NEPAL
NEW DELHI
Lucknow
Jaipur
Agra
Kanpur
Bettiah
Muzzafarpur
Darzeeling
Kurseong
Kalimpong
Chunar
Allahabad
Jhansi
Gaya
Patna
Latonah
Hazaribagh
BANGLADESH
BURMA
Calcutta
Arabian Sea
(Bombay) Mumbai
INDIA
Bay of Bengal
Hyderabad
Bangalore
Madras
INDIAN OCEAN

INDIA - 1999

PREFACE

This is the true story of a girl born in India in 1940.

'Minnie' survived without anyone to counsel her in the background of Indian and Anglo-Indian culture during and after the British Raj in India. Her father had disappeared a few years after her birth and no one seemed to know of his whereabouts. She had only the memories of him up to the age of three-and-a -half years, his fair skin, his blue eyes and the sound of his voice on which to conduct her search which took her to the United States.

The American agencies; the FBI and the CIA as well as the Jesuit Order of Catholic priests and missionaries knew the whereabouts of Michael DeLisle Lyons at all times, yet his own family believed he was in India.

Her deeper search for identity led her to discover her French and Irish ancestors who had migrated to the States of Michigan and Ohio in the eighteenth and nineteenth centuries.

The autobiography was written with the encouragement and help of friend, the late Dr. W. A. Suchting, Retired Reader of Philosophy, Sydney University. The author has changed the names of some of the living characters to protect their identities.

CONTENTS

1. 1922 – Detroit USA ... 9
2. 1991 – Sydney, Australia ... 23
3. 1942 – India – My father leaves ... 24
4. 1947 – Mother tries abandoning ... 39
5. Aunt Natasha's home town ... 61
6. Orphanages and homelessness ... 72
7. Fr Evans tells a Lie! ... 82
8. A stable life in a family ... 93
9. 1951 – At last an English school! ... 102
10. The facts of life ... 113
11. Is my father living ? ... 126
12. Humanitarian ... 138
13. Uncle Eddie dies ... 144
14. The Discovery ... 151
15. Superstitions and prejudice ... 161
16. My mother's story ... 165
17. High school certificate ... 172
18. A Rejection and a Recovery ... 179
19. From pigtail to perm ... 186
20. Secretarial job! No not for me! ... 191
21. Violet's first love and a public humiliation ... 197
22. A change for the better ... 205
23. When I fell in love ... 212
24. Broken engagement leaves its mark ... 217
25. A visit to the south ... 225
26. And he proposed to me ... 229
27. My trip to the USA and the search ... 240
28. Denver, Colorado, 1965 – The father I could not claim ... 254
29. Return to Motherland ... 272
30. Yet another rejection and suicide ... 279
31. Days of the nervous breakdown ... 287
32. A recovery and a winner ... 292
33. A model and a teacher ... 303
34. An attempt to find a husband ... 307

35. A popular woman of the year 1969 311
36. A desire for a respectable marriage 317
37. Another superstition and yet another rejection 326
38. Arrangements for immigration 330
39. Challenges of a new country, Australia – 1971 334
40. A marriage to remember 341
41. A mother with a family to care 349
42. 1981 – Living in Australia 355
Epilogue – American relatives with French and
Irish ancestors! 367
Bibliography 392

ILLUSTRATIONS

between pages 150 – 151, 278 – 279, 340 – 341

FAMILY TREES

pages 393 – 402

BITTER SWEET TRUTH

1

1922 — Detroit, USA

Michael Patrick Lyons sat at the end of the table with a glass of his favourite liquor, while his wife, Bertha Ida, sewed a patch on her husband's trousers. Life was difficult for her, with six children and a husband who continually lost his job and consoled himself with excessive drinking. Michael was shocked when their eldest son, Michael DeLisle, spoke of his desire to join the Jesuits as a missionary.

"Come on Papa, don't look sad. I'll visit you when I can. Besides, Chicago isn't far." Michael put his arms around his father reassuring him.

His father said nothing. He didn't approve of his son entering the church as a priest even though it was considered an honour at the time for Catholics to have a priest in their family. Often the eldest son joined the priesthood and very many went to India as missionaries.

Michael was young and slightly built. He was handsome, his clear, deep blue eyes reflected compassion as well as the brightness of intelligence. He had inherited the looks of his French ancestors, rather than his Irish.

"I don't know what is to become of us, with you gone, your brother Frank cannot help much. I have no job and your four sisters are very young. Did you not consider us before making this decision? After all charity begins at home!" Michael Patrick bellowed, shrugging his son's arms from his shoulders and taking a big gulp from his glass.

Michael Patrick was distraught with uncertainty. He knew he was a failure and unable to provide for the woman he loved so dearly and his children whom he adored. He had neither the qualifications nor the skills to compete in the work force. His father, Daniel Lyons was a blind broom maker in Springfield, Ohio, where he had settled with his mother, brother Michael and sisters, Johanna and Catherine. They had migrated from Cork in Ireland, during the height of the Potato Famine. There was no record of what happened to his grandfather. His grandmother, Ellen Lyons, spoke very little about her husband and where she came from. Ellen died in 1889 at his cousin Michael Reading's home in Springfield. She had been living with them for a long time and not with any of her own children.

Daniel Lyons, was a hard working man able to buy a few properties with his brother Michael, in Springfield, Ohio. He rented out one and lived in the other with his family of seven children. All went well until his wife, Catherine Leonard, died while giving birth to their eighth child. About the same time, his tenant refused to pay him rent. Since his notice to evacuate the house, was ignored, Daniel had no alternative but to force the tenant from the house. He climbed onto the roof and covered the chimney with a blanket while a fire was burning in the fireplace inside. The fire died out and the house was filled with smoke causing the tenants to leave. Daniel's brother, Michael and wife, Mary Ryan, took possession of the house by putting a lock on the door, but as Daniel came down from the roof, the tenant's wife hit him with a frying pan on the back of his head, which sent him blind. Never regaining his eyesight, he became dependent on his brother and sister-in-law at 36 Gallagher St. Springfield, Ohio, along with his children.

Michael Patrick had been just nine when his mother, Catherine Leonard died in childbirth. His sisters, Mary and Ellen worked as servants to support the family. His one brother Daniel Junior, became the editor of the Collier in Ohio and is reported to have written a dictionary which was used in New York schools for many years. After his father, Daniel Senior, died in 1885, Michael Patrick went to Detroit in search of employment. It was there that he met Bertha, his beloved French wife. He had great difficulty in finding permanent work, the frustration causing his alcoholism. He placed hope in his eldest son, Michael DeLisle, to shoulder his responsibilities and help support the family financially.

Bertha Ida came from an affluent French family. Her father, Peter Bienvenu dit DeLisle was a State Representative from the

Fourth District of Wayne County, 1903–1904. He was a Legislator and Justice of the Peace in Delray, Michigan and a prominent member of several fraternal societies as well as a Democrat in politics, who lead the movement to merge Delray with Detroit.

The scrapbook of his political career was kept in the Burton Historical Collection at the Detroit Public Library. Bertha's grandparents, Peter Bienvenu DeLisle and Zoe Riopelle, had the timber contract for Fort Wayne when it was built on the Detroit River. Her grandfather, Peter Bienvenu DeLisle was also known as "Welcome DeLisle" by many in the Delray and Detroit area. His mother, Monica Livernois, the daughter of Joseph Livernois, owned the land where the fort was built. The street, which started at the entrance to Fort Wayne, is called Livernois Avenue after them and is one of the longest named streets after a French family in the city and suburbs of Detroit.

Welcome DeLisle was a descendant of an old French family which came to Detroit early in the history of the settlement and owned a tract of land in the western part of the city. From there the DeLisles moved to River Rouge early in the 1800s and took up a tract of land adjoining Dearborn Road on which the old DeLisle residence is still standing. Welcome DeLisle was prominent in township affairs for many years and held the offices of Treasurer, Highway Commissioner and School Inspector. Bertha's ancestor, Francois Bienvenu dit DeLisle was born in southwest France, in the parish of St. Pierre, La Rochelle. He was the son of a very wealthy mother, Helen Guyard. Jehan Guyard, the father of Helen Guyard was a Royal Notary in Fontenay, France.

Francois Bienvenu was called DeLisle as a nom de guerre, or military nickname. He moved to Canada as a soldier. Lieutenant DeLisle accompanied Father Angeliran, a Jesuit, on missionary visits to different Indian groups. Father Angeliran was Superior of the missions to the Ottawa's at Missilimackinac de Ste. Marie du Sault (Sault St. Marie), to the Miamis, to the Illinois, to the Puans of the Bay and to the Sioux. He also accompanied explorer Antoine Cadillac on his foundling voyage to establish a trading post in what is now Detroit, in the state of Michigan, in 1701.

Bertha's grandmother, Zoe Riopelle was the daughter of Angelica Bondy. Through the Bondy family she was related to Francois De Chavigny de Berchereau and his wife, Madam Eleonore de Grandmaison. Francois De Chavigny was the Lord of the Region of Champagne in France. They migrated to Canada in 1640 and soon became one of the richest and most significant families at that time. Through the Bondy family she was also related to the Premier of Quebec, Maurice DuPlessis.

"Ah," moaned Bertha as she came back to the present. The needle pricked her finger and the blood stained the trousers.

Her husband shouted, "What have you done? That's the only pair of good pants I have. Tomorrow is my job interview. What will I wear?"

"I'll wash the bloodstain in time for your interview tomorrow," assured Bertha.

Her husband was forty-two but looked ten years older. Bertha remembered when they met in the church in 1900. He was handsome with blue eyes and dark hair. She had been engaged to be married to a wealthy Frenchman. She heard Michael's strong and resonant voice in the choir at 'All Saints' and it won her heart. She developed a friendship with Michael, which ended her engagement. Bertha and Michael were married against her parent's wishes and brothers, George, Francis and Louis DeLisle were disappointed because she was their only sister. They tried to prevent her from marrying an Irishman without resources, born in Ohio. She was stubborn. Her parents and brothers threatened to disinherit her. But being headstrong, nothing could stop her marrying Michael Patrick Lyons who was thirteen years her senior.

Bertha had won many beauty contests and was called the "Belle of Delray" by the press in and around Delray. She was spoilt and loved by all at home and in the French Colony, but the marriage with the Irishman had placed her outside her community. Life became very difficult, but it did not bother her initially. Her first child was born in Delray, in her parents' home on the 26th of September 1901, ten months after their marriage. Her father, Judge Peter Bienvenu DeLisle, named him Michael DeLisle Lyons. Over the years Bertha gave birth to nine children, three of whom died in infancy. As long as her parents, Peter Bienvenu dit DeLisle and Adeline Catherine Payette (Piette) were alive they helped her financially and gave her all the support she needed. Things only became difficult after their death but being extremely religious she learnt to have faith in God, which helped her in raising a big family, with little or no means.

When her eldest son, announced his desire to join the Jesuits' missionaries of Chicago, she was happy that he had the vocation. She believed that God had blessed them by choosing one of her children for missionary work. She trusted that with God's blessings she would manage somehow. Unfortunately, her husband did not share her pleasure. He was proud of his eldest son's achievements and hoped that one day Michael would get them the better life they had been dreaming of.

"Stop it! He has the right to choose his own way of life. He has done enough for us. Now he has to think of himself. God has given him the vocation to become a missionary, let him go in peace. I am sure the Lord will take care of us," Bertha said putting her sewing away.

She walked towards her youngest daughter, Marie, sitting quietly in one corner and looking bewildered. Marie was just six and a half. Bertha had lost two children, a son who at nine died of blood poisoning and a daughter who was crushed to death accidentally. She was left with six children, two boys and four girls. Her eldest son, Michael was leaving them at the age of twenty-one. She remembered him as a little boy, sitting at the back of the house, dismantling the parts off the radio and then re-assembling them together, just to find out how the radio worked!

In 1917, Michael had become the radio instructor at Cass Technical High School at the age of sixteen. Later he acquired the licence of the ham radio and in 1919 was the secretary of the *Detroit Radio Association*. He became the president and the editor of *The Detroit Radio News*.

Her son, nicknamed 'Meno', built *8MK*, the predecessor of *WWJ* Radio Station, in the backyard of their home on Green Avenue in Delray. Later he built the first apparatus for *WWJ*

Radio Station with his brother Frank. He made the first broadcast in the world from *WWJ* radio on 20th August in 1920. Michael and his brother, Frank, had also installed the first Police Car radio, capable of broadcasting and receiving, in Toledo, Ohio.

Bertha put her arms around Michael, "Son, I will not stop you. If you have the vocation to be a priest, then go and serve the Lord. He will take care of us. Keep us in your prayers. God bless you. We will visit you sometimes."

"Thankyou Mama. You have always inspired and guided me with your love and faith in the Lord. The Jesuits have promised that my sisters will get free schooling and Papa may get some work. There are many others suffering in the world, much more than us. I am going to help others. The Lord wants me to help them too." Michael replied.

"But Papa needs you. We need you here when Papa is without a job. You can go later, what is the hurry Meno?" fourteen-year-old Helen said. Her two sisters, Margaret, twelve and Loretta, eight stood quietly by her side and watched with sad expressions.

"Frank will take care of you. Papa will find something eventually, but the Lord needs me to take care of the many who have no one to depend upon. Have faith in the Lord, Helen. God who provides for the birds in the sky will take care of you all."

"Well, if you have decided to leave, then you'd better go now." Frank said picking up his elder brother's box. He was tall and well built. He had always worked with his brother, Michael and was sad that his brother whom had always been his guide and support was leaving. He desperately wanted to stop him, but he knew no-one could do anything once Michael had made up his mind. Michael was headstrong and stubborn like his mother. He always knew what he wanted and did what he wanted.

On August 6, 1922 Michael DeLisle Lyons entered the Society of Jesus, Missouri Province from Detroit. He spent his first years as a scholastic at St Stanislaus Jesuit Seminary in Florissant, Missouri. In 1927 he attended St Louis University for philosophy studies. At the end of the year he informed his parents of his decision to go to India as an American Jesuit missionary.

"But Meno, India is so far away! I am told that the country is full of wild animals; tigers, leopards and elephants. The wild animals and poisonous snakes roam the streets everywhere," Bertha despaired.

"My dear Mama, it is not as bad as that. The British have made the place much better than what it was before. They need missionaries to convert the pagans in India. I must save those souls and bring them to the Lord. The Jesuits have promised to take care of the missionaries' families, while we serve in India. Don't worry about me, Mama, God will take care of me, just pray and have faith."

But, that was not what his father, Michael Patrick wanted of his intelligent son. His second son, Frank was working very hard to support the family, but he was also planning on getting married. Helen, his eldest daughter then eighteen, was working in place of Michael and taking care of her younger sisters' education. Since Michael had joined the priesthood, all the good he did was forgotten. The *Detroit news*, the Cass Technical High school, *WWJ* radio, all forgotten. He had joined the priesthood to live a humble and insignificant life.

Father Michael Lyons left for India at the end of 1927 with ambitions to convert the pagans and to bring them to the fold of the Catholic religion. When his ship landed in Bombay, he was appalled with the poverty of the Indian people. It was something he had never imagined.

In 1928, he was assigned to a mission at Shembaganur, India, while he was still a scholastic. The next two years he taught at the Catholic Mission, Bettiah, Champaran District. He joined the Jesuit missionaries of the Patna diocese in the state of Bihar, North India and worked in the various villages. He was confronted with the plight of the poorest, the untouchables – low castes, who were treated roughly by the Hindus of the high caste. Missionaries found it easy to convert the starving into the Catholic Religion by tempting them with food and a Rupee each at the time of conversion.

Father Michael Lyons had a better idea for the speedy

conversion of the people in India and Asia: In the PHYSICS BULLETIN of the American Association of Jesuits Scientists (Central States Division), St. Louis University, St. Louis, Missouri, Volume VI, Number 3, dated January–February 1927, he sent his article: *Plan to utilise radio to hasten the conversion of Asia..*

He wrote: –

"It seems plausible that radio broadcasting could be used with excellent results now in the work of Christianising the billion inhabitants of the continent of Asia.

The advantages of radio are chiefly these: –

Catholics should do for religion what the British are about to do in India for sanitation and hygiene and education. They are erecting two high-powered broadcasting stations and intend to erect receiving sets for whole villages to listen to.

The intellectual apostolate is needed badly now. If we get the leaders we shall easily get the masses. Radio will carry our message right into the palaces of even maharajahs and the leaders of the sannyasis.

We cannot get enough nurses for the apostolate to the women, who are often enclosed and who offer a mighty obstacle to the conversion of the races, – at least for decades. Radio will carry nursery rhymes and medical advice and spiritual advice right into the zenanas.

Countries now inaccessible, as Nepal, Tibet, etc., (which the present Holy Father desires evengelized now) would have the word of God, brought in past guards and sentries.

One good speaker would do for a whole people. One priest learns Prabatiya, another Tibetan, etc. and each talks to one nation. The intellectual apostles at seminaries could fight the intellectuals of the other camp.

Programs, – just as they are now delivered in the West.

Stations with ranges of 300 miles radii would cost between $1000 and $5000 complete, omitting salaries of installers. If they are well placed they should reach nearly 100,000,000 souls each.

The rich, whom we seek to reach especially, can easily afford receiving sets. Europeans would be glad to hear us. There must be interest in radio in India, for already there are two stations each in Calcutta and Bombay and one each in Karachi and Madras, besides one in Burma and several in China and Japan.

Asia needs and can use broadcasters better than we can in the States, for here in the States the air is crowded with 600 Stations and Catholics are taken care of by 30,000 priests. If Asia is to receive a great increase of Christianity before it hardens we must act quickly and use something the Lord has sent us, – radio.

Cost, – suppose that $3000 was allowed for each station and $4000 for the travelling expenses and salary of a Catholic radio operator or engineer willing to sacrifice himself for the great work. The installation would then cost not over $25,000.

Financing. Money could easily be gotten in the United States from American Catholic and even non-Catholic radio fans. The novelty of the idea would appeal to their generosity.

Some slogan as this could be used: 'English Catholics pay the government for the privilege of listening in. You pay a fee of one dollar a year for the Asiatic stations in gratitude to God for your radio set.' 'Buy a machine gun for the New Crusade.'

These stations could be erected in the following places:

St. Mary's Seminary, Kurseong, Dargeeling, India

Shembaganur, Madura District, India.

Catholic school, Agra, India.

Father Simon Tang's mission, near Canton, China.

Cathedral, Pekin, China.

Catholic University, Tokyo, Japan.

Ateneo, Philippine Islands.

These centers were selected because these missionaries would probably be very glad to have these stations. Kurseong should be the first, as it is the center for influence in Bhutan, Nepal and Tibet.

The maintenance is very small. The greatest item is that of cost of an operator. Some Brothers could easily do this work in connection with seismographs and other scientific instruments."

✣ ✣ ✣ ✣ ✣

Father Michael Lyons had been the student of Father Macllwain, the seismologist of St. Louis University, USA, where he learned the elements of geology and established the foundations of an interest in the science and an eye for its practical application. Geology and radio had become his hobbies. He installed wireless in the convents for the foreign nuns to hear news of their countries in the villages of Bihar.

While he was at the mission in Shembaganur, he made a short visit to Bettiah, where he was asked to help on the annual sports day of the Catholic Girls School. He was at the field helping Father Batson with 'threading the needle' race. The girls ran towards their partners on the other end of the field and, after threading the needle, ran with their partners towards where he and Father Batson were standing. A very pretty young girl ran towards them and as she approached Father Batson, she tripped and fell. Father Batson, a fat, middle aged American priest, doubled up holding his stomach. She had bumped into him and accidentally dug her right elbow into it. Father Lyons ran to help Father Batson.

"I am very sorry, I did not see Father standing in the way. How is he? I am very sorry, please forgive me," said the young Indian girl of about fourteen years.

Father Lyons turned and looked at the girl. She was beautiful with her pale light skin and black, thick, long hair, which was neatly plaited and trailed down to her knees. She looked so innocent and ashamed that Father Lyons could not help putting his arms around her affectionately, "It was an accident, my dear. You are not to be blamed. Beside, he is all right, just needs a bit of rest… What is your name?" he asked.

"I am Agnes. I live here with the nuns because my village is very far. My mother is very poor." She replied, "Are you sure, Father Batson is going to be all right?" She asked again in Hindi with a Bihari accent. Father Lyons knew the Hindi and Sanskrit language. He studied Sanskrit from the books of Whitney and Lanman written by the Belgian Jesuit priests, before going to India. He also studied Santhali and Hindi in India so he could teach in Santhali and Hindi schools. He assured Agnes that everything was fine in the same accent as hers.

"She worries too much, Father," another girl said.

"And who are you?" Father Lyons asked looking at the girl next to Agnes. She seemed to be of the same age group, but taller and a little darker in complexion.

"I am Natasha. I live in Bettiah with my parents. Agnes

spends her weekends at my house sometimes. My parents like her very much and we are good friends," she replied.

"Your friend is a very fast runner, you should be proud of her." Father Lyons said looking at Agnes.

"She also has a very good voice. You should hear her sing in the choir at church. She is also good at playing the harmonium and Sister is teaching her the organ. Agnes is also very good at drawing and embroidery work. She is very clever," Natasha said.

"Then I must come to hear her sing in the church this Sunday," Father Lyons said as Agnes blushed. Unfortunately he could not attend that Sunday as he was ordered to return to Shembanganur but he thought of her often. The following year he was returned to Krist Rajah School in Bettiah, where he again met Agnes, grown into a beautiful, shy young lady. She had stopped wearing the long skirt and blouse, a lahanga and choli, instead she wore the elegant white *sari* and blouse. He was always in the Church to hear her sing solo at the choir and play the organ. While at Bettiah, he received the sad news that on 28th September 1930, his father had an accident in Detroit. He was hit by a streetcar and instantly died.

From 1931 Father Lyons was a student of theology for two years and on 21st November 1933 he was ordained in Kurseong and remained as a student at St Mary's until the end of 1934. In 1935, he was at St Stanislaus College, Hazaribagh, Bihar. By then his brother Frank was living with his wife and many children, his sister Helen had married a Protestant in 1928, much to his displeasure. Father Lyons blamed his mother for not being strict with her, but she was dependent on her daughters.

Father Lyons spent 1936 at Krist Raja High School, Bettiah, where he met Agnes again. She and Natasha were still good friends and even had a big party to celebrate their friendship – '*Dosti*', as it was called in those days when two people proclaimed that they were good friends to the community. As two good friends they shared the same interests and even dressed alike in the same colour and pattern of *sari*. They studied together in Bettiah up to Class Seven in the same Catholic school, trained as Primary Teachers and joined the convent to become Sacred Heart nuns together. Agnes was liked by everyone in

Natasha's house. As a nun, Agnes became 'Sister Cecilia'.

While Father Lyons was in Bettiah, there was an earthquake. The old Catholic Cathedral went crumbling down. Many buildings collapsed and several people died. Father Lyons was helping in the Primary school on the day the earthquake occurred. He was checking the school premises and the classrooms when he saw Sister Cecilia being trampled by her Class Three students. They were all trying to get through the one door. If it were not for Father, the children and she would have perished under a wall of the classroom, which came crashing down just as they were evacuated.

"Thankyou, Father," she said as she rushed into safety with the children. Father Lyons stood dumbfounded. He had never been able to forget Agnes from the first time he had met her as a teenager at the race.

For the following year, 1937, he was assigned residence at the Bishop's House, Bankipore, Patna District, where he served for two years as a pastor of the pro-cathedral, director of sodalities and missionary. He learnt the many native languages of the villages all over India. While doing his missionary work, Father noticed the principal occurrences of radioactive minerals in India, with particular reference to thorium-bearing sands in South India and urani-nite in Gaya District, Province of Bihar and in the Chief Commissionership of Ajmer-Merwara, Rajputana. He was able to "translate" his geological language into terms comprehensible to the villagers whose sometimes amazingly extensive information about the occurrences of various kinds of rocks and minerals in their own localities were very interesting for him. At times he even indulged upon getting the villagers to hand pick the various minerals, especially 'beryl' in Bihar and shipped them to the USA. The money he received from the sale of the minerals was used for the poor in his mission.

It was while he was in Patna that he received the sad news that on the 31st March 1937, his mother, Bertha Ida, died of pneumonia and depression. She became a fatalistic and believed in tealeaf reading and fortune telling. She had been continually treated for depression after the death of her husband. About that time Father Michael Lyons was becoming disillusioned with the Jesuits, who according to his observation were spending more on their own comforts and less on the poor suffering people of India.

From 1939 he served at the Catholic Church, Gaya for two years. He made frequent short trips to Bettiah. He met Natasha by chance who informed him that her friend, Sister Cecilia, was not happy in the convent there. Her superior was unfair towards her because of her popularity with the students and parents and because she had won two art competitions in the State.

"They are all jealous of her," Natasha added.

"Well," said Father Lyons, "if she is not happy then she should be transferred to my parish in Gaya where I am the Parish Priest."

A few months later, both Agnes and Natasha went to Gaya. Father Lyons made sure that they were appointed as Kindergarten teachers in his mission school. He employed Agnes' only brother, Simon, from the village of Latonah, as his cook. Agnes was overjoyed and grateful since this was the first time she had her brother and his family live near her.

Father Lyons took ill with malaria and asked for 'Sister Cecilia' to nurse him. She was pleased to repay him for his kindness over the years. Her devotion and care got Father Lyons strong and healthy. He discussed resigning from the Jesuits to set up a home with Sister Cecilia as his wife.

A few months later, Natasha left the Convent with her friend, Sister Cecilia, who was carrying the priest's child. Natasha's conservative family in Bettiah were mortified. They had felt honoured when their daughter, joined the convent but considered it a disgrace when she left. Her family did not want to see her unless she promised to have nothing more to do with a friend of such reputation. Natasha however, loved Agnes very much and decided to support her friend and help her through her ordeal.

On 27th November 1940, I was born.

✣ ✣ ✣ ✣ ✣

My father, had done a lot of good for the untouchables in India and several times met Mahatma Gandhi and Pundit Jawaharlal

Nehru, but he could not find a proper job in British India to support our family.

In 1944, he was forced through unemployment to return as an active Catholic priest again. He joined the Secular priests of Allahabad Diocese and was appointed the chaplain of the British and Italian soldiers and prisoners of war.

During 1945, 'Father Michael DeLisle Lyons' maintained his interest in and expert knowledge of geology. He was qualified to make surveys and keep in touch with the Planning and Development Department of the Government of India on behalf of the American war effort. He secured permission of his ecclesiastical superiors to place his services temporarily at Federal Economic Administration (FEA) for locating the strategic minerals of India (ie. beryllium, which is used to make triggering mechanisms for atomic weapons). In this official capacity, he travelled alone in 1945 over 25,000 miles in India, mostly by jeep and sometimes by plane or railroad. By then he could speak many Indian languages and could fluently converse with the villagers in their accent.

Father Michael DeLisle Lyons returned to the United States in 1946 on the instruction from his Bishop, to raise money for the missions of India. He did this by smelting beryllium in Arvada, Colorado, for the Rocky Flats Nuclear facility. He built and sold radios and antennas to the people living west of Boulder, Colorado. Father Lyons wrote to his brother, Frank informing him of his movements but requested the information be kept confidential.

2

1991 — Sydney, Australia

I sat beside my mother's bed at Royal Prince Alfred Hospital in Sydney, watching her gasp her life away. As I did, my thoughts ran back to my childhood, when my mother was the only anchor in my life, my only means of survival. In fact, she had been the only pillar on which I could always lean during my first fifty years.

There she lay, a small, insignificant-looking woman from India, with little ability to communicate, but whose heart had always been full of a mother's love, strong enough to battle successfully against exceptional and terrible odds to keep her two daughters alive and well. Many a time I thought she did not understand my feelings or needs; but that was because we never had the leisure to sit and talk to each other. Besides, since the day I had discovered the circumstances of my birth I found it hard to reveal my feelings to her although, I loved her very much, as I had loved my father.

But on that day, the ninth of May, 1991, when the doctors told me that they could do no more for her, I knelt beside her wasted body and took her Rosary in my hand, saying it as I had done when I was a little girl and only had prayers to turn to, while her life was too busy with work to support us.

As I knelt, my lips repeated the *Hail Mary* and the *Our Father*, which I had said over and over as a child. My mind continued to wander over the fields of my memory, as far as it would go: 1944, when I was a child of three and half years of age, in Saharanpore, a city in Northern India and she a woman of thirty-two, petite, soft-spoken and beautiful, her thick black hair reaching to her hips, trying to wake me from my slumber...

Tears rolled down my cheeks as I tried to come to terms with those memories . . .

3

1942 India — My father leaves

"Minnie! Look who is beside you!" I heard my mother say. Immediately I sat up to see who it was. To my delight, it was my dear Papa, fast asleep. I saw him only from time to time. I was told that he was a very busy man and had a lot of important work to do.

My father was very handsome, with fair skin and dark hair. He had the most beautiful blue eyes, so different from the others at home. I loved him very dearly, especially because when he was at home I received all his attention. I would sit on his lap for breakfast and he would feed me with pieces of buttered toast dipped in the egg yolk. He played hide-and-seek with me and enjoyed throwing me up into the air and catching me just before I fell on the ground. Mum would stand by and beg him to stop – she was scared that I would fracture my head. But Papa knew what he was doing. We would continue playing and laughing at Mum's concern. It was so much fun! I loved him so much!

I put my head on Papa's shoulder and watched him open his eyes and smile at me. Papa then embraced and kissed me, making me feel all-important and loved. The year was 1944, when I was three years and eight months old. I lived in a big house with my baby sister Violet, my mother, Uncle Eddie, Aunt Natasha and their two daughters, Enid and Helen. Enid was six months older than Violet and Helen was five months younger.

Violet was only six months old and Papa found her too small and helpless. He would hold her for a few minutes only. He gave me much love and attention.

I remember the time before Violet, Enid and Helen had arrived and I was the only child. We were living in Mirzapur, a small town in the north of India and Papa stayed home most of the time. He was the editor of the paper called The Poor Man's

Voice and had a lot of typing to do. Uncle Eddie was not with us then. Seven-year-old Cajeton and five-year-old Julius were living with us. They were my companions, related to Mum and Aunt I was told and I enjoyed playing with both of them. Cajeton played in the sandpit with me. I was two and a half and he pinched my cheeks to make them red.

I was fair like Papa with light brown hair and eyes. Cajeton and Julius were both dark with black shiny hair. Cajeton had mischief written all over his face and both Aunt and Mum were ever ready to pounce on him for his pranks, to protect me. One day Mum caught Cajeton kissing me on my cheeks and told Aunt Natasha that the boys were no company for a little girl, so they were sent away immediately. Cajeton was returned to his parents in Bettiah and Julius to his home in the village of Latonah. It was sad without them and I could not understand all the fuss about kissing.

Soon after they left, Aunt Natasha married Uncle Eddie in the city of Meerut. We moved to Saharanpore, where Enid and Helen were born. My little sister Violet was also born in Saharanpore. On our move to Saharanpore, Papa took a job, which kept him away from home most of the time.

Uncle Eddie was a good man but had a bad temper. One day Aunt Natasha complained to him about the *dhobi* (the man who collected dirty clothes and brought them back washed every week). She used to keep an account of every item of clothing she gave him to launder. Almost every month, when the time came for payment, there was an argument between the two. On one occasion she called out to Uncle Eddie and complained that the *dhobi* was cheating her. I heard a loud argument between the two men, which ended with Uncle hitting the *dhobi* hard with his fist. Aunt stopped complaining and restrained her husband. The poor *dhobi* ran away with a bleeding nose and I never saw him again. We soon arranged for another person to launder our clothes.

Uncle kept pigeons and hens in the backyard. He had built large pens for them and took great pleasure in looking after his pets. He had a variety of pigeons and enjoyed training them to obey his command. There were also a few ducks and two big geese, which Papa bought for me! He too seemed to enjoy poultry when he was at home. Papa and I would feed the bird's together. I enjoyed carrying the grain on a plate and getting into the pen with Papa to help feed them. The geese frightened me as they always chased me when I went near them. One of the geese bit me near the left eye one day when I eventually decided to be more adventurous and develop a friendship with them. Papa was very angry and the next day both the geese were served up roasted at the table for dinner.

We had curry and rice with *dal* (lentil soup) for lunch and European meals for dinner. Both Uncle and Papa loved curry and rice. Uncle enjoyed eating fresh red-hot chilli with hot curry. He would perspire throughout the meal, but that did not stop him! I was given special mild curry, as Papa did not think hot curry was good for me. He preferred me to have plenty of fruit and milk instead.

Papa and Uncle were good friends and often had long conversations in English. They went away together for days, Uncle always returning earlier than Papa. Uncle Eddie was a tall and well-built man. He was taller than my Papa was, but although he was fairer than both Mum and Aunt, he was not as fair as Papa. Uncle had a yellowish fairness whereas Papa was more pink and whitish. He had dark brown curly hair and brown eyes and the features of the people from the hilly region, heavy cheekbones and slanting eyes. He had an authoritative loud voice.

I adored Papa. He knew everything and even managed to persuade Mum to give Violet orange juice and baby food between feeds. Mum knew the Indian way of bringing up babies, which was to give them only breast milk till they were at least a year old. Papa made her give Violet tinned milk and baby food available in those days of the British Raj. He even managed to persuade Aunt Natasha to do the same with her babies. When Violet developed bad blood dysentery at five months, Papa was able to save her by having Mum give her only apple juice and boiled rice in place of milk. He was also a linguist and, I was told, he could speak several languages. He spoke to Mum and Aunt in fluent Hindi and the dialects spoken in the state of Bihar.

In front of our house in Saharanpore there was a huge plot of land which ended at the railway lines. I often watched the trains, including the slow-moving goods trains, which carried sugarcane. Very often the local poor boys would jump on the slow moving goods train and steal a few sticks of sugar cane. I enjoyed watching them jump off the train and run to their homes. They always seemed to be in a hurry and feared being caught red-handed. There was a Christian cemetery on one side of our property and on the other side were the servants' quarters.

Tulsi was our maidservant who helped Mum and Aunt with the housework. She washed all the babies' nappies daily. She was a good cook and made European and Indian dishes. Papa did not like Mum doing all the housework without a helper. He also liked her to take the servant with her for shopping, to carry the groceries. Papa was very concerned about Mum and saw that the servant carried an umbrella over her when she went out on a sunny day. I remember Papa had a black car in Mirzapur and drove Mum and Aunt for shopping himself. But since we moved to Saharanpore we did not have any transport and had to depend on *tongas*. (A cart driven by a horse used for transportation instead of a car).

I especially remember one day when Mum and Aunt had closed the windows and doors in the large bathroom that had a cement floor, two cold water taps and a pedestal toilet with a wooden seat; they had already massaged the babies with warm mustard oil making them ready for bathing. But Tulsi had not brought the hot water from the kitchen. Aunt asked me to run and hurry her up with the hot boiling water. I had been sitting quietly in one corner, watching the babies being massaged. Since I always enjoyed doing things for Aunt and Mum, as it made me feel a grown up, I ran towards the door blindly in my effort to please Aunt and failed to see Tulsi, who was then about to open the closed door with boiling water in a huge container which tilted, the hot water falling over me scalding me badly. I screamed with pain and both Mum and Aunt immediately rushed towards me. I heard someone saying that the white of raw eggs should be put on the burns at once. This was done and I was soon surrounded with dozens of eggshells. I felt better, more because of all the attention I received than from the effects of the egg whites. Unfortunately Papa was not at home.

✣ ✣ ✣ ✣ ✣

Parvati, our sweeper, was about fourteen or fifteen years old. She was a pleasant girl who sometimes played with me. She lived in one of the servants' quarters built of mud, but very clean and neat, because their occupants swept and lined the floors with cow dung and mud every day. They had made pictures of Hindu gods and goddesses on the front walls. There were lots of stray dogs, cows, goats and poultry around the houses. Every evening there was loud Indian film music and meetings of men. Women stayed indoors working or chatting among themselves. Occasionally they would come out to fill the men's hookahs with tobacco, or rekindle them with hot coal. Whenever the women came out they covered their head and faces with their *saris*. It seemed to be the custom amongst them to show their faces only to their husbands. Children played all around the place, making as much noise as possible over the music. We, in our big house, would sit on our verandah in front and look on, listening to the songs and the talk. Sometimes they would end up in a brawl using filthy abusive language I did not understand, but Mum and Aunt would take me inside the house saying I should not listen to them.

Parvati used to make me beautiful bead necklaces and bangles. She had even made a lovely bead curtain for her house. I came to know that she was to be married. Her mother showed Mum and Aunt all the embroidered sheets and tablecloth she had made for her wedding. She did such things very well, but she could not read or write. Then one day there were loud film songs coming from the loudspeaker erected on the top of Parvati's house and many women assembled to decorate both her and her house. The mud house was brightened with flowers, especially marigolds, the holy flower in all Hindu temples. I was given a *sari* to present to her. In the late evening a procession arrived with the bridegroom on a white horse and men with musical instruments loudly playing some Indian film songs. I could not see the bridegroom's face as it was covered with flowers on long strings. The music and holy chanting went on for a long time and I fell asleep to the sound of it. Suddenly, in the early hours of the morning, I woke up to the sound of loud crying, which I knew came from Parvati's house. There was also the sound of people talking, shouting and laughing. Just then I heard Mum telling Aunt that Parvati had tried to run from her room after the wedding: her husband had wanted to consummate the marriage but she was frightened, had refused him and then climbed on the roof saying that she would commit suicide. But they caught her and pushed her back into the room. I did not really understand what was going on: I only knew that I felt sorry for her. Next day I saw her crying. She looked pale, but the parents sent her away in a *palki*, which is a box-like carriage containing the bride, carried by hand, beside the bride-groom's horse. After she left her house was quiet again. Her mother started working for us. A few weeks later Parvati came to visit her parents and us. She looked very sad, so unlike the happy friend I once had who used to run and hide round the house. She cried and told Mum that her husband and his parents used to beat her and that she still did not like sleeping with her husband because he was always drunk and was cruel to her. The husband was much older than she, perhaps in his thirties. But her mother told Parvati that this was her fate and since she was married, she belonged to her husband. I hated everything that had happened to my friend. I could not under-stand why her parents sent her back again, even if they cried when they did so, since they could have kept her at home away from the man she did not like. Her husband never brought her back to visit home again and that was the last time I ever saw Parvati.

✣ ✣ ✣ ✣ ✣

The 27th November 1944 was my fourth birthday. Mum kissed me and gave me a box, which she said, came from Papa in Delhi. I opened it and found a beautiful fine clay doll. There was also a lovely pure silk *sari* for Mum, pale yellow with a black border and irregular geometrical patterns.

"Is this *sari* for you Agnes?" Natasha asked as she entered our room.

"Yes, Mino sent it for me," Mum replied.

"When my husband buys things for me, he buys for you too – I make sure of it – but when Mino sends things, they're only for you. I never forget that we were once very good friends and always wore the same design and colour of blouse and *sari*. Everything we bought was always the same for the two of us. I've done so much for you and Mino, but you both seem to forget it all, you are both very ungrateful." As she said this, Aunt Natasha picked up the *sari*, looked at it and then, flinging it back on the bed, stormed out of the room. Meanwhile, Mum continued combing my hair, which was so scanty and soft that it curled round my face. I had a new dress and a pair of shoes to wear that day. Once I was ready Mum dressed herself in a *sari* from the cupboard.

"Why don't you wear the one Papa sent, Mum?" I asked, picking up the new *sari* and the doll box.

"Leave it where it is Minnie. I don't want any fights with Natasha. Come, let's go. Do you want to take the doll?" Mum asked.

"Yes, Mum, but I want to carry it out of its box to church," I said.

"Don't be silly! You have to carry it in the box or forget it," Mum replied. But I insisted on taking it out of the box.

"What is the problem Agnes? Why aren't you coming? We are late already," Natasha grumbled as she walked into the room.

"Minnie wants to take the doll to church, but without the box," Mum said.

"Well, I can't see any harm in that. After all, it's her doll. Why can't she carry it without the box?" Aunt said. Then she hurriedly cut the strings, which held the fine clay doll inside the box and gave it to me. I was thrilled and hurriedly moved towards the door following Aunt Natasha, while Mum was instructing the *ayah* about looking after Violet. At the threshold I tripped and the doll slipped out of my hand falling on the cemented floor. It broke and lay there in small pieces and I could do nothing about it. I heard Mum gasp and come towards me, perhaps to hit me, but Aunt came to my rescue and quickly took me in her arms saying, "Don't do that it was only an accident and besides it's her birthday today."

"She should have listened to me," Mum said and walked out of the room, Aunt and I followed.

Throughout the service I sat tormented. My beautiful doll, sent to me by my darling Papa, was broken; but I could not cry, because I felt guilty that I had not listened to Mum, I was to blame. I also felt guilty about upsetting both Mum and Papa by breaking the doll.

When we returned home after the service I went straight to the room where the pieces of my doll lay. Parvati's mother was there sweeping the floor. She looked at me and said: "Baby, why did you not listen to your Mum? What a beautiful doll it was! Your Papa had sent it to you with such love and affection and you broke it the day after it came!"

What could I say? I just stood and watched her pick up the pieces.

I was distracted by Mum's scream "Well, if you think that Mino shouldn't have sent a *sari* only for me but for you also, then take it!" Mum used to address Papa with his pet name, "Mino," which was given to him by his mother, I was told.

"Why should I take what he sent for you only? All I'm saying is that you all are ungrateful and thoughtless." Natasha was speaking to Mum. I turned to go into Aunt's room just in time to see Mum rush into our room, pick up the *sari* and dash out into the kitchen, from where she came out with a match box. Before I knew what was happening, she put a lighted match to her new *sari* saying to Aunt Natasha:

"Here, will this satisfy you?"

Aunt stood and watched in shock and silence as the *sari* turned to ashes and then walked back to her room. Mum had left after the flames had taken hold of the *sari*. I was stricken - first the doll had gone and then the *sari*. It was all finished with and everyone was calm. Tulsi who watched in silence started sweeping the ashes, once both Aunt and Mum had disappeared into their rooms.

"Papa, you've left your glasses on the table," I shouted as I ran towards the door.

Papa returned a few months after my doll was broken. We

had a wonderful time together. He played with me and often took me out on long walks. But Mum did not seem happy. I often saw them together talking in the room, Mum crying and Papa consoling her. Uncle Eddie and Papa were also often engrossed in long conversation. This was the first time that Papa had stayed for so long in Saharanpore. I was very happy! He was my dear companion who made me feel so important in the house. Uncle and Aunt were always concerned with their two babies. Mum was busy with Violet and I was usually alone except when Papa was home I had him to myself. He read beautiful picture books to me and I loved listening to the stories.

One day I sensed tension in the house. Mum had been crying all morning and Papa had been speaking to her softly. After breakfast I saw his suitcases being packed. Then a *tonga* was called; perhaps my beloved father was going back to work…

He took me to the room, cuddled and kissed me and left me with my favourite sweets. While I was enjoying the sweets I saw his sunglasses on the table and took them with me, calling Papa.

He was getting into the *tonga*. I called out to him loudly and he stopped. I ran towards the gate as Papa left the *tonga* and walked towards me. He picked me up and once more cuddled and kissed me. It was then that I noticed tears in his eyes. Certainly something was wrong. I began to cry too, saying "Papa don't go. Don't leave me. I want to come with you, Papa."

"Don't cry, Minnie, I'll come back soon. Look after Mum and Violet." He wiped my tears and his own and tried to put me down, but I clung to him. I believed that if I did not stop him leaving, I would never see him again.

"Agnes ise ko ley jao," (Agnes take her away) he said in Hindi and forced me into Mum's arms, who held me so tightly that I could not get back to him. Soon the *tonga* bearing Papa and Uncle disappeared. I cried and sobbed. Mum took me back to the room and I noticed that she too was crying.

"Why are you crying, Mum? Isn't Papa coming back?" I asked trying to wipe her tears as well as mine.

"Yes, he said he would come back soon," she said very quietly but without much conviction.

Uncle returned after seeing Papa to the train. Darkness fell and Mum busied herself lighting the lantern and making a bottle of milk for Violet. I felt alone and miserable.

✣ ✣ ✣ ✣ ✣

Not long after Papa left, Uncle Eddie took me on his bicycle to a nearby Convent School for the first time. I was given a new school bag with a slate, a box of chalk, an exercise book and a pencil. I was thrilled because, apart from having a new dress and shoes, I was going on Uncle's bicycle and everyone was making much of me.

I sat in front on the bike weaving through the bazaar, to a large building next to the church. I was taken to a lady who was teaching little girls like me. When Uncle turned to go I cried not realising that he was not going to be with me at school! I sat sobbing the whole morning until Uncle came to take me home again.

Mum said I had to go to school every day and eventually I got used to the idea.

Mum also cried often. Aunt Natasha argued with Mum. Violet caused problems, her dysentery had gone but she cried a lot and developed a great hunger for milk. One day while Violet was drinking it, Mum turned to speak to me when Violet threw the glass milk bottle down and started crying again. She did that often. Mum slapped me for not attending to Violet but I did not cry because I felt that I had let Mum down.

I think Violet broke about fifteen bottles in a week throwing them, as soon as she found the person holding them was not paying attention to her. I wondered when Papa would come back to help Mum. Uncle Eddie was mostly at home but he was with Helen and Enid. Enid was able to walk and was given much attention. She was lovely - very plump with very curly hair.

✣ ✣ ✣ ✣ ✣

One day when I was nearly five, I was playing outside in the big playground – it was September 1945, Uncle Eddie and Mum came towards me with a gentleman who looked like my father: he was fair skinned, had blue eyes, but was dressed like a priest.

I ran to him calling "Papa", but Mum grabbed me, saying that he was not my papa but a 'dost' (a friend). I was confused, I was sure he was. I could not understand why Mum said that he was not. The man looked at me and smiled the way my papa did, ran his hands over my head and patted my cheeks before he turned and left with Uncle Eddie. I stood in silence watching him leave. Mum stood beside me but said nothing.

✣ ✣ ✣ ✣ ✣

Everything changed since Papa stopped coming home; Mum expected me to help her with Violet; Uncle and Aunt were always with their children; Aunt Natasha and Mum were not so friendly; I was scolded or slapped when I did something wrong. I once found a small pair of scissors and went about using them on everything I could find. I was curious and intrigued at how they cut things! Suddenly I heard Aunt say: "Who cut the new table cloth I spread on the table?"

"I did it Aunt, see," and I proudly demonstrated how I'd used them.

She called Mum, complaining how useless and brainless I was and how I had added to the financial problems. Mum slapped me without asking for an explanation. Then the *ayah*, collecting the dry clothes reported that some clothing had been snipped. Mum locked me in the toilet after a few slaps on my cheeks. As there was no electricity in the house, we used lanterns and I thought I could see wasps in the room. I was very scared of them and of the darkness. I cried bitterly, begging to be taken out. I didn't understand why I was being punished, but no-one paid attention to my cries. I was kept there for thirty minutes crying hysterically when Aunt said the punishment had been long enough. I decided I would only do what I was told; help Mum and Aunt with Violet, Enid and Helen.

Soon Violet became a problem, whenever she saw Helen struggling to stand with the help of a chair or bed, she would push her down, which led to an argument between Mum and Aunt. As soon as she was able to walk Helen went for Violet — Uncle and Aunt thought it funny.

Violet was fair-skinned like me and had very thick black

hair. She always did what she wanted. Violet loved food and would devour an enormous amount in a very short time and still complain of hunger. Aunt and Uncle nicknamed her 'greedy guts'.

One day, about six months after I started school, Uncle did not come to pick me up afterwards. I waited outside the gates and when every other child left, I cried. The nun on duty saw me, took me to the chapel and asked me to wait. I remember sobbing and while tears trickled down my cheeks, I prayed with folded hands for Uncle to come.

After a long time Mum arrived in a '*tonga*' for me. She looked worried "Where is Uncle, Mum?

"I don't know. I was unaware that he couldn't collect you today. I am sorry that you had to wait."

When we reached home Uncle and Aunt were in their room. Perhaps there had been a quarrel! From that day onwards Birju, the new servant, took me to school and home again. He was often late collecting me because he had to complete housework first. The nuns were very fond of me, I was always quiet in class and sat alone during playtime. Sometimes, the nun on bus duty would take me for a couple of trips around town dropping the other children home until Birju collected me.

I did not like to be in school for very long because I developed a great anxiety of a fight breaking out at home between Mum and Aunt or Uncle. Also I was afraid that Violet may be in trouble due to her difficult nature. I felt I had to be with Mum and my sister all the time to protect them from fights and trouble. The teacher at school had been teaching us about Jesus and His goodness. She also taught us prayers, which I started saying very often. I was very impressed with all she taught us about Jesus and began loving and trusting in Him as if He was a real person and beside me all the time. I visited the chapel in my recess and lunchtime, praying loudly to Jesus to protect my mother and sister when I was not at home. I developed great faith in Jesus. I believed that He understood my feelings and would help me out in the absence of my father. I remembered to thank Jesus for his kindness when I found Mum and Violet safe at home after school. Somehow I could not feel carefree like other children.

Once when we were out on the front verandah, Violet was playing with Helen, while Mum and Aunt were sitting on cane chairs talking. Enid was on Mum's lap, since she was very attached to my mother. I was playing with Parvati's sister in one corner of the verandah. Suddenly I heard a scream and turned around just in time to see Violet being attacked by a bull. It had picked her up between its horns, flung her down and was about to do so again. I ran crying to save her. Violet had wandered off near the herd of cattle that were grazing in front of the house. Parvati's father hit the bull with a stick. I pulled up Violet and dragged her towards Mum.

Not long afterwards Enid fell sick and her condition was serious for a long time. She was under medical supervision day and night for typhoid. She wanted to be looked after by my mother all the time since she was very affectionate and caring. Mum would leave Violet with me and the '*ayah*' and take care of Enid with Aunt and Uncle. One day her eyes became fixed for a short while which made Aunt cry hysterically. I began praying it Jesus for her recovery. I liked Enid very much because she was very quiet, whereas Violet and Helen fought all the time and were the cause of arguments between Mum, Aunt and Uncle.

Mum loved children and even fed Helen with her own milk while nursing Violet, because Aunt Natasha did not have much to give her child. I was told that her students were extremely fond of her when she was a kindergarten teacher long before I was born, because of her loving and caring disposition.

Papa wrote to Mum every now and then. His letters were always in Hindi. She brightened up on the days the letters came. On my fifth birthday, I received a pretty frock, some coloured crayons and a colouring book from Papa. In the evening of my fifth birthday, Uncle was playing on the bed with his two daughters, I sat at the end of the bed and watched them play the way my Papa used to play with me. I started playing with Uncle Eddie's shoes and managed to pull out a nail, which I put into my mouth. Something made me laugh suddenly and the nail went straight into my stomach. I told Uncle that I had swallowed a nail from his shoes. He could not believe it at first, thinking that I was making an excuse to get his attention. But since I persisted he yelled out to Mum and warned her about it. Both Mum and Aunt were in a panic. Immediately Mum called a *tonga* and rushed me to Dr Austin, our family doctor. He advised Mum to give me plenty of boiled potatoes that evening.

About six months after my fifth birthday, when I was playing in front of the house with children from the servants' quarters, I heard screaming and shouting coming from our house. I stopped playing and immediately ran towards it. Inside I saw Uncle holding Mum by her beautiful thick, black plaited hair and shoving her head into the hot charcoal fireplace. She was small, while Uncle was tall and heavily built.

"Stop it Eddie, it's over! Forget it!" Aunt Natasha was saying, pulling him away. I ran towards my mother to save her.

"Bloody woman, you think we have lived on your Mino! He bloody well left you all on us and has suddenly disappeared. Who is going to meet all the expenses? It was all very well for him to ask me to look after you all, but where is the money to support you and your children? He must have given it to you. He could not have left without providing for you all. I am sure you have the money but you will not give it for use in the house." I heard Uncle saying all this to Mum in his loud angry voice as he let go off her hair.

"Yes, I have a lot of money left by Mino and I am a bad woman! I am to be blamed for everything and I have ruined things for everyone. I should die! I wish God would take me away now," Mum said.

"God won't bloody well take you away – you take yourself away. Here, here is a knife to cut your throat with. We'll be rid of you then and your darling children can go off into an orphanage." Uncle said.

Mum took the big shiny breadknife, which Uncle thrust at her and held it to her neck. I caught the knife in the middle with both hands, keeping it from her throat, pleading with her at the same time, not to do so. My hands began to bleed.

Uncle stood by smirking whilst Aunt watched for a moment and then ran to my aid.

"Agnes, stop it! Look, Minnie's palm is cut."

But Mum persisted. "Leave me. I'm fed up with my life. I'm not the only one to blame. Mino found it easy to run away, I'm left to face the world with these children. It's all hopeless. Let me die." She continued sobbing.

"Agnes, stop it. We are sorry. We shall manage somehow if you swear you have no money and you do not know his whereabouts." Uncle suddenly became aware that Mum was serious about wanting to kill herself.

"I told you he left me no money. He said he would send some, but he hasn't and I haven't even had a letter from him for some time. I don't know where he is," Mum said.

I did not know what they were talking about; I only wanted to save my mother. She was all I had. Mum left the kitchen and went sobbing towards our room. I followed her and when she sat on the bed I sat beside her, putting my arms around her. It was then that Mum realised my palms were cut. She kissed me and bandaged my hands without saying a word. Then she cuddled me and we both sat there crying. For a long time I was haunted with that horrible scene of the fight and I was full of fear and apprehension about my dear mother's life. All the more I wished for the return of my Papa. I had felt safe and secure when he was at home and now it had become a nightmare.

In 1946, I did not receive any birthday present from Papa on my sixth birthday. I had not seen him for a long time and wondered when he would again return but no one answered my question. Everyone maintained silence on the topic of my dear Papa. The schools remained closed for a long time since there was trouble over the struggle for independence from the British. There were times when we could hear a lot of screaming in the distance. I once overheard Mum and Aunt talking about some clashes between the Hindus and the Muslims about separate areas once India was independent.

4

1947 — Mother tries abandoning

As conditions became worse I heard Uncle discussing a move from Saharanpore. The clashes between Hindus and Muslims often ended up in violence. Many people were killed daily on the ground of religious differences. Prices of foods went up. Some things were not available in the market at all, like kerosene oil so we used candles at night.

The days and nights were filled with the noise of people screaming and crying. All schools were closed indefinitely and most people stayed inside the house. Although Hindus and Muslims were killing each other they did not touch the Christians. They spared the houses which had the sign of the Cross either drawn across the door or put up on the roof.

One day I found our things packed into boxes and loaded into two *tongas*. Aunt, Uncle, Enid and Helen got into one *tonga* while Mum, Violet, Birju, our servant and I were made to sit in the other. Mum had to force me in because I was waiting for my Papa to return to the house. The platform at Saharanpore station was packed with people and their belongings. Mum was carrying Violet and dragging me along by the hand. Aunt and Uncle carried their daughters. Birju carried some luggage as well as supervising the four porters who were heavily laden with our tin boxes full of kitchen utensils and clothes.

We pushed ourselves through the train door. Even though our berths were booked in the sleeping coach of the third class compartment, there seemed to be more people than seats. The people were everywhere: not only inside the coaches, but also on the roof and hanging outside the doors and windows. Some even sat on our boxes and we could not object. Uncle was irritable and lost his temper with the porter over payment. He punched the porter on the nose. Luckily the train started before a crowd could gather.

I was exhausted and worried that Papa would not know where we had gone when he came back to Saharanpore. No-one else seemed to think about that!

When I woke the next day we were in the mountains, a few hours from Darjeeling, in the great Himalayan ranges of north India. We changed trains to one that was short and travelled fast on winding tracks. The air was fresh and I could see snow in the distance. There were many eucalyptus and pine trees, the women wore *saris* different from those of Mum and Aunt. They spoke a different language *'Nepali'*, they had different ways of farming. The fields were arranged in steps and they mostly grew tea.

I hated the bus ride up the mountain, because the roads were narrow and winding. Mum and I felt giddy and sick. We reached Kalimpong at about three o'clock in the afternoon. Uncle had arranged a house which belonged to a Britisher who had returned to England and wanted someone to stay in it while he decided about its sale. Uncle Eddie said it would be a safe town to live in during the Hindu and Muslim riots over a separate area for Muslims (Pakistan). I loved the bungalow and the garden with its trees, flowers and butterflies and easily imagined that fairies and elves would be completely happy living there too.

Mum used to read me the stories from the Old and the New Testament from the Hindi Bible. She was very religious and never went to sleep without saying her prayers. Every Indian employs a sweeper, who belonged to the lowest caste, to do the menial work in the house. Servants were very cheap in India and every family had at least two. Indians are very conscious of class and caste and therefore it becomes necessary to keep servants, since people of higher caste cannot perform many types of work, even in the privacy of their own house, because of social norms.

I remember the day Mahatma Gandhi, the man who was responsible for the independence of India, was shot dead by a Hindu fanatic. Uncle read about it in the newspaper at the breakfast table and announced that the shops would be closed for some days as a sign of mourning. There were many days before we could buy food in the market again.

Uncle was out of a job. Since we moved to Saharanpore, Papa had started work with the U.S. Foreign Economic Administration surveying the strategic mineral deposits of India for the war effort. He had to frequently travel to the high mountain ranges of the Himalayas. He employed Uncle Eddie to help him on his trips. Since Papa stopped coming home, Uncle never seemed to have a permanent job.

✣ ✣ ✣ ✣ ✣

One morning we had a visitor, a young man in his late twenties. Aunt Natasha was very happy to see him and welcomed him affectionately. He was introduced to me as Uncle David. I soon discovered that Uncle David had been invited by Aunt Natasha to live permanently with us in Kalimpong.

Soon Uncle David accompanied us on our long walks instead of Mum and Aunt. I thought him quite good-looking with his brown complexion and black curly hair, but nowhere near as handsome as my Papa. We children were expected to call him Uncle. In India, amongst the Hindus, everyone who is older is given a status of respect as Uncle, (*Chacha,* if he is the brother of the father, or *Mama,* if he is the brother of the mother.) Aunt, (*Chachi,* if she is the wife of *Chacha,* or *Mami* if she is the wife of *Mama*). The sister of the father is called *Phuphi* and her husband is *Phupha.* An elder sister is called *Didi* or *Bahen;* an elder brother is called *Dada* or *Bhai.* But the Christians and the descendants of the British in India addressed everyone older as Uncle or Aunty out of respect, irrespective of whether they were from the father's side or the mother's. The older sisters and brothers were called by their names as were the younger ones.

I was told that I had to go to a boarding school and given to believe that it was my Papa's wish. I was told that Papa would eventually visit me at the school. A lot of clothes were made for me, as well as shoes and other things were packed into a black tin box. Then one morning, my mother took me to the big school on the top of a hill. Aunt Natasha, Uncle David and Uncle Eddie watched me go with sad faces. Mum had sold one of her heavy 22-carat gold necklaces to buy all the things required for me at the boarding school. Since Uncle Eddie's sister, Agnes Wright, was educated in the same school run by the Loretto nuns, he was confident that it had to be a very good English school for me. It was expensive and only the rich could afford to study there, but it was arranged by the Bishop of Patna. My mother had written to him. I was to be adopted overseas, I came to know later. I could not help crying when Mum left me at the convent with a foreign nun. Though the nuns were kind, I kept crying incessantly for days. I could not understand why Papa could not visit the home where my mother and sister lived and why I had to be put into a school for him to visit me. I hated the dormitory where I had my bed. I was the youngest boarder, just six and half years old.

I was there for a fortnight when I became seriously ill. Mum was called and had to take me home for medical attention. While I was away they'd changed houses. Uncle Eddie had got himself a permanent job in a sugar cane factory at Tamkuhi, in the plains of north India. His work lasted for nine months of the year, but he received salary for the whole year. The British owned the factories and only the Anglo-Indians and the domiciled Britishers were employed.

I was referred to a doctor in Darjeeling. We stayed in a hotel while I was treated. Mum paid a large fee to the private doctor. Mum and Uncle David took me for a daily injection for two weeks to a large hospital. Uncle David carried me on his shoulders and let me go horse riding at the Mall, right in the middle of the shopping centre. He also bought me a lovely little red car to play with in the room. There was such peace and we were happy there, Mum seemed relaxed and without worries.

Mum disclosed to Aunt and Uncle that Papa and she had a joint account in the State Bank of India. She said that Papa had left about twenty-five thousand *rupees,* a huge sum of money in those days, for her in the bank. She said that she had forgotten about it. Unfortunately, when Mum went to withdraw some money, she was informed that all the money had been transferred into another account in New York and then withdrawn. Uncle Eddie lost his temper at Mum's secretiveness and for her losing the money. Up until then Mum had been pawning and selling her gold jewellery to make ends meet. She had plenty of 22-carat gold jewellery, as Papa had presented her with many pieces because Indians prefer to invest in gold jewellery rather than keep money in the banks.

Soon after we returned to Kalimpong we changed our house once more and lived at 'Seven Miles'. We lived on the ground floor of a double-storey timber building. Mr and Mrs Green lived on the first floor. Mr Green was an Anglo-Indian like Uncle Eddie. Mr Green was married to a *Nepali* woman and their only daughter was studying in England. Every British or Anglo-Indian married to the native Indian woman preferred to send their children to England for education in those days.

The building was at the side of the main road to Darjeeling. On the other side of the road was a high hill covered with trees and bushes. On top of the hill was the Catholic Church and a mission school, St. Philomena's convent, run by the nuns. The medium of instruction there was *Nepali* and the school was for the poor Catholics. At the side of the school, a short distance away, was the English boarding school, where I had been admitted before I became ill.

We kept poultry and while Uncle Eddie was on holidays he had time to make cages for the hens. My job was to open them in the morning and then close them in the evening, as well as cover the boxes with *gunni* or jute bags. Very often I did not like doing the work: Helen, Enid and Violet were always playing and I was made to work, something that I felt was unfair. One evening I closed the hen's cages, but refused to cover the boxes: something within me stopped me from picking up the *gunni* bags lying on the ground. Uncle was very angry with me for defying him. He stood in front of me and insisted that I pick them up. Eventually, with tears in my eyes, I bent down to pick up the bags. As I lifted them, Uncle screamed: "Run." Then he called out: "Natasha, bring the stick - there is a cobra under the *gunni* bag." Mum came running and pulled me away. Uncle killed the snake with the stick and threw it on the side of the road. Everyone stood by in a state of shock and wondered how it got there. After that day Mum made sure that the woman who helped with housework also saw to the poultry.

✣ ✣ ✣ ✣ ✣

Uncle Eddie had to return to his place of work. The day Uncle left, Enid cried bitterly. It reminded me of the day my Papa left in Saharanpore and I felt sorry for her. I hated anyone leaving because I feared that they too, would not return.

One morning, Mum and the teacher who lived next door, took me to the poor Catholic school for girls at the top of the hill. The classes were conducted in the *Nepali* language. I was admitted to Class 2, as I was seven years old. In India children start schooling at the age of five. The Principal gave concession for my monthly fees.

There is no social security or welfare organisation in India so Mum opened a small shop in a tent at the side of the road near our house. Mum sat on the floor and sold cigarettes, *pan* (betel leaves), snacks, biscuits and homemade lollies for the children. She also received orders for embroidery work on the vestments, which the priests wore during Mass and the Altar clothes. She also took orders for sewing and embroidery work on bedcovers and tablecloths. She would sit till late on her hand machine or the embroidery work every night and start early in the morning on the cooking for the shop. Mum and Mrs Green, her good friend went to watch the football match in the city practically every weekend.

I climbed up the hill in front of our apartment every morning to attend the school. I enjoyed it during the day when Mum was busy at work, but ran home immediately after, to be with her in the evenings. I learnt to read in *Nepali* and enjoyed reading storybooks myself every night while Mum did sewing or embroidery work for her customers. At times I read the stories to Violet.

The pupils at school came from very poor homes and could not afford uniforms. There were both Catholic and non-Catholic students. Mum always dressed me in socks, shoes and pretty frocks that she designed and stitched; besides, I was much fairer than the other girls in the school so everyone made a fuss of me. My light brown hair always had new ribbons and bows.

I always did well in maths and reading. The first year I

was awarded a lovely hand knitted blue pullover on prize-giving day for coming first in the class of forty-five students. I felt nervous yet proud to walk up on to the stage and accept my prize. Mum was unable to attend the function, but I knew she would be happy with my performance. After school I ran towards home with my award under my arm. As I passed the school gates, some big girls stopped me and asked to look at the prize. I could not refuse as they were big, strong senior students. I watched them unwrap it and saw the blue pullover which I had received as an award being worn by one of the girls. I could do nothing but look on in despair. The girl was fat and pulled a stitch which brought tears to my eyes. They gave me back the pullover after each of them had tried it on. Mum seemed very happy to know of my success, as was Uncle David. I wished that my dear Papa was around to share my achievement too. The pullover was too big for me so I gave it to Mum.

✣ ✣ ✣ ✣ ✣

Uncle David was always thoughtful and kind to Mum. Aunt Natasha did not like it and one day I heard the three of them quarrelling.

"David, I must remind you that she is much older than you. I don't like the way you give her attention and take care of her children." I heard Aunt saying. Then she turned to Mum and said in a very angry voice, "Agnes, I hope you are not getting any ideas about David! He is younger than you are. You have your bastard children. Look after them and leave David alone."

"How can you accuse me of such a thing, Natasha? I consider David my younger brother. He is being nice to my children and me that is all. You are making such a heinous story out of it all. Can't anyone be good to my children and me! Can't I have a good friend and a brother to help me sort out my problems! Why do you always consider me bad – what have I done, except made a fool of myself by falling in love once with someone who did not have the right to love! " Mum asked.

But Aunt Natasha continued saying things I could not understand and scolded Uncle David. Though he was twenty-eight, he was very quiet. Aunt was older than he was so he would not answer her back because this would have been contrary to the way in which he had been brought up. That evening he packed his box and went to live at Mrs Green's house. Mum was thirty-six but looked much younger and prettier than everyone else. I hated to see her unhappy.

Mum met Uncle David near the cinema in the city whenever she went to watch a football match. She loved both the football and Indian films. I went with her to the cinema a couple of times to the only picture hall in Kalimpong which was made of tin and corrugated iron. When it rained, the roof made such a noise that no one could hear what was being said. There were rows of collapsible chairs on the bare muddy floor where we sat and watched the film. After the film the floor was always littered with peanut shells, fruit peel and other debris.

I remember the three of us watched a film called *Sindoor*, about a widow who fell in love with a man, to everyone's disapproval. She had a son who wanted a father. I shared his feelings. The film had some very sad songs in it, which brought tears to my eyes as I thought of my dear Papa who had left me and not returned. I thought of him every day and wondered where he was.

One day Mum took me to a butcher's shop and I noticed one of the young butchers staring at me. I did not like his gaze so I tugged Mum's *sari* to show her that I wanted to leave. Two days later, on a Sunday morning, Mum asked me to mind the shop while she went home to make some more lollies. We had just returned from the Sunday Church service and I was still in my best clothes. The butcher boy walked past the shop making signs to follow him up the hill. He walked up the hill for a distance and before long, he was beside me dragging me by the hand to a bush. He sat down on the grass and started pulling at my underpants. I struggled to get free but he was much stronger. To my relief, the schoolteacher called from the shop below and the butcher's fingers loosened. I pulled myself away and ran down the hill. I must have looked upset and shaken. The teacher asked why I had left the shop unattended. I could not speak and sat down on the floor ready to sell the things. I could not tell Mum what had happened, but I made sure that I never visited the butcher's shop ever again with her and avoided being alone outside the apartment.

✣ ✣ ✣ ✣ ✣

Mum closed her little wayside shop, as she did not make much out of it. She caught the bus early in the morning to a fish market and bought baskets full of fresh fish to sell door to door every day. She continued sewing and embroidery 'on order' as before.

On one of her rounds with the fish, Mum met an Englishman and his wife. The wife was a South Indian who could not speak English. When the couple discovered that Mum had a certificate to teach, they asked her to tutor the wife. Mum gave up selling fish and taught her some English words, table manners, tasteful dressing in *sari*s and cooking. The couple had two children, Hector and Barbara, who were later sent to England for education.

One day Mum's friend, Mrs Green, invited us for lunch for the Hindu festival of *Dushera*, which celebrates the day when the Hindu God Rama left for the forest with his wife Sita and brother Luxman. Mrs Green put out some home-brewed liquor with, *jadh*, which was milky in colour and tasted so good that I had three glasses of it. The 'glasses' were made of steel so that they did not break. Everyone, was busy chatting and no-one noticed what I was doing.

After awhile I felt light-headed and flushed. It was about two o'clock and time for lunch. The food was ready and everyone sat in a line on the floor, legs folded, like *yogis*. Mrs Green and a servant placed steel plates in front of each of us, in which the delicious yellow *pilaf* rice was served. Another servant followed her with a most appetising pork curry, which was served next to the *pilaf* on everyone's plates. *Puris* followed next. I began feeling giddy and sick. I remember becoming conscious again on Mrs Green's bed with Mum sitting beside me and saying it was time to go home.

"But where's my food?" I asked.

"It's four-thirty and everything is finished. That will teach you never to touch adult drinks again!"

She looked so angry that I thought it best not to question

her any more on the subject. But I was hungry and felt sorry for myself on account of missing the lovely food, especially the pork that I liked more than anything else.

✢ ✢ ✢ ✢ ✢

I missed Papa very much and whenever I went to a film with Mum, I used to cry listening to sad Hindi songs. The songs seemed to express my feelings of love for him. We had a gramophone at home and I would sit beside it sobbing for my dear Papa while listening to the sad songs. Many years later I discovered that those songs were sung for lovers, but the sad tunes mattered to me, they brought tears to my eyes and I associated every word with the disappearance of Papa and my empty feelings of loss. I wondered how he could forget my mother and me. I prayed daily to Jesus for his return. I stopped asking Mum about him because it either made her sad or angry; in any case, she did not know where he was.

No one seemed to know!

I thought it best to keep my feelings to myself and pray. I searched for his familiar face in the crowd whenever we went out and any attention or affection given to me, reminded me of him and brought tears to my eyes. I became a dreamer and a sensitive introverted child always lost in my thoughts. I was only eight years old and found it difficult to be carefree like the other children. I pitied myself for not having a Papa. I had so much to ask but trusted no-one to answer my questions. I feared being humiliated besides Mum was busy working to provide for us while Aunt Natasha was pre-occupied with her own children.

✢ ✢ ✢ ✢ ✢

Through Mrs Green we came to know Mrs Kingsley who had a large property and offered us a piece of land. Uncle Eddie built a good cottage out of mud and bamboo sticks. The walls were plastered with mud inside and outside. The flooring was of brick and mud plaster The cottage had a thatched roof, with three small rooms but only one room had a door. Uncle, Aunt and their children lived in the big room with the door. Mum, Violet and I occupied one of the rooms without the door. It opened into the kitchen, the other third one belonged to Uncle David.

The toilet was repulsive. The door was made of a tin sheet with a latch but we had to sit on two bricks over a hole where there was a tin can at the bottom. Indian people always use water to clean themselves instead of toilet paper, they consider using water cleaner and more hygienic so a bucket of water and a mug was placed daily at the side. There was always soap near the tap to wash the hands.

Mrs Kingsley was a *Nepali* Indian woman of a big build. *Nepali* women have the same features as people from the hilly region: rather flat face, yellowish smooth complexion and small slanting eyes. She wore a gold ring in her nose and large heavy gold earrings in the ears and a number of bangles, all 22-carat gold. When she drank tea, her long nose ring dipped into her cup of tea. She chewed *pan* (betel leaves) which stained her teeth black. Mum and Mrs. Kingsley became very good friends. Aileen Kingsley was a very good friend of mine. We had great fun running up the sloppy land and the green fields. We lived in the lowest terraced land, the Kingsleys lived on the top of the hill. There was a lot of terraced land in between.

While Uncle Eddie was on holidays he grew vegetables at the back of the house. He loved dogs, gardening and farming and we kept the poultry. Uncle bought a cow and Mum milked it with the help of a servant. A few goats were added to our list of animals. Mum seemed to enjoy looking after the farm animals, but she hated dogs and cats.

Mrs Kingsley was a very kind lady with eight children of her own and she adopted many local children whom she helped with education. In turn they took care of her big house and land. She allowed many poor *Nepali* families to live free on her property. They grew crops and gave her part of the produce. She was very respectful towards the Catholic priests and they had a high regard for her because of her charitable nature.

✣ ✣ ✣ ✣ ✣

I was a very sickly child in Kalimpong. Very frequently I suffered with fever and bad throat. The local doctor told Mum that I needed my tonsils removed. Mum heard about an English specialist visiting the small government hospital in Kalimpong. She made an appointment for the operation in the local public hospital. The doctor carried me in his arms after the operation, back to the little recovery room, since there was a delay in finding the nurse and the stretcher. He took special care of me because he said I reminded him of his own daughter back in England. The operation was a success and from then I did not have frequent attacks of cough and colds, but my health remained delicate. There were times when I had spells of giddiness and feelings of fainting in the school. I often felt the sinking feeling with great thirst and saw stars in front of my eyes. But I did not tell Mum about it, as I did not want to add to her worries.

Uncle David carried me on his shoulders and bought me chocolates. He called Mum, *'bahen'* meaning 'sister'.

I used to be very frightened of thunder and lightning. I cried with fear, closed my eyes and put my fingers in my ears, to dull the sound. Uncle David always picked me up and put me in bed beside him, covering me up with a blanket so that I did not see or hear anything. There were times when I used to sleep in Uncle David's bed, listening to the wonderful stories of Gautama Buddha which impressed me greatly as did the stories from the Bible which Mum read to me. I liked Uncle David because he gave me attention like my Papa.

Mum worked at the sewing machine till late in the night, to earn money. I remember one night her right index finger caught in the machine and the needle went through it. Uncle David helped to get it out while Aunt reprimanded her for working so late at night under the light of the lantern. Her finger was bleeding profusely and there was no doctor available. She found a piece of her old white *sari* and wrapped the wound. I was worried and concerned. I found it hard to sleep because I did not know how to help her.

Mrs Kingsley was very kind in helping Mum with sewing orders. Mum did all sorts of jobs to support Violet and me. She was always working and had lost a lot of weight since Papa had disappeared yet I never ever saw her resting in bed even when she was ill.

By then everyone at home was fluent in the *Nepali* language. Mum, Aunt and Uncle David spoke in Hindi amongst themselves but spoke to us in *Nepali*. Uncle Eddie spoke to Aunt and Mum in Hindi as Papa had done. He had studied up to Class Seven in English but he was also fluent in *Nepali* having grown up in Kalimpong.

About that time I was preparing for my First Communion and Confirmation. I learnt all my prayers in *Nepali*. Every Sunday Aileen Kingsley and I had to stay back after Mass for Catechism with other children to prepare for the two Sacraments on the same day. I enjoyed watching the coloured slides about the life of Jesus on the whitewashed wall of the room. Once in a while, as a reward, we watched a silent film in black and white with Charlie Chaplin.

On the day I received my first Communion and the Confirmation, Papa's absence made me very sad. No one seemed to bother about my feelings. Everyone else seemed happy celebrating my First Communion, but I could not forget Papa, especially when I watched other children with their fathers. Where was my Papa? Why was he not coming back to his Minnie? I was forever plagued by these questions but afraid to ask anyone.

After the long service, we were served breakfast in the hall near the church. Uncle David took photographs. We had the Kingsleys over for lunch and Mum killed the biggest rooster we had. Only Mum could cut the rooster's neck. I used to run as far as I could go, away from the scene, because I could not bear to see the blood or hear the poor rooster cry before dying. Mum poured a teaspoon full of mustard oil and a clove of garlic, into the rooster's beak before killing it. She said it made the rooster tender to eat. I thought it was all very cruel and never ate any fowl killed at home. However I enjoyed eating all types of meat, as long as no one reminded me of where it came from.

✣ ✣ ✣ ✣ ✣

Mrs Kingsley's children went to the English school on top of the hill. I attended the *Nepali* school for the poorer local children. After school and on the weekends, I loved to play with little rag dolls I made myself out of Mum's old *sari* pieces. I played with them by myself for hours. I wrapped the rag pieces onto a stick to form a figure and dressed them in *saris* or *dhoti-kurtas.*

Sometimes Aileen Kingsley and the poorer children joined me. We built huts out of twigs and mud for the rag dolls and played real family life dramas. In my doll's family, the father was either dead or had run away and the mother brought up the children. We arranged marriages between our dolls and had small parties after the weddings. Sometimes, when Mum was at home and in a good mood, she'd make a sweet dish for us to eat during the wedding reception. The boy doll always took the bride away with a big dowry of real sweets and clothes, like pieces of rags as *saris*. We used silver foil to make jewellery for our rag dolls. Sometimes the father of my dolls was bad and he would beat his wife and the children. I enjoyed my make-believe world of the dolls. Violet, Enid and Helen were too small to join in and spent their time in the house with toys bought from the shops at Christmas time.

✣ ✣ ✣ ✣ ✣

Not long after my First Communion we all went for a picnic to the banks of the River Teesta, a few kilometres from home. Mr and Mrs Green, Mrs Kingsley and her children and the Messys joined us. We set out in the morning on foot, carrying containers of both cooked and uncooked food. The picnic spot was between three and four kilometres downhill. Uncle Eddie and Aunt Natasha took it in turns to carry Helen. Mum held Enid's hand and Violet was with Uncle David. I enjoyed running ahead.

On the way we passed many small streams trickling down the side of the big rocks onto the road. There was a very steep drop on one side full of green trees, beyond which, in the distance was the Himalayan ranges with snow capped-peaks. We met many *Nepali* and Tibetan men and women on the way carrying long baskets on their backs supported with bands from their heads. They always carried a T-shaped stick each, so when they were tired, they could support the basket on the stick and stand erect. They chewed tobacco as they walked bent under their heavy loads.

The place was very beautiful and there was no one else there except us. The picnic things were placed in one spot and while some began gathering wood to light the fire, others put bricks and stones together to make a fireplace. The fire was lit and the big container with rice was placed on it. Another fireplace was made to warm the cooked meat curry which we had carried with us in a large aluminium container. Most of the women cooked while we children rushed into the cold river. Uncle Eddie came along with us. Enid, Helen and Violet were allowed to go into the water wearing just their cotton knickers, while I was told to remain in my petticoat because I was older. We splashed about in shallow water as we could not swim. I enjoyed watching Darryl in the distance, yodelling and plunging into the deep water

When the curry and rice was ready we sat on the *dari* (a carpet undersheet) spread out on the sandy banks. Each family had brought plates. Most of us ate with our hands, as cutlery was too heavy to carry; only the adult men used forks and spoons which had been brought for them.

We finished lunch and washing around four o'clock in the afternoon. Darryl, his sister Philomena, Uncle David and the other men played cricket. We children were making a sandcastle, while Aunt and Mrs Messy watched us. Mum, Mrs Green and Mrs Kingsley wandered around the sandy bank, chatting and exploring. They noticed a large wooden box buried in the sand, not far from where we were playing. I heard Mrs Kingsley say to mum:

"It must be some treasure!"

"No, no, it must be the statue of the Goddess Durga thrown into the river after the festival." Mrs Green said.

"Well, let us see what it is," Mum concluded, walking towards the box eagerly.

The others followed. Uncle David stopped playing and joined the three ladies as they opened the lid. I saw them bang the lid shut as soon as they opened it and walk quickly away from the box.

"What is the matter?" called Aunt Natasha.

"There is a body of a young bride in it – dressed in all her bridal clothes, a red *sari* and a lot of jewellery," Mum replied.

Later I heard that the dead body was that of an eighteen year old bride who had committed suicide on her wedding night because she had not wanted to marry the man her parents had forced her to marry. The *Nepalis*, as do most Hindus, throw their dead into the river with or without a coffin. In this case, the box had buried itself in the sand after being carried downstream by the current.

We turned for home late in the evening. It was exhausting walking uphill following the main road and took us longer than in the morning. By the time we lit the lanterns and were ready for sleep, it was midnight. Mum made me go to the toilet. She stood waiting outside the toilet door, holding the lantern for me. Just as I was leaving the toilet, we heard the weeping of a woman as if in great pain. Mum looked frightened and asked me to hurry; indeed, she literally dragged me inside the house and locked the door.

"What is the matter Agnes?" asked Aunt from her room. Even Uncle David came out of his.

"Can you hear the crying sound?" Mum asked in a frightened voice.

"Yes, it sounds like someone in great pain!" Aunt said.

"It may be the ghost of the dead woman you all disturbed by opening the burial box," Uncle replied.

"Say some prayers for her soul and go to sleep," Aunt said.

I don't know when the crying stopped because I dozed off, cuddling up to Mum on one side while Violet lay on her other. The next day, Mrs Kingsley said that even she had heard the sound between her house and ours. The crying sound continued for many nights after that. It started a little after midnight and went for an hour or more. But each night it sounded further down the road, until it was very faint and one night it stopped. Uncle David said the ghost of the dead woman must have followed us and then had returned to its burial place at the banks of River Teesta.

Many years later I heard that Darryl drowned at the age of eighteen even though he could swim very well.

✣ ✣ ✣ ✣ ✣

On my ninth birthday, Uncle David presented me with a pair of brown boots, hand-made by a Chinese shoemaker from the city. I remember the day I first wore them, Aunt Natasha enquired from Mum how much they had cost and how she had afforded an expensive item without a permanent job. Mum looked uncomfortable. I tried to defend her and said before she could speak:

"Uncle David bought them for me, not mum."

"Uncle David! When did he give them to you?" asked Aunt.

"Yesterday, when we went to the Chinese shop in the city," I replied.

"Uncle David is very good to you, isn't he!" Aunt said sarcastically and walked away. I noticed Mum looking very worried. I did not know the reason, nor did I know how to help her.

A little while later, when I was playing in the garden outside the house, Aunt came to me again.

"Has Uncle David been very often to the city with you and your mother?"

"Yes, he meets us every time we go to the city and we watch films together. Uncle said I needed a pair of good boots. Do you like them Aunty?" I was very excited about my new boots.

"Of course they are very nice, especially when your mother didn't have to pay for them," Aunt said as she hissed her way back to the house, full of temper and venom.

That evening there was another serious fight between Mum and Aunt. Fortunately, Uncle Eddie was not at home, as he was at work in the plains at Gorakhpur.

"So, you are still after David! There is a difference of twelve years between you two. He comes from a good respectable family and is a bachelor. He has his whole future before him. You are enticing him because you want to palm your bastard children off on him! He has been calling you *bahen* (a sister), but behind my back you have been trying to get him to shoulder your responsibility! I will not let David get involved with you and your children", Aunt screamed.

"Natasha, why are you so suspicious? Yes, David has been out with me and has bought those pairs of boots for Minnie, but as I said before, I have always considered him as a younger brother. He loves Minnie and only wishes to help us. David is scared of your suspicions and that is why he has been meeting us on the quiet, only to be a good friend and brother. I know my responsibilities and duty towards my children. I still love Mino and no one can take his place in my life." Mum replied.

It made me very sad. If only Papa was here things would have been better for Mum. That evening I sang sad songs and prayed to Jesus for Papa to return to us in Kalimpong.

Shortly after the fight, Uncle David left for his home in Bettiah, in the plains. I watched him cry bitterly before leaving. Later I heard that he had joined the Indian army from where he resigned to join the Jesuits in the Patna Mission as a lay Brother. Aunt seemed very proud of the fact when she got the news, since it was considered an honour to be a man of religion. Mum continued with her tuition and visits to the city with Mrs Green and Mrs Kingsley. They were good friends and had great sympathy for her.

✣ ✣ ✣ ✣ ✣

Mum was very quiet after Uncle David left. I felt that she was planning something. I noticed that she often wrote long letters to the bishop in Patna or to a priest in Muzaffarpur. Then one day she told me that I had to go back again to the same boarding school up on the hill which was run by the Loretto Nuns. She again told me that Papa wanted me to be in the boarding school and that he would visit me soon in the place.

Just before I left for the boarding school, I overheard Aunt telling Mum one day:

"How can you part with your own children! I stopped you from putting Minnie in an orphanage soon after she was born and now when she is growing up so well, you wish to send her off to America for adoption on the advice of Bishop Wildermuth and Father O'Brien and give Violet for adoption to Father O'Brien's American sister!"

"I am doing what I think will be good for the children's

future. I cannot give them the good education and the standard of living they deserve", Mum replied in her quiet and calm manner.

I was taken to the same English Convent School where the Kingsleys went a week later. I was not happy about it, but Mum insisted that it was good for me and I had to go. She put me into the boarding school during the Easter holidays when all the other boarders were at home and the school was closed. There were only two big girls in the boarding school at the time, because their parents were overseas. I cried when mum left me, but it had no effect on her. She had an indifferent expression on her face. I struggled to follow her, but a fat nun held me back. However, I decided I would return home to my mother somehow and very soon.

I was in the boarding school for about ten days and I cried every day. I missed my mother very much and worried about her welfare. I did not want her to disappear like my father did. I also missed home and my friend Aileen. I missed all the fun we had playing in the big field, running wildly and free. At the boarding school everything was timed and routined. It was a very gloomy and depressing place. I wanted to find my father. I missed all the love I had from both my parents when we were in Saharanpore. I was very confused about what was happening. Why was I always put into a boarding school when other children stayed at home. I could not understand why everyone said hurtful things to my mother and she cried so much. I knew how hard she worked and she was very clever because she could do so many things but why did she cry often? She put me into the boarding school against my wishes. I had done nothing wrong to make her cry or be angry. Sometimes she'd to slap me after a fight she had with Aunt Natasha or after the dolls play when there was a disagreement with Aileen or other children. She afterwards cuddled me saying, "I am sorry Minnie, I know it was not your fault. When they complain I feel so hurt and angry with myself. I slap you instead because of my frustration. I hate any conflicts. I cannot fight back because they all condemn me saying I cannot take care of my children. I have no money and I have to depend on others for help. When anyone complains, even when I know it is not your fault, I still punish you because I don't know what else to do. I am sorry. I am so sad with my life; I don't know where to take you two and how to manage it all. I love you two so much but I don't know what to do for the three of us." Mum then cried and I forgot her beating me for no reason and cried along with her.

"It is alright Mum, I don't mind you slapping me. I am sorry that I have made you cry. I will let the others do what they want, even take my doll away or eat my lollies. I will not fight with anyone, I promise. I will be what you want me to be, but don't cry." Mum was all I had. She often cuddled Violet and me at night when she thought we were asleep and kissed us quietly. But why was I put me into the school? Had I done something she did not like? I wanted so much to get back to her and tell her that I was sorry. I was pretty sure that she was crying and I needed to go to her and assure her of my love.

There were two girls, about fourteen or fifteen, with me in the boarding school. They had not gone home for the holidays and they informed the nuns of everything I said and did. They enjoyed staying at the school and eating the European food but I missed the curry and rice I ate at home. I often cried at mealtime and told them I would kill myself eating the leaves from the plants outside if they hassled me too much about eating. I wanted to go home to my mother and that was all I wanted, not the food or the beautiful bed or the toys. Nothing interested me, I felt like a prisoner suffocated with all the goodies they offered at Easter. All of the things given to me after the midnight mass were lovely but I did not want them. I wanted my mother and home.

The school was very expensive: ninety *rupees* per month, which included education, board and lodging. (In 1949, ninety *rupees* were a large amount: you could buy a loaf of bread for only ten *paisa* or one tenth of a *rupee* and a month's groceries cost only ten *rupees*.)

Aunt Natasha came to see me on Easter Sunday. With great difficulty she was allowed to meet me for a little while. Aunt told me that she had come to take me home but the Reverend Mother had refused it because Mum had not left any such instructions. I came to know that Mum and Violet had left Kalimpong for a place in the plains called Muzaffarpur. They left two days after I was put into the boarding school. Aunt was alone with Enid and Helen waiting for Uncle Eddie and then they too were to go back to the plains. I cried when Aunt left and that night I planned to run away from the convent the next day. I wanted to go with Aunt to the plains where I had the chance of meeting my dear mother and sister.

The next morning as usual we three girls were ready to go for breakfast. But before doing so, the older girls went to the morning Mass in the chapel with the nuns, while I was made to sit out near the dormitory steps and play with some toys. I was waiting for this opportunity. As soon as I saw the girls disappear into the chapel I jumped up and ran towards the long steps which went all the way down the hill, past the poor *Nepali* school I had been attending and down on to the main road. I ran as fast as my legs could carry me. When I was at the foot of the steps, I looked back up the hill, in the distance I could see the heads of the two girls looking down at me. I crossed the main road and used by-ways and short cuts to reach Aunt's house.

Aunt was sitting at the table having breakfast. Enid and Helen were still sleeping. I was out of breath for I had covered about two miles, non-stop. Aunt was shocked to see me, but she lovingly made me sit and have breakfast with her before she started asking questions. I told her I was not returning to the convent. She sat and watched thoughtfully as I ate.

I was enjoying my *parathas* (Indian homemade bread) and mince curry, when the two girls arrived. They were breathless too, as they had come running the long way, by the main road. Aunt made them sit down and served them with tea from the teapot covered with a fancy tea cosy. After breakfast she took me back to the convent school with the girls, promising me that she would get permission for me to be at home for the holidays. She also promised to write to mum, asking her permission to take me down to the plains and to Muzaffarpur, where she and Violet were.

When we reached the convent, the Reverend Mother looked very concerned. She stared at me and spoke to Aunt.

"I don't think I can keep her here against her wishes. She is old enough to know her own mind and is fretting for her mother. I cannot look after her for twenty-four hours a day. She is a very headstrong child. It would be best if she is returned to her mother. I'll write to Bishop Wildermuth in Patna and tell him the story.

"I was delighted and ran out of the convent gate with Aunt. All I thought about was that I had won and was going home to my dear mother and sister! Little did I know then what sort of a future I had won with that freedom.

5

Aunt Natasha's home town

We had to wait at least a month before Uncle Eddie could come home to us. Aunt had packed the entire luggage with the help of the servant, but she could not travel alone with the children and so we had to wait for his arrival.

One day while packing a huge black metal trunk Aunt found a white envelope containing a few strands of soft golden hair. She said they were mine. I was born with only very scanty golden soft hair. Mum and Aunt decided upon having my head shaved by the barber a few months after I was born. They were confident that a thicker new growth would follow. The hair grew again but this time light brown in colour and thin.

I missed my mother and sister very much. Somehow I felt that Mum did not want me and that this was why she left me and went away with Violet. I could not understand why first Papa left then Uncle David and finally Mum and Violet. Everyone seemed to leave me and go away. Aunt Natasha was the only one left, so I was determined to hold on to her. I made sure that I was always with her in case she decided to leave me too. I slept in the same room with her, next to Enid and Helen and followed her everywhere throughout the day.

✣ ✣ ✣ ✣ ✣

One day Mr and Mrs Douglas came to visit Aunt Natasha. Mr Douglas was an Englishman. Mrs Douglas looked like a fair skinned *Nepali*. She was dressed very tastefully in the most beautiful white silk *sari*, with a thin gold border. She had very thick black hair which was done up into a large puff in front and then neatly folded into a big bun at the back. She wore a very bright red lipstick as a contrast to her black hair and white skin. Mrs Douglas was a very softly spoken and gentle lady.

After they left I heard Aunt talking with our maid-servant

that Mrs Douglas was once a very poor local woman, who used to survive by picking up coal pieces from the railway lines and selling them to earn some money. A photographer once took some photographs of her carrying a heavy basket of coal on her back. He enlarged the best photograph and had it displayed in his shop, as an advertisement of his photographic skill. Mr Douglas took a fancy to the photograph when he saw it and bought it for his house. Not long after, Mr Douglas saw Mrs Douglas walking up the hill with her heavy load of coal. He recognised her as the lady in the photograph and offered her a friendly and caring hand. Slowly he won her heart and they were married. He taught her to read and write and to become a good wife to him. They were to leave for England soon and settle down there.

✣ ✣ ✣ ✣ ✣

Uncle Eddie came a few days later and one day we all boarded the bus to Darjeeling, from where we caught the train to Bettiah, a city in the state of Bihar, north of India. Aunt said she had informed Mum and she would meet me at Muzaffarpur, which was on the same route to Bettiah.

I felt sad leaving Kalimpong because I was used to its beauty and the landscape and I was unsure where we were going. Aunt did not enjoy good health in Kalimpong and was keen to return to the plains. She had to leave behind many luggage bags in the house, as we could not carry all of it with us. Aunt asked Mrs Kingsley to look after it, as she was sure we would return; if not, she would send for them. The big black trunk, which contained the hank of my hair, was also left behind.

It took a few days and nights to reach Muzaffarpur where Mum took down my entire luggage from the compartment. I was happy to see her and enjoyed her fussing over me, but suddenly when I realised that the train was moving and that Aunt was about to leave me, I started crying to go with her to Bettiah. I felt I had to do so, because she had brought me home from the boarding school, whereas Mum had left me. Perhaps I was still angry with Mum. Uncle pulled me up into the train again, telling Mum to pick me up in a week's time from Bettiah.

Mum said nothing; she and Violet simply stood amid my luggage at the station as the train sped past.

After a few hours we arrived in Bettiah. We hired three ekkas (a cart, pulled by a horse, with only a high platform to perch upon). The ekkas carrying the luggage and us were driven through narrow streets filled with people, unlike those at Kalimpong. The men and women were dressed differently and the children ran about naked, which would have been impossible in Kalimpong, due to the cold weather. Aunt was familiar with the language, which the ekka drivers spoke. It was very different from the *Nepali* language. She seemed very happy and excited.

The drivers kept hitting the horses with whips to make them run faster. On both sides of the street were rows of houses. There was hardly any greenery. Suddenly the ekkas stopped in front of a house, which was plastered with mud and had a red-tiled roof. The wooden door was open. A girl of about fourteen was playing outside. As soon as she saw us, she began calling to the people inside the house saying that *bahen* (sister) had come. At this, a number of others came out from the house to welcome Aunt, Enid, Helen and Uncle. I heard a dark skinned man of about twenty-four asking whether I was Agnes *bahen's* daughter, Minnie. Aunt replied that I was and that I had come to stay for a few days with them, after which I would be taken back by Agnes, my mother. I suddenly felt I did not belong there. In the excitement even Aunt forgot me. This was the first time I realised that Mum and Aunt were not real sisters, that Aunt had her own seven brothers and four sisters. My mother was Aunt Natasha's friend and they addressed each other as sister (*bahen*).

The dark man took me by the hand and led me through a narrow corridor into a wide courtyard, which was tiled with bare bricks. The verandah around it was plastered with mud over the bricks. All the walls were plastered with mud. On the other side of the verandah were a few rooms. At one end of the courtyard was a pump to draw up fresh water. The part of the verandah nearest to the water pump was closed off to form a kitchen. In the kitchen there was a double fireplace on the floor, made of mud. Coal and wood was used as fuel. Many utensils, most of aluminium and brass, lay neatly stacked up in one corner of the kitchen. Opposite was a flight of three cement steps, leading to a small room. This was the only cemented room in the house and I was told later that it belonged to Aunt Natasha. She had had it built for herself when she was teaching in Bettiah.

Our luggage was taken into the cemented room. I was taken to two ladies sitting in the middle of the courtyard. The older lady looked at me closely and said that I looked like my father whom she remembered very well. The two ladies were Aunt Natasha's mother and grandmother.

On one side of the courtyard sat an old man with hardly any hair on his head. He was introduced to me as Aunt Natasha's father.

Minnie was also the name of Aunt Natasha's youngest sister who became my friend and together we climbed the terrace steps without railings. The steps were very steep and I had to hold on to the walls on one side whilst climbing them. Minnie would spread the washed clothes for drying on the terrace roof and tell me stories about fairies and giants while doing her work. From the terrace roof we looked into the neighbours' courtyards. The lady on one side of their house was happy to see me, as she said that she knew my mother. Everyone who saw me seemed to look closely at me and then start talking in whispers amongst themselves.

The courtyard opened onto a large garden at the back, which had many fruit trees. Uncle Noorat had a pet monkey, which he kept tied to a tree. Uncle Norbert, Aunt's brother, frightened me with ghost stories and saying that he could turn me into a monkey with his magical powers. He was the real life of that house, full of jokes and fun. Many years later, he became a very religious Jesuit priest in Patna and died as the Rector of the Jesuits in the city of Patna.

I liked being in Bettiah because there was so much to see and so many people to meet. Aunt had a lot of relatives and she was invited over by everyone. This was the first time she had come to visit her parents and relatives after her marriage. She had married on her own and out of their caste to an Anglo-Indian. In Bettiah the marriages are arranged even amongst the

Christians. Aunt's relations were angry with her at first, but since she had been writing to them continually, they had accepted the fact, though they felt awkward at first to meet a *sahib* (the name given to the British and the Anglo-Indians by the native Indians) son-in-law. Once Aunt and Uncle were in Bettiah and in the house, the relations poured in from everywhere to see them and invite them over, as was the custom. Uncle looked awkward and out of place, as he was brought up in British ways and did not know the local language well enough to communicate. Aunt's relations were all staunch Catholics, but they followed Hindu ways since it was their original background.

I discovered that everywhere I went with Aunt Natasha and Uncle Eddie, people made much of Helen and Enid. I had to sit very close to Aunt to be noticed. When they did take notice of me, they would always ask the same question:

"Is this Agnes's daughter?" Then look closely at me and say, "She certainly looks like her father." After that they would forget my existence and continue fussing over Enid and Helen. Very often Aunt's sister, Minnie, would discreetly coax me to leave the room when visitors came to meet Aunt and take me upstairs on the terrace roof to listen to her stories or to play hide-and-seek.

Aunt Minnie took me to her school one day. Education was not free and compulsory in India, I was not allowed into my appropriate class but given permission to stay with Aunt Minnie as a visitor for the day. It was a private school run by the nuns. I realised that even the nuns looked at me in the same critical manner and spoke in whispers to each other as did everyone else when Aunt Minnie told them that I was Agnes *bahen*'s daughter.

During the break she bought me some powder in a small packet called *churan*. It was so sour and salty that it burnt the skin on my tongue and even made it peel. Later Aunt Natasha scolded Aunt Minnie for giving me churan as she said it contained some arsenic-like ingredient and could be harmful for a child of my age. The school did not have a canteen and so the students bought food and snacks from the hawkers who sat outside the school gates. Hawkers sold things from baskets, which they carried on their heads and went from house to house, calling out what they were offering. They carried a light cane stand under their arms and when anyone wanted to buy something from them, they put the basket on the stand to display and sell. I ate a variety of homemade sweets and peanuts bought from hawkers.

Uncle Eddie returned to his job at the end of the week promising Aunt that he would find accommodation for her close to his place of work. He said he was very ill at ease in Bettiah, as, besides being the only Anglo-Indian amongst all the Indian Christian relatives, he was also not used to a big family.

Before Independence, all converted Christians preferred English names of the saints as the British Government rewarded the Christians and the Anglo-Indians with good jobs. Some even went to the extent of changing their surnames. But since Independence it has become a fashion, even among Christians, to keep an Indian name and in particular the surname, in order to show their caste. All Indian surnames show the caste one belongs to. After Independence most Christian names have been replaced by Sanskrit names having the same meaning, eg. Norbert is turned into Daleep, Violet into Malti and Michael into Savannand.

✣ ✣ ✣ ✣ ✣

Mum arrived after ten days to take me back to Muzaffarpur. I was happy because I felt that I did not belong at Bettiah, as Aunt Natasha was too involved with her relatives. Besides, Aunt's mother and grandmother were full of questions about how mum intended bringing up the two of us by herself.

"They are my children and I will do everything I can to raise them myself." I heard Mum responding to Aunt Natasha's mother.

✣ ✣ ✣ ✣ ✣

Arriving in Muzaffarpur late at night, Mum took me to the teachers' quarters behind the small Catholic primary school. There were three other teachers with Mum living in that building made of brick and tiles. Each teacher had a separate room but shared the kitchen and toilet. There was a sink on the verandah for washing if the bathroom was occupied.

I slept cuddled up to Mum and Violet. She explained that she had managed to place me in the good school at Kalimpong with great difficulty and effort, that it was for my future welfare and she said she didn't understand why I ran away.

"Anyway, I'm glad to have you back, I missed you a lot. We will leave it all in the hands of God and trust in Him and His mercy" she consoled.

Next morning after breakfast of bread and butter with tea, Mum took us to meet the American parish priest, Father O'Brien. I realised from their conversation that he was a friend of my Papa and intended helping us. He seemed displeased with me for running away from the boarding school in Kalimpong.

"You have kicked your future away by doing so Minnie," he said to me. "You would have had a good future in America later on. You ruined everything by running away like that! What can I do for you all now?" He spoke in perfect Hindi with a Bihari accent like my Papa did. I had heard Mum speak the Bihari language with the other teachers and in Bettiah. By then I could also speak the language a little, along with *Nepali*. There seemed to be many similarities between the two languages.

"She is only a child Father," Mum said. "I think I will keep them both with me. I shall work hard to support them."

"So you're not going to send Violet to my sister in America?" Father O'Brien asked.

"No, I don't think I can part with them, they too, cannot live without me either," Mum replied.

"It is your decision and your life Agnes, but it is going to be very hard. I cannot keep you here for long. I have my own staff, I don't really need another teacher. Besides, many people know you here. There will be gossip and scandalous talk which could give this school a bad name. I cannot risk that, nor would the new Bishop Wildermuth like it to happen. So you will have to make your decision soon and then, I am afraid, leave the city."

"I shall go to Patna and speak to the Bishop myself. Perhaps Mino has written to him and sent us some money. Bishop

Wildermuth was a good friend of his, I am sure he will help us," Mum said.

"It is most unlikely, but you can try. I shall pray for you," Father O'Brien concluded.

We walked back to the teachers' quarters. The others seemed to be very sympathetic. They were mostly from Bettiah and advised Mum to see the new Bishop, as she had planned. Mum had very little money; she was entirely dependent on Father O'Brien's charity. Mum took us out of the school compound the next morning on purpose so she did not confront any of the parents and the school children. She was once teaching as a nun in the very school and therefore it seemed appropriate for her to avoid them by staying out of the premises during school hours. It was a very hot summer day and we did not have enough money to buy a cool drink. When we returned that evening the teachers offered us their leftover food, which was all we had that night. It was strange being without Aunt Natasha and her two daughters. I missed them and wondered why we were not living together anymore.

Soon the school closed for two months of summer holidays and Mum was busy sewing for the church while we played outside our room every day. Father O'Brien paid Mum for the work and she used the money to buy food for us. One day Mum announced she was going to see the Bishop in Patna for some help and would be back within two days. She left by train that evening. We were left in the care of a teacher who had not left for summer vacation.

Although the teacher was very sympathetic towards Mum and said she would take good care of us, after Mum left she complained about all she had to do for us. Violet was only five years old. We were used to sleeping with Mum in one bed and Violet had the habit of rolling and throwing her hands and legs about the bed in her sleep. In India children mostly sleep with their parents, girls with the mother and boys with the father, till they are mature, chiefly because they lack accommodation and have to make do with one room and very often with one bed. That night we slept with the teacher. In the morning she was full of aches and pains. We had a visitor that afternoon: a neighbour of Aunt Natasha from Bettiah came in to spend few hours in Muzaffarpur Catholic Mission, while waiting for the connecting train to Bettiah. She told me that we should have gone to Bettiah and stayed with Aunt Natasha whilst waiting for Mum's return from Patna. Immediately I got ready to go with her, but Violet refused. That afternoon I left with the lady and went back to Aunt Natasha, who was very happy to see me again.

"So your Mum has gone to ask help from the new Bishop. As if he will be bothered with her! Why doesn't she come and live with me over here? " Aunt said.

I felt safe and happy in Bettiah. It did not matter any more that everyone made much of Enid and Helen, as long as Uncle Norbert and Aunt Minnie took some notice of me. It was also good to have enough food.

Uncle Cherobim, one of the brothers of Aunt Natasha, told me that he had once saved my life.

"One day when you were about a year old, I found you sitting at the edge of the well facing us, with your back towards the hole. You were digging the ground with a sharp knife. The well did not have any boundary wall around it. If you had just turned back in panic, you would have gone straight into the deep well. I crept quietly from behind, leapt over the well and picked you up. Your mother and Aunt were paralysed with fear."

"Yes and what about the time she sat covered in honey under the bed!" Aunt said. "Your father had bought a big tin of honey for you and kept it under the bed. Somehow you had crawled under the bed, knocked the tin over and spilled its contents all over the floor. We found you sitting there, in the middle of it, honey all over you, licking it up hungrily."

I was happy knowing that Aunt Natasha's people loved and cared for me. I liked being with people who knew me. It made me feel accepted and loved. I felt a sense of belonging and security. But a few days later Mum came for me. I could not refuse to go with her. No one asked me to remain, even though I was hoping they would.

"Did the new Bishop give you any help?" Aunt asked. "Was there any message from Mino? Bishop Wildermuth and he were good friends once!"

"Bishop Wildermuth has promised to see to the education of the children. He has given me ninety *rupees* for the time being. There is no message from Mino and the Bishop does not know where he is," Mum replied.

"Why don't you stay here and work as before?" Aunt asked.

Mum did not want to stay and teach in Bettiah. She said she wished to live independently with us and away from everyone who once knew her. That same evening she took me back to Muzaffarpur.

✣ ✣ ✣ ✣ ✣

For the next few weeks she was back on her embroidery work for the church. Mum was extremely religious and attended the service every morning without fail. She received the Holy Communion daily after fasting from the previous night, not taking even a drop of water till she had received the sacrament.

I missed the life we lived together with Papa. I also missed Aunt Natasha and the life in Kalimpong when we were all living together. I liked living in a family and with many people around. One day I took the liberty of asking Mum:

"Where is Papa? Why doesn't he come to us any more!"

"I don't know where he is. He has left all the responsibility on me and escaped. I don't want to talk about him anymore," Mum replied.

I felt uncomfortable. I did not really understand what the talk of responsibility was about, but I wondered whether my Papa had actually forgotten me.

"Mum, why are we not living with Aunt Natasha anymore?" I asked again.

"They haven't got a place of their own and I don't want to live in Bettiah. Besides we have to live on our own and not depend on others," Mum replied closing the conversation.

I liked living in Muzaffarpur, especially when the teacher went away and we had the whole place and the kitchen to ourselves. Mum worked in the church daily, decorated the altar with clean linen and changed the flowers and the candles. She cooked us good meals and seemed happy that she was able to attend the church service every morning. She made sure that we also said our evening prayers and the Rosary with her daily before going to bed.

6

Orphanages and homelessness

The summer vacation was coming to an end. One day I heard Father O'Brien say to Mum:

"Agnes, you cannot slave to provide for the two children all your life. They need more than just food, love and care. They are growing up and need proper schooling. The Bishop has not sent you any help, nor is there any sign of their father. It will be best for you to leave the children in the orphanage at Jhansi and start a life for yourself again. You need to consider your future too. I can arrange for you to take the children there. It would be best for all of you."

At first Mum ignored the offer, but eventually had no choice when Father told her that he could not allow us to stay on in his teachers' quarters, once the school re-opened.

Once again we were on the move, this time towards the city of Jhansi, where Mum said we were going to start our schooling again, as it was important to be educated. We had not been to a school for quite some time. Mum told us that she would also stay in Jhansi and try to teach in the same school.

It was a long journey to Jhansi, a city of the brave Rajput queen who fought the British for the independence of her kingdom. I sat near the window in the third compartment of the train, which was steaming through the wide expanse of, reddish earth, on which there roamed peacocks and cattle. I was feeling sad and even unhappy. I was tired of always moving to different places. There seemed no stable and permanent place to live. I wanted a home, like the one we had in Saharanpore. I was frightened and confused and still missed Papa and worried that he would never find us because we moved so much. I hummed the old sad songs and asked the good Lord Jesus for the return of my father. Tears rolled down my cheeks as I prayed and sang. Things had been so much better when he was with us. There were no fights between Mum and Aunt when he was with us and we all lived together in one big house with servants to help out. I liked it the way it was in Saharanpore: Mum seemed so happy with Papa then and I did not to have to worry about Mum and Violet.

After twenty-four hours we arrived at the station of Jhansi which was a different state, people spoke in Hindi, different to Bihari and *Nepali*. But again there were some similarities, so I could understand them. The women also wore their *saris* in a different way. We took a *tonga* to St Phillomina's orphanage. I was rather nervous and upset because I was afraid that Mum might leave us there once again and disappear, even though she had promised she would not.

Mum gave the European Reverend Mother the letter, which Father O'Brien had sent about us. She read it and said:

"Well Agnes, I will take the children and keep them here. I agree with Father O'Brien that this is the best for both you and the children." I caught hold of Mum's hand and squeezed it hard.

"Can I stay here for a few days with the children before I leave?" Mum asked.

"Well, we don't generally allow that, but I shall let you stay for a few days only." the Reverend Mother replied.

"I am a middle trained teacher. Could I have a teaching position here," Mum said.

"Certainly not. This is an orphanage and we do not allow any parents to stay here. Agnes, get hold of yourself and start your life again. The children will survive here without you. They will make their own life later. You take care of yourself." Then she turned and left the room and the Indian nuns helped Mum to carry our luggage inside.

This was an orphanage exclusively for Indian girls. Our things were taken to a dormitory, which had cubicles for the staff at the end. The girls' beddings were on the floor in two rows. Ours were placed beside the others. I wanted to cry. I wanted my Papa to help us. Where was he? He had loved and cared for us so much, how could he have forgotten us? Mum was given a bed in the cubicle with a teacher.

The girls of all ages wore blue cotton frocks. We were provided with similar. None of the girls wore shoes, so ours were taken away. We walked barefoot on the hot and rugged ground of Jhansi where the summer temperature reached 52 degree Celsius. We were there in June, the hottest month of summer in India. The church was about six kilometres from the orphanage. Between the church and the orphanage was the English Convent school for the rich children. We had to walk barefoot twice on Sundays to the church, once for the Mass in the morning and again in the afternoon at four, in the heat of the day, to attend the Benediction. Mum had never allowed us to walk without shoes and socks both in Saharanpore and in Kalimpong. Without shoes it hurt so much to walk over the hot road, but there was no escape as we were given to understand that we had to do penance to save souls and also to reach heaven when we died.

The food at the orphanage was terrible. Once a week the big girls would knead the plain wholemeal flour for the *chappattis* (home made unleavened Indian bread). The girls rolled out the kneaded flour into circles, then baked them over the coal fire and kept them in a big wooden box for the week. Spinach or lentils were boiled every day and served with the stale *chappattis* from the box for dinner. Often I found streaks of slime coming out of the bread when I broke a piece of it. The hot weather made everything go off quickly. But we had to eat what was given to us or go hungry. We sat on the ground in rows and silently ate our watery spinach and stale bread with our hands, after thanking the good Lord for the meal and our lives. We were served the same thick stale bread for breakfast with a glass of watery tea made in the same container in which the spinach was boiled. It smelled of spinach. There was hardly any milk or sugar in it. The girls found the dry *chappattis* hard to swallow and managed it only by drinking dark tea with every bite they took, so we too tried to do the same. At lunchtime we received thick boiled rice with watery lentil soup. Meat was a luxury and served only when there was a feast-day of some saint. It was served in watery gravy and everyone received just two pieces of the meat each. We could not ask for more food than was served to us – not that I would have, as I found it repulsive. But we were told that we should be grateful for what we got as it was free and that if we were on the streets we would have lived on food from garbage bins or starved to death.

The school was closed for two months holidays, so we did not attend any classes. We spent each day praying and doing house work. After the holidays we were to attend the poor school next to the English school where Hindi was the medium of instruction.

Mum was served with the good food enjoyed by the nuns and the teachers. She felt very sorry for the two of us. She had managed to stay a bit longer than permitted because a sick newborn baby was left abandoned on the doorstep a day after we arrived. The nuns were happy to use Mum in caring for the baby for a month. One day with the nuns' permission, she took us out. She bought us a good meal that evening. We both ate as though we had not done so for days. Mum watched us with a very sad expression on her face.

After the meal we visited the palace of the famous Rajput *Rani* (queen) of Jhansi and the grave of her loyal horse. This is when I grasped an opportunity to corner Mum with the questions, which plagued me most.

"Mum, when are we leaving this place? I don't like the food here". I was still under the impression that it was only a school and that Mum would take us with her when the term was over. Her answer made me worry about her intentions. I made sure I kept an eye on her movements at the orphanage: I was not going to let her leave us there and go away. I felt I had to go with her wherever she went.

One day I heard Reverend Mother telling Mum the baby was well again and that she'd been given enough time and that she should leave as soon as possible, as her presence meant we were being treated differently from the other orphans.

"Don't leave us here Mum, I beg of you." I pleaded with her that evening.

"I have nowhere to take you both, nor any means to support you. They will see to your education and well being. You will both be better off here than with me," Mum replied.

"No, I will go with you wherever you go. I will run away from here if you leave me, or I will eat something and die." I started crying while Violet watched. "Why don't you write to Aunt Natasha? She will help us and keep us," I said, putting my arms around her. She was crying with me. I kissed her as I realised that she did not want to leave us and that she loved us. I decided that I would make her take us with her wherever she went. I was not bothered about education or anything else; all I wanted was to be with my mother who loved me, since Papa had disappeared. She was all I had. I could not understand why we had to be with the orphans. I did not think we were orphans! We had a loving mother and our father wasn't dead, he had just gone away somewhere. He said he would return soon. Why did Father O'Brien and the nuns want to make us orphans when our parents were alive!

Mum did write to Aunt Natasha and also informed the Reverend Mother that she could not leave us behind and was going to take us back but needed time until she heard from her dear friend, Natasha. The Reverend Mother, a German nun, shook her head and told Mum that she was being foolish and ruining her young life.

"The children will survive here. They'll forget everything in good time. No one will want you if you have two children. People will gossip wherever you go."

Aunt Natasha wrote back and said that she was overjoyed to have us live together again. They were moving from Bettiah to Allahabad, to be closer to Uncle Eddie's work. Allahabad had good English schools. They were going to stay with a friend, Mr de'Cunha, an Anglo-Indian conductor-guard in the railways.

When the British ruled India, most railway jobs were given to Anglo-Indians, because they could communicate with everyone since they were half-Indian and half-British. The Anglo-Indians themselves were very loyal to the British, and considered themselves more British than Indian. The British also gave them preference over the Indians.

The Indian community did not want to accept the Anglo-Indians, as they were half-breeds and products of the British, whom they disliked, being the rulers with a different religion and cultural background. Because an Anglo-Indian might have been born as a result of an affair between a British officer and the poor Indian woman who did domestic work in his home, they were mostly fairer than the average Indian. There were also the Anglo-Indians born of marriages between officers and Indian girls from well-to-do Hindu or Muslim homes who had been disowned by their parents. The Indians were very strict about marrying their children into their own caste and class. No outsiders were ever welcomed. They believed in family status and maintaining purity of caste and race. Therefore Anglo-Indians born of such alliances had no option but to follow British ways and religion. They were accepted in the Christian religion but never by Hinduism, as they had no caste. Many Anglo-Indian children were born on the tea and the coffee estates and where the indigo factories were. The British Government provided them with work, while the Christian churches helped them with education. As far as possible they were brought up according to western ways.

Most Anglo-Indians who could prove their British background left India and immigrated to England and Australia after the independence of India. The British made special provisions for their immigration. The few who were brought up as orphans, along with those who could not establish their British background, stayed back with some who preferred India and lived as a separate minority community. But they still followed the same British traditions and culture and considered themselves as British. The Anglo-Indians preferred intermarriage with their own community. The religion and the cultural difference made it difficult for them to assimilate with the other Indians.

✣ ✣ ✣ ✣ ✣

I was very happy with Mum's decision to take us back to Allahabad and to Aunt Natasha. They had a proper home for Enid and Helen.

We travelled in the third-class compartment on the train to Allahabad, Violet went to sleep on Mum's lap. The general compartments in Indian trains have no allocated seats, people just buy tickets and pile in and seats are a matter of first come first served. There were people carrying their baskets of fruits and vegetables and other things such as honey, milk and home-made ghee, mostly for sale at the nearby village markets. I kept my head out of the window to watch the dimly lit villages passing by but found I could not keep my head out of the window because of the fragments of coal dust from the engine which kept getting into my eyes. I pulled my head in and closed the window before snuggling down on the narrow seat.

After two nights and two days in the heat of mid-summer, we arrived at the station. The porters helped carry our two trunks of clothes, utensils and bedding. They carried the luggage on their heads, while Mum, holding our hands, dragged us behind them through the crowd. The Reverend Mother in Jhansi had paid Mum some money for attending to the sick baby so we hired a *tonga* to carry the luggage and us. It took us along a wide road into a narrow lane, which had double storey buildings on each side. We went through a narrow gate into the first building on the left side. This was Block 128. Mum went up the steps to flat No.2 which belonged to Mr de'Cunha and introduced herself as Aunt Natasha's friend telling him why she was there. He told Mum that Uncle Eddie and Aunt Natasha had not arrived from Bettiah. They had not mentioned anything about us, so he told Mum to come back when they arrived. Mum pleaded with him to let us stay at his place waiting for Aunt Natasha as we had nowhere to go.

"I cannot allow a strange Indian woman with two white children stay in my house. I live alone here and I cannot allow any gossip and scandal to start by your staying even for an hour. Besides, I am a railway guard and have to be on duty tonight. I cannot leave strangers in my house. You could steal things and disappear," he said and walked into the flat.

"What will we do, Mum?" I said, feeling very unhappy.

Mum did not answer but directed the driver of the *tonga* to a Catholic Church in Allahabad. The man did as she requested and the horse was once again galloping through the hot air of the midday heat.

There was hardly anyone on the streets except some stray

dogs and a few people with covers over their heads. This was June, the hottest month of summer. The school hours in the plains in North India during the summer are between eight in the morning and one in the afternoon. The summer starts in April. There are two months of summer holidays, from mid-May to mid-July. The rich people usually leave for the hill stations near the Himalayas and to the south of India, the poor and those who cannot afford to travel, prefer to spend their afternoons sleeping indoors cooled by fans or air-conditioning, or under the shade of a big tree. The heat of the sun can cause immediate heat exhaustion. People often collapse, some go insane. In heat like that we searched for a place to spend a few days, in an unknown city.

Mum directed the driver to a big building at the side of the cathedral.

"I want to see the parish priest. Is he in?" Mum asked a lady nearby.

"Yes, Father De'Mello is coming out soon," she replied.

I realised then how tired and weak Mum was looking. A dark-skinned priest with a long beard came out, he was a secular Indian priest from the south of India. He looked at mum and then at us in the *tonga* full of luggage.

"Who are you and what do you want?" he said.

Mum explained.

"I am sorry, I don't know you, so I cannot give you a place to stay. Even if you are a Catholic, you might run away with things." He said in Hindi.

"Father, please at least keep my things here and help me with some money for food and the conveyance. We'll wait at the station until my friend arrives." Mum pleaded.

"Sorry, I cannot look after strangers' goods. They could be stolen or may get me into trouble." He then reluctantly pulled out a ten-rupee note and gave it to Mum.

Mum wiped her eyes and took the money. She asked him if he knew where Father Evans lived. Father De'Mello informed Mum that Father Evans was not in Allahabad, but lived in a place called Chunar, a few stations away.

As Mum walked towards us, the lady who had spoken to

her first said she knew Father Evans and that the train to Chunar left at 8.00 at night.

"I live close by, come to my house and relax before going to the station."

"Thank you very much," Mum replied. The lady sat with us in the *tonga* and guided us to her house. As we left the church gates Mum looked to the right side where there was another gate.

"Who lives there?" she asked the lady.

"That is the English convent school, run by the German Loretto nuns," Mrs Dawson replied.

"I'll ask them to keep my children in the boarding school," Mum said and immediately had the driver take us through the gates. Mum insisted to the watchman she wanted to see the Reverend Mother of the convent. He reluctantly informed the nuns and returned with three of them.

"Who are you and what do you want?" the fat nun asked in her broken Hindi, noticing that Mum was an Indian, dressed in a rather dirty *sari* from the journey.

Mum explained that we needed education in a good Catholic school as we were Catholics. We had come to stay with a friend in Allahabad who had not arrived. Would she keep the children as boarders till they came?

"This is not an orphanage nor a shelter, it is an English convent school. Only the students who can pay the high fees are taken into the school or are boarding here. Your children would not fit in with our students, they are all from good homes and speak English. Besides, we are on summer holidays now, go to the parish priest, ask for his help." With those words the nuns walked away, ordering the watchman to close the gates after we left.

Mum returned to us dejected.

"Don't worry. Spend the day with us and then go to Chunar," Mrs Dawson consoled Mum. "Father Evans is a kind man. He will help you. We know him very well; he visits us whenever he comes to Allahabad. You can leave your luggage at our place. I will lend you some money for the journey."

Mum put her arms around my shoulder as the *tonga* drove

on towards Mrs Dawson's house. I felt bad for putting my mother through the trouble just because I wanted to stay with her and not in the orphanage. It was over 50 degrees Celsius that day, even the bitumen on the road started melting.

Mrs Dawson paid the *tonga* when we reached her small cement house not far from the cathedral. I jumped off in a daze and hurt my head on the *tonga* roof. But the pain did not hurt so much as the fact that everything seemed to be so dismal. A few days later I felt the pain, which kept me awake for many nights.

Our luggage was placed in one of the two rooms the house had. Mrs Dawson served lunch for us and her three children, who were of similar ages.

"Thank you very much for your kindness. I had given up hope and was thinking of putting an end to our lives by jumping into the river," Mum said to her afterwards.

"You must never think like that," she said, "God will help you. Look at your children – they are so pretty and innocent. How could you think of taking their lives! Where is their father?"

"I do not know where he is," Mum replied.

"He must have been a foreigner because your children are fair," Mrs Dawson said as she served the rice.

After lunch Mum and Violet went to sleep, but I could not so I got out of the bed and played with her children, until 7.00 o'clock that evening when the rickshaw came to take us to the station.

The Dawsons were kind and kept our luggage. I felt that Mrs Dawson would have allowed us to stay at her house until Aunt Natasha came, but her husband, an Indian Christian was reluctant so we had to leave for Chunar after all.

Later I learnt that when Mum was a nun she had worked with the German Loretto Order in Bettiah. She knew some of the nuns in Allahabad and so she sought their help.

7

Fr Evans tells a Lie!

We took an ekka at Chunar station, because no rickshaws were available. Chunar was a small station with two railway lines. Not all trains stopped there.

We passed rows of mud houses with thatched roofs. The streets were very muddy. The only large building made of brick was the Catholic Church and the school. Next to the church was the small brick building for the parish priest. At the back of the church was the graveyard. A small pale-faced priest came out of the house when Mum rang the bell.

"I am Agnes and these are Mino's children. Do you remember me? I met you once in Allahabad when Mino was in charge of the army men?" Mum said to him.

"Yes, I remember you very well. Michael was my friend and a very fine man. I am well aware of the problems he had. Well, how do you happen to be here? Where is he? The last time I met him, he was planning to visit the USA without the help of the Jesuits, because he said that if he asked their help, they would only give him a one-way ticket. He was going to collect enough money to visit his country and return soon," Fr. Evans said, looking concerned.

"He left in mid-1946. No one has heard of him since. I don't know what to do. It has been very difficult for us. I was to meet Eddie and Natasha at Allahabad, but they have not yet arrived at the address given to me. I had nowhere to go, the parish priest in Allahabad did not help me at all, so I took the liberty of coming to you for shelter and help until they arrive," Mum replied.

"Well, now that you are here, I will help you, but unfortunately I have no permanent accommodation. Also the people here remember Michael, he worked for the poor and the needy in this little place and was able to convert many in the depressed class to Catholicism. Do not mention his name in their presence," he said to mum and then looked towards us. "Bring the children in and have some dinner. I'll arrange for beds."

We were given a room to ourselves in the building where Father Evans lived. We slept like logs that night, as we were exhausted after the train journey and the ordeal of Allahabad. The next day we had our four meals as in Kalimpong. Breakfast was at 8.00 in the morning consisting of fried egg and toast. Lunch was boiled rice, meat curry and *dal* (made from red lentils boiled in water and garnished with butter and cumin seeds, the favourite dish of the British in India and the Anglo-Indians, to go with spicy curry and rice). Afternoon tea consisted of some biscuits and tea served at 4.00 in the evening and then dinner was at 8.00 in the evening, consisting of *dal* again, vegetable curry, meat curry and *chappattis*. Father Evans' servant prepared the meals and served them to him and us at the same time in our room.

The three of us slept in two *khats* (beds made of bamboo sticks and strong jute ropes) joined together. Mum spread two mosquito nets tied to four poles on each *khat*, to protect us from swarms of mosquitoes during the summer and the monsoons. Violet and I slept on either side of mum as we had done in Kalimpong.

Father Evans was an Anglo-Indian and his only sister had settled in England. He was about fifty, the same age as my father. The people loved and respected Father Evans because he was very kind to everyone. He knew the homoeopathic medical system and would treat the poor sick people by giving them tiny sugar balls saturated in medicinal drops. He carried a small wooden box full of homoeopathic medicines on the back of his bicycle and travelled throughout Chunar and the neighbouring villages treating the sick and the poor.

The next morning, while we were fast asleep, Mum attended the service performed by Father Evans. Later, she talked with Father about our future. He said that he would arrange for us to be boarders in Jeolikote near Nainital, at the foothills of the Himalayan range, further away from Darjeeling. He suggested that Mum take up nursing as a career. He knew the matron of a hospital in Allahabad who would help. I heard all the advice Father Evans gave Mum but did not know what to do as I had caused a lot of worry to Mum by making her take us out from St Philomena's Orphanage in Jhansi.

That evening Mum took us for a walk towards the river, which was not far from the church. We sat on the bank and watched the muddy water move slowly past. There were many people bathing there.

While I watched the river flowing by I saw something white bobbing up and down on the water some distance away. I pointed it out to Mum. She explained that it was a dead body and that fish and turtles were eating it from underneath. I felt sick; I had not realised that fish ate human flesh. Mum explained the religious difference between the Hindus and Christians, that the Hindus sometimes cremated their dead and sometimes threw the dead into the river Ganges and Jammuna, whereas the Christians always buried their dead.

On our return I saw many people, including women and children, sitting at different places and excreting. Mum told me that they were people from the mud houses with thatched roofs. They had no toilets beside their mud houses, so they used the fields and the space beside railway lines. They carried water in small tins, or brass utensils called *lottas,* to wash themselves afterwards. The people in the fields looked so strange with their backsides pointed towards the road! Perhaps, like ostriches, they thought that if they did not see anyone, then no one would see them. But I would rather have seen their faces!

✢ ✢ ✢ ✢ ✢

That evening I roamed around the church to explore the stone building constructed some centuries before by the foreign missionaries who came to India converting the poor and the oppressed. Chunar was a British settlement and General Warren Hastings had taken over the fort from the Hindu Rajah. Later in the 1940s Chunar was used to accommodate Burmese evacuees.

I walked into the graveyard. I could not read the names on the gravestones as they were all in English, but could read the dates to see how old they were. Most of them were from the 17th and 18th centuries and of the British settlers. The graves had beautiful marble figures of angels over them. It made me sad to think that everyone had to die at some time or other. I hoped that I would never see anyone dying and that my dear mother and sister would never die.

"What are you doing in the graveyard?" I jumped with fright and saw that it was Father Evans. I told him what my thoughts were.

"Everyone has to die to be able to meet Jesus in Heaven," he said "Jesus loves us and has given us each a guardian angel to look after us while we are on earth. Our guardian angel helps us to live according to the wishes of Jesus and helps us to reach heaven after death."

"Did you know my Papa?" I asked him suddenly.

"Yes, I knew your Papa very well," he replied after a moment of silence. "He was a good and intelligent man. He used to visit Mahatma Gandhi very often and would sit with the Untouchables helping them in the Ashram set up by Mahatma Gandhi in Bihar. He was a very kind man and did a lot for the poor and the needy."

"Do you know where Papa is? I want to ask him why he does not come to us any more. I want to bring him back to us again," I said with some hopes.

Father was quiet, then he put his hand under my chin and petted my head lovingly, saying: "Your father is in Heaven with Jesus. He is dead. You should pray for him and take Jesus as your father. Jesus took your father away because he was too good for this earth. Now Jesus is your father, you ask Him for anything you want and pray for everyone you love on earth. Jesus will listen to your prayers He is your father now."

The news that my father was dead made me extremely unhappy. I felt that I had to look after Mum and Violet for Papa and make sure that they too would not die and leave me, like Papa did. We were sort of orphans after all and that is why there was the effort to put us into the orphanages by the various understanding priests. But, we still had our mother. I was not going to let her abandon us into any of the orphanages.

Father Evans left me and went towards his house. I walked into the church and, kneeling in front of the altar, I prayed to the statue of Jesus, which looked so real:

"Dear Jesus, you took my dear Papa away. Now you have to be my Papa and look after us. Keep my Papa very happy with you and tell him that I love him very much, I miss him and I wish he were not dead. Please Jesus, help me to look after Violet and Mum."

I walked out of the church feeling somehow very satisfied with myself. I also remembered that my guardian angel was walking beside me as Father Evans had said. For some years after that I often talked to my imaginary friend, the guardian angel and Jesus, my father, whenever I was unhappy and misunderstood. I tried my best to be good in order to make my guardian angel and Jesus happy. Jesus became my father and I spent all my free time praying and talking to Him. I consulted Him on all matters as I would a human father. I prayed in church with my eyes closed and meant every word said in the prayers. I never felt the need of a friend of my age, as I was lost in my own world of Jesus.

When I reached our room after visiting the church that afternoon, I found mum sitting beside Violet on the bed and combing her hair. Violet had short, thick black and straight hair. Mum oiled and plaited her hair daily and put coloured ribbons at the end of it, as she did to my soft and long brown hair.

Father Evans was in the room, talking to Mum. "It's best that you tell the children and everyone that their father is dead and that you are a widow. Give them the surname of 'Anthony'. They will pass off as an Anglo-Indian rather than as Indian. You should call yourself 'Mrs Anthony'. It is no use giving them the surname of your mother 'Shah' because they do not look Indian."

I did not understand what they were talking about. At the time I was very sad and upset since Father Evans had informed me of my father's death. It made me feel lost and lonely to realise that my father was never going to come back to us and that I would never see him again.

✣ ✣ ✣ ✣ ✣

Mum went back to Allahabad for the luggage left at Mrs Dawson's house. There was no news of Aunt Natasha's arrival.

We spent a few weeks at Father Evans' house before boarding a train for the hills. It was only a day's journey to a place called Kathgodam from where we had to take a bus which travelled up very narrow and winding roads towards Jeolikote, through thick jungles of pine and fir trees. Jeolikote was a very small hill station. We went to the small convent run by the Loretto nuns again, but these taught in Hindi. The convent school was very small and mainly for the locals, but there were a few orphan Indian Catholic girls there too.

Father Evans' letter gained us immediate admittance and both of us were given places in a small dormitory with *khats* in two rows. Mum went to stay at the teachers' bungalow for the night.

I was so exhausted and depressed that I fell asleep in no time. In the middle of the night, I was awoken by Violet, who had climbed into my bed saying that she wanted to be with Mum. It was very dark and cold outside. I held her hand and led her quietly towards the teachers' cottage at about 1.30 in the morning. We passed the little chapel and proceeded towards the little graveyard of the nuns and the priests, which was on our way. As we came to the first grave, Violet stopped, held my hand tightly and whispered, "Minnie, there is a ghost of a nun sitting on that grave in front of us. She is dressed all in white and is glaring at us, let's run back."

I did not wait to see the ghost but ran back as fast as I could still holding Violet's hand. We jumped into one bed and slept huddled together.

The next morning we told Mum when she came to visit us. She looked very disturbed and put her hands around us affectionately.

"Why can't we live with you Mum? There are many other children who have no Papa but they live with their mother. Why do you want us away from you?" I asked. "Tell Father Evans to let us stay in Chunar. Papa has gone and now you too want to leave us. Please don't leave us Mum, I promise to be good and do everything you want me to." I started crying as I spoke. Mum looked at my thin pale face with a very sad expression. Violet came closer, held her by the hand and she too started crying.

There were a few Indian teachers in *saris* standing nearby, who came to mum and said to her, "Poor children, it is very sad for them. They are old enough to know their mother. How can you leave them and go away from their lives? They are going to fret for you."

Mum stood quietly then said, "All right, I shall take you two back. We shall face whatever comes. God only knows what is in store for us next."

I do not know what she said to the nuns, but before long we were back on the bus to Kathgodam and then to Chunar. The Indian nuns were friendly and helped Mum with sufficient money for our return. They advised Mum to stay with Father Evans, as he was a very kind and understanding secular priest. They even advised Mum to take up nursing with the help of Father Evans and make a career for her to support the two of us.

✣ ✣ ✣ ✣ ✣

Although Father Evans was not happy about our return, he was understanding and gave us a room in the school building to live. Mum was given some teaching work. We attended the same Hindi school.

The room we occupied must have been a classroom once, because it was very large. Mum was able to put two *khats* together with mosquito nets. On one side of the room she kept a stove on a table and she placed two big buckets full of water on the other side of the room for washing dishes and utensils. So we had every thing in one room. In the morning we brushed our teeth and washed in the school toilets and the outside washbasin. Very often we could not afford toothpaste, so we used salt to rub into our teeth instead of toothpaste, or the small bitter twig from the *neem* tree to chew and clean our teeth.

There was no electricity in the whole of Chunar so everyone used lanterns at night as in Saharanpore and Kalimpong. Father Evans had huge cloth fans hanging from the roof in his office, which were pulled by his mission helpers with a rope, to create a breeze during the hot summer afternoons. Everyone slept outside at night when it was hot.

We had just moved into the room when Uncle Eddie, Aunt Natasha and their two daughters visited us. They came to take us back with them, as they had eventually settled down in Allahabad. Mum refused to join them, saying that she had settled into a teaching life and could manage us independently.

Uncle seemed to have met Father Evans before, so he spent time talking with him while I was glad to have Aunt spend time with us. I wanted to go back to Allahabad with them after lunch, but couldn't leave Mum and Violet. Aunt said we were always welcome to live with them in Allahabad.

Aunt wrote to us often and in one of her letters said that Uncle Eddie always had two extra plates laid for us on the dining table every day and hoped we would soon join them. She said Uncle Eddie missed us and that Allahabad was a better place for us to live as it was a city and had a good English school.

I replied to Aunt's letters in Hindi because I wanted to let her know my feelings towards her. I learnt Hindi as fast as *Nepali* because Hindi has the same alphabet as *Nepali*. I was able to read Hindi books and even speak and understand it better. Until then I could only speak and read in *Nepali*.

We lived in Chunar for a while but Mum often lost her temper with us, as she had to attend to her teaching, as well as all the house chores. Perhaps she was also under great mental tension. We washed our own plates after meals and I repaired my frocks when they were torn. Mum had little patience teaching me to sew. There were times when she slapped me for what I considered no reason because I did not understand what she was trying to teach me. I was always willing to help, but messed up because I was clumsy. Violet refused to do anything but somehow managed to escape punishment. I wondered whether Mum was angry with me for ruining her efforts to leave us at Kalimpong or Jhansi. But at night when she kissed me while she thought I was asleep, I felt she did love me after all. One night I asked her why she lost her temper so often with me. She replied that she wanted me to be strong and learn right from childhood to survive in the cruel world. She said that life was hard and she was teaching me to do the right thing in spite of all obstacles. She did not want me to get into any trouble later on in life. I asked her why she loved us only when she thought we were asleep. She loved us but did not want to spoil us, she said. Once she said she was fed up with life and wanted to kill herself but that she realised she had to live for us. Especially for me because I was always following her around. She knew that I loved her too much and could not leave me. That is why out of frustration she would slap me for my mistakes.

Every night we knelt in front of the small altar in the room and said the Rosary and the night prayers, before going to sleep. I had to fast from midnight every Saturday as Mum did, in order to receive Holy Communion on Sunday morning. Even though we were eventually allowed to have a cup of tea one hour before church, Mum still wanted me to fast from midnight with her. She played the organ in the church and sang solo during church services. She prayed before cooking and before and after meals. The nuns of the Order of St Anthony ran the Hindi school and liked Mum very much for her caring and efficient disposition.

She read us stories from the Bible every night before we went to sleep. Mum kept a Hindi Bible under her pillow. Violet used to doze off but I stayed awake till the end of the story as in Kalimpong; I loved the stories from the Old Testament. Mum described Hell as the most horrible place where there was never-ending fire and devils, with horns and spears. The devils used the spears to push people back into the flames, Mum said. There was, she said, a big clock at the gateway which kept ringing "never, never" to the people who had led sinful lives on earth.

"There is no escape from Hell once you reach there," Mum would say. "The snakes and the bats keep flying and attacking at you. You can never see God or the angels in Hell".

I became very frightened of committing sin. She said swearing, telling lies and being lazy were all sins, so I tried to do whatever she wanted me to and avoid sin. Mum also encouraged me to read the Bible in my free time. She also bought me many short Hindi storybooks. They were cheap and were about the heroes and legends of India. All the stories had morals. Mum loved reading and spent all her free time reading Hindi books and magazines. Violet, on the other hand, enjoyed playing with her friends, most of whom were boys. She never showed her tears even when she was scolded or thrashed but could spin tall stories to get herself out of trouble.

Mum looked sad often her salary was very small and she kept us isolated from everyone around so we were friendless. Father Evans was the only one who visited us. The English-speaking descendants of the British, the Anglo-Indians, wore good clothes to Church on Sundays. Their seats were reserved in the front benches close to the altar. Their family names were written on brass plates and nailed to the pew. I often wished that we could dress like them and speak English. They were called the *Sahibs* and the *Memsahibs* and their children were called the *missy babas*. I wanted so much to be friends with them but could not.

Although there was a cinema in Chunar, we couldn't afford it, instead on the weekends and holidays we went for long walks to the river or to the historical fort of Chunar. Sometimes I walked alone to the creek not far from the school and watched the small tadpoles and tiny fish in the water. I imagined myself with a big fishing line, catching fish. I also dreamed of riding on a horse and galloping fast like the Indian Princess and Prince from the past.

✣ ✣ ✣ ✣ ✣

One day Mum developed pain in one of her teeth. She was treated at the Government Hospital but they did not have a dental surgeon, so we travelled to Allahabad. Violet and I spent the day at Aunt Natasha's place.

Mum came back from the dentist in great pain. Her face was very swollen and her mouth was bleeding. We caught the train and returned to Chunar. She was admitted to the Government Hospital that evening for stitches as the dentist had severed one of her arteries when extracting the teeth.

We visited Allahabad a couple of times after that because Father Evans was trying to place Mum in a hospital for training as a nurse. We always travelled back to Chunar without tickets because Mum never had enough left to return. When she was finally selected for training, after Father Evans reduced her age to satisfy admission requirements, we moved back to Allahabad.

Mum gained admission to the Midwife Training Course at the Kamala Nehru Memorial Hospital, where the matron was a Catholic lady and had great respect for Father Evans. According to the rules Mum had to stay in the hostel at the hospital so we were left with Aunt Natasha and her daughters at Mr de'Cunha's place.

8

A stable life in a family

Uncle Eddie and Uncle de'Cunha (Uncle Dick) were good friends. Uncle Eddie had been among the first batch of boys brought up at Grahams' Home in Kalinpang, so he had to help in the building of the Home as it stands today. The boys in the Home had been disowned by their parents and depended on charity and the British Government. They walked barefoot and grew up amongst great hardships. Their education was in English but lasted only up to Class 7 or middle school, which was considered sufficient to get jobs in the railways and other Government departments. They were given English surnames and called Anglo-Indians.

Uncle de'Cunha's accommodation consisted of two large rooms, a small storeroom and a toilet. It had verandahs and balconies on both sides. The kitchen was downstairs in the servants' quarters, from where meals came four times a day, in dishes, well laid out on a wooden tray, cooked by Cheronji, the cook. Cheronji had a fat grubby wife and three children, living next door to the kitchen. Uncle gave him money each day to buy fresh groceries and meat. He never asked for an account.

One of the large rooms was used as a bedroom. Two double wooden beds were put together in the centre. At one side of the room were wardrobes and a dressing table. The small room was on the right of the bedroom which Uncle used as his storeroom and on the left was a large toilet which had one pedestal-type toilet and a large metal tub under the tap for storing bathing water. The water supply often did not reach the first floor because of low pressure, so Uncle had a number of metal buckets to store water. A woman used to sweep and mop the cement floor of the whole house and the stairways. She used phenyl with water to mop the floor after sweeping. The pedestal-type toilet was cleaned every time someone used it. She lived with her family in one of the servants' quarters allotted to Uncle de'Cunha. In return for the free accommodation, the sweeper cleaned the house and the toilet.

The other large room was used as a family room. On the front verandah was a stand where Uncle hung his hats. The front verandah had a door leading to the next door neighbour's flat. It was always kept locked. When Uncle de'Cunha was off work he enjoyed drinking rum, sitting on the front verandah near the steps.

When we moved with Aunt Natasha, a single bed was put along the heads of the two double beds for Violet and me. Mum visited us every week for three hours and once a month for twenty-four hours. She had to be back at the hostel by 10.00 pm every time as the gate was closed at 10.30pm. Whenever she stayed with us for the night she had to get a night pass.

Uncle de'Cunha was often on night duty, but when he was home he slept on one side of the double bed, Enid and Helen in the middle and Aunt on the other side. When Uncle Eddie came home during the off-season, he slept alongside Aunt Natasha.

Not long after we went to stay with Aunt, she had Uncle Dick build a high brick and cement fireplace on the verandah outside the dining room. She told Uncle that food got cold while being brought up to the house and she told him that Cheronji was stealing money from him every day. So Aunt began running the house. Uncle Dick gave her the housekeeping money each month when he received his salary and she gave Cheronji money for meat and bread but she bought the large ration of food every month.

Aunt Natasha wrote every item in her book and checked Cheronji's accounts daily. There was always a dispute over a few *paisas* or *annas*. (In those days twelve *paisas* made one *anna* and sixteen *annas* made one *rupee*. A loaf of bread was only two *annas*.) The men selling meat, vegetables and fruit, delivered them in flat baskets carried on their heads. Aunt paid them herself. Their accounts were written in their account books and in Aunt's book. Although the men were illiterate they could count well using their fingers, they got Aunt to write the account down in their books, in front of them. In spite of this, there was always an argument when the payment was to be made, as Aunt claimed that they cheated when counting to get extra money, their counting being based on memory.

✣ ✣ ✣ ✣ ✣

On Father Evans' references, we four girls were admitted to a school in Allahabad, called St Anthony's Convent, where the instruction was in Hindi. I was placed in the third class although I was nearly ten. In Saharanpare I learnt the English alphabet and counting because there I was placed in a convent school where everything was taught in English. I had to restart my schooling in the *Nepali* language at the *Nepali* school in Kalimpong and then again in Hindi at Chunar. Then I was again in a Hindi Convent school.

St Anthony's Convent was near Mum's hospital. The daughter of her medical superintendent, Sumita, was also admitted to the same school after us. She was the only daughter of Dr Samant Chowdhry. The doctors had their bungalows in the hospital premises and were allowed to live with their families.

Sumita's father was a pilot and was mostly away from home. He belonged to the families of Indian *Rajahs* whose kingdoms and land had been taken away by the Government after independence. Sumita's mother, Dr Samant Chowdhry, was often on duty, so she would ask Mum to babysit Sumita, whenever Mum was off-duty and not at home with us. Both the doctor and Sumita loved and respected Mum even though she was only a nurse and Mum was trusted with the whole house. I used to visit Sumita whenever I went to visit Mum at the hospital and enjoyed playing with her. She had a room to herself and plenty of toys, most of them from overseas, as her mother often visited Europe and the USA. The furniture and the kitchenware in her house were modern and very expensive. Sumita had a music teacher visit daily to teach her classical Indian music and singing as they were considered a good qualification for girls. Rich families wanted to have daughters-in-law who could sing and play musical instruments; as well as a good English education and a large dowry.

✣ ✣ ✣ ✣ ✣

The hospital where Mum was training was behind the house of the then Prime Minister of India, Pandit Jawahar Lal Nehru. His house, Anand Bhawan, had a huge area of land around it, so, after the death of his wife, Kamala Nehru, who died of tuberculosis, he had the hospital built on a portion of the vacant land. At first the hospital was only for women's diseases and childbirth, but later on dental, cancer and radiology departments were added.

The female family members of Prime Minister Nehru preferred to be treated at Kamala Nehru hospital and had special reserved rooms and treatment given to them. The poor patients paid very little for the treatment and they were provided with free medicines. The rich paid for the private room and the medical care, as well as for the medicines. The hospital was financed by charity and the Nehru Trust Fund. The Board of directors mainly consisted of members of the Nehru family.

After Mum passed her training as a midwife, Dr Samant Chowdhry recommended her as a special nurse to her important patients. She considered mum an efficient and caring nurse. Mum attended both the daughter of the Prime Minister, Mrs Indira Gandhi and his niece. Mrs Indira Gandhi, became the Prime Minister after the death of her father, and was a good friend of Dr Samant Chowdhry. Her two sons, Rajiv and Sanjay were good friends of Sumita.

While at Sumita's house I met Professor Bachan's sons, Amitabh and Ajitab. Professor Bachan was from the University of Allahabad and wrote many books of Hindi poetry. Amitabh Bachan later became a famous Indian film star, and later a politician, when his friend Rajiv Gandhi, the grandson of Pandit Nehru and son of Mrs Indira Gandhi, became the Prime Minister. Sumita became the Director of Social Works. I used to play with Sumita and her friends often, because there were times when I would stay the weekends with Mum and spent most of the time at Sumita's place, during the time Mum was at work.

Allahabad is full of the descendants of rich *rajahs* and *nawabs* who are well-educated and live aristocratic lives. It is an old city and with one of the oldest universities in India and considered a centre of education in the ancient times. It also has many ancient Hindu temples and is where the holy rivers Ganges, Jammuna and Sarsavati meet. The Hindus consider this sacred. Every Hindu, rich and poor, like to make a trip to Allahabad, to have a dip at this junction once in their lives. They believe it cleanses them from their sins and secures them a better birth in the next life, according to the philosophy of *karma*. It is believed that a lot of the events which took place in the epic, *Mahabharata*, happened in and around the city of Allahabad. The rich in Allahabad are highly educated and religious. They worked alongside the British for some time and later were the members of the Indian freedom movement. Allahabad is the next big station to Benares (Varanasi) or Kashi. It was once known as Prayag.

✣ ✣ ✣ ✣ ✣

Deepak, a grandson of one of the *Rajahs* was in my third class at St Anthony's Convent. On his birthday we were each given a booklet, made up of a collection of his photographs, poems and congratulatory letters from relatives and important people in India and overseas. We were also served a lot of sweets. Deepak had come to the class that day in a rich blue velvet suit and shoes, which were bought for him in England. I am told that when Prime Minister Nehru was young his clothes used to be sent to Paris to be laundered and he studied at Oxford University. The rich in Allahabad preferred to send their sons overseas for education during the British Raj. They still live a very luxurious and lavish life.

✣ ✣ ✣ ✣ ✣

Every Christmas we visited Mum and attended the Christmas tree in the nurses' hostel. The Catholic matron put on a big show when members of the Nehru family were invited to watch the nurses' performances. Once I was asked by Mum to perform an Indian dance in front of Mrs Indira Gandhi, the daughter of Prime Minister Nehru. I loved Indian music and dancing, having picked it up from the films I had seen. Mum was always proud of me for being able to dance and encouraged me with her praise and admiration.

We were at St Anthony's for the year in which Mum did her midwife training. Father Evans kept in touch with us. Whenever he came to Allahabad he visited Uncle Dick and us. He advised Mum to continue her training for and become a general nurse, but unfortunately she could not, because Aunt Natasha refused to keep us without an increase in the money for our board and lodging.

Mum had to abandon her ambitions and stayed at Kamala Nehru Hospital as a midwife. She continued to stay at the hostel while we were with Aunt Natasha. Mum came every month with her salary and paid the bills Aunt presented on account of us. The board money kept increasing every year as Mum's salary increased.

It was after I joined Aunt Natasha again that I realised how much Mum loved us two. Everything she did was to give us comfort and I understood her hardships. Aunt Natasha was not the same person I knew in Kalimpong and Saharanpore. She was more concerned about her daughters, always praised them and criticised us for our little mistakes. Whenever Uncle Eddie came home on leave he and Aunt took the four of us to the shopping centre called the Civil Lines. They bought Enid and Helen new clothes and shoes while Violet and I watched. Sometimes Violet complained.

"Ask your mother to get your shoes, I have my own children to take care of." Aunt Natasha would tell her with sarcasm.

Violet always wanted to be treated like Enid and Helen. She answered back when she was asked to do chores in the house while the other two did not do anything.

"It is easy to give birth to children but difficult to take on the responsibility of a mother. She is having a fine time living at the hostel in the hospital while I attend to you two for such a small amount. Then you want the same treatment as my children. They have a respectable background. I come from a high caste Brahmin family. My children have breeding. You two may be fair skinned but have no breeding. The cheek you have, to answer me back when I have given you shelter in my home! Have you forgotten the orphanage where the two of you were rotting? You should be grateful to me for offering you my home and a family life."

I did not understand some of the things she said but I knew she gave preference to her own daughters. Sometimes I felt that we were burdens. She had to stay in the house all the time to take care of the four of us, while Uncle Eddie was away and Mum was working. Perhaps she was lonely and bored and was taking it out on us two!

Aunt Natasha would make Violet and me feel inferior to Enid and Helen, I really could not understand why. I thought we were all children of the same God and everyone was equal in His sight, so why was there arrogance of background and caste? What was a background after all, I would often wonder? What was a high caste and how did it make them different from Violet and me, I didn't understand grown-ups' talk. I often sat alone in the verandah thinking about it. Sometimes tears came to my eyes, other times I imagined myself a princess living in a castle and belonging to a high caste. But most of the times I talked to Jesus complaining and asking for help.

Once I told Mum what Aunt had said which caused a big argument.

"So Minnie told you what I said? It's true. I have a big family my children can fall back on. What have your children got? You are what you have become because of my help. You have forgotten the days when you often had to abort the babies fathered on you by Michael and I was the one who counselled you two into having Minnie and establishing some sort of a family life for her. I left the convent to help you, my best friend, and gained a bad name along with you. Now you are trying to be independent after I have done everything for you. I am still burdened by your children and their care. Without me what would you do? Send the children back to the orphanage I suppose!" Mum left in tears, saying she would never enter the place again.

For a long time Mum stopped coming to the house to see us. Instead she met us at the steps and took us out to see films.

Films were the cheapest entertainment for us. Often mum had a free pass given to her by patients who owned cinemas. Allahabad had movie cinemas. It is a big city.

Mum made me a beautiful green printed dress with bows and ribbons for my tenth birthday and came to give it to me near the steps. Mum had not seen Aunt Natasha for more than a month. Aunt came called her up, saying that because of my birthday all ill-feelings should be forgotten. I decided never again to mention what Aunt said to us in temper. Most of the time she was very thoughtful and kind to us. She'd forget the things she said but I could never forget them and fretted for days. I felt it was the absence of my father that made it possible for Aunt to lash at us with those words. I prayed to Jesus often and said that He should not have taken my father away from us.

✣ ✣ ✣ ✣ ✣

One day, shortly after my birthday, Uncle David, Bro. Rai, visited us on his way from Hazaribagh to Patna. I was happy to see him again, but found him changed. He was very religious. I just stood and watched from a distance. He was someone I loved in Kalimpong because he gave me the attention which had made me forget Papa for a while, but he seemed a stranger to me. Mum took half-a-day off to meet him. He suggested that we two should be placed in a boarding school in Hazaribagh.

When the New Year started in January 1951 Mum took leave to put us in the boarding school arranged by Uncle David. Hazaribagh is a small town in Bihar, where the earth is reddish in colour and at night the ground glitters with pieces of mica scattered amongst the mud and rocks.

The convent had two grades of boarders, ones who paid full fees and were given good food and beds to sleep on and the other boarders, who slept on the floor and had plain, leftover food. They had to help the nuns after the classes with cleaning and the kitchen work. These were mostly the Anglo-Indians and the Catholic children. The others were children of rich Hindus and Muslims. Fortunately, the nuns knew Uncle David and, as we were admitted as his nieces, we were kept amongst the rich boarders, even though our fees were not paid. The teaching was in Hindi, English being just one subject.

I felt sorry for the other poor boarders and always saved some of my food for them. I felt comfortable with the poor Anglo-Indians and spent more time with them. Mum wrote to us regularly and I sent her letters with drawings and kiss-marks practically every day. When the Easter holidays came Mum took us back to Allahabad and we managed to persuade her into not sending us back to the boarding school. Perhaps Mum missed us too, because she agreed without much hesitation. Aunt was happy to have us back. She said that she too missed us, as did Enid and Helen.

9

1951 — At last an English school!

After the Easter holidays, Uncle Eddie decided that we should attend an English school. Father Evans suggested he speak to the Bishop of Allahabad. We set out in a *rickshaw*, Violet and I on the footstand, Enid and Helen on their parents' laps on the seat.

It was the place where Father De'Mello had refused us help before but Uncle Eddie asked for the Bishop. The way Uncle spoke in English and his air of authority made Father De'Mello act courteously towards him and personally guide us to the adjacent building where the Bishop of Allahabad lived.

I watched Father De'Mello disappear into the building to inform the Bishop of our visit. A tall, well-built, fair skinned South-Indian man in a white gown, purple satin belt, purple satin skull-cap and big stone-studded gold ring on his finger came out of a room to meet us. Aunt immediately knelt down and kissed his ring as he mumbled some blessings.

"Yes, what can I do for you?" he said in a very loud, clear voice.

"I am Mr Wright, an Anglican with a Catholic wife. These two are American Catholic children. You must know of them as they are the children of Michael Lyons who was attached to your diocese before he left for the USA. He seems to have disappeared into thin air." Uncle said this with an air of superiority and added, "My wife and I are doing what we can for the poor children, but I think you should also take some responsibility."

"What do you mean?" the Bishop bellowed in his loud voice looking at the two of us. "What do you want me to do for them?"

"The children need an English education. My wife and I are bringing them up with our children since their mother has to work and stay in the hostel at the hospital. I cannot afford to give them good schooling though I feel very sorry for them.

The church should help in the absence of their father. He has been working for the church since 1923. It is shameful the way they have been abandoned and ignored by the Jesuits." Uncle said in a very aggressive manner.

The Bishop Raymond tried to defend himself from Uncle's accusations and demands. I took Violet's hand and pulled her further away from them while the heated argument continued. Uncle was red in the face and shouting. Finally the Bishop pointed towards the English School on the other side. Uncle turned and they both walked towards us saying, "I am glad you have accepted the truth and undertake to put Michael's daughters into the English convent school. In fact, all four of the children should be placed there as a mark of gratitude for what my wife and I have been doing for them when the Church should have done it long ago."

"All right, ask the nuns to admit the four of them," Bishop Raymond said looking rather disgusted as he walked back into his room.

The Reverend Mother was waiting for us when we arrived the following morning, as she had already heard from the Bishop. We were all admitted free into the school and were given free school bus service. There were other Anglo-Indian Catholic students in the school besides us, who had to pay only for the use of the books. According to the law, Christian schools had to have a certain percentage of Christian students in the school. Since most students came from poor homes and could not pay full fees, the schools took them in free. In the English Convents, the Anglo-Indians were admitted free due to their English background. Mum was not able to gain our admission because of her Indian background and not having command of English. St Anthony's Convent, where we were admitted initially was meant for Christian students with an Indian background. Since the fees in that school was less than at the English school many middle class Hindu and Muslim students were also admitted there, while only the rich were enrolled in the English school, St Mary's Convent.

"Agnes, remember that, though we managed to get your children admitted to the English school along with ours, you will have to see to their uniforms and other needs." Uncle said to Mum when she came to see us that week. You will also have to increase the money for your children's board and lodging and undertake to share the cost of the electricity and other extras."

"Eddie, I shall try my best, but I am only a midwife nurse and I don't get much money," Mum replied.

"Either pay your bills or take your children to live somewhere else. We have to cater for the needs of our own," Uncle said.

Mum looked sad. She was pleased to know of our admission into the English school but it made her unhappy to know of the expenses. I felt sorry for her but I did not know how to help.

"I shall ask for extra duties from Dr Samant Chowdhry and try to give you what you want," said Mum.

✣ ✣ ✣ ✣ ✣

On the first day of our new school, Aunt woke us up at 4.00 in the morning instead of the usual 6.00, because she did not have an alarm clock and was very excited. We sat ready in our new navy-blue uniforms and white blouses, waiting for the bus that was not due for two hours. We yawned but our eyes were glued to the road.

I was made to repeat Year Three, the others were all placed in the Kindergarten. I was the tallest and the oldest in my class. Students start school at the age of five in India and generally they finish Year 10 at the age of fifteen.

The school hours were 9.00 am to 3.00 pm., except in summer when they were between 8.00 am and 1.00 pm. Our lunch was brought daily by Cheronji in tiffin-carriers, consisting of four steel containers, each holding a different food, such as boiled rice, lentil soup or *dal*, meat curry and vegetables. He also brought plates and cutlery for us to use. There was a large sheltered area near the gym hall where everyone could sit at the table for lunch. The school had no canteen.

We were assigned ranks according to the total marks of all the tests given. Violet started coming within the first fifteen students, though Enid and Helen had problems. I had no one to turn to for help and would come towards the last in the class. Mum came twice a week, as a visitor at home but had no time to look into our books or report cards; she would only smile and tell us to try harder next time. Mum was living in her own world. She thought of me as the most beautiful girl in the world and a genius; she praised me to all her friends and the doctors. I could not hurt her feelings by crying about my inabilities and failures!

Whenever Mum was at home, she did my two long plaits and made two big puffs in front with a few curls over my forehead. She applied thick black *kajaal* (black paste made from soot of pure ghee and peppermint and used as eye-liner, supposed to be good for the eyes as well as beautifying them) around my brown eyes and a small black dot on my chin. She said the black dot was a beauty spot and would ward off any evil eye. One day Sister Joanna, a German nun, called me at recess and very affectionately told me to stop applying the black stuff around my eyes, because she said my pale face was too thin for the thick dark lines. I objected to it the next time Mum was there.

"I think it makes you look prettier. The nuns know nothing about facial make-up. Anyway, I shall only put a black dot on the chin so no evil eye can harm you." Mum said with a smile and did this whenever she could.

I liked most of the nuns at school because they were kind and religious. The Catechism teacher, Sister Magdalene, made a great impression on me. Although I found it difficult to read English, I was always able to answer the questions the next day because I listened carefully to what was taught the previous day.

All subjects were taught in English, Hindi being taught as just another language, only once a day. The English books were all printed in England and were very expensive. We poor Catholic students were given the second-hand books on loan for the year. We had to pay for hiring the books and the cost of stationery once a term. The school year had two terms. The year began in January and ended at the beginning of December. We had one month's holidays in December and two during May and June for summer.

I liked the headmistress, Sister Seraphica, a German nun, tall and very slim with the most beautiful blue eyes – perhaps they reminded me of Papa's! She was my Art and Science teacher and taught me Catechism. Later, Sister Seraphica was calm and quiet with a lovely voice. She sang solo in the church choir. The first day in the new school, when Sister Seraphica came to take our roll-call and called my name, 'Esther Anthony', I was not sure what to do. I heard the giggles of the girls in class as I remained standing. Sister Seraphica put her hand on my shoulder and indicated to sit down. (We stood for roll-call and as she called our names, we sat down. The headmistress went from class to class in the first period collecting the rolls.) Her hand was gentle and caring. I wanted to do well so that I would always gain her attention.

Throughout my school-life I imitated Sister Seraphica in every way; her style of writing, her walk, her way of talking and praying. (We said the Our Father at the beginning and the end of every lesson. Sister Seraphica always kept her eyes closed when she said prayers. I even went to church regularly so that Sister Seraphica would know that I was doing what she taught us. She was the person I wanted to be like, perhaps a second mother, intelligent and full of goodness, one that was there to guide me. Unfortunately, Sister Seraphica was too busy to notice my efforts. At the time I was extremely introverted and sensitive forever escaping into the world of fantasies where I was recognised as the most beautiful and intelligent person and much loved by everyone. I also had Jesus, my Father to consult and talk to.

At home I tried to read the comic page in the Sunday Standard newspaper Uncle Dick bought. I put the sound of the letters together to read it. The pictures helped me understand the words spoken. Neither Mum nor Aunt could help because they did not know much English, nor did they have time for me. But soon I was reading and speaking English. I borrowed books from the school library. Whenever I read new stories, I told them to Violet.

Violet preferred to make up stories herself, which were very long. We started drawing comic stories of our own with stick figures, at the back of our school exercise books and then tell them to each other. We got into trouble at home and in school for wasting the expensive exercise books, which ultimately made us give it up. By then I had started coming somewhere in the middle of the class. Violet still did better than me.

I missed Papa particularly when I saw other students with their fathers. Generally, the rich non-Christian girls did not like the Anglo-Indian or the Christian girls because of cultural differences. During playtime the girls stayed in their own little groups, according to their religion and cultural background. Although I had a few Anglo-Indian friends from the class. I felt more secure to be in the school chapel during recess and lunchtime, at first to impress Sister Seraphica, later out of habit. I started enjoying my conversations with Jesus rather than being with the others in the playground. I was extremely shy and found it hard to make friends. Often I felt everyone criticised me and looked down on me. I liked to be alone and by myself. I also started frequently abstaining from food, lollies and drinks as penance for the souls in purgatory, in accordance with what was taught during Catechism lessons. Every evening I said an extra Rosary in the solitude of the stairway at home after dinner and before going to bed. I lived in my own world with no friends to avoid the real world, where I felt I had nothing. I would talk to Jesus who was my father figure and knew Him to be gentle, kind and understanding and I did everything I considered Jesus would want me to do. Very often I felt sick and giddy. I was very pale with dark circles around my eyes.

Uncle Dick had taken a liking to me and comforted me with smiles and words. He was scared of Aunt and in her presence would simply ignore the situation. On paydays he called all four of us one by one and give us each two *rupees* for our monthly pocket money.

Uncle Dick nicknamed me "Praying Mantis" and Violet was called "Black Eyes" because of her beautiful big black eyes and thick black hair, in contrast to her white skin and pink cheeks. She had a lot of friends at school and in the neighbourhood as she possessed the gift of the gab and could impress everyone with her tall tales.

✣ ✣ ✣ ✣ ✣

During Christmas break Uncle Dick enrolled us in the Christmas-tree functions, held at the Coral Club, meant only for the Railway Anglo-Indians and their families. Uncle paid Rs. 5.00 per head for us to join. Mum and Aunt would give our presents on 23rd December to be placed under the Christmas tree. On the evening of the 24th December, Father Christmas gave us our presents and packets of lollies. Once Violet, Helen and Enid, were selected to take part in the Christmas play as angels. During the Christmas week many groups came to our house from the Church singing carols.

Most guards at the Railway colony were Anglo-Indians, who lived along strict British lines and while we were living at Uncle Dick's house, we learnt to live in the Western style of the Anglo-Indians. We ate European meals, mild curry and rice and red lentil soup, sitting at the table and using knife and fork. We had to be on our best behaviour during the meals. Uncle Dick sat at the head of the table on one side and Aunt sat opposite and the four of us on either side. We said Grace before every meal. Every Sunday we attended Church and after the service, while Uncle and Aunt chatted with other families from the colony, we stood still and waited for them in silence. The servants and shopkeepers called us 'Baby or Missy Sahib' and they called Aunt 'Memsahib' and Uncle 'Sahib', as they did the British family members in Chunar.

One Sunday Aunt recognised one of her and Mum's ex-pupils from Bettiah. The young lady was Mrs Medley, a daughter of a Britisher. She became a good friend to Aunt and Mum and we visited her often. Here 23-year-old brother settled in Allahabad and visited us daily and would say he wanted to marry me. I avoided him out of dislike as I had no idea of marriage when I was nearing only my eleventh year.

Mum also introduced us to a young south Indian man of about 24 years of age, the brother of one of the nurses. One day I heard Mum telling Aunt that he had taken a fancy to me and asked if he could marry me. Mum refused saying, I was too young, but he had left his address with Mum saying she could contact him. He was supposed to be financially secure and was looking for a wife. He had found me to be a girl of his dreams, whom he could educate and mould to his taste as his wife. Aunt had very good judgement and gave me a feeling of security when she told Mum not to consider it. I loved Aunt for that.

Mum said that she was concerned about our future and wanted us both to be settled respectably in life. At the time it seemed to be a good proposal, even though I was very young and he was more than double my age, but he was rich, a Catholic and had promised to educate me and give me a good home.

One weekend Mum took a few days off from the hospital and journeyed to Patna City again to visit Bishop Wildermuth regarding some financial support for us. Both Violet and I stood in the verandah while Mum went to see the Bishop. She looked sad when she returned. Later she told Aunt Natasha that the Bishop had given her some money for our return to Allahabad and promised to help financially once he was able to contact 'Michael'. I did not know who Michael was and why Mum wanted to find him. The Bishop said he did not know his whereabouts himself. I remember making two more such trips to Patna with Mum. Each time it was the same answer. Mum looked very disturbed and disappointed every time. We also went to Gaya to Fr O'Brien SJ. and stayed for three days. Father O'Brien was from Mazaffaspur who had transferred to Gaya. Fr O'Brien told Mum not to mention Fr Lyons' name because the people remembered him for his charitable and missionary work there. He was once the parish priest of Gaya and had built the church for his parishioners. It made me wonder who Fr Lyons was and why there was such secrecy about him. I could not ask Mum or Aunt about Fr Lyons or 'Michael' because they were either angry or upset with him and I was scared of being told off.

Father O'Brien could help Mum with little financially.

Some time later, Mum told Aunt that Fr O'Brien had developed pleurisy. We visited him in the Patna Civil Hospital. As usual, I was made to stand outside while Mum went into the hospital to see Father. I eventually refused to visit both the Bishop and Father O'Brien with Mum after I realised that she visited them asking for financial help for us. I begged Mum not to do so, saying that we should not ask for charity. I overheard Aunt telling Mum that we should not be embarrassed by her futile frequent begging for financial assistance.

"You should bring up your children on your own and forget Michael."

Aunt stayed in the kitchen while Cheronji cooked, because she claimed that he put aside part of what was cooked for his children and threw it in small packets to them from the back balcony. One day, while he was cooking, his headgear fell off and onions rolled out of it. Aunt couldn't help laughing heartily, but Uncle Dick paid dear Cheronji off that night, after he'd worked for five years in the house. From then on Aunt did the cooking and other household chores. A casual lady came each day just to clean the dishes and the utensils.

Later, in 1951 Uncle Eddie returned for his annual leave and both he and Uncle Dick went shopping for a red Echo radio. We had never seen a radio before. It had been invented and introduced to India just prior to their expedition. They kept the radio in the drawing room. At first we girls wondered where the noise was coming from and believed what we were told — that people actually lived inside it and were responsible for the singing and talking. Helen was afraid to touch the radio knobs in case they grabbed her hand, but I doubted the idea of people living inside; after all, the back was sealed!

Only Uncle Eddie and Uncle Dick were allowed to handle the radio, so when we wanted to listen to the music we asked one of them to switch it on for us. We were allowed to listen to the radio for a limited time daily. Every morning Uncle Dick listened to the BBC News and then, at our request, he would switch to the Hindi film songs program broadcast from Ceylon Radio. (The local stations mainly broadcast classical Indian music and songs.) Apart from the BBC News most programs were in Hindi and did not interest Uncle Dick.

One afternoon when it was very hot and it was impossible to sleep on a mattress, everyone decided to sleep on *daris* (cheap, hand-woven cotton carpets) on the cement floor with the ceiling fan on and with all doors and windows closed. Outside the hot sun caused the air to blow as a sweltering wind called *looh* in Hindi. Many Britishers and their families died of heat stroke and heat exhaustion because of the *looh* in summer. The rich slept in air-conditioned houses. The hot summer wind caused heat exhaustion and sudden collapse from cholera and dehydration. I walked out of the room and sat in the corner of the verandah reading a book of Hindi short stories. Suddenly I heard the shouts of a man who was selling vegetables, which he carried in a basket on his head. I looked at him through the balcony rails. The poor man looked so hot and tired in the temperature of more than 45 degrees.

The book I was reading said that one should be kind and generous to the poor. Without a second thought I called out to him and asked him to wait near the stairway. Then I ran to the icebox, poured a glass of cold water and ran down the steps. The man was squatting by the steps, hoping I'd buy his vegetables. "I haven't come to buy vegetables, but I have brought you some cold water. It must be very hot for you in the sun. Drink some of this and you'll feel better," I said, offering him the water. He looked angry at first, losing a sale, but the sight of a thoughtful child with a cool glass of water pleased him. During hot summer months plain cold ice water is sold for the price of a loaf of bread. Cold water with lemon and fresh crushed mint was more expensive. It was also possible to buy crushed green mangoes and mint in iced water or freshly crushed sugar cane with ice. He stretched out his hand towards it but quickly pulled it back, looking at me questioningly. Obviously, I did not look like a Hindu and they would not trust something to eat or drink from the hands of a Christian since Christians do not believe in the caste system and also eat meat of various types and are considered to be like low caste or even casteless people. First the man shook his head to show he did not want it and then he said: "No, I don't want any water from you." He then heaved a deep sigh and prepared to replace the basket on his head. I assured him that the glass was clean and the water untouched. But he just placed the basket on his head and walked off as fast as he could, without another word. I was miserable because of his behaviour: had not Sister Seraphica also said that to give water to the thirsty was an act of charity? I had not realised the depth of the caste system among the Hindus.

Disappointed at what had happened I went back to my seat and scribbled comic characters on sheets of paper, making picture stories. This gave me great satisfaction. Later I would show them to Violet and she would enjoy listening to the stories and looking at the pictures. No one else had any time for him or her. I had the ambition of writing a novel one-day which would take the world by storm!

10

The facts of life

Every afternoon after our nap during the summer holidays, we four girls went into the bathroom to play with water while having a bath in the big bath tub. After our bath we lined up for our hair-do and powdering by Aunt. One day just as she finished doing Helen's hair, Helen pointed at my chest.

"What's that you're hiding?"

I looked at myself and for the first time noticed two lumps on my chest. What were they? None of the other three had them! Fortunately Mum had heard Helen's question and came to my rescue.

"Don't worry, it's natural," she said to me. "You're eleven and developing into a woman. You should not bath with the others from now on."

I looked at Mum and Aunt. Yes, they had two lumps too! I felt miserable. I did not want to grow up; I wanted to be like Violet, Helen and Enid.

At school I started paying attention to the senior students they had lumps too. I did not want to be like them, so I took a razor blade to the toilet one evening and decided to cut off those bulges. I sat on the toilet trying to gather all my courage, but the thought of blood and pain stopped me. I remembered how a few weeks back; something sharp had hit me on the edge of my left eyelid and caused it to bleed profusely. Aunt Natasha had panicked and Uncle Dick rushed me to a doctor who stitched it. The bandage was over my eye for a week. That's it! An idea struck me – stitch the front of my cotton petticoat tight to flatten the bulge!

From then on every time I went to the toilet I took a needle and cotton and stitched the front of my petticoat from the neck to the navel, so tight, that the bulge were flattened and did not show through the dress. But this was successful only for a few months, because after that the bulge still appeared, no matter how tightly I stitched. In fact my petticoats started to show holes and I could not stitch them firmly enough. Mum noticed the holes in the front of the petticoats so she bought a small-sized brassiere and made me wear it. I sobbed as Mum fixed it on me because I did not want to look different from other girls at home. Mum and Aunt thought it all very funny and laughed to their hearts content while I cried. They never explained the facts of life, nor did the school.

✢ ✢ ✢ ✢ ✢

That year Uncle Eddie had permission from his boss at the sugar factory to take along his children for a short stay with him in Tamkhoi. Ever since Uncle worked at the factory, which was under British management, all his co-workers had Anglo-Indian or European wives and were given bungalows to live in with their families. But Uncle had his job on the condition that he would never bring his Indian wife to live with him, though he could bring his children. Most of Uncle's friends from Kalimpong were also working with him.

Since it was summer holidays I accepted an invitation to accompany Uncle Eddie, Helen and Enid to Tamkhoi. Violet did not come as she preferred to stay with Mum and Aunt in Allahabad.

We changed trains at Gorakhpur on the way. Somehow, I began feeling ill and missed Mum. But there was no way I could return immediately.

Tamkhoi was a small village where Uncle had a large bungalow to himself. He had a servant named Ali who was about eighteen, who did all the housework, including cooking. Uncle saw that we three were happy and got whatever we wanted. He bought me a lot of Hindi magazines and easy English storybooks to read.

I enjoyed the first two days in Tamkhoi, but from the third day I started pestering Uncle about our return to Allahabad. I noticed blood-stains on my panties which frightened me as I believed I had developed tuberculosis and was about to die. I wanted to return home to my mother and sister. At first Uncle ignored me and instead further loaded me with more magazines. I did not confide in him about my fear of tuberculosis, but showed the stained underpants to Helen which made her believe that I was very sick and about to die. Helen joined me in harassing Uncle persistently to take us back home. The backaches that followed made me cry often and I looked pale. Eventually Uncle became worried about my condition and sent a telegram to Aunt. We had been in Tamkhoi for only a week when both Uncle Dick and Aunt Natasha came to take us back.

Aunt was furious with me, saying that I had spoilt her daughter's holiday with their father. I felt guilty, but I could not tell her how ill I felt. I had developed pains in my legs, back and thighs and was sure that my death was close.

We boarded the train for our return to Allahabad the day after Aunt arrived. As before, we had to break our journey at Gorakhpur for two or three hours to catch a connecting train. We spent those few hours in the first class waiting room with Uncle Dick. I was bleeding profusely by then, so I called Aunt into the toilet, confiding in her my belief that I had tuberculosis. It was the seriousness of my expression perhaps which sent Aunt into a fit of hysterical laughter. I was shocked – it wasn't funny. I stood confused in the toilet while Aunt went back to the waiting room. I heard her saying something to Uncle and then I heard the two of them in fits of laughter together. I felt worse. How could Uncle and Aunt laugh when I was dying from tuberculosis!

After a short time Aunt returned with some long pieces of cloth and cotton-wool. I had no knowledge of human biology and was under the impression that the stomach was like a big balloon where food and blood could be stored. Aunt wanted me to tie the cloth like a belt and secure the cotton. I refused and started crying. Aunt began laughing uproariously again! After she had forced me to use the cloth and the cotton wool, she left me standing sobbing, while she went away in fits of laughter. I felt very sorry for myself and wished my mother was with me instead. Both Helen and Enid sat very quietly in one corner of the waiting room listening to the conversation and laughter of Aunt and Uncle.

We caught the train for Allahabad at 4.30 that afternoon. I sat in one corner, huddled up, groaning with pain all over my body and praying that Jesus would save me from death till I reached my dear mother. After Enid and Helen were asleep, Aunt made a place for me to lie down next to them on the same berth. We reached Allahabad the next morning at 6.00. Mum and Violet were at the station waiting for us.

"You look so pale!" Mum said as she kissed me affectionately.

"She needs some instructions on development from a girl to a woman. Minnie is so stupid. She spoilt the holidays for my children with her tales of dying," Aunt said angrily.

Mum put her arms around me comfortingly as we sat in the rickshaw. She explained that I had grown into a young woman and that every month I could expect that to happen. If this was growing-up, I hated it!

✣ ✣ ✣ ✣ ✣

Aunt Natasha had a beautiful peach-coloured georgette *sari* with a gold border. She kept it hanging very carefully in her cupboard. One day I asked her why she did not wear it as often as she did the others.

"It is my wedding *sari*. I like to preserve it so that I am buried with it when I die." Aunt said.

"What colour did Mum wear for her wedding, Aunt?" I asked her.

"Ask your mother what *sari* she wore," Aunt replied in a sarcastic tone and smiled. But I never had the chance to do so.

My mother could draw and paint and did beautiful embroidery work. One day on her way home she saw a girl walking at the side of the road with a magnificent pattern on her pullover. The following day Mum started a pullover of a similar pattern for me. It was finished in a week and everyone admired it. She never followed a pattern from a book because she could create her own or reproduce one after seeing it only once. Aunt told me how Mum used to sing solo in the church while in Bettiah. I had heard her sing the Latin hymns and play the harmonium and the organ in Muzaffarpur and Chunar.

Mum's patients said she had a very gentle hand when giving injections and she was the only one I could trust whenever I had to have one. Mum was also very efficient and gentle whenever she had to lance any of the boils I used to get every year, especially in the month of September.

Once Mum introduced us to a lady living opposite our flat who was in her late forties and had eleven children. Her husband, Mr Gurmukh Das, was the stationmaster. They were Sindhi (from the north of India, near the River Sind). They spoke Hindi as well as their own Sindhi language. Their eldest son was married and had a very young son. All eleven children, the daughter-in-law, the grandchild and Mr and Mrs Gurmukh Das lived in the same sort of accommodation as ours. The married couple and the grandchild lived in the small room, while the rest of them were distributed all over the rest of the two room flat. They were also using their servant quarters as rooms for their grown up sons who attended the University of Allahabad.

Mum met Mrs Gurmukh Das in the hospital. One night they invited us for dinner. I met their fourteen-year-old daughter, Padma and stayed friendly with her for years. I visited their place every evening to chat with Padma about Indian films and my favourite Indian film stars. At the time I had only been watching Indian films and did not know that English films existed. I had started speaking Hindi fluently and had survival knowledge of English. Everyone at home spoke Hindi and had forgotten the *Nepali* language. The two Uncles and Fr Evans, spoke to each other in English but they all spoke in perfect Hindi to Aunt, Mum and us.

Violet often accompanied me to Padma's house since she had developed a crush on Padma's eighteen-year-old brother, Laxman. She thought he looked like Dalip Kumar, the Indian film star famous at the time.

Padma's second oldest brother, Mohan, came to see Mum one day about some medicine for his mother and was entertained by Aunt, as Mum was at the hospital. He was a tall, thin, slimy-looking man. I never liked him, but both Mum and Aunt seemed to have taken a fancy to him. He was in his early thirties, wore loose pants like pyjamas and shirt as did most

Sindhis and was unemployed. He became a regular visitor to our house, whether Mum was at home or not. Uncle Dick did not seem to like him much. Being an Anglo-Indian, Uncle Dick considered Indians below him, as did the British in India. Perhaps Mohan noticed Uncle's dislike of him and started visiting the house in his absence. He took the liberty of walking straight into the bedroom to lie on one side of the bed. Aunt seemed to like his company and they talked in whispers for hours in the room. Mohan started having his dinner at our place and would leave long after we were all fast asleep, about two or three o'clock in the morning. Not long after he began spending most of his nights in the house in the absence of Uncle Dick. Aunt would say that she was afraid to be alone with four girls and so was glad that Mohan could stay over.

One night I felt someone's hand moving about in our bed. Our heads were towards where Aunt used to sleep and since Mohan was sleeping in that place, he could easily slip his hand over the bedheads into our small bed. I froze when I felt his hand on my neck and groped my small breasts. Aunt moved and the hand shot away. I realised that I hated him.

At the time I was reading the life of Maria Goretti, a teenage martyr, who was stabbed to death by a twenty-five-year-old man in Italy, because she did not allow him to touch her. I too decided that I would die rather than allow Mohan to touch me again. The following night I made Violet sleep in my place and I slept on the other side of the bed. She experienced the same problem as I had the night before and was furious when she got up. She was then about nine. We decided we could not tell Aunt or Mum so we kept our pillows piled up on his side of the bed and slept huddled up together on one end, well out of his reach. We did not feel his hand again as we did the same every night.

✣ ✣ ✣ ✣ ✣

One morning a very dark lad of about seventeen came to the house. Aunt Natasha was happy to see him. Cajeton was her brother from Bettiah who had lived with us when I was just two. He had been in trouble with the police and fled Bettiah. Natasha was his only sister living outside the state of Bihar, so he came to her. At first Aunt did not want to keep him, but when he promised to give up his bad old ways and complete his high school, she agreed to his staying. He was given the little room for living and studying.

Cajeton and I became friends. He confided in me about his girl friend and why he had to flee Bettiah. Once he said to me, "Well, if a thing is in the market for sale then why can't I also make an offer for it!" I asked him what he meant. "Either you are pretending or you are very simple and innocent. But you must realise that Mohan is after you." I half-understood him.

I sat in the small room with Cajeton and discussed his philosophy of life. He seemed to be very intelligent and also conventional. Cajeton was sensitive and upset because he considered himself to be neglected by his parents, since there were so many people at home, no one gave him any attention. His bitterness made him lose all religious values. I enjoyed discussing human values and religion with him at great length. I had developed an idealist view of life and was fanatical in my religious beliefs. Perhaps I was trying to convert him back to religion. Cajeton sometimes helped me with my maths homework. He designed and painted beautiful photo frames with cardboard and wood. I felt that he was a good friend and looked up to him as an elder brother. There were times when he told me to leave him alone because I was too stupid to understand his feelings and was better off doing my homework than talking in an infantile way to him. Aunt did not like me visiting Cajeton's room too. She spied on us whenever we were together. Although she always found us talking or doing homework, she would often ask me to leave him alone with his study and do my work in the dining room with the others. I was then twelve years old with a very well developed body but an innocent mind.

The one good thing that came of his staying there was that Mohan stopped staying over at night. This made Aunt extremely unhappy. She started finding fault with Cajeton and wanted him to go back to Bettiah.

Cajeton was admitted into a High School. He started coming home late which made Aunt angry. On one occasion he came to my school during the lunch-hour and asked me to tell Aunt that he had seen me outside the Church about 3.30 in the afternoon and told me that he was returning late home that evening because he was going for some tutorial classes. So the first thing I did when I reached home was to tell Aunt what Cajeton wanted me to say. I felt proud in being entrusted with an errand by my dear friend. Aunt looked at me questioningly and then said, "Perhaps he came to your school to tell you to say so, but for your information he is at home already. I don't know why he trusts you with his stories – I hope you are not having ideas on him!"

I did not understand her, but I was angry with Cajeton for getting me into trouble and making me tell lies. He later explained to me that he was to go out with a girlfriend that evening but their plan was cancelled, so he had rushed home to be in time to stop me from carrying out his request. He had not realised that I would blurt out the news to Aunt as soon as I stepped in the house.

"You are stupid, you cannot keep your mouth shut even for a moment."

I felt worthless and shed tears because even my good intention was misunderstood. I intended to help but both Cajeton and Aunt were angry with me. I felt let down by Cajeton whom I considered my best friend. I decided to stay closer to Jesus, my imaginary father and friend whenever I was hurt and had problems.

✣ ✣ ✣ ✣ ✣

I met Dolly, who lived in the flat recently built close to ours. She was about fifteen. Her brother, Stanley, was seventeen and they also had a sister of six. The family was South Indian Christian. I began seeing Dolly often since Padma was busy with her final school examinations. Dolly and I discussed Hindi storybooks and Indian films. She told me that her brother Stanley had given up studies a few years back and was unemployed. Soon I noticed that he would always hover around the house whenever I went to visit Dolly. But I never spoke to him – I was very shy of boys.

One day, while waiting for the bus, I noticed that someone

had scribbled in Hindi and in large red chalk all over the cemented area that covered the drain: "I love Minnie". I told Aunt and Uncle Cajeton about it when I returned from school that afternoon. Of course, by then it had been rubbed off. But the next morning it was there again in white chalk. It was there again on the third day in red chalk. I told Aunt and Cajeton about it that afternoon. Cajeton walked us to the bus stop the next morning and saw it, then walked towards Dolly's house, where he forced Stanley to write my name in Hindi on a piece of paper. It matched with what had been written near the bus stop. Eventually Stanley admitted he had done it. Cajeton brought him to the bus stop and pushed him at my feet.

"Say sorry to her! She is like your younger sister, not your girlfriend and don't ever think such things about her, you bastard. Say sorry at once or else I'll hand you to the police for defaming a young girl's name," Cajeton yelled.

Stanley begged for forgiveness as did his mother and Dolly on his behalf. Just then the bus came and we left.

In India feelings of love are not displayed in public. In big cities, like Delhi, where people are westernised, it may be accepted to some extent, but in most parts of India it is not. Even husbands and wives do not display affection for each other in the presence of their elders and children. That is why Stanley's expressing his feelings about me in public was considered in a bad light, as it was taken as reflecting upon my name and so he had to be punished with a public beating and apology. I had no idea of teenage feelings of love. I looked at everything in the light of religious values. Everything to me was as the Catechism teacher taught us. In particular, sex was never something I could even imagine. Personal and biological development was never taught as subjects in school. My mother and Aunt did not explain any facts of life to us and it was considered shameful of children to enquire about the subject from parents. Most children learnt from friends or books they read, without letting the elders know of their knowledge. Since I was busy nursing my own hurt feelings and escaping into my fantasy-world of Jesus and religious values, the realities of the world had no meaning to me.

I stopped seeing Dolly after that morning. I felt protected and cared for by Cajeton and Aunt Natasha. She had approved of Cajeton's actions. She said I was too young and such ideas should never be encouraged. It gave me a great sense of security.

Every year, the Dolls' Fair was held in the middle of the road, not far from our house. The shops spread over a kilometre. You could buy all sorts of Indian-made toys of plastic, clay and cloth. Many of the beautifully coloured clay toys were images of Hindu gods and goddesses. On both sides of the road shops sold gas-filled balloons, trinkets and glass bangles in a variety of colours and designs, clothes, utensils, toys and food, especially locally made Indian sweets. Adults and children thronged, blocking the streets to vehicles. The *rickshaws, tongas, ekkas,* as well as cars had to honk their horns and proceed very slowly. The loud music from the soundtracks of Indian films came from most shops and making it difficult to hear any conversation. I enjoyed the Fair with Mum or Padma, as there was so much to see. I would buy clay toys, which were very cheap but lasted only a few hours. But I soon discovered at the age of thirteen that the crowded fair was not a place for me as a young teenager in a dress. Some ignorant and mentally sick men found the crowded fair to be a place for cheap thrills. They enjoyed pinching or touching young defenceless women and disappearing into the crowd.

Such men tried to put their hands on women even at the picture halls. Once I went to see a film with Mum. We were sitting in the front row which was the cheapest. Mum had little money at the time. I was engrossed in watching a film in which my favourite actress, Nargis, was acting. Suddenly, I felt someone's feet pressing against my bottom. I complained to Mum.

"Put your feet down!" Mum said angrily to the dirty-looking man at the back. "You should be ashamed of yourself! Haven't you got a daughter of your own? Isn't this child like your own daughter or a sister?"

"What is the matter, *bahenji*?" someone asked in the dark.

"I am sorry *Mataji*. I shall not do it again," pleaded the man accused, putting his feet down.

I realised that I had to sit at the back row, next to the wall or at the end of the row, so that no one could slip his hand beside me and pinch me or toe me from behind.

Some cinemas had ladies' class. There was also a separate window to buy the tickets. But even at this ladies' window there was usually a crush since no one believed in the queue system. Mum was once caught in the stampede. Someone in the crowd at the ladies' window pushed her so hard that her *sari* was pulled out and had to be rearranged. This was the plight of the poor and the middle class. The rich just telephoned and booked their tickets or had them collected by a servant, then attended to watch the film from the balcony, just as it started. I never liked going to the toilets in the cinemas, even though they did have one for ladies, because they smelled of urine and spittle. Even the outside side walls smelt, as most men urinated near the walls. I hated all this, but I loved watching films because they lasted for three hours and contained songs as well as stories about people's lives. I bought the little song booklet after the film and tried singing the songs, which had words so real to my plight at home.

✣ ✣ ✣ ✣ ✣

Uncle Dick had started to kiss Violet and me in a very peculiar way whenever he found us alone. He would put his grubby, rum-smelling mouth on our lips and push his slimy tongue right inside our mouths. Then he would pat us on our cheeks, saying:

"If you need anything, just tell me."

Violet and I hated his kissing and our only way of avoiding it was to keep out of his way. Violet told Aunt about it once, but all she said was that we should not let him find us alone.

"Perhaps he just means to show his affection to you," she concluded.

At the time the girls at school collected autographs of the teachers and friends in a special notebook. I had one such small book and one of my friends had written, 'Never kiss an old man – his nose is always leaking and his lips are never dry.'

Naturally, I thought of Uncle Dick when I read it!

✣ ✣ ✣ ✣ ✣

About that time we had a new neighbour next-door. The Anglo-Indian family who had lived there had retired from the railways and had emigrated to England, as many Anglo-Indians in that line of work were doing in the 1950s, soon after the Independence of India. Educated Indians were fast replacing them in the railways. The new neighbour was a young Indian couple, a young man, the husband's younger brother who had come from the village to study at the University of Allahabad. I looked much older than fourteen. Most people took me for sixteen as I was well developed, but I still had no interest in boys and knew nothing about the facts of life.

A few weeks after the new neighbours came, I noticed that every night when I was saying the Rosary, next to the steps and the balcony, the young man from next door would also stand on his balcony and whistle softly. Then I also noticed that every day after school when I got off the bus and walked down the lane towards the flat, the same young man would be walking up towards the road, whistling and making some sign with his right hand. I did not understand what all this meant, but his whistling at night distracted me as I said my Rosary.

One night I heard the whistling near the door that closed off the verandah leading to the other side, so I walked up to the door and stood behind it. To my surprise I saw a tiny roll of white paper in the door. I pulled it out and took it to the toilet, where I could be alone. It was a short letter, disclosing his love for me and requesting me to meet him somewhere alone. It was signed 'Gopi'. I never replied to it. I often found such letters stuck in the little hole in the door thereafter, which I would read and destroy immediately so that no one else would read it. I blushed whenever I saw Gopi, but I did not have the courage to write back to him or meet him alone anywhere. I was shy and also afraid, although I was flattered by the idea that someone loved and admired me like in the Indian films! But I was not interested in anything except that of the happiness of my mother and sister. Besides I did not think that Jesus would like me to meet a boy alone.

Cajeton had finished his high school examination and returned to Bettiah for holidays. One Sunday after Cajeton had left, on our way back from Church, we noticed a man selling fresh fish in a basket under a tree, not far from our flat. As soon as we reached home, Aunt gave me money to buy her some fish from the man. I liked doing things for Aunt because it made me feel important, since this meant that she considered me responsible and efficient. I walked towards the main road and the banyan tree, under which the small man sat with his big basket of fish. There were a few people around him making purchases. Some of them moved aside so that I could also reach the man. I asked him for a *seer* of fish. (In 1950s weights were measured not metrically but in *seer* and *paw*, a part of a *seer*.) He weighed the fish in his scales with the heavy iron weights on one side. I bent forward to pick a good fish to put on the scale. As I did, a hand grabbed my right breast from under my raised arm. I straightened up making the man standing beside me remove his hand. I was disgusted and embarrassed, I threw the right money to the man, picked up the fish wrapped in a newspaper and ran home, hoping that no-one was following me. I could not tell anyone about it or there would have been violence and a scene, like the time Cajeton beat Stanley. I just felt that it was a terrible thing to have grown up and have a woman's body. I constantly had to protect myself from being pinched or grabbed. As a result I became more introverted and sensitive and started walking with a stoop, always keeping my eyes cast down towards the road.

I combed my hair into two plaits without any puffs in front, as Mum used to do. I also applied a lot of hair oil to keep my hair flat on my skull. I wanted to look very plain. Indians believe in putting oil on the head to keep the brain cool and also for the good black, thick growth of hair. My mother applied so much oil that her pillowcase always had oil stains on it. She believed, as do many Indian ladies, that hair oil took her headache away. Her favourite hair oil was Amla Hair Oil. There are other hair oils as the Coconut Hair Oil and Scented Castor Oil. Poor people use pure Mustard Oil for their hair. My mother used any soap to wash her hair and we did not know about shampoo until I finished high school and started working in 1962.

11

Is my father living?

The daughter of the Rajah of Bhadri, who lived on a small estate some 200 kilometres from Allahabad, was sick and bed-ridden. She had a plaster cast on her back since she had tuberculosis. Mum was sent by her superintendent to work for the princess as a private nurse.

Mum had been away for a fortnight when our short holidays began and since the Medical Superintendent's daughter, Sumita, was going to visit the Rajah of Bhadri and his daughter, Violet and I were offered the opportunity to accompany her and visit our mother. We travelled by car.

Bhadri was one of the many little independent states ruled by a Rajah. The Rajah of Bhadri once owned a large amount of land and the surrounding villages. After Independence, although the government of India had taken away most of his land and the title, he still had his palace and the surrounding land and continued to receive the same respect from his people as before. The Rajah had his own aeroplane and a small airport.

Our car stopped at the gate and we saw Mum coming towards us in her white uniform. She kissed us all and took us to a very well dressed man sitting under a banyan tree. She introduced him as the 'Rajah *Sahib*'. Of course, Sumita called him '*Chachaji*' (Uncle), as her parents and the family of the Rajah were very good friends. Sumita's father was also the son of a rajah of a small principality in Allahabad District. As I folded my hands to say *Namaste* to him, I heard Violet cry out. She saw a large cat tied to a tree nearby and walked up to it, much taken by its attractiveness. The animal was a tiger cub and, disliking Violet's touch, had dug his nails into her leg. The Rajah immediately ordered it to let go and warned us not to go near it, because he said it disliked strangers. We learnt that the Rajah was fond of rearing the white tiger cubs. White tigers were a rare species and fetched him a good income from their overseas sales and from the many zoos in India.

Mum took us inside the beautiful palace, which had two storeys each with many rooms. The floors, the stairways and the balconies were all white marble.

We were introduced to the sick princess who was lying on the bed. She was an eighteen-year-old girl with very long hair tied up in plaits. We were then taken into the huge kitchen attached to the banqueting hall for lunch, before taking a little rest.

There was a large marble table in the kitchen with strong wooden benches on the sides for seating. We sat on the benches and were served from big rectangular steel plates (*thallies*), with compartments for rice, *chappatis* layed with pure ghee, meat, two varieties of vegetables, homemade fresh and creamy yoghurt or *dhai* and *dal*. There was also a sweet dish made of carrots and cream. Fresh fruits from the palace orchard were also served. Water was given in large steel glasses. (Indians drink only fresh water during and after main meals and fresh water is always served with every meal.) Everything was served piping-hot, straight from the huge mud and brick fireplace, which used both charcoal and wood. (Indians like freshly prepared food at all meals.) I was told that the Rajah and his family used pure silver plates. There were large copper and steel pots and pans for cooking, neatly kept in the cupboards at the sides, as well as huge brass and red clay pots filled with water. The kitchen had cement flooring with tiles all around the wall and a big steel sink in which people washed their hands. (Hindus are very particular about washing hands with soap before and after eating as most believe in eating with hands rather than using forks and spoons. They think it is more hygienic to eat from one's own hand than with cutlery used by someone else. They also gargle and clean their mouth and teeth before and after a meal.)

There was another dining room attached to the kitchen with a huge modern polished wooden table and chairs, the Rajah used this for formal dining on social occasions. The quality furniture was bought from the various cities of India and overseas. Mum said that the main bedroom of the Rajah and the *Rani* (his wife, the queen whom we did not meet) was the best, but we could not see it. The other guestrooms were also well decorated with fine rosewood furniture and silk used for important visitors only. The main drawing room had beautiful carpets on the floor. The walls were covered with mounted heads and skins of deer, antelope, lion and tiger, as well as swords and rifles. The rajahs enjoyed hunting. There were huge paintings of the Rajah's ancestors on the wall. The sofa sets had satin cushion coverings. Everything was spotlessly clean, as there were many servants to dust and clean. These servants were the people who lived on his land and had to find time to work free for the Rajah. They also attended to his cattle, goats, buffaloes and horses. There was a stable with a few horse-wagons, a *tonga* and an *ekka*. The Rajah enjoyed horse riding and hunting on horseback.

We were introduced to a few of the children in the kitchen. Some of them had their meals with us, while others helped in cooking, serving and dishwashing. They had their meals after us. These were aged between eight and fifteen and were the children of some poor distant relatives of the Rajah's family who had become poor or orphans, or the children of the farmers who owed money to the Rajah. So they helped in the house and were allowed to attend the village school. The girls were married off at an early age but continued helping with the domestic work in the palace. Some of the boys worked in the fields or attended to the cattle. The relatives' children were allowed to study further, provided they also worked for the Rajah after school hours, as well as after their education was completed. One such relative of the Rajah was Dinesh, a boy about ten who befriended Violet.

The Rajah had been educated in London. It was then, as it is to this day, a status symbol for the rajahs and the rich people of India to send their sons overseas for education, London being then the most important place for study. The Rajah's only son was in London studying engineering. We saw his photograph in a silver frame kept next to that of the princess, in the drawing-room glass case. The *Rani-ma* spent her time standing for elections and doing social work for women in the State of Uttar Pradesh, where her estate was, while the Rajah enjoyed the luxury of his palace and attended to the maintenance of his land and business. The sick princess was once a boarder in an expensive Loretto Catholic convent in Lucknow, another large city near Allahabad, the capital of Uttar Pradesh. A good English education was essential for girls to get a rich husband, as it is even to this day. All rich Hindu bachelors prefer convent-educated girls for wives as well as with a fair complexion and a good dowry.

At night, after dinner, we were each served a glass of fresh buffalo milk with a thick layer of cream floating on the top. People in India believe that a glass of warm milk at night promotes sound sleep. At home Aunt bought cow's milk because it was more digestible than buffalo milk. We used it for our tea, as we could not afford to drink a glass of milk every night. Aunt said pure milk always had a thick layer of cream. It was bought fresh from milkmen who brought it in cans and had to be boiled to purify before use. The milkmen added water to increase the quantity for sale. There were milkmen who brought their cow or buffalo to the door and sold pure milk freshly drawn at a greater price, but somehow they always managed to thin the milk with water even then. Some liked goat's milk but I thought it smelt; it was not popular. So when we were each given a glass of pure rich buffalo milk at the Rajah's palace, we relished it.

That night we all slept out on the terrace under mosquito nets since it was summer and quite warm. Mum was in the room with the invalid princess. The electricity generator worked only for a short while, after which we used lanterns. I woke up in the middle of the night with a severe stomach pain. All that cream from the buffalo's milk had made me sick and I had to run to the toilet. Unfortunately, the toilet was somewhere downstairs in the house; the door to the inside of the palace was locked once we had got into the bed on the terrace. I sat in great pain throughout the night. In the early morning when the door eventually opened, I was able to run into Mum's room for the change of clothes and to the toilet.

I had a very sensitive stomach which could not handle rich

milk or very hot curries, whereas Violet could digest anything and in any quantity. I could not eat much of the sour, raw tamarind, which most girls enjoyed eating with salt, without getting sick. Most of the tasty and spicy food sold by the wayside hawkers made me ill.

The next day we toured the estate in a *tonga* belonging to the Rajah. I enjoyed our trip into the forest where I saw the peacocks dancing. The beautiful palace set in the middle of forest land where all types of birds and nature existed made my imagination run wild and I fantasised myself as the princess many a time, well loved and spoilt by the *Rani-ma* and the Rajah. Unfortunately, we had to leave for Allahabad after a few days while Mum remained at the palace for another month. I felt sad leaving her because she worked hard day and night attending to the invalid princess who treated her like a paid maid-servant rather than a nurse.

On the 15th of August 1955 Uncle Dick turned fifty-five, the retiring age in India. We celebrated his birthday and retirement at a Chinese restaurant, the Nanking, in the Civil Lines. I was nearing my fifteenth birthday and had never visited a restaurant for a meal nor had I tasted Chinese food.

Because of his retirement we had to leave the railway quarters. Uncle looked for accommodation in the Anglo-Indian colony, the *Bundhwah* Club, on the opposite side of the shopping area and on the same road as our school and the University of Allahabad. *Bundhwah* Club was a huge area of land leased to the Anglo-Indians for sixty years. There was a dance club in the midst of cottages built by the Anglo-Indian Trustees. There were a few old cottages around the club, which belonged to the Club Trustees and were rented to the Anglo-Indians.

Anglo-Indians with birth certificates to prove their identity as descendants of the British were the only ones who could become members of the Anglo-Indian Association of Allahabad and buy, build or rent a bungalows at the *Bundhwah* Club Trust Property, at 27, Thornhill Road, Allahabad. There was a huge gate installed, at the section of the property, bearing a signboard saying that it belonged to the Anglo-Indians. There were no boundary walls or wire fences around the property. Each cottage or bungalow had servant quarters attached. They could be rented out to them for a small rent.

The dance club was a large old building, in the centre of which was the large hall where great dances were held on every Christmas, New Year, Easter, as well as on 15 August, India's Independence Day. Every Sunday there was housie and gambling for the members and liquor was available at the bar. Only members of the Anglo-Indian Association or a child of a member could attend the dances. An Indian or a non-member could enter as a guest of an Anglo-Indian member. Men and women had to wear formal clothes.

Not far from the Anglo-Indian Trust Property was Muirabad, a colony established by Methodists. The people there were all Indians with British surnames given to them when they converted from Hinduism to Christianity. Some say they were mostly low-caste Hindus who accepted Christianity to better their lives, the same as the low-castes Hindus had done in the villages of Bihar and other parts of India, under the influence of the American Jesuit missionaries. The converted Indian Christians of Muirabad were well-educated and hard-working, God-fearing people. They were all brought up in a Methodist mission and community and were able to get scholarships and sponsorships from America for higher education overseas.

Both the Anglo-Indians and the Muirabad Indian Christians lived according to British culture, but the Anglo-Indians were generally fair complexioned, with blond or brown hair, some even had blue eyes. They spoke only English and broken Hindi, since they regarded it as below their dignity to speak Hindi fluently, taking pride, as they did, in their British blood. They always dressed in Western clothes. The Indian Christians of Muirabad were dark, some very dark in complexion and could speak both English and Hindi fluently. The women mostly wore *saris*, except when they were old and retired, then they wore dresses to their ankles. The men always wore suits and never the *dhoti-kurta* of the Indians, because, like the Anglo-Indians, they too considered themselves above the latter's station in life. The Christians of Muirabad were fanatical in their religion and had their church in the middle of the colony.

There was always a tension between the Anglo-Indians and the Indian Christians rooted in the question of purity of the British race and inheritance.

Uncle Dick was a member of the Anglo-Indian Association and was able to rent half a bungalow at the colony. The day before we moved to our new home I found another roll of paper in the hole of the door which connected our verandah to next-door. The note expressed Gopi's sadness at our moving out and asked for my new address. I scribbled the new address at the back of his note and slipped the paperback into the hole for the first time.

I felt sad leaving the railway quarters in September 1955. Emily and her family had already transferred to another city, Kanpur, earlier in the year. Mohan had joined the army. Cajeton was in Bettiah since his exams were over. So much had happened whilst we lived there: it was where I had grown up into a young lady and a *Missy Baba*.

Once we had moved into the new house the school bus picked us up at our gate. Mum took a few days off work to settle us in, but then returned to work and her hostel life.

About a week after we moved, one Saturday morning around ten Aunt was on the verandah talking to Uncle Dick, whilst he read his newspaper. Suddenly, I heard the postman call at the steps. I wanted to run out and collect the mail because that night I had a dream that Gopi would send me a letter, Aunt would open it and I would be in great trouble. I was sitting in the dining room anticipating the letter. But instead sat frozen. There was silence for a few minutes; perhaps she was going through the mail. Then I heard her say to Uncle:

"Hello, where did Minnie get this postcard from?" And after that: "Look at this, Dick. She is getting love letters already! Minnie, where are you? Come here!"

I wished I could have disappeared through the floor but I hurried to the verandah, very frightened.

"Have you been writing to this boy? You are not yet fifteen and already your head is full of boys! I should have known that no good could come from someone of your background. You will never be educated. Very soon you'll run away with some boy and be sold as a prostitute. But I shouldn't be surprised. After all you don't have anything in your parentage to make you a decent, respectable person. Eddie and I have done so much for you two, giving you security, a home and education, thinking some day you would live a respectable life in the community and this is what we get in return!" Aunt continued with her accusations and humiliating words.

I just stood in silence with tears in my eyes. It was useless to tell her that I had never spoken to Gopi, nor did I have anything to do with him, beyond giving him our new address. I had never confided in anyone at home about him and his behaviour towards me, because I was afraid they might create a scene at his house, accusing him of making passes at a minor. I did not wish to get Gopi into trouble for what I considered to be nothing.

That evening when Mum arrived, the whole episode was related to her and she lost her temper with me. She slapped my face a couple of times.

"You stupid, bad girl! I have spent all my life looking after the two of you, hoping to make something of you. Your father disappeared, shirking his responsibility, leaving me alone to face the world. I have had to bear the consequences of whatever happened all by myself. I never thought that you too would let me down. I have sacrificed my own happiness to give the two of you a good and comfortable home and life. I thought one day the two of you would have a respectable life of your own!" She burst into tears. "I wish I had killed you, rather than live to see you getting involved with boys so early and make a disgrace of yourself. You fool! I am suffering for my mistake, I don't want you to suffer the way I do."

I could not bear to see her like that and between my sobs managed an explanation.

"Mum, I have never spoken to Gopi. It's just that he used to put papers through the hole in the door, I read them out of curiosity and then replaced them in the hole. On the last day only, I wrote our new address and put it in the hole for him. I don't know what made me do so, perhaps I felt sorry for his feelings for me. I am sorry I did so, I did not think there was any harm in his knowing our new address."

"You swear that you are telling the truth and that you used to say your Rosary till eleven at night and not speak to the boy?" she asked me, wiping her tears.

"Mum, I swear I am telling the truth! I always said my prayers and the Rosary near the steps. How could you think that I was talking to him? I would never do a thing like that. I said, "Mum, you said just now that Papa went off and left us. Is he alive then? Where is he?"

"He left for the USA. I don't know where he is now. Before going he said that he would soon return to us, but he never did. He just disappeared." Mum said "Promise me that you will never see or speak to this boy. Don't ever write to him either, or I shall leave you also and disappear like your father did."

I put my arms around my dear mother and gave her my promise. But why did my father leave us and go to the USA? I wondered.

Where was he now?

Why did Father Evans tell me that he was dead?

Does he ever think of me?

From that day I prayed for my father's return and developed a strong desire to visit the USA to find Papa myself. I wanted to bring him back to my dear mother. Memories of my father and mother living together in Saharanpore came crowding back and the desire to find my papa became a compulsion.

I often noticed Gopi cycling past our house but I ignored him and stayed out of sight. He never wrote again.

✣ ✣ ✣ ✣ ✣

The half-house we moved into had only two small rooms. It had a modern flush toilet, something new for me. The little kitchen at the side of the verandah outside had a high brick-and-clay plastered fireplace, where coal was burnt for cooking.

One of the two rooms was made into a bedroom with the double beds put together in the centre for Aunt, her children and Uncle Dick. The single bed, where both Violet and I were to sleep, was placed near the wall at one side of the room. All the tin trunks containing our clothes were kept under the beds. The wooden wardrobes were also crammed in one corner leaving very little space to walk to and fro. The small altar with the pictures of Mary and Jesus was arranged on the little wooden plank nailed to the brick wall. We had to say our Rosary every evening together. The story of the three children of Fatima and Our Lady's appearance to them requesting that the Rosary be said daily for the salvation of the human race, had made a great impression and the statue of Our Lady was being taken around to the Catholic homes in Allahabad at the time, to encourage the families into saying the Rosary daily.

The second room was made into our dining room with a big table and the six chairs. The large wooden cupboard with wire netting was placed against the door connecting the landlord's portion of the house. Unfortunately the furniture for the sitting room had to be placed on the verandah, closer to the kitchen.

There was a good deal of land at the back and the front of the house. Our landlord, Mr Simon and his wife were very fond of gardening. Every morning, he would work with the *mali* (gardener), in his front garden. They also kept a few poultry and had a good vegetable garden at the back of the house.

The Simons had four children, two daughters and two sons. The children were all married but for the youngest, Terence. He was just ten and used to visit us very often. I soon discovered to my great disappointment, that Violet had a crush on him. He would sing English love songs loudly from his verandah addressing his "lovely Violet" and that he loved her very much. Of course, Mrs Simon was very angry when she heard him and took an instant dislike to Violet. To my great relief, Aunt Natasha and Uncle Dick only laughed at it all. They said that Violet was only a foolish child and it was best to ignore all their childish fancies. They had not thought like that about Gopi and me, perhaps because he was a Hindu and much older than me. Besides he had actually written a letter expressing his love! Uncle and Aunt always spoke badly of Hindu men, who, they said were very different in culture. Uncle said that Hindu men considered the innocent young Christian and Anglo-Indian girls cheap and much below their standard because of their caste based religion.

I had been watching many Indian films where the oldest sister always made all the sacrifices for the younger brothers and sisters. So I had become very protective and caring towards Violet. I always gave her my share of food at the dining table. I also used Aunt Natasha's sewing machine to make dresses for Violet out of any piece of material I came by. In many ways I was trying to be a mother to her. I had decided that I would make every sacrifice to see that my sister was very well educated and perhaps become a doctor. Mum would be happy if one of her daughters became a doctor.

The old maidservant who did the cooking was sympathetic towards us. Knowing Violet's voracious appetite, she always cooked a few extra *chappattis* and secretly give them to me for Violet. She had no children.

The old *ayah* was very gentle and lady-like. Although she was illiterate, she was able to keep the daily account very accurate and up-to-date. Aunt measured the flour daily and gave it to her for making the *chappattis*. She also counted the *chappattis* after the *ayah* had made them. This upset the *ayah* because she felt Aunt did not trust her, besides she had somehow to manage extra ones every day for Violet. Aunt gave her and the sweeper woman all the left-over food after it had been kept in the cool wire cupboard for a day or two, before it went bad. This was done in most Indian houses. "Food is hard to get and should not be wasted," Aunt would say, "the poor servants can make use of it even if it is stale."

There were servants' quarters next to our garden which was fenced off with wire netting. They lived in one-room mud houses with hay-thatched roofs and a mud fireplace in the corner. They swept the room a couple of times a day and covered the floor and walls with a mixture of mud and cow-dung by hand freshly prepared every few days to freshen the air and kill germs. I often watched women and children picking up the fresh cow-dung from the streets and storing it in front of their mud houses. They would later either use it for plastering their house floors and walls, or flattening it with hands to dry and use as fuel for cooking.

Aunt bought meat and vegetables each day from the men who brought them in flat baskets carried on their heads. She also bought bread, teacakes and similar things each day from the baker, who came on his bicycle. In his tin box he also had pats of fresh butter, very carefully kept over a container with ice, some pastries and eggs. He carried a red book in which he kept a record of items bought on credit. Bills were paid monthly. Most vegetable men and women were Hindus, but the baker and the meat men were Muslim.

12

Humanitarian

Uncle Eddie visited us and liked the cottage. He said he was looking forward to his annual leave when he would set up a fowl pen. He planted chillies, mint, coriander, corn, okra and brinjal (eggplants) at the back before he left for Gorakhpur. Aunt argued with the *mali* over a rise in pay after Uncle left and he refused to work unless he got what he wanted. I took over the gardening which I found it to be very interesting. Mr Simon, our landlord, did most of it and I had watched him. I trimmed the henna hedge planted larkspurs, marigolds, roses and phlox. It gave me much pleasure to watch them grow and flower. Each morning I watered the plants with the iron watering can before I caught the bus to school. I eagerly waited for Uncle Eddie's return to show him my flower garden. I felt that he would appreciate my work, as he too loved gardening. Aunt kept herself busy with the vegetable garden at the back. Helen would often try to plant the flowers of her choice and her way, which upset me.

✣ ✣ ✣ ✣ ✣

There were many stray dogs around the Club and the servants' quarters. They came into our garden through the henna hedge and the wire fence. Most people did not like dogs and threw stones at them. Some servants threw hot boiling water and hot coals at them. Once I treated one with a bad burn on the back; the skin had lifted and the raw wound could be seen for days. I treated it with mercurochrome and boracic powder until it was well, but after a few days it was caught and put into the municipal dog pound. The dogcatchers came around every six months to catch strays and killed them. For a *rupee* the dogcatchers would free any dog caught, but unfortunately I was at school at the time. Yet another generation of pups was born by the time the dogcatcher returned. Violet and I felt very sorry for the stray dogs and saved food from our share of meals to give to them.

I managed to get permission to keep a small brown pup as a pet, on condition that she was always kept outside the house. I called her Susie and fed her from my share of dinner every night. Susie grew up to be a fine dog. Every morning she saw me to the bus stop. One day Susie ran across the road and was hit by a bus. I nursed her with medicines which Mum brought home for us. She soon recovered but when she was having her pups she died, because of a deformity of the hip-bones resulting from the accident, her pups were unable to come out and she had high temperature and blood-poisoning. I tried to feed her with a spoon while she was sick. No one helped me to treat her, nor did anyone tell me that she should be taken to a vet. Ultimately, one day when I returned from school, I found that she was dead with a half-born pup. I felt very unhappy and buried her in a corner of the garden. After Susie's death I was more concerned about the other stray dogs and attended to their mange, itch and wounds. I even cured a dog with a broken leg by bandaging a stick to the leg, until it had mended.

The servants living near our hedge started asking me to treat them and I enjoyed acting the doctor by attending to their wounds, boils and fever. I was sixteen then and simple medicines helped them so they trusted me.

✣ ✣ ✣ ✣ ✣

I was able to travel independently and I began visiting Mum at the hospital after school and on weekends when she could not come home. I caught a rickshaw from our gate to the hospital. I liked watching her work, observing the medicines she gave the patients and the way she looked after them. The nurses and the doctors were kind to me. Most of the nurses were simple, from poor homes, perhaps a young widow with children to support like Mum, or unmarried because of the inability of her family to pay the large dowry demanded by South Indian Christians. A few had husbands out of work or invalid. They all had problems, which drew them to nursing. In the 1950s, there were very few options for Christian women, most could only choose between teaching or nursing. Very few wanted to work. They were not educated enough to take up any other profession. Education is not free in India and only the rich can afford higher education. Remarriage by widows among the Indians was and is still, not approved by the Indian community even though there is a law to support it now. Most of the nurses were from Indian Christian homes, but all the doctors were female Hindus, because that was a hospital specialising in gynaecology. An Indian woman, especially one coming from the villages, never allowed a man, other than her husband, to see her face after marriage. She always covered her face with a sheet. An Indian village woman would rather die than see a male doctor for any female ailments. The *ayahs* did the job of nursing-aides. These *ayahs* were mostly illiterate and would do as they were told. The nurses only had survival English. Mum told them I was an intelligent girl studying English and I impressed them with the few words of English I had learnt in school.

Mum received Rs. 125 per month as a midwife nurse. Out of this she had to pay Rs. 40 for her board and lodging at the hospital and Rs. 25 each for the two of us plus half the house rent and the electricity, as well as any extra Aunt wanted. Fortunately she was able to get private work now and then at the hospital, The money from this covered our extra expenses. At times she would work twenty-four hours a day; she would do her regular hospital work and then at night take up the private nursing to earn extra for us.

✣ ✣ ✣ ✣ ✣

One night, I overheard Mum telling Aunt about a woman who had approached her to abort her unwanted child. She had offered Mum one hundred *rupees*. She had already received Rs.50 from another man for aborting his daughter's six weeks' pregnancy. The girl was about to enter into an arranged marriage and so her father would rather have had her killed than let her bear a child whilst unmarried. No one else would have married any of his other children if there was an unmarried mother in the house and the village would have considered the parents outcasts. The entire family would have suffered throughout their lifetime as a result.

I knew from Catechism lessons at school that abortion was a mortal sin. The revelation that Mum had done such a thing to earn money made me feel ill and I started sobbing. Mum stopped talking to Aunt and asked me what was wrong.

"I didn't know that you murder unborn babies to provide for us."

"I have no other way of earning money to buy all the things you need. Your father found it easy to disappear and desert the two of you. I can't help doing whatever I can to provide for you both."

"You don't have to do it. I don't want any new clothes or other things! I will stop eating and never talk to you, if you continue." I said.

"All right, now go to sleep and I promise I will not take that woman's abortion case."

I really do not know if she kept her promise, but I do know that she never mentioned such matters again. However, Aunt Natasha would say sarcastically. "So your mother has been able to buy you a pair of shoes after all. Perhaps she did an abortion to earn extra money. She seems to have no conscience whatsoever!"

It upset me very much so I decided to start work immediately after finishing High School. I wanted to grow up fast and earn a living to support us and help my mother in providing higher education for Violet.

✣ ✣ ✣ ✣ ✣

Uncle Dick began drinking heavily since his retirement. He often visited the De'Mellos who were also retired railway officers living at the colony. He would return home very late.

Aunt Natasha was upset with Uncle Dick's behaviour. One morning she lost patience and told Uncle to go and live with the De'Mellos since he had no consideration for her. She said she could not manage with the small sum he contributed towards the running of the house while he wasted his money on drink at his friend's place. Uncle was taken aback and for a couple of days he did not speak to Aunt; instead he sat on the verandah drinking neat Indian rum. He later told me that he was hurt by Aunt's remarks since he had done all he could to support her and the children, the family of his best friend, Eddie. He was extremely fond of Uncle Eddie and had stood by him even though there were difficulties in having Eddie's family stay at his house while he was in the railways.

A few days later he returned from the De'Mellos and told Aunt that he intended to immigrate to England. While making the necessary arrangements, he would stay with the De'Mellos. He asked Aunt if she wanted any of his furniture otherwise he would give it all to the De'Mellos. This made Aunt very angry.

"Dick, how can you consider such a thing! Every piece of furniture is going to remain in this house with me since I've looked after you and your house in every way for many years. Your house was a mess. Your servant was fleecing you. There was no one to look after the place. I made sure you bought a proper hot case and icebox and that you had proper meals. Now you consider your friends more important than me! No – you may leave with your boxes only, the furniture is going to remain with me."

And that is what he did the very next day. He was teary when he was leaving but he asked Aunt to contact him if she ever needed his help. He said that he would come to see Uncle Eddie in a month's time when Uncle Eddie was back on his annual leave. I felt sad to see him go, he had been kind to us, giving Violet and me pocket money every month. It was in his house at the railway quarters that we learnt to live like Anglo-Indians and had the security of a stable home. It was also in Uncle Dick's house that I was recognised as the *Missy Baba,* a name given to the British and Anglo-Indian girls by the servants.

Aunt did not seem upset after Uncle Dick left. She concentrated on Uncle Eddie's return. He had written that some of the Britishers from his factory were leaving for England as the factory had been sold to the Indian Government. Uncle had bought a dining set and some other things for the house, which he said he would bring when he came home on leave on the 26th of August, two days before Helen's birthday. In his letter to Aunt he had specially mentioned that he would celebrate both Enid and Helen's birthdays well that year because he had had a promotion to the position of Supervisor. Aunt was delighted with the news.

13

Uncle Eddie dies

Aunt Natasha suffered pain during her monthly periods and always drew attention towards her sufferings. She was unable to endure physical pain; even a small amount was exaggerated. Mum helped her with free medicines at such times and advice as well as treatment for small ailments. Mum took Aunt to her hospital for a consultation regarding her problems. The doctor diagnosed fibroid cysts, which made a hysterectomy necessary. Aunt refused to have anything done until Uncle returned home. Mum gave her regular injections of vitamin B complex, calcium and iron, painkillers and other medications.

In spite of Mum's gentle care of Aunt during her illnesses and the free medications, Aunt Natasha never forgot to charge Mum for any extra expenditure during the month. According to her we were a big responsibility and whatever Mum did was just a small return for her kindness in keeping us. Aunt had financial problems since Uncle Dick left and had to do with whatever Uncle Eddie sent. She lived to Anglo-Indian standards and found it very difficult to maintain. Mum was the only one she could fall back on for sharing the financial problems and hence she made Mum pay half of all the expenditure. It was unfortunate that Aunt would not discuss the budget with Mum since she considered the house to be hers and us as boarders living with her due to her kindness. This attitude of arrogance and superiority made it difficult for me to understand her even though I loved her next to my own mother. She was the only one I knew as a relative. Aunt gave us the security we needed as children.

There were times when Mum did not finish work until nine at night on the first of the month, but she still came home by ten or later at night, to pay Aunt the money, though the transaction often ended in a quarrel. There was always extra expense in the running of the house recorded in Aunt's account book or Mum had been unable to bring enough and asked for a day or two more to make up the full amount. Aunt would push back the chair or throw down the pencil and the money saying that she could not afford the whole business and that her house was not a rest home for people. Aunt would abuse Mum, calling her a woman of bad character and even a prostitute; Mum would just sit in silence. She was always on the receiving end and would finish by leaving the house in tears, saying that she would take us away soon. But she'd return the next day with the amount required and things would seem better again with Aunt. If she didn't have the amount on the day Mum got her salary, she became very nasty to both Mum and us. In every other way she seemed sympathetic to our plight though.

Violet and Helen were forever fighting. Violet could not understand why she had to give in to Helen even when she was in the right. It made Aunt very angry and she would call Violet a badly behaved and ungrateful orphan. I often lead Violet away wiping her tears and consoling her. Later I would lock myself in the toilet and cry, praying to Jesus. Aunt's sarcastic comments, made Helen feel superior and she treated us with authority rather than friendliness. I loved both Helen and Enid as my only cousins and it hurt when they said things about our background and breeding without understanding its meaning. I did realise that Aunt was under great emotional and financial stress but whatever she said made a deep impression on me.

I worried at the unkind things said to us and questioned why they were said, deciding that it may be because our Papa had deserted us. I became introverted, always afraid that I would do something to earn me abuse and criticism like I suffered at home. Praying and talking to Jesus was the only way I could feel better. Violet became extroverted and made a lot of friends in school. She joined various church organisations like "The Legion of Mary" where there were young boys and girls. She won everyone's attention with her tall tales and jokes but it made her unpopular at home.

A few days before Uncle Eddie was to return in 1956, Violet found a pencil and was delighted because we could afford only one pencil at a time. When Helen saw the pencil she at once claimed it for herself. Violet refused to give it to her. This started fighting between them. Aunt intervened and took the pencil from Violet, calling her names and, as usual, reminding her of her status in their house. After things calmed down I walked up to Helen and, plucking up my courage for the first time, said "Helen, why are you always picking fights with us? I wish you didn't have a father either and then you would know how we feel without one." I sobbed a lot after that in the solitude of the toilet.

A few days later the torrential monsoon rains began and one afternoon, just after we had returned from school, a telegram arrived with the news that Uncle Eddie was seriously ill. The telegram was two days old, as the rain had held up its delivery. Aunt panicked and decided to leave for Tamkhoi with her children the next morning. But, an hour later, two more telegrams came together. One said that Uncle Eddie was being rushed to the hospital at Gorakhpur, some sixty kilometres away, as his condition was serious. The other said that he had had an operation. Both telegrams were twenty hours late. Aunt was desperate. She looked at her watch and said that there was just one hour before the evening train left. She quickly packed some clothes. A message was sent to Uncle Dick at the De'Mello's house. He decided to join them on the journey, just as he was, in his pyjamas. Violet and I were left with the *ayah* and a message was sent to Mum through a rickshaw man. Mum took a few days off from work and visited Uncle Eddie with us the following day. I was filled with guilt for having said what I had to Helen a few days prior and prayed that nothing would happen to Uncle. That morning before school, as I was brushing my teeth, one of Helen's shoes fell off the shoe rack. It had happened accidentally; but I believed that Uncle had died. Later I discovered that he had passed away at that time, six in the morning.

I stopped at the little grotto of Our Lady of Lourdes in the school garden and prayed for Uncle's soul, making a promise to him that in his absence I would look after his two daughters as my own sisters and also care for Aunt. I understood the feelings of a fatherless child. I was also full of gratitude for all that Uncle Eddie had done for us by giving us his home and family to live with.

We reached Gorakhpur the next morning but were told that the funeral had already taken place the day before. Uncle's friends had taken aunt and her children to Tamkohi but one of Aunt's, only came to know about Uncle after Aunt arrived in the morning. Uncle had died on or at the very time that Aunt's train had arrived at the station. When Aunt reached the hospital at 6.30 in the morning Uncle had already been placed in the mortuary. There are no funeral homes in India and therefore the funeral had to take place the same day, before sunset. Aunt and her two daughters were just in time to attend the funeral.

Usually the body is taken home from the hospital and kept on the bed for a few hours with blocks of ice under it, to enable people to pay their last respects. Hindus lay the body on the floor. The dead body of a Hindu is carried by male relatives on a narrow bier to be cremated, the eldest son putting a flame to the mouth. The ashes are then immersed in the river Ganges. Some Hindus throw their dead into the river straight away. The dead body has to be buried or cremated before 6.00pm the same day!

After meeting Aunt's brother we caught another train to Tamkhoi. There, amidst tears, Helen reminded me of what I had said to her. What use was it to say to her that I had not really meant it and had just been provoked by her constant fighting with us?

✣ ✣ ✣ ✣ ✣

In Tamkhoi Aunt Natasha, Enid and Helen stayed at the house which Uncle Eddie had shared with a few other Anglo-Indians. I remembered the previous year when we visited Uncle for a fortnight with Aunt. Since the sugar cane factory had been sold to the Indian Government and most Britishers and Anglo-Indians had left for England, Aunt was able to visit Uncle and stay with him for the short school holidays. The cottage was a very large, four-bedroom house with two toilets. Ali was the young cook who served us with good English meals. We went for long walks in the village of Tamkhoi. On one such walk a few village women stopped and gossiped about Aunt: they had never seen a woman wearing an overcoat over her *sari* and so were discussing whether Aunt was a man or a woman. We found their puzzlement astonishing. The cottage had no permanent electricity supply, because it was available only at certain times, furnished by generators.

The night before we left for Allahabad, on that earlier occasion, Violet and I went to the toilet which was at the back. Everyone was sleeping outside in the garden under the mosquito nets because it was so hot. I had to wake Violet in the middle of the night to accompany me. We walked together with a lantern. She went into the toilet first whilst I stood with the lantern near the door. Then it was my turn and Violet did the same. I was on the wooden seat when I saw a *kerait* (a snake which is as poisonous as the *cobra*) crawl in under the door which opened into the garden. I bade Violet to keep absolutely quiet. She stood frozen still at one corner of the wall and I sat similarly, not blinking an eye. The snake crawled to the middle of the bathroom, then under the wooden toilet seat on which I was sitting and finally disappeared under the door, which opened, into the backroom of the house. Once it had disappeared into the house we ran through the outside door and went to sleep. Though the whole place was infested with poisonous snakes, when we told Aunt and Uncle about our night experience at the breakfast table they did not believe us, saying that we were either making up a story or had been dreaming. But when we were packing up our luggage later that morning, Uncle opened a wooden trunk in the room to take out something, he saw a belt among the old bits and pieces and was about to pick it up when it moved. It was probably the snake we had seen at night. Uncle and the servants immediately killed it with large sticks. "So you two were not telling stories after all!" Uncle said smiling

It was sad without Uncle in Tamkhoi. His things were all packed up ready for his return home for the annual leave. He had been suffering with stomach aches, but had ignored them saying that he would have it treated once he was in Allahabad. A week before his leave was to commence Uncle suddenly had a severe pain in his stomach. He was taken to the doctor in the village who gave him an enema. Uncle could not pass the enema; instead his pain grew intolerable. With the enema still unpassed, Uncle was rushed to a large hospital, in Gorakhpur, travelling sixty miles in a jeep over rough roads. His appendix was inflamed and must have burst under the pressure of the enema and the jolting. An emergency operation was performed on arrival at the hospital. It was unsuccessful and he survived only one night more.

After three days, we all returned to Allahabad. Uncle had only a thousand *rupees* in the bank as his saving and no other funds. So there was next to nothing left to support Aunt and the girls.

✣ ✣ ✣ ✣ ✣

Aunt had her operation within a month of Uncle's death. Mum arranged for her to have it in her hospital and nursed her. We four were allowed to stay in Mum's room for two days after the operation. Mum took leave and looked after us as well as attended to Aunt in the hospital as her private nurse. After Aunt recovered, she looked for a job as a Hindi teacher. She was able to get one in the boys' English school called St Joseph Collegiate, next to our convent. Since she was only a Middle Trained teacher, she was to teach Hindi as far as class four only.

A month after Aunt recovered and had found the job, there was another serious quarrel between Mum and Aunt over money. Aunt said that Mum had to increase the amount of our board and lodging again since Uncle was dead and she had to live within her small income of only one hundred and twenty *rupees* a month as a teacher. She told Mum that if she could not pay she would have to take us away. Mum was stunned, considering all she had done for Aunt at the hospital, obtaining free medication and good care through her friends. Mum was hurt and decided she would keep us near the hospital in a small flat. Our things were packed and she called for the rickshaw to take us away. As the luggage was loaded into the rickshaw, I watched Aunt sitting near the outside table, smoking a cigarette. Her face betrayed no emotion. I had been waiting for her to stop Mum while our luggage was being packed, but she had not. I wondered how she would manage without our small contribution for board and lodging. I felt she needed us even if she did not realise it and that it was her financial state and feeling of insecurity which made her ask for an increase and therefore, I should not leave her.

"Mum, I cannot leave with Uncle no longer here to support Aunt. She needs us. Let us stay together and forget all ill feelings." I said.

Mum was in a very bad temper.

"You don't realise that she does not want us. I have tried my best to please her and show her my gratitude, but she does not understand my problems. I cannot increase the money at this stage, I don't have any more, I am stretched to the limit. If I manage to find a flat near the hospital we can live for less than what I pay here. You'd better come with me as I have planned, or else I shall never come again to take you nor will I ever come to see you again."

But I refused. I was torn between my duties towards Uncle and his family and my mother. I chose to stay with Aunt in her sad predicament. Mum left in a huff, threatening she would never return. Our luggage was lying at the gate. Violet stood near it puzzled. Aunt did not move. I went up and kissed her cold cheeks. Then she cried, tears streaming down her face. She told us to take our things back into the room where they were before. Enid and Helen helped us put our luggage back. They had been standing aside in silence watching.

Mum visited us after all when she had her next day off. I made her understand and she increased our board and lodging by just a few *rupees*. I know she had a lot of problems in doing so. Though we never left Aunt till we grew up and started working, Mum had to face a lot of other small nasty arguments about money. I started dreading the first of the month when Mum came with the money to pay. Eventually I decided I had to work to help Mum as soon as I had completed High School.

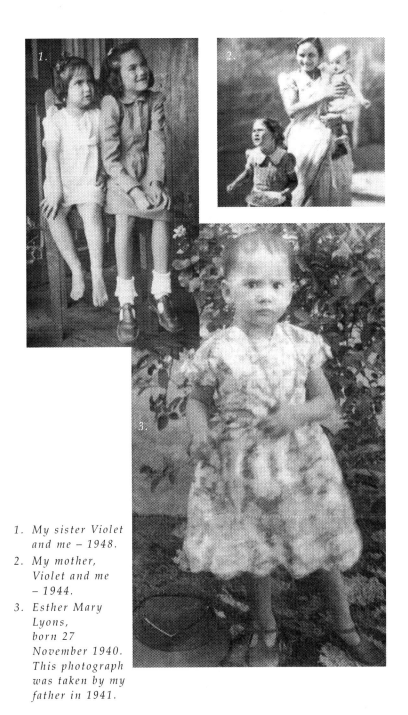

1. *My sister Violet and me – 1948.*
2. *My mother, Violet and me – 1944.*
3. *Esther Mary Lyons, born 27 November 1940. This photograph was taken by my father in 1941.*

1. *Graduating with my Bachelor of Education.*
2. *My sisterViolet at 21 years.*

1. *Winning the 1969 May Queen Beauty Competition.*
2. *Femina Beauty Contest.*

Both Pages.
Various commercial modelling jobs I did over the years in Delhi India – 1968-1969.

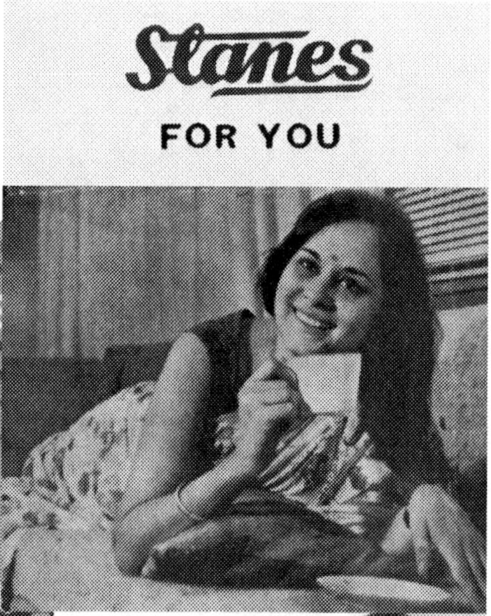

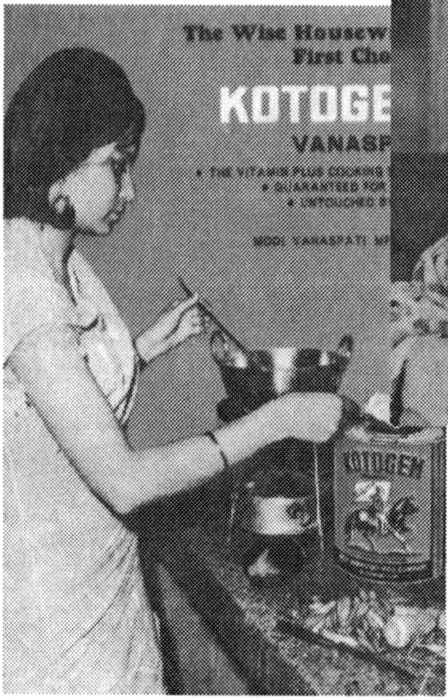

मनोरमा
आज हर महिला को क्यों पसन्द है ?
एक प्रति का मूल्य ६० पैसे वार्षिक शुल्क ७ रुपये
मित्र प्रकाशन प्राईवेट लिमिटेड, इलाहाबाद-३

Saharanpore 1946.
Left to Right:
Mother with Enid, Violet, Uncle Eddie, Helen, myself and Aunt Natasha.

14

The Discovery

Not long after that argument I was looking through one of Uncle's trunks for the tuft of my hair, which Aunt had shown me in Kalimpong. Aunt was visiting a teacher friend with Enid, Helen and Violet. I came across a file and some photographs which were neatly tied up. The file contained a mass of carbon copies of typed sheets addressed to the American High Commissioner, to Bishop Sullivan and Bishop Wildermuth of Patna Jesuit Mission, to the President of America and to the Anglo-Indian Member of Parliament, Mr Frank Anthony. All the letters mentioned me and Violet. From the letters I discovered that Uncle had been fighting for us, as we were the children of an American Jesuit priest who had deserted us. My father's name was listed as 'Michael Lyons'.

There were also letters written by Papa in his own handwriting, asking Uncle Eddie to look after us and to give me the best education possible in a good English school. They were written from different parts of India. One letter asked Uncle to use money he had left with him for us. Some of the letters were written on US Foreign Economic Administration (FEA) letterheads. One such a letter mentioned that Papa had been given dispensation to work for the US Foreign Economic Administration in India as he was best suited for the job, having a good knowledge of the language and the culture of the Indian people.

There was a State Bank pass book which had a balance of twenty-five-thousand *rupees* in the joint names of Papa and Mum and an American passport, issued in 1920, when Papa had first come to India as a Jesuit missionary, which had expired. I found two addresses, one of Papa's brother, Frank Lyons and the other of his cousin, Mrs Emma Trombley. The photographs were of Papa's sisters Margaret and Helen, of his brother Frank and his children. They were in a packet labelled, "Might be useful to Minnie later". I kept the file by me in my box. It gave me great joy to read my Papa's letters expressing his concern for my welfare. They showed that he loved me very much. Suddenly the mystery of who "Fr Lyons" and "Michael" was solved and I understood why Mum had been visiting the Bishop in Patna and also Fr. O'Brien.

Although I felt proud to be the child of an American I felt compelled to keep the secret of who my father was. I was unable to claim that my father was alive because I could not tell anybody who he was, so I was forced to continue with the lie that my father was dead. Violet was still unaware of the fact. I did not disclose it to her. It hurt me bitterly to continue saying that my father was dead when I knew it was a lie and so I further avoided people and spent more time in prayers and by myself.

I could not understand why everyone called us by the surname "Anthony" and not "Lyons" our real name. I didn't understand how my father could be a Jesuit priest and have us two when priests were not married. Slowly it became clear to me why Aunt Natasha had been saying that we had no background and all the other nasty things.

I told Mum what I'd discovered. She instructed me to keep it secret. "Why are we 'Anthony' and not 'Lyons'?"

"He did love us very much and promised to return soon from USA. I don't know what happened. So it was best that no one knew about it. Father Evans suggested 'Anthony'. It was best to let people think that your father was dead or had deserted us. Yes, he was a priest and we were not allowed to marry. I considered it best for him to return to the priesthood. I asked him to do so after Violet was born. He promised to keep in touch and support the two of you since he loved you both dearly."

It didn't make a lot of sense to me, but because I did not want my mother sad or upset I accepted what she said. I did not realise the consequences of being the daughter of an American priest. That discovery aroused my great desire to meet my Papa – if only to ask him why he deserted us – if he loved us as Mum said.

✣ ✣ ✣ ✣ ✣

Uncle Dick left for England shortly after Uncle Eddie's death and we never saw him again. His letters were addressed to Aunt in the beginning but later he wrote to me about how he missed me, his 'little Marie Gorette' and 'the Praying Mantis,' and how he would like to hold me in his arms and kiss me. He wanted me to join him, willing to pay my fare if I would marry him, as he wanted to give me a good home and all the things in life that I had never had before. I had always respected him as an Uncle who was as old as my father. His letters depressed me to a great extent. I could not believe that the man I grew up calling Uncle would eventually propose marriage to me. I was fifteen and he was fifty-seven at the time. I stopped replying to his letters and did not discuss them with anyone. Eventually we lost contact with him altogether.

✣ ✣ ✣ ✣ ✣

One Sunday as we were returning from church, a rickshaw pulled up near us and a very fair lady with jet black hair and deep blue eyes asked Aunt Natasha to accompany her as she said she lived near our house. So Aunt got in with her and went home while we four walked.

I recognised the lady, Mrs Clarke, as one of the teachers from our school. She and her husband were domiciled Anglo-Indians of Irish descent and lived in one of the apartments, not far from our cottage. Her husband was an ex-school teacher who once used to be a religious Irish Brother. He was about twenty-five years older than his wife and had become senile, losing his memory.

From that day on, Aunt Natasha started going to and from church every Sunday with Mrs Clarke. She even started visiting her after school to consult about any sort of problem she had with Enid and Helen's class-teachers. Mrs Clarke would help in resolving it with the teachers in the school. It was because of her intervention that they discovered that both Enid and Helen were in need of spectacles and that their failure in class were a result of their poor eyesight. Soon we began calling Mrs Clarke,

Aunty Clarke out of respect. We also came to know her mother, Mrs McNamara, who was a lady of seventy-five. She had a rather dark complexion.

I felt that although Mrs Clarke seemed to love her dark-skinned mother, brother and sister, she was embarrassed to acknowledge them because of their complexion.

Mrs Clarke was easily irritated, even though she was only in her early fifties. Her husband was in his seventies and just a few years younger than Mrs McNamara. The Clarkes had two sons. Both the boys looked very Irish with the light-coloured eyes of their father.

Mrs Clarke was very strict about the diets of her mother and her husband as they both had diabetes.

"You are my wife, you should listen to me. Instead, you are always bullying me." Mr Clarke said to her one day.

Granny McNamara received a pension from the British Defence Services which helped her survive. She had one good eye, the other was of glass. She told us that she had an eye infection some years earlier when her husband was alive and had to go to the eye hospital for treatment. She stood in a queue for a long while to see the doctor. When at last she did, she found him busy talking to a nurse and somewhat inattentive towards the patients. He put some drops into her eye as he talked to the nurse. As soon as the drops were put into her eye, she screamed with pain. At this the doctor discovered that he had used the wrong drops. But it was too late, for her eye had already been damaged beyond treatment. To make up for what he had done he gave her a glass eye free!

Granny McNamara was fond of her daughter, Anne Clarke, but scared of her temper, because if she was in a bad mood, she would often say things that would hurt. One evening Granny McNamara came to see us in tears at about five in the evening, complaining that Anne had been rude to her. Granny had simply asked Anne what she could do with her kerosene oil stove, since she was not using it any more and Anne had replied:

"Mum, I am teaching, I don't want to be disturbed. You'd better light the stove and sit on it. Now get out and don't bother me."

Aunt Natasha tried to comfort her and gave her a nice hot cup of tea but after she left, Aunt was hysterical with laughter over what Aunt Clarke had said. She thought it funny as well as unkind. Mrs Clarke always gave private tuition between four and five in the afternoons and did not like to be disturbed at that time. Teachers' salaries being very low in India, every teacher tried to do some private teaching after school to help them survive.

✣ ✣ ✣ ✣ ✣

Another evening Mrs Clarke visited us about six. She looked very upset. Her husband was nowhere to be found. He had insisted on taking a walk and since Mrs Clarke had been busy giving private lessons, she became irritable and told him to go away, though she yelled out after him to return soon. He had been gone for two hours and there was no sign of him. Since then she had looked for him everywhere he could have gone and had notified the police. She spent the entire night praying for him and crying with guilt over her rudeness to him.

The next morning, when we were going to school, I was looking out of the bus window as usual, when suddenly I saw old Mr Clarke, covered with blood, in a rickshaw, going towards the city. As soon as I reached school I ran to the staffroom and informed Mrs Clarke about what I saw. Immediately she took leave and rushed towards the city government hospital. She found him in the emergency ward, guarded by the police. The rickshawman had dumped him at the gates; saying that he had found him lying at the side of the road in a place called Katra, quite a distance from our house. The rickshawman had then taken off, never to be seen again. It remained a mystery what happened to him.

Mr Clarke's skull was broken and bleeding, as were his hands. After he had been bandaged and treated he was allowed to go home. At home Father Cyril George an old student of his, gave him the Last Sacrament and that same night he died.

Mrs McNamara's second daughter, Sybil, decided to take her mother back with her to Calcutta after the funeral and place her in a Widows' Home nearby. Granny McNamara died within six months of leaving Allahabad.

Mrs Clarke was left alone. Aunt Natasha became friendly with her and visited her often. I felt drawn to her also and as long as we were living in that house I too visited Aunt Clarke with my problems and fears. Aunt Natasha had confided in her about my father being a priest and so Aunt Clarke was sympathetic towards Violet and me. She tried to guide and help me grow out of my problems. Violet had a mind of her own and her world was full of boyfriends. She was indifferent to what was said at home. Nothing seemed to upset her. She only thought of dressing well and having many admirers. As she grew older she started looking upon me as a rival.

Every evening we knelt in front of the altar at home and said the Rosary. Each of us said one decade of the Rosary loudly. When it was my turn, I stressed every word, my eyes closed, sometimes as if in a trance, imagining the happenings of the Mystery of the decade. Hearing me pray the way I did annoyed Violet. Especially when everyone praised me as a good, saintly girl. When Violet's boyfriends would also praise me, Violet would come home and pick a fight with me. We hit each other, threw shoes, or pull each other's plaits. My long plaits reached my hips, Violet found it easy to pull them and hit me. Mum or Aunt intervened and saved me, because I always got the worst of it. I often ended up crying because I could not understand what had happened to make Violet so hostile. However, there were times when Violet was nice to me – usually when she wanted to borrow something. Once Mum made skirts for both of us with matching blouses. Violet wanted to borrow the skirt and blouse I was wearing before we went to the Benediction one afternoon. She had heard her friends say nice things about me in my new clothes. So she came to me and said, "Minnie, would you like to wear my skirt and blouse, as yours does not fit you very well? Perhaps it will fit me better and mine would do the same for you."

I was ready to do anything to please my sister. So off she went with the clothes that her friends had praised me in and I was in her clothes which were too big for me. Violet had grown taller and was of bigger build than me. I needed a belt to tighten the skirt around my waist and looked a drab. Mum noticed it in the Church and was very angry at Violet, but it made no difference. Violet boastfully told her friends that she had fooled me and taken my clothes and that Mum spoilt me because I was stupid and simple. People called violet a tomboy. I, on the other hand, loved her and always wanted her to be happy. I continued to protect her by taking all the blame on myself. I understood that Violet wanted to get attention and so tried in every way to help her get it from her friends. I remained introverted and forever engrossed in my own thoughts and prayers. I got all the comforts I needed in talking to Jesus in the solitude of the chapel and the back of the house as I was too frightened of criticism in the world I lived in, trusting no one.

We were members of the Sodality of Mary at the convent and had our prayer meetings every Sunday afternoon just before the Benediction at the Cathedral. So on Sundays we attended the Sunday Mass, then the Sodality meeting and the Benediction in the evenings. Mother Seraphica sang solo in the Church choir. After the Benediction, Enid, Helen and I walked home, but Violet stayed back for the Legion of Mary meeting with boys of her age.

✣ ✣ ✣ ✣ ✣

One day I discovered a large boil at the back of my right ear. A few years before there had been a small boil in the back of the same right ear while we lived in Chunar. Mum lanced it and treated it at home. Then when we were at the railway quarters, I had another one, which was dealt with by the medical superintendent of Mum's hospital. But this time it was much larger and throbbed painfully. The boils always came in September after the monsoon and before winter. Father Evans tried to treat it with his homoeopathic.

Mum took me to the hospital as Father Evans' homoeopathic medicines were not doing any good. The following morning the medical superintendent said it needed a specialist's treatment. She gave us a referral to the ear, nose and throat specialist.

That afternoon Mum dressed in her nurse's white *sari* and

blouse to impress the doctor in the civil hospital and took me there. The outpatient clinic was crowded, but Mum managed to hand in her medical superintendent's letter, which had an immediate effect. We did not have to wait long. The doctor examined the boil and said that it was ready to be lanced. So I was taken to the operating room and, after a local anaesthetic, the job was done. Mum was with me all the time. Once I was bandaged, she took me home in a rickshaw. The next day I was allowed to go to school.

The first day in school was fine, but the next day, when I was waiting for the bus after school, I started feeling giddy, so I sat down on the bench in the school verandah. My right arm and shoulder began jerking, I felt cold and faint for a few seconds. I caught the bus with great difficulty. When I reached home I told mum what had happened and she took me to her hospital. She described my symptoms to the doctor, who just laughed and said it was only a child's fear and fantasy and all I needed now was a good dose of a laxative, castor oil. There and then, Mum forced me with the thick repulsive castor oil and took me back home..

The next day was Saturday and everyone was at home sitting on the verandah, enjoying the morning sunshine. I felt shivery but the sunlight made me feel good. After about thirty minutes I felt sick and brought up all the castor oil. Mum helped me to the toilet. She discovered that my temperature was 104 degrees. She gave me an aspirin and put me to bed. Mum gave me another aspirin before she lay down to sleep beside me that night.

I woke up feeling very thirsty in the middle of the night and wanted to go to the toilet. With Mum's help, I got out of bed, but as I stood up I felt weak and giddy and then blacked out.

When I came around I heard Mum's muffled voice calling out to Aunty Natasha who quickly came to help. By then I was conscious, my lips were blue and I was very pale. My temperature was near 105 degrees. Aunt ran to Aunt Clarke's place to call a doctor. Aunt Clarke knew Dr Burke whose two daughters were in my class. So she guided Aunt Natasha to Mrs

Baker, who had a telephone. (In India a telephone is a luxury and it took years for the connection, unless a bribe was used.) Mrs Baker was a secretary to a rich Muslim family and it was they who had the telephone installed in her house for convenience. Since it was just after midnight, Aunt Natasha got the doctor to come to the house. (There were no after-hours doctors in Allahabad, so we had to use the government hospitals and wait for treatment in the casualty.) Unfortunately we had no conveyance and at that hour of the night it was dangerous to travel by a slow rickshaw.

Dr Burke diagnosed meningitis, as a result of the operation on the boil. The ear, nose specialist had left pus under the mastoid bones, which had travelled towards the brain. He had not given me antibiotic to kill the infection. Dr Burke gave me just twenty-four hours to live unless the antibiotic he used was successful.

The next morning, the parish priest administered the Last Sacrament to me. In the afternoon I was visited by my favourite nun, Mother Seraphica and another nun. They asked me if there was anything I wanted especially and promised to pray for me. I was much taken by all the sudden concern and the attention. I had not realised the seriousness of my ailment. I was then seventeen. No one was to disturb me except Mum and Aunt. The doctor visited three times that day. My backbone was very stiff and he kept a watch over it, making me try to bend. The next day he declared me out of danger. The nuns visited me on the following three days. I also had visits from most of the people from the Anglo-Indian colony, many of whom I had seen but never spoken to. A very dark lady, Mrs Carver, came to visit me one evening with gifts of a Rosary and a medal of St Jude. She said she knew Mum from the hospital. She ran the Housie at the Club every Sunday evening. She visited me on three consecutive days and each time she sat and prayed for my recovery. She left a little dachshund pup for me. I called him Rex and he became my closest companion. When I recovered I was told to stay home from school for the rest of the year and take it easy. But after a fortnight I insisted on returning to school for my final examination, as I felt well. I was in Class 9 then.

Mum borrowed to pay the doctor hundreds of *rupees* for my treatment, there was no health insurance scheme and no one helped her.

I was sick for fifteen days and convalesced for another fifteen, but when I returned to school my sole desire was to show Mother Seraphica my gratitude for her visits when I was sick. So I studied hard for the examinations and to everyone's astonishment I came first in the class. The doctor had informed Mum that the high temperature and the brain infection would leave me somewhat backward and dull! But it had the reverse effect. I came first in the class that year. I retained my position thereafter.

The wealthy Hindu girls finally accepted me because of my examination results. These were the same girls who used to avoid me in the beginning because I looked very sickly and they were afraid that I had some contagious disease.

15

Superstitions and prejudice

My mother was respected by the new parish priest, Father Alva, a South Indian from Mangalore. Every week she gave him accounts of the babies she baptised before they died in the hospital. Father Alva was very keen on making every Catholic fervent and religious. He took a long time to complete his service on Sundays because he had so much to share during the sermons, which he delivered very loudly. He also took longer than most saying the prayers slowly and meaningfully.

It was during his time, in 1957, that free butter oil, wheat and powdered milk were sent from the USA for the poor in India. The Indian Government allowed the food to be given to the churches for distribution. Once a month it was distributed to the Catholics only and Aunt queued up to get the rationed amount. Another day it was distributed to the Protestants only and there was a day set aside for the non-Christians when there was always a stampede and the police had to be called to restore order.

The butter oil was good for cooking but the powdered milk was used only for tea at home. In the school the nuns served it to the poor Catholics to drink during the recess. I hated the taste yet I was forced to drink by the nun in the infirmary. She considered me very pale and weak. Violet drank two or three glasses at a time. Unfortunately this USA food soon started appearing in the markets also and the churches stopped receiving it. Aunt Natasha was very disappointed, as it was a help in the house.

About that time Aunt brought a round object like fungus on a plate from school and told us that it was a gift from God. She told us that a person suffering from a cancerous wound in his leg had been praying for recovery. One day he dreamt that he was bathing in the river and an object touched his leg where the wound was. He was cured, because he believed that it was sent from God. He was told in his dream to take the object and keep it in a flat plate and to pour black tea over it every day. On the seventh day the object would double in size. This should then be given to someone else, so that it was in every house and people would know God's mercy and love. The man was supposed to have bathed in the river after he had the dream and just as in his dream, a round fungus-like object did touch him and he was cured. So he brought the object home and distributed it all over the city of Allahabad amongst the believers in God. No one could name the person who discovered it, but every Christian house had the object on their altar at home where it was kept with reverence and worshipped as a gift from God. Aunt even drank a bit of the tea poured over it for the cure of her recurring physical ailments; I was given some, as were the other three at home. Father Alva did not comment about it because he said he had no proof that it was true, but if the people believed and it healed them, he would not stop them. Even non-Christians heard of it and put their hopes on it for a cure. News of it was on the front pages of the local papers so the scientists took it for investigation. To the shock and horror of everyone, it was found to be a sea fungus full of deadly bacteria. A warning about it was published in the popular press and that was the end of that. Ours went out into the garden that very day, straight from the altar and no one spoke of it again!

One afternoon during the winter holidays in 1957, Cajeton Uncle appeared from Bettiah and stayed with us until he found a job in a factory at Naini as a welder, then moved into a friend's place.

One day Aunt came home from school in a violent temper because she heard that Cajeton had resumed his relationship with the daughter of the school cleaner. The girl had a reputation for promiscuity. Aunt lost her temper with her brother when he next visited. He confirmed that he was friendly with Mary adding she was a good girl and going steady with him. Aunt claimed that her family were Brahmans converted to Christianity during the time of the famine in Bettiah, when as a result of the nine days novena, said in the Catholic Church, at the time of a saintly bishop Hartman, it had rained and practically half of the city of Bettiah had turned Catholic. But Mary's family included sweepers and low caste converts, besides, Aunt worked as a teacher in the same school where Mary's father was only a cleaner, so it was humiliating for her. Apart from being caste-conscious, Indians are also very class-conscious. They look down on such jobs as cleaners, drivers, cooks and even welders and workers. They look up to academic jobs, which need an educational background. They will not entertain anyone in lower professions as equals.

Cajeton was neither concerned about what people said nor class-conscious and left the house in a huff. Aunt told us how one afternoon she saw Mary's father sweeping the playground and spoke to him very harshly about allowing his daughter to be with her brother. Soon after that Cajeton found another job a few stations from Allahabad. He told Aunt that she was correct about Mary. Aunt was pleased to hear the news and happy with Cajeton. About a month and a half later, she was informed by Father Alva that Cajeton had married Mary. Aunt decided to have nothing more to do with her brother.

A fortnight after her decision, Cajeton visited us again. Before Aunt could order him out, he cried and told Aunt that he had left Allahabad to get away from Mary but that she had turned up to his new place suddenly one day saying she loved him and could not live without him. He had let her stay at his place for three days, but on the third day he was visited by the police and the local parish priest, charging that he had kept an under-age girl, who had run away from her house. Cajeton was thunderstruck. He had the option of being jailed or of marrying Mary immediately. He chose the latter, because, apart from the fact that he did not want to lose his job, he also considered that, since Mary had lived a decent life for the few days that she had been with him, marrying her might bring about a change for the better. Unfortunately, he soon learned how he had been tricked into marrying her. She had come to him because the police had caught her making love to a rich Hindu in public in Allahabad. The police noted Mary's name and address to file a charge against her. Her parents made her flee Allahabad. The only place she could go was to her former boyfriend, Cajeton. So they sent her there and later informed the parish priest that their daughter had disappeared, adding that they thought that she was with Cajeton. The parish priest, Father Alva, contacted the priest of the place where Cajeton was and together with the police they forced their immediate marriage. Father Alva thought he was doing the right thing by marrying a young girl to a good Catholic boy. We felt sorry for Uncle Cajeton. Mum persuaded Mary to take up nursing after they returned to Allahabad and Cajeton took up his old job at Naini.

16

My mother's story

By the time I was eighteen I was well known among the servant quarters and the rickshaw men around the Anglo-Indian colony as the *memsahib* who gave the free medicines and tonics. Since I was a regular visitor to mum's hospital, I'd learnt a lot about medicines and caring for the sick. I used the stock Mum brought home, it gave me great satisfaction to help and treat them.

Rehman, an elderly rickshaw man once came to me with a bad cough, which he had suffered for sometime. I guessed it to be tuberculosis and strongly recommended that he see a doctor in the Civil Hospital. My guess was correct and he had a list of medicines and tonics to take which I got from Mum. I helped Rehman for months till he improved. Then one day an old woman came to see me with a deep burn in her hand, which had become badly inflamed. I cleaned it and treated it with medicine and dressing till it was cured.

Sometimes I visited Mum in the hospital and waited for her in her room. I tidied her cupboards then read Hindi magazines and novels. Mum had a pile of them which I found very interesting. Once I read a short story book about sexual crimes against women. It was the first time I had read about sexual assaults and forced prostitution of young girls from poor homes. It horrified me to learn that some poor parents sold their daughters for prostitution to get money. I prayed intensely for those victims.

When Mum was off duty we sometimes saw a film in the afternoon. More often we sat chatting on her bed. One day I asked her about her childhood and her parents. I had never met her family and knew nothing about them. She told me that she was born into a farming family in Latonah, a small village, in the state of Bihar, in northern India with a population of over 700 Catholics. It was an old Capuchine settlement of converted

Catholics and orphans brought from different parts of Bihar. The people who were re-settled in Latonah were the converted low caste Hindus, Muslims, abandoned Anglo-Indian offspring of the British working in the indigo factory in that area and Santhal Tribals (Aborigines). In 1921, Latonah was entrusted to the Jesuits of Patna Diocese, who originally came from the Illinois and Michigan States in USA At the time, late nineteenth century, the British established indigo factories around the area and there were many abandoned Anglo-Indian children born of the British officers and the native women. The missionaries brought up many such Anglo-Indian children in the orphanages. To start with they were brought up according to Indian ways and language, but later it was decided to give them a British education and cultural background.

The entire population of Latonah attended church twice daily. Once in the morning for Mass and in the afternoon for Benediction and the Rosary.

"There are no railway lines to Latonah and no proper transport to reach the village," mother explained. "The missionaries travelled by jeep and boats over muddy land and across the ever-flooding River Kosi. The missionaries found the poverty-stricken people of the State of Bihar; very simple and willing to convert in the Catholic religion in order to get some food and a few *rupees*. They needed to survive and keep their children alive. Most of them were farmers and farm labourers, who depended upon the Monsoon for the growth of their produce in the fields.

There is no electricity in my village. The people of Latonah use clay pots for cooking and firewood for fuel. They live on rice and lentils and meat is a luxury. The parish priest supports them financially, providing them with land to farm and mud houses to live in. Imported toys and clothes are distributed for Christmas and Easter, donated by the Catholics in the USA

The parish priest's house and the church are the only two brick buildings in Latonah. The church is built in the middle of the village dividing it into two parts, Mariam Pura (colony of Mary) and Joseph Pura (colony of Joseph). Next to the church is the primary school, which provides the children with sufficient knowledge to read the Bible and the prayer books both in Hindi and in the *Maithli* languages. Every year the intelligent and talented students were taken away by the nuns from Bettiah (a nearby city), to study in the Catholic High School and then later to enter the priesthood or the convent as nuns. The remaining children grow up in the true Christian spirit of praying and serving the Catholic Church and tending the land and the cattle. There are no factories or industries around the village to employ them. The people have blind faith in their parish priest, trusting him for his prayers for the cure of their physical ailments and in most cases avoid attending the small Government Hospital. To the people of Latonah the parish priest is in the place of God and they will do anything for him.

I was born in 1912 in that village. My mother Elizabeth, was a Muslim convert."

"How was she converted! I thought Muslims are staunch in their religion?" I asked.

"She was only three when the foreign nuns found her in a place called Fakirana not far from Latonah, after a flood. Every year the Kosi River floods during the monsoons and many houses and fields are destroyed. The nuns kept her in their orphanage and baptised her into Catholicism. Six months later, her parents, a Muslim couple, belonging to the family of rich jewellers with the surname of Shah, came looking for her, but when they discovered that she was converted to Christianity, they decided to abandon her. My mother, Elizabeth grew up in the orphanage with the nuns and married an orphan, my father, Keilu Julius Didacus, a fair skinned boy with blue eyes and red hair. They were given a small piece of land by the church to live on in the village of Latonah.

My father, Keilu (the word Keilu in the Maithali language meaning a person with blue eyes) and my mother, Elizabeth, had two sons and three daughters. I was the second youngest. At the time of my birth, a poor but shrewd man sold my father, Keilu Julius, for forty *rupees* to a tea estate in Assam. My father went with the man thinking he was acquiring a good job but soon discovered that he had actually been sold. It took three years for the parish priest to get him back to the village as a free man. In the meantime, my mother, Elizabeth gave birth to me, on the 4th July 1912."

"That was terrible!" I said, "How did your mother manage with so many children?"

"It was very difficult for her. My mother had no means to support us, she earned some money for food by cutting grass and selling it as feed for the cattle; apart from what the parish priest handed her as help. Every day she would carry me, since I was just a few days old, to the fields where she laid me on the grass while she did her daily grass-cutting. I must have been around three when my father returned to the village as a free man. I remember my mother crying with joy when he walked through the door, a tall, well-built man with red hair and blue eyes. He was so striking with very white skin. My mother held me to him as his youngest child born after he had left. At first I did not want to go to him, he was a stranger to me but he held me affectionately and said I was his child, so I began to trust him. He was a very soft-spoken man and I soon loved him very much. Unfortunately he died a year later. He worked hard as a slave in the tea plantation and was physically run down. At the time of his death, my mother had another child by him who was just a month old. My mother brought us up in great hardship thereafter, but she was extremely religious with strong trust in God and prayers.

"I attended to the goats and the cows for the other people to help support the family financially from the early age of five like my brothers and sister did. I attended the church primary school in my spare time to learn about Jesus and our Catholic religion. The nuns in the school found me intelligent and talented in music and art. I was nine and in the third class in 1921, when I was taken by the foreign Bettiah nuns for further education and as a future candidate for an Indian nun. They told my mother they would educate me and give me a future, as well, they would ask the parish priest in Latonah to support my mother more financially to help my brothers and sisters. The village people were honoured and proud to have a child from their village selected to join the convent. I remember I was crying when I left my mother. She was a petite beautiful dark skinned lady who was known for her kindness, compassion and charity in the village. I was allowed to visit Latonah and my family once every two or three years. I joined the convent as a nun and when my mother died I could not attend her funeral, nor those of my elder brother and the younger sister."

"When did you become a nun Mum? Sister Benolda in our St Mary's Convent School says she knows you from Bettiah, is that true?"

"Yes, she was one of the foreign nuns in Bettiah. I worked for the foreign nuns and priests in Bettiah as their helper after they brought me from Latonah village. I was asked to do all sorts of domestic work and spent spare time in prayers and learning to become a nun. Later in 1932 I became a Kindergarten and Primary teacher after passing class seven. The German Loretto nuns granted the Middle Class Teachers' Training Certificate to me. In 1934, I joined the Sacred Heart convent as an Indian nun. Aunt Natasha was a very good friend of mine throughout my school days. She lived in Bettiah City. I often got permission to spend weekends and holidays at her place. Her grandmother loved me very much. Aunt Natasha decided to join the convent as an Indian nun as well. The Indian nuns, unlike the foreign nuns, were expected to live like the general Indians, eating and sleeping on the floor and speaking the native languages. They did not have to learn the English language; instead their duty was to teach Christianity in the native language to the poverty stricken, low caste Hindus of the state of Bihar in India. I learnt to play the organ and the harmonium in the church. They said I had a beautiful voice. I sang solo all the Latin hymns during the religious services in the church."

"Aunt Natasha also said you won state awards for embroidery work and painting, twice at the State Exhibition Centre in Bettiah." I said cutting her short, "Is that true? I like your drawing and embroidery. You are a genius! Please sing for me even though I have heard you sing during Benediction in the Cathedral. When did you meet Papa?"

"I have lost interest in all those things, besides I have no time and my voice is getting bad with age. I did win State awards for my work. I was asked to send some to the State Exhibition

Centre twice, but the Superior stopped it after the second time because she was afraid I would become too proud. The Superior asked me to put down the name of another nun on my work the third time. Aunt Natasha, who was my best friend among the nuns, made me realise how unfair it was to do so and therefore I disobeyed the Superior.

I met your father when I was teaching in Khrist Rajah High School in Bettiah as Sister Cecilia. He knew me from the days I was working for the foreign nuns as a domestic hand in Bettiah. I was twelve or thirteen I think. He was a young American Jesuit novice who later went to Khursiyong for his ordination. He was always full of admiration for me. I was a nun and teaching in Bettiah, Muzaffapur and Gaya. Your father was the parish priest in Gaya and Chunar."

I asked Mum how Aunt Natasha and Uncle Eddie met and she told me that after I was born Papa lived with us, as did Aunt Natasha. It set her people gossiping that Papa had two women, so he found it necessary to find a husband for Aunt Natasha. Papa had received dispensation from the Church to work for the US Foreign Administration as a geologist even when he was a Jesuit priest and travelled to the Himalayan ranges looking for precious and semi-precious stones. He was allowed to take along men on contract to help him. It was through that scheme that he came to know Uncle Eddie, a young hard-working Anglo-Indian. Papa discovered Uncle Eddie was an orphan and in due course they became good friends. He arranged for Uncle Eddie and Aunt Natasha to marry. Papa trusted us with Uncle Eddie. He made us settle down in Saharanpore and returned to the Church as a Secular priest.

"Both Natasha and I left teaching and lived as housewives. Your Papa frequently visited us, at times staying over for few days at a stretch. Your Papa loved us very much and I never thought he would ever leave us as he did without any financial support." Mum said.

By then, knowing Papa was a priest, I realised he should not have fathered us. I was taught at Catechism lessons that priests take a vow of celibacy. I dared not question my mother as to why she had allowed those things to happen because I did not want to hurt her. Perhaps also I did not want to know the truth and loved my parents too much to ever accept their part in wrongdoing. I was told it was a Mortal Sin for a priest to have a family and children. But I did not want to condemn them. I understood that the heart knows no reasons and they loved each other as humans having the right to do so. But I could not understand how Papa could remain a priest when he had already broken his vow of celibacy by having us. Which was more important, being a father to his own children or pretending to be a pure celibate and ignoring his children and the woman he loved, and not facing his responsibilities?

I wondered how Father Alva could think it his moral duty to marry Cajeton and Mary because they lived together for three days, though no one saw to arranging my mother and my Papa's marriage even though they were living together and we two were born of their love and union. I also wondered why a marriage vow made in the church could be broken and accepted, but a priest who breaks the vow of celibacy and fathers two children who cannot be accepted. I could not understand why an educated, civilised community and the church, would make an innocent child born out of wedlock, a victim of humiliation, while letting the father, who actually helped create the child, go free with respect.

Why such injustice towards the innocent child?

I prayed for my Papa and wanted to meet him just once.

To me he was just my father. I did not care whether he was white or black, whether he was American or Indian, what race or religion he was. It mattered only that he was my father and I was his daughter and I loved him. I wanted reassurance of his love. It hurt me more to know that I was born of a priest, than out of wedlock. I felt everyone, including Aunt Natasha, thought badly of us for being the daughters of a priest. Also I felt sad because my poor mother was the victim of the situation and had to carry the burden of the love which both she and my father shared. My mother brought us up alone and no one thought of her feelings and courage in doing so. She was constantly humiliated by the peoples' remarks. I eventually understood why Mum did not want to stay and work in Bettiah.

17

High school certificate

When school re-opened in January 1958, I was placed in Year 10, which ended in the middle of 1959 with an Indian High School Certificate. Most of my friends, Dr Burke's two daughters, Bulbul Ghosh, Shrmilla and other rich Hindu and Muslim girls, were placed in a separate Year 10 which prepared for the Senior Cambridge examination, set in England at the time, and sent out to English Schools in India.

My few Anglo-Indian and Christian friends who did not do very well in the Year 9 examinations, were placed with me. I came first in Year 9, yet I was put there because the nuns said that being poor, I would not be able to afford further study and therefore would end up working or marrying. They thought it best for me to get an Indian High School Certificate and enter the workforce. We were given ranks in class according to our marks in the final examination. There were 45 students in Year 9. All the students who ranked up to 25, except me, went into Senior Cambridge Year 10, the rest from 26 to 40 were placed in the High School Year 10, as I was. The girls who ranked after 40 failed and had to repeat Year 9. Every class had 4 or 5 failures every year who repeated because they did not score an average of 40% marks in all the subjects. One could repeat the class twice, the third year if she did not pass then she had to leave school.

I could neither question the nuns' decision nor expect Mum or Aunt to do so as they did not know much English, nor had enough time or knowledge to plan for my future. The school had no career advisers. I made very little contact with any teachers or nuns, as I was timid and introverted. I did not even discuss it with Aunty Clarke. I accepted the nuns' decision with a heavy heart. I felt it was unfair but I could not say anything. After me, Violet, Enid then Helen, all took up the Indian High School Certificate. The nuns made the decisions and we had to follow, because we were students who paid no fees. Most Catholics and Anglo-Indian students were poor and received free education in the Catholic schools. Most of the students in the Christian schools in India were non-Christians who pay large fees. The Christians were taught Christian doctrine and the Bible in the first period every day while the non-Christians were taught Moral Science, but everyone, Christian or non-Christian stood up and made the sign of the Cross and said the *Our Father* and the *Hail Mary* before and after the lesson.

Miss Caston was my teacher in Year 10, a spinster and in her fifties. She was an extremely religious Anglo-Indian, a long time-member of the staff and an ex-student of the school, well-liked by the nuns. She and Mrs Clarke were good friends. Mrs Clarke praised me to her in the staffroom as an extremely shy, introverted, talented, but intelligent person, badly treated by Aunt Natasha. That made Miss Caston over-protective of me. I was the quiet introvert who wore long dresses and prayed often even during the recess and lunchtime and I walked around the school with my eyes downcast.

Mr Williams taught St John's First Aid in first term. He demonstrated bandaging on me, because he said that from my face it seemed I did not understand what he taught, that I had the expression of stupidity. He was surprised that I knew all the answers when he gave us the written tests. Throughout Year 10, I maintained my first rank in the monthly tests.

Our classroom was at the end of the school building, next to the Teacher Training classes which were co-educational. Whenever I crossed the school playground, I heard the young male trainee teachers banging on the desks and singing: "When the saint goes marching by—". It made me blush scarlet and I'd hurry past the college with my eyes towards the ground.

Art was one of my elective subjects for the Indian High School Certificate. Sister Seraphica was the art teacher while Miss Caston taught most of the other subjects. Maths was my other favourite subject. I did all my homework with the radio on, listening to Indian film songs. In between the homework, if the music was good, I'd dance Indian dancing to the tune. The others at home would be busy studying at the dining room with Aunt.

In spite of all the dancing and singing, I still topped the class.

Every year we had a Retreat for three days, when a Redemptorist priest came and gave us sermons on improving ourselves. We stayed silent and spent all our school time praying and listening to the sermons. The Redemptorist priests were usually from the USA. Since I'd discovered my father was an American priest, I wondered if any of them were my father. Throughout the Retreat I dreamt of each priest being my father. I tried my best to attract each one's attention. I prayed with sincere hope that the priest, who I imagined to be my father, would at least acknowledge me. At the end of each Retreat it greatly disappointed me to find that the priest did not acknowledge me as his long lost Minnie.

I had a few Anglo-Indian friends, Jean Mackrot and Thelma Becham, in my class. During the Retreat in Year 9, I heard Thelma was kidnapped from the picture hall where she was watching a film with her younger brother. It seems that a foreign-looking man they had entertained the previous evening called her out of the hall and that was the last time anyone saw or heard of her. She just disappeared. Some said she eloped with the man, others said she had been kidnapped. What happened remained a mystery. Jean Mackrot persevered till the end of the year and left to take up a typist's job, so I was eventually the only Anglo-Indian left in my class to complete my High School Examination.

✣ ✣ ✣ ✣ ✣

I visited Aunt Clarke every day after school and on weekends. She was my saviour whenever I felt hurt by criticisms at home or upset about schoolwork. Aunt Clarke was determined to get us fair treatment in school. The only thing I disliked was that she considered me very simple and I felt that the school staff, especially my class teacher, Miss Caston, over-protected me. There were times when Aunt Clarke too called me a 'praying mantis' because, she said I prayed too much for my age.

Every year we celebrated Teachers' Day when the students came dressed in casual clothes and gave presents to their teachers. The nuns helped organise concerts with the students, to entertain the teachers. At the end of the concert, all the teachers were called on stage and the whole school sang songs praising and thanking them.

The school held annual concerts where the parents and friends paid to watch. Once they put on 'Snow White and the Seven Dwarfs' with lots of music and singing. Sumita, who went to the same English School from St Anthony's Convent, was Snow White. Mostly the rich Indian girls had the important roles; perhaps to draw more audience and funds for the school.

Sister Elizabeth gave private tuition in piano and another nun taught art and painting. The certificates for all subjects came from England. I wished I could have taken up Art and Music, but unfortunately, I did not have the means. We were able to just survive on Mum's salary. There was no money for luxury or developing any talents we may inherit.

Although I prepared myself for the High School Examination from the convent, I was assigned in 1959 to Allahabad Government High School as my Examination Centre. It was a long way from my house. I took a rickshaw every morning at 7.30 to reach the place exactly at eight and returned three and half-hours later. All the other students from my convent school also went on their own. The Government High School was only for boys. Every time we went we were confronted with rude remarks and teasing from them till the doors to the examination hall opened and the examination supervisors presented themselves. It was a nightmare to be there before and after the examination. I hired a rickshawman from near the Club and requested him to be there promptly when the examination was over so I could disappear without delay.

We were all given examination roll numbers in Hindi. Although I spoke only Hindi at home to both Mum and Aunt, my medium of instruction at school was English and Hindi was just one more subject for me. I read Hindi well and understood it, but was never taught the numbers in Hindi. Anyway confident that I knew my roll numbers in Hindi I never bothered to have someone read them out to me. We wrote the roll numbers on every test paper, which I did. One morning, after I completed three examinations, the examination supervisor announced just before the fourth examination was to start, that someone was using a wrong roll number and so he went through everyone's examination papers as he collected them. When he came to mine, he exclaimed, that I was the fool who had been writing the wrong number. I wrote number seven, when it should have been nine. I felt embarrassed and upset. I had written the wrong roll number on every paper that far. It did not match the serial numbers given to the centre. They were therefore able to discover the mistake. I was asked to correct it from then on, but I did not understand the consequences of having written them wrongly.

One Sunday evening during the examination period, Mum came home with passes for a Hindi film. Everyone was delighted and got ready for it. I had a mathematics examination the next day and so I did not want to go, but Mum insisted, saying that she could not think of leaving me alone in the house at night. The films in Hindi lasted about three hours which had them finished at 9.30 at night and then returning in a rickshaw from the city took another forty-five minutes. I had to go along and sit there in tears worrying about the examination the following day. Mum was confident I would do well and that I needed some relaxation. She was right, for I got a distinction in maths!

That day, after the examination was over, I realised I had forgotten to ask Mum for sufficient travel money. Since students in India generally do not have a part-time job, they are entirely dependent on their parents till they graduate from the university and take up a career.

I returned home in a rickshaw as I could not have walked the distance and asked Aunt for *twenty-five paisas*, or less than an Australian cent. Aunt fished out the amount from somewhere, grumbling at the same time, "Can't your mother leave enough money for you when she knows you are doing your examination? Why should I have to pay for your expenses? She has no sense of motherhood; all she cares about is wasting money on films. I will not be able give you any more, so go and get money from her for tomorrow."

I felt humiliated and decided then and to take up some job after I had finished high school and become independent. I was too embarrassed to ask for money for everyday needs. We did not get pocket money after Uncle Dick left.

After a month and a half, the high school results were published in a special issue of the Patrika newspaper. Everyone else from my class had passed in the II and III Divisions, but my name was not there. I was thunderstruck. Cajeton went to my examination centre to make inquiries and was told that my results were being withheld. It was at least a relief to know that I had not failed. On Aunt Clarke's advice I went to see Miss Caston, my Yr. 10 teacher. She was expecting me to come in the Ist Division and was very upset too, but when I told her what Uncle Cajeton had found out, she became hopeful and took me to the nuns. We had a new Reverend Mother, who was also German but unlike the old one she was very kind and caring. Reverend Mother Angela immediately rang up the High School Board of Education and learnt that there had been some confusion between my roll number and that of another student from somewhere outside Allahabad. In the first three of my examination papers, I had actually written the other student's numbers and thus caused the confusion; and so both of our results were withheld. For fifteen days I stayed home unable to face the people who considered me a failure.

After a fortnight Miss Caston, Reverend Mother Angela and another nun took me to the Education Office in their black Morris car, driven by their faithful old driver. At the office I was given a pile of test papers of both the two students. I found it easy to separate mine from the other student's, because his was all in Hindi while mine were in English. Then I was told that they would let the principal know the result the following day. Reverend Mother Angela seemed very happy as we returned that afternoon as she had seen the marks and was confident of a good result. In my anxiety to separate the papers I had no time to look at the marks.

The next morning Reverend Mother announced that I had passed in the Ist Division and I was the only one in 1st Division from the convent with a distinction in maths that year. I was very happy but suddenly remembered my Papa, whom I thought, would have been overjoyed and proud to know that his little Minnie had done so well. I was filled with depression and sadness. I wished I knew where he was so I could tell him about it. I felt the same after every occasion of joy or celebration. So that evening I sat on the steps beside the toilet and cried for my Papa. I pleaded with Jesus, my substitute father, to help me find him soon.

18

A Rejection and a Recovery

Since I had finished my high school, Aunt advised Mum to consult the nuns about an appropriate career for me. I expressed my desire to become a nurse to Mum but she did not want that for me. "Nursing involves a lot of hard work with no appreciation", Mum said "I would like you to be a doctor instead."

She took me to see the Reverend Mother regarding my continuing studies at college as she wanted me to complete the equivalent to Year 12 and then to continue at the university. However, Reverend Mother dismissed the idea.

"It is no use your planning to study further Esther, you will not be able to afford it. You could not take up science in high school since we could only offer science to students who studied for the Senior Cambridge. Therefore, it will be impossible for you to take up medicine. Give up the idea of studying further – it is very expensive, your mother cannot afford it. You should take up typing and help your mother financially. Speak to the Bishop, he will help you with the fees for learning typing."

We returned home disappointed. Later I discovered my name was in the merit list and I could have received a scholarship from the government for further studies if the Reverend Mother had helped me apply for it.

That evening after Rosary I sat alone thinking about a career for myself. I did not like the idea of becoming a secretary, because I wanted to serve and care for the suffering. Nursing would have been ideal, but since Mum was against it, I could not. Suddenly I was struck with the desire to become a nun. I thought of joining the Society of Blessed Virgin Mary (IBMV) like the nuns of the convent I attended. So I went back to see Reverend Mother Angela the next day, this time alone. I told her my desire.

"My dear, I would be delighted to have you with us as a nun, but unfortunately we cannot receive you. I don't know if any other congregation could take you. Perhaps Mother Teresa's might. Anyway, write and ask her, we definitely cannot."

"Why not Mother?" I asked shocked. "Have I done something wrong?"

"I am sorry my child, but our rules do not allow anyone of your background to join the convent," she said, looking rather uncomfortable.

I felt humiliated and for a moment I could not speak. Then I summoned up my courage and asked her in a low voice:

"Is it because my father was a priest ?" The nun nodded.

Suddenly I realised what being a priest's daughter meant – I was not only an unwanted child but one who was also disowned by the Church on account of something for which I had no responsibility. I realised that Church and society would never really accept me because my parents had broken the Church law. I would never have freedom of choice throughout my life in the Catholic Church. I could not understand why it taught to forgive and accept when the Church could not forgive my father and accept me, the innocent child of the priest. I did not write to Mother Teresa to join her congregation, because I did not feel like joining a convent under restricted choice. I felt that I had the right to the freedom of choice like every other human being. I was certain that the Church, which preached justice and charity towards the innocent children, was treating me very unfairly. It hurt me very deeply.

That one rejection changed my entire life. I set out to prove my innocence and became determined to find my father. It became an obsession for me to prove that I was an intelligent and capable individual with a respectable background, that I did inherit the genes of my parents, both being talented and respectable people, I was also as capable as them, irrespective of the fact that I was born out of wedlock and of a priest who took the vow of celibacy.

I was created from my parents and God had willed it so. Nothing happened without the Will of God the Creator, that is what I grew up believing. I had a free choice, like everyone and therefore, I had to prove that.

I had to live a life of goodness to prove that individuals, irrespective of where and how he / she comes on this earth, have their choice of living a life that is good, or evil. The parents or family does not make that choice for the child. Experiences and circumstances, in the long span of lifetime, makes them into what they become. Every child is born innocent; they are not bad or good because of the wrongdoing of the parents. I set upon proving myself as an individual that was unjustly and deeply wounded in spite of my many good intentions and abilities.

I did not tell Mum about my desire to become a nun nor about the nun's rejection; I did not want her to be hurt too. I still prayed as before in Church and at home, but there was a change in me. I became very conscious that my father was a priest and that he must be saying the Mass as a priest at the altar in some other part of the world. The fact distracted my thought at the Sunday Services and the priest saying the mass reminded me of my father, the injustice and the hypocrisy. I often found myself imagining during the Sunday service what would happen if and when I eventually met my father. I felt strongly that my mother and father had loved each other and should have been allowed to marry and settle down as husband and wife. The Church should have seen to it in order to avoid the further sins of lies and pretence. The desire to meet my father grew stronger in me. Violet was busy in her own world and I could not discuss my feelings with her nor could I with anyone at home.

One evening when Father Evans visited, I confided in him the fact that the nuns had rejected me. He was angry and sympathised with me. He told me that he had known my father as a very kind and caring man who did a lot for the oppressed classes in India and converted many of them to the Catholic Church. He said that my Papa was full of religious fervour and enthusiasm to start with but once he fell in love with Mum he wanted to leave the Church and settle down with her and father his children. Both Mum and Papa were excommunicated as long as they lived together. Papa was later forced to continue as a Catholic priest but kept in touch with us as long as he was in India.

I asked Father Evans why he had told me that my father was dead. He replied that he had no option; that it would have been better for my mother and us to remain unknown so that we could live peacefully, without people becoming aware of the scandal and isolating us socially. He wanted to save us the pain of realising we were unwanted children. That is why he had changed our surname to 'Anthony', which enabled us to pass over as Anglo-Indians, rather than as an Indian with the name of 'Shah'. But since I had come to know the truth and was old enough to handle the situation, Father Evans could tell me that my father's real name was 'Michael DeLisle Lyons' and 'Anthony' was fictitious. Father Evans added that he had told lies for the good of our future and that his conscience was clear.

I was upset at the thought of all the lies that had been said to hide our existence. At the time I was full of idealism and hated any kind of lie and deceit. I believed that we must speak the truth at any cost and must be strong enough to accept the consequences resulting from our mistakes. I did not consider it right to carry on with a false name after I discovered the truth. Therefore the first thing I had to do was reclaim my true name.

I looked at my birth certificate. It mentioned only my mother's name. I wrote to the Church in Calcutta where I was baptised and asked the priest, Father Ameye, S.J., to give me a correct birth certificate with the right name. "Surely", I wrote, "I could not have been born without a father!" The priest knew who my father was. How could he tell a lie when he baptised me? How could he lie in God's house and not give me a surname, when he knew the truth himself? Would Christ have done so? I challenged him and asked him in the name of truth and Jesus, to give my father's right surname on my birth certificate. The effect of my letter was as I wanted. I promptly received a proper certificate with my father's name as Michael D. Lyons, but the priest added that since my father was not doing any work at the time, he had to write the occupation as "unemployed". At the time Papa had resigned from the Jesuits in the Patna Mission and was unable to get any job in British India, as an ex Catholic priest.

I did the same for Violet and got hers corrected from

Saharanpore. Next I had it published in the local newspapers that I had changed my surname from 'Anthony' to 'Lyons' and I henceforth wished to be known by the second. I consulted no one on the matter and did it all by myself because I was hurt by the rejection I received from the nun. I did not realise the consequences till acquaintances started inquiring why I had done so. Mum had problems with her friends at the hospital, but she said nothing to me. She just told them that her full name was 'Anthony Lyons' and that I wanted to be known as the latter. Aunt solved the problems of her friends in school where she worked by telling them the truth about our origins. Perhaps unwittingly I caused more tongues to wag. I acted in what I thought was the correct way. I did not regret doing so then or later, because that was the truth and it gave me an identity, even though I exposed a scandal, for which I was being unjustly victimised.

Later, Uncle David came to know from the Jesuits in Patna that my Papa had left the priesthood in the USA, he had finally received dispensation to do so and had settled down with an American woman. It further embittered me against the rules of the Church which did not allow Papa to settle down with Mum even though he had fathered two children by her in India, but gave him the dispensation in the USA to live with an American. His bishop, Bishop Sullivan of Patna Mission had retired and returned to the USA in 1946 at the same time as my father did. Bishop Wildermuth became the new Bishop. He did not wish to hear about us and we were left to our fate and to face the wolves in the pagan country. We did not matter to them any more. We were considered best forgotten and non-existent.

Once Mum completed her training and was able to work and support the two of us, she did not consider it necessary to visit Patna and the new Bishop Wildermuth, as it seemed a futile effort. He always denied knowledge of the whereabouts of my father. He made my mother feel humiliated and guilty about having the two of us. The Bishop reluctantly saw her at the door of the Bishop House whenever she went to ask for help making it sure that she left Patna the same day by handing her an amount sufficient for the train fare to return. He did not want anyone to know that we existed. Mum soon decided to forget the past and concentrate on bringing us up herself.

I began to understand my mother's plight. I admired her courage and determination to shoulder her responsibilities alone, even though she came from a small poverty-stricken village of Bihar. Perhaps a mother is a mother, no matter which part of the world she is from, a mother gets her courage from the circumstances she is placed in and works for the interests of her children. Race, colour and religion make no difference; motherhood is a woman's inborn quality.

"Your mother and father were ready to put you into an orphanage as soon as you were born. The parish priest of Calcutta advised them to do so, but I made them keep you and helped them to settle down to a family life for your sake," Aunt Natasha said to me one day.

In spite of Aunt's remarks, I felt closer to my mother. I realised that she had stood by us even though it was hard for her to keep us with her and face the world alone. I even felt respect for Aunt Natasha, though she gossiped and never spared us her taunts. She was just being a mother to her own children and perhaps understandably a bit jealous. After all, she had made it possible for us to live in a family and a home, making it easier for Mum to support us without putting us into an orphanage. I also realised that Aunt was under great financial and mental stress. She had come from a very caste conscious Brahman family. Aunt had been the friend who had guided and lead my mother. Mum became independent and worked to support us financially, while Aunt took care of us four girls at home. Aunt remained in poor health after her operation.

The bitter truth of being a priest's daughter had changed my entire life.

I suddenly grew up into a different person from what I had been as a child. It changed me from an innocent child into an adult, full of responsibilities and care, determined to find my father and my identity. Although I remained a good Christian and could never forget Jesus Christ whose teachings I followed throughout, I could not attend Mass the way I did as a child. I could not come to terms with the unjust treatment given to me and the fact that I had limited choices in life because I was the daughter of a Catholic Father, and a Religious, who once in his youth took the vow of celibacy.

19

From pigtail to perm

"The nuns said that Minnie should do a typing and shorthand course," Mum said to Aunt one evening, "but I have no money to pay for her training."

"Why don't you go to the Bishop and ask him for help?" Aunt asked.

So the next day Mum and I went to the Bishop's house near the Cathedral. We met the tall, well-built man, whose stature commanded respect. Bishop Raymond was the one who got us into the English Convent School on Uncle Eddie's request.

Mum and I knelt and kissed his ring while he blessed us. Mum begged him for help towards my secretarial training. She spoke to him in Hindi as the Bishop was fluent in both Hindi and English.

"I don't understand why the nuns would have suggested the secretarial profession. I strongly disapprove of it. Indian bosses are from a different moral background and there are many cases of harassment of our girls. Do you think your daughter could stand up to them?" He said in his loud, gruff voice.

"What career do you advise her to take up then?" Mum asked.

"I would think teaching would be a more appropriate profession for our girls," he replied.

"But the nuns said she is too quiet for teaching and would not be able to control the students," Mum replied.

"How do they expect her to control men in an office then? Still, if you want to give her secretarial training and need financial assistance, go to Father Charles, my secretary downstairs and ask him for the fees' money. You can have it from him each month till she finishes – I will telephone him now. But I still feel that she would do well as a teacher. She has no experience of men and the secretarial work is not meant for her," he said retreating into the corridor and heading towards his room.

Bishop Raymond was a good orator and his sermons were very powerful. I heard that he had been to the USA and Australia and that his sermons and speeches enabled him to collect large sums of money for the poor of his parish. He was from Mangalore, a city in the South of India. Bishop Raymond was highly educated and knew many foreign languages. He spoke in English with an Oxford accent and his Hindi was as perfect as his mother-tongue, the Mangalorian language. Every Sunday, two Masses were said in the Cathedral, one in English and the other in Hindi. Bishop Raymond said the Mass and delivered the sermon in both languages.

I was admitted to Pitman's College in the Civil Lines. For the next six months I attended the College every day from 9:00 in the morning until noon, learning typing and shorthand.

✣ ✣ ✣ ✣ ✣

I continued my visits to Aunt Clarke every day. She had started criticising me for my appearance and the style of clothes I wore, which were mostly made by Mum. I still had two plaits reaching to my waist, tied in ribbons at the end. I used a lot of coconut oil on my hair like most Indians did. Every week I washed my greasy light brown hair with soap. I still wore ankle socks and black ballerina shoes and looked like a schoolgirl. Aunt Clarke often said that I should stop praying and begin behaving like a young lady of my age.

One day Aunt Clarke visited us with a lady, Mrs Beveridge, who had just moved into the colony. She was tall, wore very heavy make-up, including dark lipstick and long painted nails. She wore high stiletto shoes according to the fashion in the 1950s and early 1960s and skin tight skirts. Mrs Beveridge's husband was a representative for a company which produced canned and frozen meat. He opened a shop in the Civil Lines. Mrs Beveridge claimed she could cut and perm hair for ladies more cheaply than the hairdressers. She informed us of Mrs Rath, another Anglo-Indian lady living in the area, who sold secondhand dresses at her residence. Mrs Rath obtained them from a US Mission in bulk and sold them at her own prices. They were good European clothes. Mrs Beveridge took Aunt Natasha and me to see Mrs Rath. We bought a few skirts, blouses and coats on credit for the four of us girls. Aunt and I arranged to pay in instalments. The clothes were cheaper than buying material and having them stitched. Some were a perfect fit while others were a bit loose, but a tight belt fixed the problem.

Soon I completed my secretarial course and found a position at the office of Mr Tayal, a wealthy, childless industrialist, who ran businesses with his two brothers in Allahabad, Delhi and Punjab. One of their lines of business was film distribution in a small area of Punjab, the head office being in Allahabad, where I was located with Mr Tayal and his accountant. My duties were correspondence, filing and book-keeping.

Mrs Clarke was delighted that I found a job, but she insisted I have my hair cut before I began. So, one evening, Mrs Clarke and Mrs Beveridge dropped in and saw that my waist-length hair was cut and permed. I was reluctant but Mrs Clarke insisted that a young Anglo-Indian girl like me should look modern and not wear old-fashioned pigtails like a low-caste Indian girl! No one at home objected. Aunt Natasha was happy to listen to Aunt Clarke's advice, because she was eager to bring us all up as Anglo-Indians. Mum too loved to show off with her daughter looking more English than Indian, perhaps she wanted me to be more up to the standard of my father. Mrs Beveridge charged nothing for doing my hair. She taught me to shave my legs and armpits, saying I was too hairy and introduced me to stockings. I also learnt to apply lipstick and other cosmetics.

Since Mum had become a nurse, she used face-cream and make-up on her eyes with the Indian black eye-liner, *kaajal*. She wore her *sari* in a dignified, fashionable way by using pins to keep every pleat in place. She loved perfumes and used good Indian *itrs* (perfumes). Her thick black hair was always well oiled and shiny, kept in a fine bun over the back of her head. Mum looked after her beautiful long hair, she said that Papa had loved her long hair which reached to her knees. Instead of using lipstick Mum chewed *pan* (beetle leaves) frequently, like the other nurses, this kept her lips red. She never used European cosmetics, perhaps because they were unknown to her; they were also very expensive. Aunt Natasha forever criticised her for her make-up and hairstyles. Aunt did not use make-up except for powder after a bath. She dressed in her simple traditional manner and found it hard to accept Mum with her fashions, saying that since Mum had two children to support and no husband, therefore she should not waste time and money on clothes and fashion.

I admired Mum the way she took care of herself. She was so petite and yet motherly and caring. She enjoyed a game of cards with us whenever she was at home and was full of fun and laughter since working as a nurse. Even though she was often unhappy due to the remarks by Aunt and the financial problems, she would easily forget and became her self again, caring and supportive of all we did. She trusted and encouraged me. She was proud and convinced that whatever I did was good and so never questioned me. Whenever Mum visited us, she had a basketful of fruits and sweets for the four of us. She treated us alike and brought home any new medications or tonic available for Aunt Natasha. With all the differences over financial problems, Aunt and Mum still called each other, '*bahen*' and were best of friends. Mum shared with Aunt all her experiences at the hospital. Aunt would add her comments and advice. We all looked forward to Mum's visit every week.

Aunt knew Mum was the only one to help her in whatever way she could, even though she found it hard to ask politely because of her arrogance and sense of superiority. When Aunt needed help, she said so in her own aggressive way and with an excuse and Mum was obliged to do as Aunt demanded, the more so because we were there and because Aunt was her friend since school days. Mum had nowhere else to take us. We had no relatives, just Aunt and her two daughters who had given us the security of a home and the belonging to a family. Aunt was taller than Mum and dark in complexion. She was intelligent and confident of herself. Since she had been living in the Anglo-Indian environment with Uncle Eddie and Uncle Dick, she had more knowledge of English and the European lifestyle, although she never forgot her background of a high caste Indian. She always held herself and her children superior to us. Mum remained the same simple, Indian woman, living and working with Indian nurses and patients.

20

Secretarial job! No not for me!

Since Aunt Natasha found it difficult to manage on the salary of a Middle Class Trained Hindi teacher, she dismissed the old *ayah* and the gardener. Helen and I took on the gardening and Aunt did cooking. The only things done by a servant was cleaning the toilet and sweeping the rooms. About that time Mrs Simon raised the rent. Aunt was angry and refused to pay the increase. After a quarrel between Aunt and Mrs Simon, we were given notice to vacate the house. Reluctantly Aunt accepted the rent rise so Mum had to increase her share. For a long time Aunt and Mrs Simon did not speak to each other. Aunt searched for another house to rent in the meantime.

✣ ✣ ✣ ✣ ✣

The day I started work at Mr Tayal's office, he invited me to his house, which was next door. He introduced his wife. I was offered tea and a snack and invited to visit his wife whenever I was without work in the office. Mr Tayal told his wife that I reminded him of Audrey Hepburn, very innocent looking and still dressed like a schoolgirl with socks and low-heeled shoes. 'My Fair Lady' was being shown in one of the cinema halls in Allahabad.

Mr Hari Gupta, was the accountant at the office. He was very polite and considerate to start with, but when Mr Tayal left for his tours to other offices in different States, Mr Gupta harassed me by asking me out for dinner with him. He was a young unmarried Punjabi man. I constantly refused his invitations saying that my parents would object. I did not disclose that I had no father because I wanted him to think there was a male member in the house and that he could not take any liberties. Mr Gupta laughed at my excuses, saying he knew about the Anglo-Indians and the Christians and the freedom they enjoyed in going out with the opposite sex. I told him I had been brought up differently. He suggested that I keep our date a secret and excuse myself by lying I was working late. I refused, saying I could not betray my mother's trust. He was annoyed and started harassing me through my pay. It was always late, first a day or two, then a week. I did not know who to complain to. I had not visited Mrs Tayal and did not think she would help. I could not confide in Mr Tayal when he was in the office. I would only stay in his office when I was taking notes in shorthand and see him again when they were ready for his signature. I was scared of men other than Aunt's brothers. I had heard from Aunt Natasha and Clarke a lot of stories about how some employers took out their young Anglo-Indian secretaries, and later abandoned and even sacked them when they fell pregnant.

Mrs Clarke was continually advising me to keep clear of them. I believed that holding hands with a man would lead to pregnancy. I had seen an Indian film, '*Bahar*', about a single mother treated badly by the man who made her pregnant and society. And, I knew Mum's plight.

One day I spoke to Aunt Clarke about Mr Gupta, as she was the only one I could confide in. Neither Mum nor Aunt knew much about careers and education, because they came from a different way of life. They lacked education or knowledge of the Anglo-Indian ways. I still spoke in Hindi at home. Aunt Clarke insisted that I speak to her in English and would check me for my mispronunciations. Violet was more fluent in English as she had a lot of Anglo-Indian friends with whom she mostly conversed in English.

I took my first pay to Bishop Raymond as a first instalment of the money he had lent me for my fees. He was taken aback. He said that this was the first time anyone had offered to pay back money. So he blessed me and bid me use the money well for my own needs. Bishop Raymond died shortly after from a massive heart attack in Mangalore, where he had gone for a holiday. I was saddened by his death.

Since I had started working, I began contributing towards my and Violet's board and lodging to Aunt Natasha. Mum met the expense of electricity and also put money towards all her other debts. She had always bought material for our dresses on credit. Every month I had money to buy gifts such as *sari*s for both Mum and Aunt. I could not treat them differently. I was also able to buy materials to make dresses for the other three girls and myself, as I felt guilty about buying material only for myself. I would buy the same kind of material for all four of us. It gave me a great satisfaction to see everyone happy.

Since there were no department stores in Allahabad, we could not buy ready-made dresses. We bought material of our choice and had dresses made up by tailors, or did it ourselves at home. Once I did venture to make my own dress, because Mum's were always big and loose on me. She used her judgement and never had patterns or sizes to follow. Although my first attempt at sewing was a mess, I did eventually learn to make a dress for myself. Later I discovered I could afford a tailor-made dress, 'more fashionable'. So her tailor started to work for us. Sometimes Aunt Natasha hired him for the day. He sat on our verandah sewing and altering dresses bought from Mrs Rath. We paid him five *rupees* an hour. He completed two pieces of work in the day. Aunt always caught him stealing pieces of material. I preferred him to work at his shop and give the result to me in a week later. He was a Muslim, as most tailors were at that time. Mum stopped sewing dresses for us, but continued knitting.

Since Mr Gupta harassed me through my pay all the time and kept me long after office hours. Finally, I decided one day, to see the film with him. I arranged the day and the hour at which I would meet him at the picture hall. When the time came I asked Mum and Aunt to accompany me. Mr Gupta looked very angry when I introduced Mum and Aunt to him. I offered to pay for their tickets, telling him I was not allowed out alone. That was how it would have happened if I were of his religion and caste. A Hindu girl of a respectable family is always chaperoned by a family member till she marries.

I sat between Mum and Aunt and Mr Gupta had to sit

beside Aunt. I thought that would teach him a lesson! Unfortunately he was even worse in paying me my salary after that. He loaded me with work and I had to stay after office hours to complete it. Ultimately I decided to resign and started looking out for another job find other employment.

Aunt Clarke had another suggestion. She advised me to see the nuns about joining the Teachers' College. She had already prepared the ground for me by gossiping to the other teachers and the nuns about my office problems with Mr Gupta. My school teacher, Miss Caston and Mrs Clarke made the new principal, Mother Hermina, realise how close I was to losing my innocence in the office men.

Mum and Aunt agreed with Mrs Clarke, and soon I was back at the Convent. Before enrolling myself at the Teachers' College, I had to decide whether I wanted to be a secondary or a primary teacher. I knew nothing about either. Fortunately, I was given the opportunity to teach the kindergarten class one-day and make my decision. I found I could not handle the little ones in a class of thirty-five to forty students. Without any aide it was very exhausting and confusing. This led me to take up training as a secondary teacher. I felt I could at least get a discussion going with the senior students. The Indian girls in the secondary classes found my personality impressive and my soft voice intriguing. I had full co-operation from the senior students throughout my training period of two years.

Sister Magdalene was head of the primary and kindergarten teacher training and Sister Bernard was head of the secondary. They were both Anglo-Indians. Sister Magdalene was actually a domiciled English lady, a daughter of Mr Roger, a widower, who visited Allahabad every year to spend time with his only child. Sister Magdalene was extremely fond of me because I had been in her Catechism class in third class. Sister Bernard had never taught me. She only taught the Senior Cambridge students for English, but she had seen me often in school and knew me through Miss Caston and Mrs Clarke. She was happy to have me and throughout my training mothered me, as did Miss Caston in Year 10. Sister Bernard was strict but fair to all the students. She had to manage with Co-education in the Secondary Teachers' College. The male student-teachers were allowed into the college premises at 9.00 in the morning but had to leave promptly at 3.00 in the afternoon soon after the bell went. Sister Bernard saw that the male students left the place on time and both she and Sister Magdalene made sure no males were on the premises during the lunch-break. The male trainees did their teaching practice at the boys' school next door. Only female teacher-trainees were allowed to teach in the convent, which catered for the girls from rich and respectable Indian homes.

The college education was not free, I had to arrange for my fees. I wrote to the Rangers' Club in Calcutta, and asked for financial assistance. I was given that opportunity. The Frank Anthony Educational Fund was also available from the Member of Parliament, Mr Frank Anthony in Delhi, but people who availed themselves of his fund had to agree to teach in any of his schools for two years, anywhere in India. Mr Frank Anthony represented the minority group of the Anglo-Indians in the Indian Parliament. He and his wife had no children of their own. He was a Barrister-in-Law and the one who took the first divorce case of the Prime Minister Jawaharlal Nehru's daughter, Indira Gandhi. He helped in passing the new Divorce Bill in the Indian Parliament. Mr Frank Anthony opened many schools in various parts of India, all in his name.

I continued working at Tayal's office for a few months more and then found that typing court affidavits part-time paid me just as much as the office work full-time. So I resigned and confined myself to doing all types of typing work, paid for by the page at home.

In the first year of my training Mrs Clarke persuaded me to take a month's holiday. Miss Caston and her brother, Gerry and an old friend of theirs were going to a hill station called Naini Tal. During summer holidays of two months, most rich Indians visit the hill stations in India, as did the British when they ruled India. Rich Indian princes and the Britishers had established the hill stations and to this day it is very popular with those who can afford to live there during the summer months.

Miss Caston had rented two bedrooms from Peter Clarke's mother for a month. Peter had taken his secondary teachers' training from our college and was teaching in one of the boys' schools in Allahabad. Miss Caston kept me very busy sightseeing. We spent most of our time around the lake, watching the yacht races and window-shopping. I was able to go horse-riding at China Peak. At night I enjoyed looking at the lights on the surrounding distant hills. There were many dances at the clubs and restaurants, but since I could not dance and the Castons did not like going to them, I only heard about them from Peter and his sister, Kay. I wrote to Mum practically every day and told her about the wonderful place, Naini Tal.

Aunt Natasha had always disapproved of ballroom dancing. She said it was indecent since men and women danced holding each other. She said that only alcoholic and loose characters went to such dances and clubs. Somehow her words always had an everlasting effect on me.

21

Violet's first love and a public humiliation

In 1960 Violet was sixteen and in Year 10 she had grown up very charming and everyone took an immediate liking to her. Aunt Natasha however, made her daughters aware of their high-caste family background and the many religious relatives in the family including her two brothers. Aunt could not forget that the two of us were born of a sinful relation and therefore were inferior to her children. Although Aunt seemed to love us because she was always there to stand up for the two of us, she could not help reprimanding us, commenting on our background and saying the most hurtful things without considering our feelings. I tried to be a part of the family when their relatives were visiting, but was always left feeling an outsider. No one from Mum's family visited us. It never occurred to me to question her about them, perhaps because Mum did not speak of them, nor did she have any photographs of them. Aunt had many photographs of her family members. Her family had lived in the city of Bettiah for generations. Mum's lived in the village but they never took photos.

Once Aunt Natasha visited Bettiah with the four of us to attend the wedding of one of her nieces. Mum didn't go because she had no leave left. Although Aunt ensured no boys got too friendly with us, as she felt responsible and protective. Violet made friends with one of the young relatives of Aunt which made Aunt furious. She did not want Violet to develop any serious relationship with her relatives; she said that Bettiah was only a small town and people wasted no time in starting a gossip. The people of Bettiah had not forgotten Mum and the scandal caused by her eloping with a Jesuit priest, she said. Violet corresponded with the young relative of Aunt's for about a month and then forgot him when she met Victor Carter.

Victor was studying in the boys' school where Aunt was teaching Hindi. At first Mrs Carter took no special notice of their friendship; in fact, with Aunt's permission, she even took Violet to a few dances and Violet learnt to dance with Victor. Of course, Aunt would have a lot to say about Violet's behaviour and character when she returned after the dance. Fortunately, Violet was indifferent to all criticism and it was I who used to brood.

Violet's happiness was short-lived, because one day Victor came home and said his grandfather was very angry with him, since he had seen Victor and Violet kissing after Church service. Mrs Carter and her father, Mr Peters, did not consider Violet good enough for their Victor, so he was ordered not to have anything to do with her. Mrs Carter also stopped coming to our house. The Carters were a good friend of Father Evans. They knew of our background, hence considered us unholy and of scandalous origin.

✣ ✣ ✣ ✣ ✣

Mum and Aunt found accommodation cheaper than Mrs Simon's, on the other side of the Alfred Park and closer to Mum's hospital. The house was new and a double-storey with no backyard. The neighbours were rich Hindus. We knew no one nearby. We had to lock our dog, Rex, inside the house when we went to school every day.

The Carters lived near the park not far from our new house. Violet's relationship with Victor Carter became closer. Since Victor had to cross the park, he and Violet did so together every day. They would wait for each other and then walk across happily.

One afternoon, the two of them were returning home along with some other students from school through the park. Mr Peters, Victor's grandfather, happened to be returning from Church and saw them. He commanded Victor to follow him home immediately. Victor refused. His grandfather went off in a temper and both Violet and Victor continued on their way rather upset.

"Victor!" They heard Mrs Carter saying. Mr Peters had sent

him home once. "Your grandfather asked you to follow him home and you are still with this girl who has no character or shame!"

Victor calmly asked her why she had taken a dislike to Violet when in the past she had praised her. Mrs Carter replied that in the past she had felt sorry for Violet's family and visited them only to help. She had not realised that Violet would go after her son. She said that she did not approve of Violet because of her background and had forbidden him to see her. She ended by taking off one of her shoe and advancing towards Violet saying:

"I will smash your face with my shoe and teach you never to have anything to do with my son in the future."

Victor immediately jumped between Violet and his mother. He caught her raised hand holding the shoe and pushed her away gently. Mrs Carter tripped and fell on the ground, by then Mr Peters had returned and while he helped his daughter up, Victor mounted the bike with Violet and cycled off as fast as she could to our house. He told Aunt he was very frightened of his mother, even more since he had confronted her. Victor said he could not return home.

When Mrs Carter confronted Victor and Violet, all the other students and some parents along with servants had stood watching. After Violet and Victor left, Mrs Carter stood in the park abusing Violet to all listening. She declared openly that Violet's parents were not married and that both of us were bad girls born of a sinful relationship and that was why she did not want her son, coming from a respectable and good home, to get involved with Violet. She also said that we were being brought up with a lady who had two daughters of her own, that the lady was encouraging the four girls to catch decent men and that we were carrying on like prostitutes. Helen and Enid were in the crowd and heard everything.

Fortunately Mrs Carter did not know our new address. The students and the people who witnessed the scene saw that it was gossiped all through the town that evening. The nuns and the staff members of both the schools also came to know of it the next day.

I was at work when it all took place. When I returned home that evening I found the house locked. I found Enid, Helen, Violet and Victor inside sitting quietly once I unlocked the doors. Helen related to me all that happened and Aunt Natasha had gone to see the Parish Priest, Fr Alva. I was hurt and upset at the insults that had been levelled at my sister and the others. I felt all the more a maternal responsibility for Violet. I felt sorry for Aunt who had to put up with all the shame and harassment.

Aunt Natasha later returned with Father Alva, who tried to persuade Victor into returning home. But he refused. Father Alva was very rude to Aunt and blamed her for her negligence and lack of responsibility towards Violet, which encouraged her to get seriously involved with Victor at such a young age. He left stating that he would speak to Mrs Carter and that Victor had to leave the house that evening, as it would be a sin for him to spend the night in a house with four young girls. Aunt sat upstairs in tears, cursing herself for having to look after Violet and me and facing such embarrassments. It made Aunt furious that her family's good name had also been ruined because of Violet's behaviour. Aunt added her opinion of Violet, calling her names and a shame to the community. She said that all along she was afraid that children like us, born of shameless parents, would one day also cause a scandal. She said she had been trying to give us a chance for a respectable life by providing us with a good education and care. At the same time she was angry with Mrs Carter for humiliating Violet and her two daughters.

Violet was stunned at what was said because she was unaware of who her father was as I had not discussed my discovery with her. She had been proud of the attention she received from the boys and never thought that it was wrong in any way to have friends of the opposite sex. She was just friends with Victor and had never realised the seriousness of having a boyfriend or what it could mean in the long term.

That evening Aunt asked me to get Mum from the hospital. Unfortunately Mum could not come till 8.00 at night as she was on duty. She was When I returned from the hospital I tried to speak to Victor myself about his going home, but he would not hear of it. It made me angry and I decided that I did not like him any more even as a family friend. Besides, I believed that my sister Violet was very intelligent and I wanted her to be well educated. It was my ambition at the time to see that Violet had a university education and became a doctor since I could not. I was then twenty years old.

In India education means a lot and everyone who can afford it acquires it whether they have the ability to study further or not. Most Indians eventually get a degree because of family pressure. India has the highest number of educated unemployed people. I, too, was one of those prestige-seekers, who wanted the highest education for my only sister and the only relative on earth. I wanted to prove to those who considered us without a respectable background that we could make a good future for our children. This relationship with Victor was something I had not foreseen and it upset me.

Ultimately Aunt asked Victor to stay in the room downstairs that night in case Mrs Carter came, or made it a police case. Aunt could then say that he was in a room by himself. Violet hovered around him, because she considered Victor a hero who had saved her from his mother. She felt she could never break-off her friendship with him. Later in the evening I lost my temper at Victor and bluntly told him how I hated him for of all the disgrace he had brought on us that afternoon. I said that if he had the slightest feeling for Violet he would leave the house and go elsewhere, if not home. Violet was annoyed at that, but it did not seem to have any effect on Victor.

Father Evans, visited us around 7.00 in the evening. He requested Aunt to permit Victor to stay the night in that room till he had personally spoken to Mrs Carter. He said he knew her temper very well and related to us an incident, which took place in Samistipur, where he was the parish priest. Father Evans said that Mrs Carter always used violence to get her way.

Father Evans kept his promise and visited Mrs Carter that night. He told her that Victor was very sorry for all that had happened, but that he was scared of her temper so he had not returned home, although he intended returning the following morning if she was willing to forgive him.

The next day, as a result of Father Evans' counselling and

advice, Mrs Carter sent a message to Victor, through Fr Evans, saying that if he returned home that morning, she would forgive and forget everything. Victor returned home immediately. Before leaving our house he made promise to Violet that he would never forget her and that he would be back to see her after he had convinced his mother of his love for her.

"My mother will have to accept you because I love you very much," Victor said as he walked out of the door, "She is not all that bad you know. She has a kind of heart, but a terrible temper." He didn't realise the effects of those hurtful words and action she had inflected on me in the heat of her temper!

✣ ✣ ✣ ✣ ✣

The nuns were kind and sympathetic towards Violet after the incident. They advised her to consider breaking up with Victor since his parents disapproved of their friendship. Unfortunately, the trouble made the tie between them stronger and they talked of marriage soon after the high school examinations. Their teenage friends showered them with sympathy and encouraged them with romantic words. Violet and Victor became the topic of gossip in the Christian and Anglo-Indian community and the town.

The two continued seeing each other. I lashed out at Victor for ruining my sister's reputation and her future, but it made no difference because Violet defended him and encouraged his visits.

When the high school results were out Victor went to get them.

"Violet, you have passed in the third division."

"How did you do Victor?" I asked.

"Don't worry about me. I failed but I am happy Violet has passed."

Victor's mother blamed Violet for her son's poor result. Violet refused to study further, both she and Victor wanted to get married immediately. Somehow, I managed to persuade Violet into taking a teacher's training. Victor decided to wait.

✣ ✣ ✣ ✣ ✣

One evening Mr Guest from the Anglo-Indian Trust Property, visited us. He owned a house in the colony and it had fallen vacant. He offered the house to us because he heard that where we were living was no place for young Anglo-Indians. Aunt was delighted at the offer since she felt secure at the Anglo-Indian Trust Property. Soon we were back living at the colony. We four were allowed to become the members, as Aunt could not, being an Indian.

Mr Guest was the representative of the British citizens in Allahabad. The Guests had rented out their second house, adjacent to their own, to two families.

We took the portion that had two rooms, a verandah and an enclosed bay with a kitchen and modern toilet. Surrounding it was a large area of land. At the back were fruit trees, while in front there were flowerbeds and an extensive lawn. Around the house was a double-brick wall, plastered and painted, with a large wooden painted gate.

Violet and I were given one room between us. The entire house had cemented floor like the majority of houses in the plains of India. Mum provided us with one single wooden bed to share. Under our bed we had our tin boxes containing our clothes. Aunt placed her big wardrobe and the kitchen cupboard in our room. We two were given two shelves in the wardrobe for our clothes. The other room was for Aunt and her two daughters. Their huge double bed stood in the centre and a wardrobe was on one side, whilst on the other was the old dressing table. All their boxes were also under the beds. The red radio was placed on the broad windowsill. Aunt enclosed the verandah with a wooden grill and made it into a dining room where we also did our homework. The enclosed bay was the drawing room. Mum paid half the rent of the house and half of other common bills, as well as those for our food and related expenses, as she had done before. I helped Mum with my share of the expenses as I was earning a wage.

Victor visited Violet every evening. I spoke to Sister Magdalene at school who advised me to persuade Violet into becoming a boarder in the Teachers' Training College for the two years, 1961 and 1962. The nuns very kindly let Violet pay her fees in instalments after she completed the training and was working.

I also joined the Teachers' College at the same time but as a day scholar. Every morning and evening Victor cycled around the college brick boundary walls, whistling. Violet often wrapped her breakfast in a piece of paper and threw it to Victor through the high metal gates. Her packet of breakfast was always accompanied with a love letter. India is a country where marriages are mostly arranged. Love marriages were and are still very rare. They are mostly amongst the Christians and the Anglo-Indians. No one dared to make it as obvious as Violet and Victor did. Sister Magdalene tried to counsel Violet.

The incident at the park between Mrs Carter and Violet left me deeply hurt. I realised that Violet and I were unwanted by both society and the Church. I started feeling confused about the Church and began moving away from it, although Christ still remained my guide and I prayed to Him reverently.

The only place I could sit and sing out my sadness was at the back of the house, sitting on the toilet steps. Rex, my dog, always sat beside me, licking my toes and hands, when tears dropped down my cheeks. I was melancholy when sad and the thought of my father who had forgotten his children, surfaced. I still loved Papa and felt that he was not to blame but it was circumstances, which made him leave us.

Violet's behaviour made many tongues wag and Aunt Natasha, out of frustration, supplied information about our origins to many of her teacher friends. Everyone seemed to know of my father and our illegitimate birth.

22

A change for the better

Not long after we moved back into the Anglo-Indian Trust Property, Mr and Mrs Moore, their daughter Audrey and son, Francis visited us. The Moores had moved to the Trust Property and recognised Mum and Aunt from Mirzapur where Mr Moore was the District Magistrate. My father was the editor of his paper, 'The Poor Man's Voice'. The Moores knew that Mum, myself as a baby of a few months and Aunt were living with him. At the time, Papa was trying to get the dispensation to marry Mum and live respectably. But the Church was determined about his returning to active priesthood and working for the missions in India.

I discovered from the Moores that my father was involved in improving the lot of the oppressed classes. The Jesuits worked very hard to do the same and were able to make many conversions giving them food and money. As a Jesuit priest, my father restored many old Churches and started many Catholic schools, including the one in Gaya and the Bishop House in Patna. On many occasions he worked alongside Mahatma Gandhi and the Indian Reformists for the freedom of India from the British. Father Lyons was a very promising priest and did a lot for the Church and the poor as a missionary. He was liked by everyone, including his Jesuit superior, Bishop Sullivan, in Bankipore, Patna. The poor in the missions remembered him for his compassion and understanding. The Moores came to visit Aunt and Mum to renew contact.

Later Audrey attended the same Teachers' Training College and took the secondary teacher's training with me and we became good friends. I enjoyed being with the Moores because I could talk to Mr Moore and learn about my Papa. Mr Moore was a very affectionate and extremely religious man.

Mrs Moore spoke very little English and preferred to eat

in the kitchen after Mr Moore and the children had eaten, according to the custom of good Hindu wives. She did not eat meat but cooked very good meat dishes in European and Indian styles for her family. I sometimes ate with them at the table.

Mr Moore became the President of the Anglo-Indian Association and attended the dances at the Club to supervise. Mrs Moore never attended the Club but Audrey and her brother went with their father. Once Audrey and her father insisted that I accompany them to the dance at the Club. Aunt reluctantly gave me permission to do so. I wore the deep blue dress I had bought from Mrs Rath. Audrey was a good dancer and had many young Anglo-Indian admirers. She spoke English fluently and insisted I speak English more often. She corrected my pronunciation and grammatical mistakes. I had a crush on a young trainee-teacher at the college, Michael Flynn. The mention of his name made me blush. I was then over twenty-one. Audrey danced the waltz and the fox trot with her father, whilst I sat and watched.

Suddenly I heard a soft voice asking me to dance. It was Michael Flynn! I could not dance, yet I could not refuse him. He must have regretted asking me because I trod on his toes or he on mine. The floor was overcrowded and I think he was relieved when a tag dance was announced and someone tagged him to dance with me. Michael never returned to tag me, but I was tagged by so many young men that by the end of that evening I had a little idea on dancing the fox trot! I loved music. I learnt the cha-cha-cha, twist, waltz and the Jive steps quickly. From that day on I accompanied Audrey to many more dance nights and took an interest in myself. I became aware of fashions and good clothes. We polished our nails and used lipstick before every dance. Aunt Natasha grumbled when I returned late from the dance, but I could talk things over with Audrey and forget Aunt's disgruntlement. My mother saw no harm in dancing and music. She admired all forms of art. Mum approved of my going to the dances, because it made her feel I was growing up according to Western ways and, besides, I never went alone, Audrey and her father were always with me.

Audrey read Mills & Boon romance novels which she

bought from Jeff Wright, a man selling secondhand English novels to Anglo-Indian homes. They could also borrow the books from him to read at a cheaper price.

I became interested in the novels of Barbara Cartland and Thomas Hardy. My favourite being Tess and, Far From The Madding crowd. I also remember reading Little Women and Jo's Boys. At school we did all the plays of Shakespeare from Year 9 onwards. We also did Lost Horizon. There were no televisions in those years and so we loved reading novels. I read the books in both English and Hindi, while the others could only read in English. The novels helped me dream a bit more and live in my own world of fantasy of love, romance and a happy family life.

One day I met Mr Jeff Wright at Aunt Clarke's house. He had a library of secondhand books. Audrey and I visited his house a couple of times. Mr Wright was an Anglo-Indian who was very literate and educated but found it hard to communicate as he could only converse about books of all types. There were very few people to listen to him, as we found him boring. Mr Wright cycled everywhere on his lady's bicycle with a book in his hand in front, reading.

He was in his early forties and not married. Aunt Clarke said that both he and his brother had inherited a good sum of money from their parents and grandparents in England where his brother was living, but Mr Wright would not leave India. Audrey often teased me about him since he always offered me his best books. She said that it was because he had a crush on me. She also teased me with a few other names of boys in the college or at the dance. I blushed, as I was still very shy and apart from dancing with young men, I never encouraged conversation with them. I still believed that I might become pregnant by sitting too close to the opposite sex or holding hands. Audrey teased me about my 'facts of life'. She told our friends that I thought children were born through a woman's navel and they all laughed, but no one ever bothered to supply me with the correct information. There was no sex education taught in the schools and no male figures at home, so I had not learnt about reproduction. Mum and Aunt believed in saving it until after marriage. It was considered indecent even to talk about it. Violet had acquired the information on sex from her friends.

I stayed at Audrey's house often and we spent time studying together or talking. The Moores went to Church every Sunday. Audrey, Francis and their father would go in the rickshaw together. Mrs Moore liked to walk.

At home Aunt found it difficult to write good English. I helped her with test marking and listing names of boys in her Hindi class. I began writing sick-leave notes and making applications for everyone, both in English and Hindi. Aunt just signed them. I enjoyed writing as much as reading and did all the official correspondence for both Aunt and Mum.

Audrey introduced me to English films and I became an Elvis Presley fan. We saw all his films that came to Allahabad. The English films, mostly old ones, were usually shown in the morning at 10.30 and only on Sundays. To be on time, we had to rush to the picture hall for the movie straight after the Sunday Mass.

✣ ✣ ✣ ✣ ✣

In the first year of my teachers' training there were twelve female and three male students. One was a young Irish Patrician Brother, Br Patrick. I never spoke to any of the boys in the college, yet they always tried to tease me whenever they found me alone, walking with my eyes cast down.

One summer holiday, I got a two months' casual job, as a trainee-teacher at a convent in Mussoorie. I had seen the advertisement on the newsboard in the colleges and applied.

I went to Mussoorie by train and bus. This was the first time I had travelled alone. The winding narrow roads made me sick. I hired a hand rickshaw to take me up to the convent of Jesus and Mary. The snowcapped peaks of the Himalayas could be clearly seen from the convent. All around were pine trees. The air was wonderfully fresh and light, like in Kalimpong.

I loved every minute I was at the girl's school. The children were all boarders, the daughters of rich parents from all over Asia and India, mostly Hindu. I especially liked a three-year-old girl whose parents had gone to England for two years further education. They had left their little daughter as a boarder with the nuns for better education and discipline rather than with the grandparents.

I taught English and geography to years 4, 5 and 8, drawing and maths to years 7 and 10. More emphasis was placed on General English and grammar in the schools at the time. It was a school where the medium of instruction was English. The boarders were provided with very good European and Indian food. They were all very well behaved, gentle girls who were a pleasure to teach.

I wrote to my mother in Hindi practically every day and posted my letters to her with pressed flowers as marks of my love. Mum's letters to me were also regular. I also corresponded with Audrey in English. Although the place was beautiful, I did become homesick.

A week after my arrival in Mussoorie, Br Patrick visited me. He lived in Mussoorie at the Patrician Brothers' Manor School with the other Brothers. He had gone to Allahabad for teachers training, as there were only three English-speaking Anglo-Indian teachers' colleges in India, one in Allahabad, another at Calcutta and the third at Madras.

I was happy to see a familiar face. Brother offered to take me down to his school, via the Mall, the shopping centre. I accepted his invitation as it was a Sunday and I had nothing to do. We set out at eleven in the morning, chatting about the college and the students.

Brother asked me about my parents, so I told him my background. I needed friendship and sympathy and Brother listened to me with understanding. He then told me that he had been sent to India as a missionary from Ireland. He was asked by his superior to take up teaching.

From a distance he pointed out his school, St Georges – the Manor House, the boarding school and the Brothers' Home which is considered the best amongst the boys' Catholic schools in the north of India. Brother said that to reach St Georges it would be best to a take short cut rather than the crowded roadway so I followed him. Suddenly I realised that he had caught my hand and was dragging me downhill. Something told me to stop. I looked down to where we were going and saw only boulders and solitude.

"There is nothing down there to see," I said, determined to return so withdrew my hand from his grasp. He glared at me, his blue eyes looked so strange that I felt scared. I walked back upwards hastily. Brother quietly followed.

"I must hurry and return to the convent, it is getting late. It would be best for you to return to Ireland and get married. I don't think you have the vocation." I said when we were back on the road.

He said nothing. When we reached the convent gates, he laughed and spoke for the first time, "Thank you for making us go back up the hill. You are a good girl. Keep it up and if you ever need anything, remember me. I will see you back in college." I did not see him again. Brother went back to Ireland for a holiday once the training was over and did not return to India. I received a postcard from him a couple of years later saying that I was right and that he did not really have the vocation, so he plucked up the courage to leave the ecclesiastical life.

I returned to Allahabad just before the summer holidays were over to rejoin the College. Mum met me at the station. She was overjoyed to see my pink cheeks and sunburnt face. Mum told me that Victor was working at the office of a Protestant church not far from our house and often presented Violet with rich gifts. We wondered how he had enough money for them.

While I was in Mussoorie, four of Mum's family had arrived from the village of Latonah. Mum had resumed her correspondence with her brother when she started working as a nurse. She sent them old clothes and sometimes money. Mum had not mentioned it to Aunt because she was afraid of her criticism. Mum's relatives were very poor in comparison to Aunt's high-caste ones, so Mum had developed a feeling of inferiority about them. Besides, Mum did not think that Violet and I would fit in with her relations from the village. Her brother suddenly died, leaving a wife, two daughters and two sons. The sons were married and settled, but the daughters were not. So she managed to get her two nieces, Grace and Marcel, enrolled in the midwifery course in Allahabad. She brought their mothers to spend a few days in the house with Aunt Natasha. As Aunt Natasha's grumbled and criticised them, Mum had to cut short their visit and sent them back. On my arrival home from Mussoorie, Aunt defensively told me how poorly dressed Mum's relatives were and how she felt embarrassed in front of the servant having them stay in the house. She said even the maidservant was better dressed than Mum's relatives were. Aunt said sarcastically that they had never seen a modern toilet and would climb on top of the toilet seat to relieve themselves. They did not know the difference between hair oil and shampoo and used the later to massage their heads, becoming shocked when it started lathering. I heard it all in silence but was annoyed at Aunt for her arrogance and sense of superiority. I did not consider poverty and ignorance a reason for thinking a person inferior.

I wanted to meet my mother's relatives. Perhaps I wanted to know some of my own, even though they were not up to Aunt's standard, but they never returned to Allahabad, having been humiliated and I never had the chance to meet them.

Mum's sister-in-law died shortly after she returned to her village.

23

When I fell in love

One weekend most of the Anglo-Indian girls from the Colony received invitations to an Air Force Ball to be held at the newly opened airforce station some fifty kilometres away. Audrey and I were delighted. We had new dresses made for the occasion that I had designed. Audrey was very short and petite, so she had to have something gathered, with frills in soft pink. Mine was of a similar pattern, in peacock blue, my favourite colour. I enjoyed the dances.

The Air Force station wagon collected us for the dance. It was a grand ball, which finished at 3 in the morning. Flight Lt Razza Sherazi, a Parsee (Zoroastrian) by religion who was very handsome with dark hair, fair complexion and a good build, danced with me most of the time. At the end of the dance he professed to having fallen in love with me and wanted to see me again the next day. I blushed, not knowing what to do for a minute; then I refused him, explaining I did not go on dates. Razza was very considerate and kissed my hand before I left for home.

The thought of being out with Razza alone made me feel bashful. I imagined what the people in Allahabad would think of me, I was considered the holy one, who said her prayers in Church with hands folded and eyes closed. I was also under the influence of Aunt Natasha who was forever speaking badly about the Anglo-Indian girls and ladies who went on dates.

Audrey met Flight Lt Brian Wilson, an Anglo-Indian, who was tall, with blond hair. I saw very little of Audrey after that dance as she was mostly with Brian in the evenings, watching English films or dining out. However, we still went together to dances held by the air force and at the Club. Every time I met Razza Sherazi, he would embarrass me with his professions of love. All his other Air Force friends seemed to know of his feelings and always saw that they were conveyed to me. According to Audrey, he did not go out with anyone and looked sad when Brian went out with her, as did the others with their girlfriends. Razza would say to them that he was waiting for me to make up my mind. I earnestly believed that I should only go out with the man I would marry and I wanted to marry only a Catholic.

Mrs Clarke was worried about my idealistic views on life. Although she was not in favour of my getting involved with Razza Shirazi, because she said mixed marriages with non-Christians never worked, she wanted me to meet some nice Anglo-Indian boy.

One evening, I was introduced to a very handsome, tall, fair-skinned young man by Mrs Wycliffe, a physical education teacher from the convent school I had attended. She was a friend of Mrs Clarke. Apparently she came to the dance with her husband and this young man, whom I later came to know as Danny, who was from the Allahabad Agriculture Institute. Danny had just joined the college from Bangalore, in the south of India. Mr Wycliffe was a professor at the Agriculture Institute and Danny was their prize student. He was an Anglo-Indian. His mother had a coffee plantation and sent him a lot of pocket money. He looked very intelligent and his arrogant, indifferent manners added charm to his personality. There was something about him I could not resist from the very first moment I danced with him. He danced with me only once that evening, as they left early.

Although I never went out with anyone I started spending hours at the back of the house praying to Jesus that, "Mr Right" would come along soon and take me away. I wanted to have a home and a happy family of my own. I had a vision of a loving husband, who was just as handsome as my father, fair and tall and who would truly love and care for me.

Soon most of the Anglo-Indian girls from the Colony were invited for another Air Force dance to mark the transfer of the first group of young officers. Audrey and I again attended the dance together. She was sad because Brian was leaving the station, but he promised to keep in touch. I danced with Razza most of the time. He asked me for my address and permission to correspond, which I gave as I was flattered by his attention. Everything was good about him, but I could not overlook the fact that he was a non-Catholic and I was prejudiced about non-Catholics.

Razza wrote to me nearly every week for about three months, poetically expressing his feelings for me. I was flattered, but I could not accept him. Sometimes I felt I should answer giving him my reasons and ask if he was willing to change his religion. While I was contemplating the idea, Mrs Wycliffe invited me to a house party at the Agricultural Institute.

Mr and Mrs Wycliffe picked me up in their van for the dance. The Institute was run by the Methodist Church and was funded from the USA. The Institute followed an American style of life.

I met Danny again at the party. Apparently he had said he wanted to meet me, so they had arranged a house party, paid for by Danny. The party was very homely. There were just three other couples besides the Wycliffes and us. Danny invited me to walk near the river while the others were dancing. He looked nervous and was very English in his appearance which I liked. Somehow we started talking about religion. He told me that though he was a baptised Catholic, he was really an atheist because he had bad memories of life as a child at the boarding school where the priests forced him to kneel and pray in Church by pinching him. I took it upon myself to make him realise the goodness of the Catholic religion. During the walk he did not even try to hold my hand; we just talked about religion and the existence of God. I decided I had to bring him back to the Church. According to Mrs Wycliffe Danny was frightened of upsetting me, but was full of praise for me. Both Mrs Clarke and Mrs Wycliffe decided that since Danny was the institute's top student and had won a scholarship to go to England for his Ph.D. in Animal Husbandry, I should take an interest in him as a good match. It was conventional amongst the elderly Anglo-Indians to match-make for the young ones. Even during the British Raj times, it was the elderly Anglo-Indian relatives and friends who took it upon themselves to find an appropriate match for the young Anglo-Indian. They would arrange an occasion for the young couple to meet and then encourage them, on the importance of marrying the right person and within the community. Aunt Clarke was doing what she considered the right thing for me since both Aunt Natasha and my mother could not. I had fallen in love with Danny and he seemed to fit my vision of an ideal husband with his background of being half-European, intelligent and a born Catholic.

Shortly after the party, Danny went on a summer vacation to his home-town, Bangalore in December 1962. Meanwhile, I continued receiving letters from Razza. I answered him occasionally in an ordinary tone, with news and reports about the weather and so on, although his letters were full of affection. One day he proposed marriage, leaving me with no alternative but to reply to him, telling the truth, that I could not marry him as he was not a Catholic. That concluded our correspondence. Many years later, Audrey informed me that Razza eventually married an Anglo-Indian girl and was a very loving husband. I realised by then, through bitter experiences, that there are good and bad people in all religions and races and that one should never generalise and be prejudiced or biased. The principle of all religion is to guide people to live good lives with honesty and love towards all fellow beings and to serve the creator with sincerity and dedication.

At the end of January 1963, after the holidays, Danny returned to Allahabad. Once again I was invited to the house parties at Mrs Wycliffe's place where I met him frequently. Danny and I went for long walks along the bank of the River Ganges, next to the Institute halfway through the party. We discussed religion and many other topics. I enjoyed those walks with him. He would often drop me home either in the Institute jeep or the rickshaw. Once he put his arms around my shoulders and tried to hold me close to him. I immediately tried to get away from him.

"Oh Esther, let me hold your hand at least," he said.

"I want to be close only to the man who is my husband," I said, getting away from his hold. He laughed with the echoing laughter of his which I loved very much. I liked everything about him but was not prepared to let him get close to me, because I did not want to become pregnant before marriage. I still believed that one could get pregnant by just holding hands or sitting close to a man.

Enid and Helen had their own respectable girlfriends and did not like dancing or having boyfriends. Aunt said that when their time came for marriage, they would have the best of husbands as they had a very respectable background.

"Well, Esther, even angels don't mind holding hands and you are only human," said Danny on one occasion when we were returning from a film. "Let me put my arms around you," which he did. Fortunately we were near my house. I jumped off the rickshaw and ran down the pathway towards our gate, not looking back to see if he was laughing the way he usually did.

Perhaps those were my best days of life!

24

Broken engagement leaves its mark

Violet was still at the boarding convent, completing her two year teacher training when she became officially engaged. Victor's job at a Protestant church office, as a clerk, paid him a salary of one hundred *rupees* per month. Aunt often said that Violet was a bad example to her innocent and virtuous daughters, but that since Violet was a product of a scandalous relationship, this was to be expected. In her frustration Aunt would discuss Victor and Violet's relationship with her teacher friends at school and innocently spread more gossip. Mum tried to speak to Violet fearing that Violet would repeat Mum's mistakes but to no effect. Violet tried to cover up for Victor but she was really not very happy about his over-possessive nature and was looking for an excuse to break off with him..

One day, close to the end of the summer holidays, I had a visitor, Jumbo, the African friend whom I had met at Naini Tal. He was returning to Nairobi, so he had come to bid us goodbye. We were all in the garden chatting when Victor arrived on his bike to see Violet. His eyes shone with anger and jealousy at the sight of Violet talking to Jumbo.

"Violet, I want you to come with me right now," he shouted as he got off his bicycle.

"Stop shouting at me Victor!" she said, walking towards him.

"Violet, we have a visitor who has come to meet the family. You should be civilised enough to give him your company. Besides, you shouldn't allow Victor to shout at you in front of an outsider," I said to Violet very calmly.

"How dare your bloody bitch of a sister interfere between us! I asked you to come away at once!" Victor said very angrily. We all stood with Jumbo silent and embarrassed. I felt humiliated at the abuse.

"Violet, if you love your sister you would return the engagement ring this minute and not allow him to disgrace me in front of everyone."

Violet walked to Victor took out her engagement ring which he had given and returned it to him saying, "Victor, how can you use that abusive language towards my sister! Take your ring back. Our engagement is off."

He was shocked and so were we.

"Come and take your ring back. You know that I love you very much and we have been friends for so long. You cannot break it off like this!"

"Let us all go in for lunch," I said and everyone had to pass by Victor to get to the dining room. Violet followed us in the end. While we were having our lunch, I heard Victor call out loudly to my sister.

"Violet, I am not leaving. I shall sit on your steps until you have taken the ring back. I love you very much and cannot leave you till death."

I told Violet to ignore what he was saying and then went to the door and spoke to him very calmly.

"Victor, it is over. I can complain to the police about your sitting on our doorstep when we don't want you."

He rose quietly and went outside the gate saying loudly, "There, I am outside, but I shall not move from here till Violet takes the ring back. I will throw acid on Violet's face if you try to fix her with another person. She is my fiancee."

We ignored him and continued with our lunch. Jumbo left an hour later. When I went to the door to see him off I found Victor still standing by the gate. Violet was in her room, calm and indifferent, reading a novel by Barbara Cartland. I thought of my friend Audrey and her father. I quietly ran out of the house in the heat of the afternoon. As I passed Victor at the gate, I looked at him with contempt. I hated him for ruining my sister's future.

Audrey and her father shared the same opinion as me and advised that in view of Victor's threat, to take the matter to the police.

"How dare Victor call you a bitch!" Audrey said, "You

should have called him a bastard."

Although I was familiar with the English spoken at the convent school and in educational books, I did not know the meanings of the two words, "bitch" and "bastard." They were not in the few Mills and Boon books I had read! I kept repeating the word "bastard" in my mind as I walked hurriedly back home. I found him still waiting at the gates.

"You are still here, you bastard!" I said emphasising the word, because it was in retaliation for what he called me; besides I also wanted him to know that even I could use good English words to show my temper.

As I reached the steps of the verandah, I turned around to see the effect of my words on him. He was not there. I looked past the gate and saw him in the distance cycling quickly towards his house. I was very pleased with myself and the impact of the word. Cajeton visited us and we related the incident to him.

"That is very good. We must see that Violet does not re-establish the relationship." Uncle Cajeton said with concern.

Violet wrote short stories, which I kept to show to anyone, who might publish them and make her an author. She also painted and drew faces well, though they always resembled me. I was proud of my sister's talents and was confident that she would do much better without Victor.

Shortly after we returned home, Aunt had visitors. They were people from Bettiah; her hometown, who had settled in Allahabad and visited her frequently. They suggested that Violet should be hidden away from Victor till the college opened a week later and offered to keep her in their house at Naini. Aunt approved of their suggestion and Violet went with them that afternoon.

Victor and his mother returned around 6.00 in the evening. They were walking down the pathway towards the house when two constables who had been put on duty for our security, stopped them. Victor and his mother stood at the sweet shop across the road and began abusing us loudly in the filthiest terms they could find in both Hindi and English. Helen and Enid stayed inside the house. I walked round the garden saying my

Rosary and praying for peace and help from Jesus, though I heard all they were saying.

"You had the cheek to call my son a bastard!" Mrs Carter was yelling in Hindi, "when you yourself have no father. People must know that all the women in that house are whores. There are no men there. The women are bringing up their daughters to be like them, prostitutes. They are not fit to live in decent, respectable communities. They should be thrown out. Ask that tall girl, who seems so saintly, who her father was! Ask her if her mother ever got married! "

The man who ran the sweet shop went on with his work. People who came to the shop wondered what it was all about. Some stood looking at our house. No one had the courage to try to stop her. The two constables stood on one side watching. Everyone from the Colony stayed in their houses. Fortunately, darkness fell at last. Aunt kept coming out and frequently urged me to come in. But I stayed out saying my rosary and begging Jesus to help and protect us, for I had the feeling that Mrs Carter was eventually going to come into the house and hurt Aunt, Enid and Helen. I felt that I had to stay outside and guard them.

Mrs Carter and Victor stayed calling abuse until 9.00 that night. Before leaving she threatened to return the next day to see that none of us left the house unless Violet went back to Victor and their relationship was restored. She took the break-up of the engagement as an insult and wanted me to apologise in public for calling her son a "bastard". Victor knew most of the *goondas* (criminals) around the area and was capable of hiring them to injure us. I was distressed by the things Mrs Carter said. Until then I had been upset because my father was a priest and I was not permitted to become a nun, but was awakened as to how Violet and I were regarded in society. I also learnt what the word "bastard" meant in relation to us.

Mum came to visit us a few days after the incident and Aunt told her what had taken place. She seemed upset, but said nothing. It was very difficult to know Mum's feelings as she always seemed calm and composed.

A day before the college was opened I went there with Violet and her luggage. The nuns were sympathetic towards us and were delighted that Violet had broken off her engagement. Mrs Carter and Victor arrived but Sister Magda*l*ene took us inside one of the nun's rooms, while the Carters were there. We stayed inside until they left.

✣ ✣ ✣ ✣ ✣

Soon after the college re-opened for our final semester, Mrs Wycliffe said that Danny was back from holidays and wanted to see me at the weekend. We went for our walk beside the River Ganges and Danny brought out a postcard. "This came to me. I thought you should have it. It has not made any impression on me because I don't care about people's gossip." Then he handed me the postcard.

I read the card quickly.

"*Dear Danny,*

I know that you are very fond of Esther. But you should know that she is a bastard, as her parents were never married. You come from a respectable home. I thought I should warn you about this girlfriend of yours who also has a bad character like her mother.

A Well-Wisher"

I was shocked.

"What is the matter?" asked Danny. "I do not believe a word of it. I know you too well. I gave you the card just to let you know what is going on and to warn you."

He put his arms around me and pushed me against the wall looking straight into my eyes and came close to my face. I panicked, fearing that I was about to lose my virginity and tried to struggle free.

"Give me a kiss, there is no one here to watch," he said.

"No," I said, struggling.

I freed myself from his embrace, but he did kiss me lightly on my cheek, which made me blush. Danny laughed sending shivers down my spine. I looked at him with mixed feelings of love and fear. He was so handsome. I was upset about the postcard and confused about his trying to force me into kissing him. Was he taking advantage of something bad written about my parents? Was he thinking that I was bad? In a split second many questions came crowding into my head and I did not know what to think or do. All I wanted was to run away from everyone, even Danny. No-one understood me. It hurt to be labelled and called bad because of my parents. I knew my parents were not bad, they had only fallen in love. I loved them. It was not fair. I hated the person who wrote the anonymous letter concerning my background.

"Esther, even angels cannot resist a kiss! You are very immature, grow up. I'll drop you home," Danny said in his very masculine voice and I snapped out of my tortured thinking.

The next day at college, Akbar, a fellow-student teacher from my class gave me a note, which said exactly the same thing as the postcard. Akbar said that he had found it on his table in the morning when he arrived. He added, "Don't worry Esther, you are like my own sister and I have always admired your goodness. Tell me if anyone worries you and I'll deal with them for you."

During the next few days more anonymous letters were delivered to other boys in college. They had taken them to Sister Bernard, our Secondary Co-ordinator, asking what was going on. She confiscated them, saying they were the products of a sick mind and should not be taken seriously. I too went to her with the note Akbar received and shed tears about it. It pained me to know that more people were informed about my background. I became aware of it all and was sensitive towards it being mentioned. The nun was concerned but calm. She took the note from me saying, "Stop crying and take hold of yourself. Forget all these silly notes. They are meant only to hurt your feelings. What happened in the past with your parents has nothing to do with you."

But I could not forget them. I decided to leave Allahabad and Mum and teach in another city. Sensitive and conscious of my background I avoided the people in the Anglo-Indian community and the Church because everyone was judging me. I never discussed it with anyone at home or with Violet, because I did not think it would help, nor did I tell Mum as I did not want to hurt her but I also thought that she would not understand.

I saw Danny a few times more after that. He never mentioned the postcard again and we spent our time watching films or going on long walks. He presented me with two Bangalore silk *saris*. The first *saris* of my own! They were beautiful, green and blue with gold work. I wore them when I visited him, as he liked to see me in *saris*. Mum helped me put them on as I found it hard to do. I usually wore dresses and occasionally wore the salwar kameez (a sort of pants suit) which most Indian teenagers wore.

At the end of the year Danny topped his Master of Science examinations in Animal Husbandry and received the Gold Medal. He also managed to receive an enrolment in England for his Ph.D.

I saw him off at the station the day he was leaving for Bangalore at the end of the year. He asked me to wear a white *sari* and to put up my hair in a neat bun. My hair had recovered from the shock of the perm and once again grown to my waist. Mum dressed me in her white full cotton voile *sari*, which she received as uniform for duty as a nurse. She dressed me as she used to wear her *sari*, very neatly, every pleat falling accurately into place.

In the distance I saw Danny's tall, slim, fair figure. He stood out in the crowd at the station. He had dark hair and a very long Aryan nose. His eyes were large and almond-shaped. His laugh showed his uniform white teeth. I found him so very handsome and even liked the impression of arrogance which he gave people when they met him for the first time. He had a very masculine bass voice that plucked at my heart! I fell in love over and over again with him.

Danny was pleased to see me dressed the way he'd asked.

"Esther, I have to leave you. Look after yourself. I'll write to you," he said just as the train was about to leave.

Mrs Wycliffe and a few other friends had also come to see him off. Mrs Wycliffe whispered to me that I should visit Danny's family before he left for England.

"May I come to visit you in Bangalore and see you off at Delhi before you go to England?" I asked.

"Bangalore is a long distance, I shall write to you when I

am going to England and perhaps you can see me off at Delhi," he replied.

"Let her meet your family in Bangalore before you leave," Mrs Wycliffe said loudly with betel leaves in her mouth. She was a slim lady with a big mouth in her small light brown face.

Danny blushed at her comment and said that I could come after Christmas. He sounded as though he was not very pleased with Mrs Wycliffe's intrusion. The guard blew the whistle and Danny boarded the train. I waved as long as I could see him and felt sad after the train disappeared. It was the first time I cared for a man other than my father. Danny was in many ways like my father. They were both intelligent, good-looking and spoke gently obvious to me that they cared about me as they made me feel important.

✣ ✣ ✣ ✣ ✣

I was so shaken by all the gossip that I decided to go over the file of correspondence between my father and Uncle Eddie. I wrote to both the addresses in 1963, left in the file by my father, those of his brother Frank Lyons, in Detroit and of Mrs Emma Trombley, in Toledo, Ohio. I told them of our existence and of the predicament we were in, pleading with them to let me know where my father was, as I needed him. I promised just to write and not in any way make any demands on him. Mrs Emma Trombley was the wife of my father's cousin, George. She wrote to say she did not know his whereabouts, but continued to correspond with me, sending us small financial gifts every Christmas and Easter for sometime afterwards. I never heard from Papa's brother, Mr Frank Lyons, even though I wrote to him a couple of times begging for information about where my father was.

25

A visit to the south

For a long time after Danny left for Bangalore, I had no news from him. I was very disturbed and spent my time gardening or visiting Mum. Eventually, the day after Christmas, his letter came informing me he was leaving for England in the middle of February. He wrote that, if I was interested in visiting him in Bangalore, I should do so immediately. I was delighted and prepared for the trip down south. Mum was pleased and helped me pack. I boarded the train to Bangalore a few days later. I travelled in the third-class sleeping coach, where my berth was reserved for the three nights and two days journey south across three States with different languages and cultures. Once I was in the state of Andhra Pradesh and closer to Madras I could not understand anyone, because they spoke South Indian languages so different to the northern languages. It was difficult to order meals at the stations. Fortunately, most hawkers understood English. At Madras I changed for Bangalore on my second train journey alone.

Danny was at the station to meet me. From the expression on his face I could see that I appeared scruffy and filthy, for he looked critical and somewhat disappointed. I had avoided the stinking toilet of the third-class sleeper compartment much as possible, as well as the washbasin outside the toilet, which was extremely filthy with the people's spittles. I could not afford the first-class compartment, which was cleaner. Perhaps that is why I looked a mess. My face was very black with the soot of the steam-train and my hair was full of charcoal pieces and untidy.

To me Danny looked even more handsome than before. I was overjoyed to see him but his grim look made me feel self-conscious. He took me to the YWCA guesthouse where he had booked my accommodation for the three days I was to stay in Bangalore. I had already reserved my return journey, because as I was to join my new teacher's position at Agra, in the first week of January.

"I'll be back in an hour for you." Danny said when he put my suitcase and the bedding in my room. "You'd better dress in a white *sari* and do up your hair."

After Danny left I had my first shower for three days after travelling in the dirty train. I'd borrowed Mum's long white *sari* petticoat to wear under all the *saris* I had brought for my stay. I possessed only three *saris*: one, Mum's white cotton voile *sari* and the two Danny had given me. I had just learnt to wear *sari*. As an Anglo-Indian I wore dresses most of the time.

While showering, my only petticoat slipped off the rickety hanger onto the wet floor of the bathroom. I had nothing else to wear under the thin white voile *sari*! It was nearly time for Danny to collect me. So I wrapped the *sari* three times round myself before putting in the pleats in the front. I wore only my underwear and the *sari*. Fortunately, the *sari* was more than six metres long. Mum got a length of eighteen metres of cotton voile material for three *saris* and cut them herself. Being a small lady, she needed less than six metres for herself. The third and the last piece were always longer than the first two. She gave me the last piece this time. I found it hard to make neat pleats in the *sari* as she did it for me, so I ended up using many pins to keep them in place.

I painted my cheeks with rouge and used a bright red lipstick. My hair I tried to put in a bun, but, although I somehow managed to do so, it was nowhere as good as when Mum did it for me the day Danny left Allahabad.

When Danny returned he looked at me critically, "So, you are going to meet my mother at last! Please take off all that colour from your cheeks, you look too painted."

He was clearly not happy about my appearance, but I could do nothing about it. Because of the many drapes of the *sari* my movements were restricted. I could only take small steps. He did not speak to me much on the way except to tell me that he had two younger brothers and a sister. They did not have a father. The family owned a coffee plantation.

We eventually reached a beautiful bungalow. His mother

welcomed me. She was beautiful, with features like Danny, but more olive in complexion. She had the same almond shaped eyes and a long nose. She was very simply dressed in a white silk *sari* and with only a light lipstick for make-up. I was introduced to his two brothers and the sister who was just fourteen years old. None of them resembled Danny, although they were all very fair. I also met an older lady, an Anglo-Indian in a long dress who was introduced to me as Danny's nanny.

Danny spoke very little during the meal. I liked his mother. After lunch Danny took me around the town for a drive and then left me at the YWCA before it got dark, promising to pick me up early the next morning.

That night I woke with a start. To my horror, a huge rat was running up and down my blanket. It must have been living inside the torn mattress! I could not go back to sleep after that.

Danny came at 8.00 in the morning. I'd dressed in one of the *saris* he had given me. He took me to his home again but this time I was more at ease with his mother. She invited me to visit Bangalore again and asked me to stay in her house the next time I visited the city. We went out shopping together and she presented me with a mother-of-pearl necklace. She also told me that she liked me and would be happy if Danny would marry me, as she wanted him to be happy. I learnt that Danny was her first son, by an Englishman, who had deserted them. She had the other three children from a British coffee plantation owner. Danny mostly lived in boarding schools. She said that she felt guilty about it all. Furthermore, the children from her second husband received a large sum of money each per month, from their coffee plantation as soon as they were eighteen years of age. But Danny received nothing. His mother had willed her share of the property to him and also gave him the same amount per month from her share, like the others did. The old nanny and housekeeper had become a part of the family. When the second husband died the children and the wife became the owners of the coffee plantation.

I felt closer to Danny after I learnt his background. I was sure that God in His mercy had finally found me the right man to be my husband.

That evening after dinner Danny took me back to the YWCA. He told me that he was happy that his mother and I got along very well as he was extremely fond of her and never wanted to hurt her.

I travelled back to Allahabad the following morning. Danny saw me off at the station with his younger brother. He promised to inform me of his date of departure from Delhi for England, as I intended seeing him off.

The journey home was boring. I was happy to reach Allahabad and meet Mum at the station. One week after I returned from Bangalore I was off to Agra, the city of the Taj Mahal for my first teaching position. Violet left for Mussoorie, while Enid and Helen completed their High School Examination and were planning their future careers. Enid decided to take up a secretarial course, while Helen was contemplating further education.

26

And he proposed to me

It was during 1963 that I began my career as a secondary teacher in the Convent of Jesus and Mary in Agra. I was sad leaving my mother and Aunt Natasha in Allahabad and starting my own life. The people were old-fashioned in the crowded main city with its narrow roads. It was difficult to move about in dresses without being whistled at or hearing sexist remarks. It was not uncommon to be pinched or grabbed at the breast by grubby-looking men in the crowd. Both sides of the road had shops above which were the apartments of prostitutes.

Fortunately, the convent was in the Cantonment Area far from the main city. The people were tolerant of Western clothes, perhaps because they were used to the foreign tourists visiting the Taj Mahal. I wore *saris* more frequently. I got used to wearing them like Mum. I was the only Anglo-Indian teacher living-in with the other two Indian Christian teachers. We each had a room to ourselves next to the nuns' accommodation. We ate together at a dining room close to the nuns and shared their kitchen. Although we were teachers, we had a 10.00pm curfew when the big iron gates were locked. The nuns kept close watch over our movements and being teachers we were expected to be virtuous.

The two Indian Christian teachers were from Allahabad and claimed to come from respectable homes. They were forever enquiring about my parents and their occupations. Unfortunately I could only tell them about my mother who was just a nurse, but I had nothing to say about my father except that he was no more. One day in the course of conversation and perhaps under pressure by their frequent questioning I made the mistake of telling them that my father was an American. This raised doubts in their minds about my background and they wanted to know how an Indian nurse could have children by an American. One of them recalled the gossip about my sister and Victor by Mrs Carter. I said nothing but listened to them in silence.

I soon discovered the corpulent Irish Reverend Mother had taken a dislike to me, perhaps the two teachers had gossiped with her. To add to that I received many letters from Danny and the incoming mail went to the office from where we collected it. I heard from other teachers that sometimes it was inspected before being given to us. So when I found one of Danny's letters open I asked Reverend Mother about it. She went red in the face and shouted at me for suspecting her of opening my mail. I tried to avoid her after that.

I once received a telephone call from Danny. Since he had a few months before he left for England, he had decided to take his brother around the historical places in the north and to my great surprise he came to visit Agra with his younger brother. That afternoon we went to see the great Taj Mahal in the moonlight.

The Taj Mahal, a white marble monument built in memory of Mumtaz Mahal, the wife of Mughul Emperor of India, Shahjahan, is one of the wonders of the world. Mumtaz Mahal died early in her life giving birth to her fourteenth child. The Emperor was heart broken at her death. He kept his promise made to her at her deathbed about building the best and the most unforgettable monument in memory of the love they held for each other. He had white marble imported from Italy which was decorated with intricate floral designs in red, green and yellow precious and semi precious stones which took thirty years to build. Inside, the body of Mumtaz Mahal was laid in full splendour. The body was kept in a small gravesite nearby while the Taj Mahal was being built. It is said that the Emperor rewarded the architect who built it with a large sum of money, but also had his hands cut off so that he was unable to design another building like it in his life time.

His son, Aurangzeb put the Emperor into prison, later in his life. Aurangzeb became the next Emperor of India but he accepted the request of his father Shahjahan by keeping him imprisoned in a fort not far from the Taj Mahal. Every day the old imprisoned Emperor Shahjahan would look at the Taj Mahal from his verandah and think of his favourite wife Mumtaz Mahal. He died one day while looking towards the monument and was buried in the Taj Mahal beside his wife. The stately and grand monument of love, the Taj Mahal still stands with all its beauty and splendour even to this day even though the precious and semi precious gems are now replaced with just colours. It draws a lot of tourists to India from all parts of the world.

It was there I remember Danny telling me about the importance of education while we sat in the park in front of the white marble monument of love. "You must do the degree course somehow. A Secondary Teachers' Training is not good enough. A degree is a must if you want to go overseas," he said and added with a smile, "It will keep you busy while I am away."

I nodded my head. "Yes, I will do my Bachelor of Arts by correspondence from Agra University." I felt that I had to study further just because Danny was such a learned person.

I saw them off at the station the next evening with a heavy heart. Danny promised to inform me the date he was leaving from Delhi. I was determined to take a few days leave from school and see him off in Delhi.

A week later I had another visitor, Helen, had decided to join a college in Simla, a hill station, some distance from Allahabad, to pursue higher studies. But she lasted only a week in the hostel of St. Bede's College. Helen was very homesick and behaved contrary to the wishes of the nuns. Having argued with the Mother Superior, she had walked out of the college and left Simla. Since she had to pass through Agra on the way to Allahabad, she stopped at Agra to see me. She had grown into an understanding young lady who, in her own way, regarded me as an older sister she could depend upon. The feeling of superiority still prevailed amongst Aunt and her daughters, more so as besides the two brothers of Aunt being the Jesuit missionaries, her distant Uncle was to become the first Indian Jesuit Bishop of Patna Mission. More of their relatives had also joined the religious life. Yet Helen had grown to look upon me with respect and friendliness. There was a better understanding between her and Violet as well. In many ways we were like sisters except for the matter of the background. I advised her to take up teacher-training at Allahabad instead. Eventually both she and Enid did this. They both became primary and kindergarten teachers like Violet.

All visitors were taken to the Reverend Mother and her permission had to be arranged in order to have them on the premises. So I took Helen to the office to explain her visit to me. Since nuns of the same Jesus and Mary order also ran the college in Simla, Reverend Mother did not seem very happy to meet Helen. In the evening I went to see Helen to the station and was late in returning to the school. It was eleven when I returned and the iron gates were locked from the inside. The rickshawman helped me by banging at the gates to have them opened. When they finally were, it was opened by the Reverend Mother. I could not even explain to her my reasons for being late because she walked away quickly in great displeasure.

I compounded my unhappy situation by applying elsewhere for a teaching position during the term. Perhaps that was a mistake, given that our letters were tampered with. Rejections kept arriving as it was just at the start of the school year and all schools had a full complement of staff by then. But, of course, the Principal became aware that I was looking for another job and disliked me all the more. The situation worsened when the problem with my left ear recurred I saw an ear, nose and throat specialist who gave me antibiotic injections every day making me feel weak and exhausted. My mouth dried up while teaching and I often had to leave the class for a glass of fresh lemon juice.

One day I wandered around the Church yard which was close to the convent. There were graves surrounding a small ruin not far from the Church. They were covered with dead leaves and soil. I liked reading the inscriptions on tombstones so I stopped near a grave and bent down to clear it. I was shocked to read 'Esther Lyons', my own name. She had been born three days after me, on the 30th of November in the 19th Century and died at the same age as I was then, but in the month of December. It scared me. I started clearing the neighbouring tombstones and found the graves of a whole family of 'Lyons' buried in the nineteenth century. Later I learnt that the entire family had died of heat exhaustion and sunstroke, then a common fate for English people. I have never forgotten that strange incident in Agra.

✣ ✣ ✣ ✣ ✣

I was lucky to get an offer of a teaching position in 'La Martiniere Girls' School', a Protestant English School in Lucknow, closer to Allahabad. They offered me one hundred and ten *rupees* a month and free board and lodging. It was a little less than what I was earning at the convent but I jumped at the opportunity. I wanted to leave Agra. The Reverend Mother was not pleased to have me leave in the middle of term, but I gave notice and left, forfeiting one month's salary.

La Martiniere Girls' was a private school run by the Board of Members. Instruction was in English and Hindi was taught as another subject, as were all English convent schools in India. There were more Anglo-Indian teachers of my age in Lucknow and most of them wore dresses. It was a boarding school for girls from all over northern India with a very good reputation which we teachers were expected to maintain with a good teaching standard.

The Principal was Miss Gresseux, unmarried and in her forties. She lived in the school building next to the office in a well-furnished apartment. The school had its own swimming pool, unlike many schools in India and had a good record in sports and swimming. This which made it more popular to modern rich Indians.

The main building was a castle with four turrets and a moat. One of the drawbridges was cemented and made into a pathway leading to the office, the other led to the staff and the students' dining rooms and then to the main building.

It was originally a palace built by the last Mughal nawab (Muslim ruler), as his wife's summer palace. All the rooms were large, one of the huge halls was the girls' dining room, next to which was the staff dining room. The servants served the food wearing white-and-red uniforms. Staff were served exclusively European meals. A large cement staircase led from the dining-hall to the first floor girls' dormitory. Six resident teachers lived next to the dormitory, each having a private room and there were terraces on either side of the dormitory. My room was on one end and had a door, which led to the turret stairs.

Every morning an *ayah* woke us up with a cup of hot tea and biscuits. She folded our clothes and made our beds, as well as cleaning the room and having the *dhobi* (washerman) wash our clothes. *Ayahs* were designated different rooms to look after. I liked my *ayah,* as she was a very caring lady who had been working in the school for twenty years.

There were new buildings built around the castle for more classes. The school had its own Kindergarten and Primary classes. I taught mathematics in Years 8 and 10, English and history in Year 8 and art in Yrs 3 and 10. I enjoyed teaching there. The Principal was very understanding although she had a bad temper when things went wrong. She took an immediate liking to me and was a great support to me in all my undertakings. Her secretary, Mrs Whitby, was her best friend. They loved drinking rum and whisky together every evening in the Principal's apartment with the lady accountant, Miss Maggie Siness.

Mrs Whitby was a divorcee. Her husband had migrated to England with the children and she never saw them again. Miss Maggie Siness also took a liking to me. She was a dwarf, in her mid-thirties. Maggie was very intelligent and did all the school accounts. She was a twin and her parents treated her differently from her sister who was normal and pretty. After her parents died the sister deserted her, saying she was ashamed to be seen with her. The sister ultimately immigrated to England leaving her without much money. Maggie lived in a small rented bungalow away from the school. Mrs Whitby often visited her for dinner and drinks.

I also met the Daniel family there. Joan Daniel was studying in Year 10; her older sister was in Year 9, being a little slow in her studies. Mrs Daniel made much of Joan because she was pretty and intelligent. The youngest Daniel was in my Year 6.

One day, not long after I joined the school, I was invited by Mrs Daniel to visit her home, because she and her husband were good friends of Father Evans and he was visiting Lucknow. He wanted to see me.

The next day, after school I visited their house. They were very fair-skinned Anglo-Indians who put up Father Evans whenever he visited Lucknow. He was given a small room where he stored all his files and papers. That day Father Evans took me to this room and informed me that he was still fighting for the rights of the Catholic priests to marry. He said that for this great work of his he wanted my help, since I had grown up. He was around sixty by then. Father Evans had stopped shaving and had long grey hair and beard. He looked very withered, with shrunken eyes and pale face. Every now and then he went on a hunger strike fighting with either the Bishop or the Pope. The Church had excommunicated him because of his obsession at the time. Although he was allowed to stay in Church accommodation in Allahabad, he was not allowed to say Mass in the Church. I felt sorry for the way he looked and asked him how I could help him.

"By marrying me, of course! You and I could make an example to the world of a priestly marriage. I asked your mother but she does not want to. You would be the ideal person, being the daughter of a Catholic priest."

I was shocked, I couldn't speak. I thought of him as the priest who had helped us when we had nowhere to go and had felt grateful to him ever since. I knew that he was once a friend of my father and had always respected and loved him. He had helped Mum take up nurses' training, enabling her to support us. And now he was proposing marriage to me! I was only twenty-three and trying to get over the experiences in Allahabad. I was trying to start a new life for myself, away from gossip and humiliation. And here was Father Evans suggesting I should take up a cause to start a new round of problems for myself again in order to set an example for the world!

"Think about it Minnie! Perhaps you were born to take up this cause. You have a purpose in life. I shall see you again in Allahabad during the coming holidays," he concluded.

I nodded my head to humour him, but from then on I tried to avoid him. I did not tell Mum in my weekly letter to her. I received Mum's and Danny's letters frequently, but always made sure I read Mum's letter in the privacy of my room, destroying it afterwards. We corresponded in Hindi and I felt embarrassed that if the other Anglo-Indian staff knew that my mother was not able to write in English they would gossip. I was also afraid that if anyone found out about it, I would have to explain to them who my father was and how I came to be born of an Indian mother and an American father. I could not tell a lie and spin some story like Violet would have done.

Father Evans battled alone with the Church till one day he was found dead in his room amongst his papers and the typewriter. He was sick and no one knew. He had not been eating with the other priests and mostly keeping to himself. He had no income and whatever he had he spent on the papers and correspondence, treating himself with his own homoeopathic medications. He was given a priestly funeral in Allahabad.

✣ ✣ ✣ ✣ ✣

Violet had kept in touch with me regularly writing about every adventure she had with her boyfriends and always asked me for advice about them. Once she wrote of a rich Indian prince who was deeply in love with her. She met him at a dance and he fell in love with her at first sight. He proposed marriage and was going to give her a house in her name if she accepted. Her letter distressed me since Aunt Natasha and Aunt Clarke always warned us against rich Hindus who took advantage of Christians and Anglo-Indians deserting them once their infatuation was over. But the very next mail brought me a letter telling me she had abandoned the thought of the prince, since she had found a true love.

Not long after that letter, I received a telegram from Violet inviting me to Mussoorie immediately to watch her school carnival. It was impossible to take leave, so I did not reply. Two days later she visited me for a day. I was teaching at the time when she walked into my class and said she had come to show me the carnival flag that she had painted and for which she had received much praise from the school. At the same time, she had been upset that I had not turned up even though she had sent the telegram. I was very much taken with her love and concern. She looked upon me as a mother and valued my approval of anything she did. We had lunch together and I proudly introduced her to everyone as my talented younger sister. I was sad to see her leave that evening. She had spent a night to reach me and her return would take another night just to be with me for a day!

I had been waiting to hear from Danny to learn his date of departure. Unfortunately, after a short silence, I received a letter from England. In his letter he explained that he had been busy during his last few days before departing could not write. He added that he loved me and would write till he returned. He asked me to wait for him and spend my time studying and teaching.

There were a few other young teachers at the school who also had boyfriends. We all spent time discussing our male friends and trying to help each other in our loneliness.

Not long after Violet's visit, Mum decided to surprise me with a visit. I quietly took her to my room as I was ashamed to let the others know that I had an Indian mother who wore a *sari* and could not speak English. I was also afraid that I would have to explain to everyone about my parents and background if they saw her and face the same humiliations and blackmailing as in Allahabad. The Anglo-Indian school staff were very British in their outlook. Most Indian Christians knew English and wore dresses as well as live British style, like the Anglo-Indians. Mum preferred to stay as she was since Papa liked her as such. Papa had learnt Hindi to communicate with her. He had never wanted to change my mother. Besides, Mum mixed only with the nurses who were poor Indian Christians. She would say that she was an Indian and would remain so and was proud to wear her *sari*.

I spent the day with Mum in my room and did not even take her to the dining- room for meals, as did the others when their relatives came. I had our meals served in my room. Mum was very quiet; perhaps she understood. She told me that she had come to see how I was faring. She spent the day tidying my room. In the evening I saw her off at the station, promising to visit Allahabad the following weekend and every holiday.

I felt very guilty after she left and cried myself to sleep. I felt helpless in the face of my fate. I loved my mother very much but I was afraid of the people around me who never spared me the pains of humiliations.

Shortly after Mum left I had a problem at work. I was caught by the Principal for covering for a teacher friend, Moira Joachim. She had been getting some students to do corrections for her in the room while she went out with her boyfriend, the father of one of the students from her class. I knew about it but did not tell anyone. Moira failed one of the students who had been doing the corrections for her. That student made a complaint against her to the Principal and Moira was immediately dismissed. I was severely reprimanded for not informing on her. I broke down when I was scolded and explained to the Principal that I had been emotionally disturbed because of the way in which I had treated my mother. I also told her the reason why. So I confided in her about my origin. Somehow I believed she would understand as Mrs Clarke had and won her forgiveness and friendship. I realised later that I had developed a pattern of behaviour according to which I would connect any failure in life to my being the daughter of a priest and thus a feeling of self-pity. I could not face rejection and failure.

I went home for the Christmas holidays. Violet also came from Mussoorie. She decided to resign from the school and take up a position in Jhansi, the place where we two had once stayed in the orphanage. She managed to find a teaching position in the English Convent next to the orphanage.

In Jhansi she met Second Lieutenant Leslie Springett, a senior student from Mussoorie who had joined the Air Force. Violet and Leslie were friendly for eighteen months. He was determined to marry her and even became engaged to her against his parents' wishes. But his parents disliked Violet, because they had heard of her flirtatious nature and her origin as the deserted daughter of a Jesuit priest, but Leslie was extremely fond of her. The Springetts were very good Catholics and proud of their family background. They wanted a good Indian Catholic girl from a respectable family for their son.

After a year of teaching in Jhansi she resigned and settled in Kanpur closer to Allahabad. Leslie still visited her but after a few months Violet broke the engagement because she received a nasty letter from Leslie's mother condemning her and stating that she would rather disown her son than ever accept Violet as part of their family.

By then Enid had also taken up a position in Kanpur. Violet and Enid, taught in the same school, while Helen stayed on in Allahabad with Aunt Natasha and taught in the English Convent School we attended as children.

27

My trip to the USA and the search

The following year, 1965, I saw on the noticeboard an invitation for any member of staff, to apply for inclusion in an 'Experiment in International Living' scheme, through which teachers and members of other professions could visit any part of the world including the USA.

I decided to apply and begin my plan to find my father. Besides, ever since Danny left for England I wanted to go overseas. I thought this to be the opportunity to enable me to fulfil both the dreams of meeting my father and showing Danny that I had also been overseas and improved my status.

I met Dr Tripathi, the representative for the scheme in Lucknow, who also organised beauty contests and other competitions. He had the reputation of being a womaniser and was always ready to oblige a good-looking woman. Dr Tripathi was a tall, thin man, in his mid-thirties, of light-brown complexion with a bald patch in the middle of his head. He interviewed me in his clinic when I submitted my application. I'll never forget his scrutinising eyes when he took my application forms. I had obtained an excellent recommendation from my Principal and a similar character reference from the parish priest in Allahabad, Father George.

Dr Tripathi asked me questions about my ambitions and aims in life. I answered idealistically and patriotically, clearly impressing him. He assured me he would see that the application was sent to Delhi and he would do his best to see mine accepted. I was wearing a straight dress and was very slim but shapely. I also had an innocent and shy expression. He may have thought me 'a tasty catch'! As I was leaving he said with a feline smile:

"When you are selected, we must celebrate with dinner and a movie."

"Of course, Sir, we will celebrate the occasion but first, you must see that I get selected," I replied with a very sweet smile.

"I shall do my best and even try and get you a scholarship which would cover most of your expenses. You would have to pay only two thousand and five hundred *rupees* towards your trip to the USA and back."

He concluded by saying that the administrators of the program preferred pure Indians, whilst I looked Anglo-Indian and had a European name, but that he would strongly recommend me because of all the character references I had and because I had promised to celebrate the success by going out with him.

I was one of the five selected from Lucknow. I had to see Dr Tripathi for a photograph to be published in the local newspaper. I was then twenty-four but looked only nineteen. While we were being photographed, Dr Tripathi reminded me of my promise. I smiled very cutely, telling him that I would definitely keep it some other time, as I was a bit too busy that day. In the crowd of organisers that evening he could not press the issue. Needless to say, I did not go out with him.

✣ ✣ ✣ ✣ ✣

I had to get two thousand and five hundred *rupees*! No one at home had money to lend. My Principal, Miss Gresseux, was kind enough to advance me one thousand *rupees* to be repaid in instalments each month from my salary until I left for the USA. Mum managed five hundred *rupees* and Father De'Souza, the new parish priest in Allahabad, who was a very kind man and told me that he had met my father when he was just a young Seminarian in Allahabad, lent me five hundred *rupees*. I promised to repay Father De'Souza when I returned. I was still short of five hundred *rupees*!

I had been corresponding with Mrs Trombley in the USA, since I first wrote to her after I had discovered her address in the file with my Papa's papers, in Uncle Eddie's box. I wrote to inform her of my proposed trip to the USA and my inability to come up with the remaining five hundred *rupees*. Mrs Trombley immediately sent me a cheque of US one hundred dollars in reply to my letter and also invited me to stay in her house in

Toledo, Ohio. That one hundred gave me enough money to pay the five hundred *rupees* and to buy her a 22-carat gold pin with Amethyst stone for her coat. She had asked me to buy a pin in the shape of a peacock with the remainder of the money.

Then clothes for the trip? I had to get a few good *saris* as I was going as an Indian. I had only the two good *saris* that Danny had given. A silk *sari* cost over two to three hundred *rupees* then, whereas my salary was only one hundred and ten *rupees* per month as a teacher. Mum earned one hundred and twenty *rupees* a month as a midwife nurse. We could not afford to buy silk *saris*, but fortunately, Mum's medical superintendent's daughter, Sumita, presented me with two of her old *saris*, which were in good condition. She also lent me her suitcase. I was ready for my trip to the USA, full of hope of finding my Papa and of meeting Danny in London on the way back.

"I hope you return, Minnie!" Mum said to me one evening. I hugged her and assured her that I would be away for only two months.

I had to resign from the school where I taught in Lucknow, since I was going overseas for two months, but the Principal, Miss Gresseux, said that she would accept me back when I returned provided there was a vacancy.

I wrote to Danny telling him of my selection and he was delighted. He invited me to visit him on my return trip. Uncle David visited Allahabad before I left and gave me the address of a Jesuit priest, a friend of his, who was living in the USA. Uncle asked me to contact him adding that his friend would know my father's whereabouts. Uncle David saw me in Delhi before I left. He stayed at the Jesuit College, St Xavier's, in Old Delhi and also arranged for me to stay at the Jesuit College guest-house for the night before I was to join the outgoing group. I was very impressed with the Jesuit College, St Xavier's and asked Uncle to try to get me a teaching position in that school when I returned.

"You will never be allowed to teach in any of the Jesuit schools in India because of your father," Uncle replied.

I felt terrible when he said that, it was like being an outcast of the Catholic Church just because my father was a Jesuit priest.

I did not have many options as I could neither become a nun nor teach in any of the schools run by the society he initially joined. I felt that I was the innocent victim of the Church.

✣ ✣ ✣ ✣ ✣

It would have been very expensive for Mum and Violet to go to Delhi to see me off, so they said goodbye at the Allahabad station. Mum promised to welcome me home on my return. Father De'Souza helped me with the passport formalities. He knew some officers in the Passport Department in Allahabad.

We had three days orientation at the Lodi Hotel in Delhi. During this time it was explained what the 'Experiment in International Living' project meant and why we should consider ourselves as delegates from India, representing Indian culture. We were to give an image of India to people who had never been to India and might never visit India. One hundred and eighty participants were there, divided into different groups. All were bound for different parts of the world. I was the only Anglo-Indian and a Christian.

There were eight of us in the teachers' group. Everyone was married and elderly except Nivedita and myself. I was the youngest. Dr Tripathi was at the orientation. He met me one day and asked why I had not seen him again, I made my excuse and promised to see him on my return; of course I never did.

Mr and Mrs Trevedi were in charge of the 'All India Experiment in International Living' scheme. On the day of the departure, Mrs Trevedi stood at the gate before we boarded the plane to wish everyone goodbye individually. When my turn came, she particularly reminded me that I was to represent India and so had to act accordingly wherever I was. It was fairly clear that, since I was an Anglo-Indian, I had to be especially warned, since they, like all Hindus, who consider themselves to be the true Indians, had a view that we were more western in outlook than Indian.

✣ ✣ ✣ ✣ ✣

It was my first plane trip. I felt lonely, since everyone spoke in different Indian languages and stayed with their own kind. I knew no one, yet I was excited, since I was going to the USA where I was determined to find my father. I found the plane journey very exciting, having come from a very poor home from a small city of India. It was wonderful to look out of the window and see the clouds. I made several visits to the toilet so I could use the many perfumed toiletries. I had never seen some of the items displayed. The food was delicious and I ate every bite, wishing at the same time that the others at home could have been there to enjoy them too. One of the teachers from our group, being a strict Brahman, had trouble with the meals since his diet was normally vegetarian and there was very little of that available, except in the form of salads. I heard the elderly vegetarian teacher demand a vegetarian egg. At the time I could not figure out what a vegetarian egg would look like! I had never tasted the variety of food served to us along with the soft drinks and juices, which were very rich and tasty. The Pan Am Air hostesses were very polite and caring and I felt like a *Maharani* (chief queen).

There were three groups for the USA, doctors, students and teachers. We all disembarked in New York where we had a day's orientation and were given the names of our host families. We were introduced to the American lifestyle and culture. The next day we were introduced to our host families. Mine was a Jewish family, Mr and Mrs Machtey.

Mr Machtey was a lawyer. The couple had a boy and three girls who were teenagers. They drove me to their home at Mt Kisco, about 60 kilometres from New York City. I was given a room to myself and had to call them father and mother as did the others, since I was to live as a family member. It was wonderful to sleep in a bed of my own with clean, soft mattress and warm covers. For the first time I saw a television it was colour!

The Machteys were kind and caring. Mrs Machtey was a tall slim lady with short grey hair, in her late forties. She was full of enthusiasm and adventure. She seemed to be the one who attended to the needs of the family and the home and was the member of many charitable organisations. Mr. Machtey was a quiet gentleman, tall and slim but bald, aged about fifty. He left for New York every morning by train and returned late in the evening, Mrs Machtey and I exchanged information on Indian and American cultures. I liked the Americans and yearned to meet my father. I wanted to confide in Mrs Machtey about him, but the thought that she could also hate me as Mrs Carter, did kept me from doing so.

I enjoyed my stay with the Machteys who were very friendly and considerate. Being brought up as an Anglo-Indian, I had no problem assimilating to the Western style of living in their home, whereas the others in the group found it difficult, especially the elderly Brahman teacher. He was unable to sit and eat his vegetarian meals at the table with his host family of non-vegetarians. Also, since he did his *pooja* (chanting of prayers with offerings of flowers and fruits to the deity) every morning, he found it difficult to find an appropriate place and water for the service. He used the water from the kitchen tap, as he felt the water in the bathroom was too impure and unholy to be used for the Gods. The people he lived with had no understanding of what he was doing. Unfortunately he could not explain to them either, as he did not have a good command of English, being a teacher of Sanskrit and never having had much opportunity to speak any other language except his own mother-tongue, Hindi.

In India fruit was expensive, but in the USA I ate it to my heart's content, as well as chocolates and other food. I felt guilty to see food wasted after the meals. I had lived in the orphanages and witnessed the poor children picking from the street bins for small particles of food in India and wished I could somehow parcel up all the wasted food from their kitchen bin to India for the poor street kids. One day I introduced the Machteys to Indian curry and rice dishes which they enjoyed.

Every few days I wrote to Mum assuring her of my love and early return. Once I wrote to Aunt Natasha and sent my love to both Enid and Helen but Aunt did not reply personally but sent her love in Mum's letter.

My stay with the Machteys came to an end after three weeks and I was very sorry to leave them. The family saw me off at the bus stop where all the Indian members were to meet before proceeding to New York City. They gave me gifts and a small amount of pocket money. That was the first time I learnt of the Jews in America. My knowledge of the Jewish community was confined to what was in the Bible, because in India I could only learn Indian and British history. I had never realised that there were Jews also in the USA.

We stayed in a hotel in the New York City for three days after our home stay period was complete. I spent the nights in my hotel room watching the programs on the colour television.

One evening we were invited to a clam-bake party, where I thought I saw a man, who resembled my father in age and appearance, as I remembered him. So I spent the entire party staring at him, trying to attract his attention and summoning up the courage to ask him whether he remembered his little Minnie! Fortunately, I could not do so. Perhaps he became aware of the Indian lady in a *sari*, trying to make a pass at him! Later, I consoled myself with the feeling that he might not be my father and that even if he were, Aunt Trombley would help me find him somehow.

Throughout my stay I searched for Papa everywhere I went. I had only the memory of him from the age of three and four. I had no photograph. Apart from his image blazoned in my memory, I remembered his voice and the sound of his last words spoken to Mum, as he left the house in Saharanpore in 1944; "*Agnes, ish ko ley jao*" (Agnes, take her away.) in perfect Hindi. That voice of his was so clear in my mind, haunting, as it was soft-spoken and concerned.

The memory of that last time was so vivid and made such a great impact on my life that I couldn't forget him. That parting left a child waiting for his return. I never considered his reaction when he would meet me again, after he had actually forgotten us, all I knew was that I had to meet him again, my Papa, who had promised to return.

The three-day stay in New York came to an end and we travelled to Washington DC in a Greyhound bus. I was amazed at the cleanliness of the buses, so different from those in India and also that they were not over-crowded. At home I found it safer to travel by rickshaw instead of bus, though it was very slow. Greyhound buses were comfortable and made regular toilet stops at clean stations. In India the toilets at the bus stops stank of human urine, like those at picture theatres. But what horrified me at the bus stops in the USA were the obscene books sold openly. I looked at them out of the corner of my eye and wondered how people could actually read them! I had never seen them in India.

I was wearing a sky-blue nylon *sari* with a maroon blouse. Just as I was trying to get into one of the buses after a short stop, I heard someone speak. "Hello there! May I help you carry your suitcase? It seems a bit too heavy for your delicate hands." It was an American young man about my age.

He took the suitcase and helped me into the bus, while the elderly Indian teachers stared at me with disapproval. The young gentleman tried to sit beside me, but Mr Joshi, the elderly Brahman Indian teacher, brushed past him and took the seat. It seemed as if Mr Joshi was keeping an eye on me as a responsible representative of India. When the bus started I heard the same young gentleman say to me from two seats away:

"Which country are you from?"

"India."

After a little silence he asked, "How old are you?"

Before I could answer Mr Joshi said "No, no, a lady's age is never asked, young man. It is not polite. What do you say, Miss Lyons?"

The other Indian teachers smiled at him and began discussing the difference between the Western and Indian cultures amongst themselves in Hindi. It was enough to discourage my young admirer from further questioning.

We stayed in a five-star hotel in Washington, DC for five days. On the first day nothing was organised, so we took a stroll around the hotel, which was by the side of a busy main road. I was a small town-girl; the other teachers were from Delhi, Bombay and Ahmedabad. They seemed rich and must have owned cars as they knew about roads and traffic rules, whereas I did not. I remember leaving the building that morning. By the time I came out the others had reached the other side of the road, so I tried to catch up with them and ran across the road.

Halfway down the street I stopped, as there was a stream of oncoming cars from the opposite direction. I had not realised that the road had definite two-way lanes. I was used to the roads in India with no set rules and pedestrians cross the road anywhere and anytime, as long as they are able to survive doing so! There I was in my green-and-white *sari* standing in the middle of the road with cars speeding on both sides. Eventually, after a long wait, I got across, having had a lesson in US road rules.

Among the many other arranged sightseeing tours I particularly remember our trip to watch the changing of the guards, the White House, President Roosevelt Museum and the Wax Museum. The Wax Museum was the last we visited before we left for Ohio and I was the first to complete seeing the place, so I sat and waited for the others near the reception desk. I was very still, staring at the people around and trying to find my father in the crowd, when a man came close to me, with his hand stretched and his finger about to touch my nose.

"What do you want?" I said sharply and quickly moved out of his way.

"I am terribly sorry, I was not sure whether you were also a wax model like the ones inside, so I was going to touch you. I was also wondering why a wax model with those foreign clothes was placed here," he was apologetic and disappeared through the exit. I was amused and could not help laughing along with those around me.

We visited department stores in our spare time. I had never seen one before and was full of plans to buy things for Mum and Aunt and the others. My Indian friends bought nylon curtain materials with small prints to use as *saris*. Nylon *saris* were very expensive in India then as they had just started manufacturing them. I managed to buy two, one each for Mum and Aunt with the money given as pocket money by the Machteys.

Our next destination was Oxford University in Miami, Ohio, where we were each going to spend a week with an American room-mate. The women were placed in one hostel and the men in another, but we met each day to discuss our experiences. We were shocked at the freedom of the sex relationships between the students. All of us felt acutely embarrassed to see young couples love-making on the lawns, as this could never happen in India, I thought. One day we saw a notice about a dance to be held in the canteen area. We all dressed our best for the occasion, only to find that the students were dressed casually. The jazz band music that was played was too fast for us! They mostly did the Barn Dance in-groups. We felt out of place sitting in our best clothes and not knowing the dances.

Everywhere we went there were stories and photographs of us as delegates from India, in the local newspapers. We were introduced to a few VIPs and visited some interesting places in Ohio, one of them was the local newspaper office. On those occasions I always looked for my father, because I knew from the papers left with Uncle Eddie he was from Michigan, being born in Detroit and I searched for him amongst the many faces in Ohio.

The time for our return to India was imminent. I had been regularly writing to my mother, giving her descriptions of my adventures, but not telling her of my search for my father. I also kept up my correspondence with Danny in England. After the university campus stay we had free time for one week. It was then I went to visit my Aunt, Mrs Emma Trombley, in Toledo, Ohio. She had paid for my fare from Oxford, Ohio, to Toledo by local airline. I remember the flight to Toledo because I met a young American air force cadet about my age, on his way home for a short holiday. He sat next to me and asked my name. He said he would like to meet an Indian girl since he had heard of their faithfulness and loyalty. He also asked me just before the plane landed in Toledo, if I would go out with him for dinner that evening. I was surprised and felt flattered, but could not accept it because of my loyalty to Danny. I made an excuse saying I was leaving the city that night.

Aunt Emma was waiting to receive me. She looked a very motherly and kind lady. On the way home she told me she was surprised at my being so fair, because most Indians were dark-skinned like Afro-Americans and had a particularly strong unpleasant smell. She added that my mother must have been a pretty and fair Indian to have a daughter like me.

Aunt Emma's bungalow was beautiful with a fine rose garden in the front. I met Uncle George, her husband and Papa's cousin. He was in his mid-sixties and very quiet but being ill, he spent most of his time in a big chair in front of the fireplace. All their children were married and had their own homes. I was again given a room to myself. In Aunt's house I liked the large bathroom best. It was pink and contained all sorts of body lotions, bubble baths and rose-perfumed bath salts. It reminded me of the great Emperor Shahjahan and his wife Mumtaz Mahal, in whose memory he built the Taj Mahal in Agra, India. During my school days I had read that the Empress Mumtaz Mahal had a passion for roses and had used rose scents in her baths as did her Aunt, Empress Noorjahan. There in Mrs Trombley's house I felt like an empress bathing in rose-scented bubbles! In India I bathed under the tap or used a tin mug to pour water over myself and had only ordinary soap with hardly any perfume.

Aunt Emma took me shopping the following day and bought me a beautiful dress with lace at the neck and sleeves and another lovely blue suit-dress with a white lace blouse. Then she bought me some underclothes, stockings, white gloves and a small hat, as she wanted me to accompany her to Church the following day. She said that she preferred me in the dress and while I was with her I wore only dresses. After the service she told me that she had taken me to Church so that my father's relatives would meet me. She did not talk with them much because they had not been good to her, as she was a Protestant. The majority of my father's relatives were staunch Catholics. They had treated Aunt Emma badly for marrying into a Catholic family and remaining a Protestant. She said that my father used to visit her occasionally before he had joined the priesthood. She remembered him sitting at the back of their old house fixing radios, as he was very interested in them. He spent hours pulling a radio to pieces and then putting it back together again just to learn how it worked. She said that my father was a very intelligent and curious child.

Aunt Emma informed me that my father visited her after

he returned from India in 1947 and had again visited in 1949 when he had eventually decided to leave the priesthood and settle down in Denver. As far as she knew he was still there, but he had never communicated with any family members since then.

I was disappointed that Aunt Trombley was unable to tell me of Papa's whereabouts as she was my best hope to help me meet him. But I was determined to find him before I left the USA.

One day Aunt said she was holding a tea party in my honour. She put an announcement in the local newspaper to give relatives a chance to meet me. Unfortunately, none of the relatives turned up for the party at which I was the hostess. A few of her friends and her daughter came. She said that my father's relations did not wish to know me because they were under the impression that I was a dark-skinned Indian. Aunt Trombley only announced in the papers, 'Esther Lyons from India is a guest in my house and I am giving a party her honour. Anyone interested in meeting her is welcome'.

The next day, I decided to ring the Jesuit priest whose address Uncle David had given me. He was delighted to hear from an Indian whom he considered as a niece of Brother David Rai, (I had introduced myself as such). He was a friend of Uncle David. After a chat he invited me to an exhibition on Jesuit Missions throughout the world. Aunt Emma encouraged me to go.

I set out in the Greyhound bus but the priest was disappointed I was wearing a dress. He wanted me to be the representative of the Patna Mission dressed in a *sari*. He had an Indian *sari* displayed on the stall, which he asked me to wear and act as a live model. I did not have a petticoat long enough to wear under the *sari*, but since Father insisted, I wore the *sari* over my blue short skirt and lacy blouse! I enjoyed my afternoon in the stall chatting about India and giving information to people about Indian Catholics converted by the American Jesuits.

At the end of the day, when Father took me to the bus stop, I disclosed to him that I was the daughter of Father Michael Lyons and asked him if he knew his whereabouts as I was anxious to meet him just once before I left the USA two days later. Father was taken aback, but was very understanding. He said that he knew about us as he was in India when it all happened and that he did know where my father was and would try to get in touch with him on my behalf. It seemed that my father had felt obligated to remain in touch with the Chicago and Michigan Jesuits and had been giving financial help to young seminarians studying for the priesthood.

We went to a telephone booth nearby, he looked up the directory and rang my father. I stood outside, my heart beating fast, tears of joy ready to fall. I had won and at last I was going to speak to my dearest Papa after so many years. But it was not to happen that way, because, to my great disappointment, Father said he was unable to get in touch with Papa as he was not at the address. I noticed that he looked red and rather embarrassed.

I asked him for my father's telephone number and told him that I would try to contact him again myself. Father seemed hesitant, but gave me the number saying that my Papa was living with a woman and that she had taken the call. It was she who had divulged that my father had left the place and that she did not know when he would return. She had told him that the place was only their office and that he did not live there.

Although Uncle David informed me earlier that my father was living with a woman, I did not want to believe him, because I didn't understand how a priest was allowed to live with a woman openly, when he was not allowed to live with his family; Mum and us two, in India. I had learnt in Catechism that 'once a priest is always a priest,' and that priests are not allowed to live with a woman and have children. I remembered from my childhood that Papa always wore ordinary civilian clothes whenever he was at home in Saharanpore. I had never seen him in clerical clothes. I was determined, in spite of the news, which the Jesuit priest gave me, to see my Papa and speak to him just once. I went to the USA mainly for that reason.

I thanked the priest for his understanding and kindness. On my return to Aunt Emma's house I told her what happened. She surprised me by saying she was aware he was living with a woman in Denver, but did not tell me because she did not want to hurt me. She advised me to forget my father and get on with my life. But I insisted that I had to make contact with him just once. Before I went to bed I rang the telephone number given to me by the Jesuit priest, a lady's voice informed me that Mr Lyons did not live there and that she did not know his whereabouts. Aunt Emma saw me off at the Toledo airport and again advised me to get on with my own life and forget the past, adding that even my father's only brother Frank had decided to forget him forever. But I knew that I had to meet my Papa and keep trying till I spoke to him just once, though did not know how I would manage it within the remaining twelve hours to be spent in New York before I left for India forever.

With a very heavy heart I left for New York the next day. We assembled in a designated hotel that evening ready to depart for India the following morning at six.

28

Denver, Colorado, 1965
The father I could not claim

Every Indian member of the group were present at the hotel in New York eager to return home. But I was upset because I had failed in my personal mission. After dinner I tried to contact my father again, but the same woman's voice said that he was not there. About 10.30pm I rang again and had the same response, since I was desperate, I said to the lady:

"Please tell Mr Lyons I am Minnie, the little daughter he left behind in India. I came here with an Indian group and have to return early tomorrow morning. I just want to talk to him once before I leave. I am speaking from a hotel in New York."

I broke down as I said those words to her. There was silence, as if she was shocked. I had to put the phone down abruptly, as I could not stop sobbing. After that I walked back to my room wiping my tears and feeling very frustrated at my helplessness and the thought that I would never meet my father.

Nivedita and I shared the room. She was very excited.

"*Beti, mei tera pita hoo*" (daughter, I am your father), he said in perfect Hindi as he used to speak to Mum.

"Papa, I know it is you, I can speak in English now," I said very excitedly. But he continued in his fluent Hindi, saying he knew I was capable of good English, but that he would like to speak in Hindi because he did not want anyone listening to us to understand what he was saying. I was a bit puzzled as to why he was so secretive. He said that it had taken him time to find out the location of the hotel where I was staying. I had only given the name of the hotel in my disturbed state of mind when I spoke to the woman. I found it incredible that he reached me.

"I do not want you to return to India. I want you to come to me in Denver. Give me the name of your Co-ordinator there and also remind me the date of your birth. As well, tell me your height and weight."

He asked me to describe myself, as he said he needed all the particulars to get me to him in Denver. I was happy that at last my dream of meeting my father was to come true. I waited near the telephone since Papa said he was going to get back to me again after he had spoken to the Co-ordinator. Nivedita remained fast asleep in her bed as I sat waiting for Papa's call. It was long past twelve midnight. He rang again about thirty minutes later, though to me it seemed an eternity. He informed me that the Indian Co-ordinator, Mr Dhawan, had not agreed to send me to him, but that nevertheless, he had already booked my flight to Denver by the domestic airline and instructed the hostess to give me twenty-six dollars cash till I reached him. He again insisted that I was to go to him and not return to India. Just as I finished talking to Papa, the Indian Co-ordinator, Mr Dhawan, walked straight into the room, without any warning.

"Miss Lyons, what is this all about? I have just had a call from someone who claimed to be your father. You have always said that your father was dead and have also stated this in your application in India. Now this American calls to say that he is your father and that he wants to see you. In your application you said that you were Indian, you never mentioned having an American father! How can that be so? I am responsible for every one of you. I cannot leave you here with anyone who has no authority over you."

Mr Dhawan was annoyed. I tried to explain to him that I had not known that my father was still alive, that my natural father was an American, I had not seen him for more than twenty years. I did not remember him, everyone said that he was dead. As I had found him I wanted to go to him.

"I am sorry, I cannot let you do so. What proof have you that he is your father? What will I say to Mrs Trevedi and to your mother in Delhi? No, you will have to return with us to India. I cannot give you the permission to stay back."

He left the room angrily and banged the door behind him. As soon as he left, there was another call from my father. He continued speaking to me in perfect Hindi.

"Minnie, I have made all the necessary arrangements for

you. You must come to me and not return to India. Do you understand? I am waiting for you here." His insistence sounded desperate.

I was dazed, not knowing what to do. Of course, I wanted to see him, but I had not expected such a situation. It confused me. I could not understand how my father, who was supposed to be a Catholic priest, could have the power to arrange for my trip to him in Denver in spite of the fact that the Indian Co-ordinator in-charge of the group was determined that I should return to India. Under the circumstances, I decided to take things as they came; after all I had spoken to Papa and learnt that he loved and accepted me. I became troubled with the situation. A thought did occur to me as to whether the man on the phone, claiming to be my father, was after all my Papa! Or, what if he should keep me back and never allow me to see my mother or sister again in India. After all, he seemed to be so authoritative and domineering! Just the same the desire to meet my father decided my fate.

After Papa's last call near two in the morning, I heard nothing further so went to bed. As soon as I touched the pillow I fell asleep. Nivedita woke me up around four-thirty, as we had to be at the airport by six. I got dressed reluctantly, still wondering whether Papa would be able to organise my stay. I went down to the breakfast-room with my luggage around five. As I sat down at the table for breakfast, two young and handsome Americans, dressed in formal dark suits, took their places on either side of my chair. One of them asked me as he sat down.

"Are you Esther Lyons?"

I told him I was and before I could question him as to how he came to know me, he explained that they were from the police department and that my father had complained to them that I was being prevented from going to him. They were going to make sure that I went to him and not to India.

"You must get onto the plane to Denver and not to India. Understand?" One of them said to me in a very authoritative manner. I did not know what to say. I felt like a child about to be kidnapped!

Mr Dhawan walked up to me and asked me to get into the Greyhound bus bound for the airport. There was nothing I could do but follow him to the bus. I saw the two young Americans disappear as I boarded the bus. I thought that was the end of them and my quest to meet my father. When everyone got in, the bus set out for the international airport. I sat at the back and looked out of the back window, to my shock I saw the two Americans who said they were from the police department in the distance, they were following the bus on their motorbikes.

At the airport Mr Dhawan made me hurriedly join the queue of people waiting to have their passports checked. As I stood there, I looked around for the two Americans since they had followed me all the way. They were nowhere to be seen. Then suddenly a voice came over the loudspeaker saying: "Calling Esther Lyons, a member of the Experiment in International Living Group from India. She is to board the plane bound to Denver and not the Air-India flight."

The announcement was repeated over and over till the American Head Office Co-ordinator walked up to Mr Dhawan and asked for an explanation. He had come to see us off at the airport. Both Mr Dhawan and the US Co-ordinator walked up to me and asked me to explain the situation. I told him that I had managed to contact my father whom I had not seen since I was a little girl of three and half, that I had been informed by everyone that he had deserted us and his whereabouts was unknown and therefore, he was assumed dead. But that I had found him and he wanted me to go to him in Denver, but that, Mr Dhawan would not give me permission to go.

"Do you want to go to him?" he asked.

"Of course, I do," I said. I did think that a visit to my father would do me good after travelling all the way to USA. There would be little chance of my ever visiting USA again once I returned to India.

He asked me my age before going to the two young police officers. Next, I saw him walk towards the telephone booth to speak to my father. After a long time on the phone, he went back to Mr Dhawan. They had a long chat, before; he came to me again and announced that I was free to go to my father if I chose to do so. I was overjoyed. As I was picking up my suitcases to follow the two police officers, I remembered my dear mother and sister who would be waiting for me at Delhi Airport. I turned to Mr Dhawan and asked him to give my mother the thirty US dollars I had saved and tell her that I was with my father and would return soon. He looked troubled, but compelled.

I watched the plane leave for India at the International Airport then felt doubts in my decision. I was also puzzled at my father's power to manage my stay. The two young officers walked on either side of me, towards the plane waiting to leave for Denver not far from the same airport. They did not leave till the plane taxied to the runway, as if making sure of my departure to Denver and my father.

I was the only passenger on the plane. As soon as I sat in my seat, the hostess gave me twenty-six dollars. She said my father wanted me to have it. I sat by the window in a dilemma. I nervous about what I was doing was right. I knew my mother would be at the international airport in Delhi, waiting to receive me. It would have cost her a lot of money to take that trip. She would have borrowed the money from a money-lender, as she often did. I worried how she would feel not seeing me return as promised, but then the thought that Mr Dhawan would give her my message and the gift, made me feel confident that she would understand. Once the plane bound for Denver was in the air, I thought only of my dear Papa and how to relate to him after so many years.

✣ ✣ ✣ ✣ ✣

It was afternoon when the plane touched down at Denver. I wore a green *sari* because I thought that my father would find it easier to recognise me in a *sari*. At the airport I looked for the tall, handsome man, I remembered from my childhood, but I could not see anyone of that description. While I was looking around, a plump, semi-bald man, about my height, walked up to me and said in the voice I could not forget.

"Minnie? Are you Minnie?"

It took me a moment to answer. Obviously, this was my father, but he was so different from the memory I had carried and loved so dearly! I could not help but stare and scrutinise him from head to toe. Shyly I smiled.

" Papa!"

He gave me a gentle kiss and a hug. I was shocked at the change in his physical appearance. Then remembered he'd left a little girl in India and was greeting a young woman in America.

I did not know what to say, so just stayed silent, observing and listening to his every word. I could not believe the truth—the bitter sweetness of it—my Papa, my father I had dreamed of, the man who had obsessed me throughout my life, the man who left me unable to lead a normal life!

He was beside me, I only had to reach across to hold his hand.

I loved him yet hated that he left me.

I longed for him to hold me again yet hated that he had turned his back on us.

I wanted him back in India with us, yet was angry with him for presumably living a happy life of comfort in the US while we were so disadvantaged.

"You have grown into a beautiful young lady, just like your mother! I remembered you still like the little girl I used to throw up in the air," Papa said as he helped me with my suitcase. He told me how he had to convince the American Co-ordinator that he was going to support me and take care of me while I was with him in the USA, as I was his very precious daughter.

Soon we were on our way to the house in his Buick car. He told me that he lived in a small place called Arvada, in the suburb of Denver. He had come to know of my visit to the USA and had planned to visit me quietly one day, just to see me from a distance. But when I phoned and told the lady-friend of his that I was leaving the next day, he became desperate, as he was under the impression I was going to be in the USA for a long time. Papa explained that Petronilla, the woman he lived with, was a Lithuanian. He had not told her anything about his family life in India. She was very understanding when I rang up and after he told her of my existence, she actually made him contact me, saying that his daughter was hers too and that he must bring me home. He then spoke to Petronilla on his car communication device, which he had invented.

Papa recalled how I used to sleep beside him when I was small, but since it was obvious I was too old to do so then they would fix up the bedroom beside theirs in the house. He was excited and talkative, while I sat quiet, listening to the voice of the man whom I had craved to meet all those years. I had such haunting memories of that soft, caring voice but he was different softly spoken, but concerned only about himself. He never once asked after Mum and Violet whom he had also left behind. He spoke only of his life with this other woman, who had taken my mother's place. We suffered so much because he had deserted us. Suddenly I found it difficult not to think of my dear mother and sister. Yet I sat there in silence beside him in his car, listening to him patiently.

We drove past the city into a wide stretch of empty, arid land, until we came to a gate, which he opened by pressing a button, after which he drove along a long driveway to a house. As he did, he pointed to the huge factory-like building in the distance surrounded by barbed wire and said that it was the Rocky Flats Plant, an atomic power station that was heavily patrolled and protected. The barbed wire was electrified and only a few people were allowed in and out. Papa said that he supplied the Rocky Flats Plant with Beryllium to trigger mechanism for Nuclear weapons and that he was the only one who knew how to smelt the Beryllium Ore from the mine near his house. Papa had to employ a couple of Afro-Americans to help him do so. He was the owner of the Beryl Ores Company. He said that he had secretly informed the authorities in the Rocky Flats Plant Station about his two daughters in India.

When we eventually stopped in front of the house, an elderly-looking woman came out to welcome me. I immediately took a dislike to her, because I could not help comparing her with my own delicate-looking mother; I felt hatred for the woman who had taken the love my father had for my mother. I thought of my mother's sufferings while this woman was enjoying the love and happiness that should have been my mother's. The woman was in her fifties, older than my mother, whilst Papa was then sixty-four, though he looked at least ten years older. She told me that Papa had spent the entire night telephoning around to arrange for my visit to him and that he had spent a large sum of money in that one night just to get me to Denver.

I was given the room, which must have been the guestroom. It had a display case containing many precious stones, both polished and unpolished. Papa had found those stones, some of them were from India, he'd said. The two shared the room adjacent to mine. The place was very quiet because it was kilometres away from other houses and the city. The two-bedroom house was on forty acres of land.

I woke early the next morning with Petronilla speaking on the radio in coded language. She was speaking to different parts of the world. She later told me that she was speaking to someone in Russia and could also speak to India where they had contacts in Madras and Delhi. Later I also realised that she was very careful about who visited them and had a bell which rang alerting them to anyone passing through the gate, which was about two kilometres down the hill. Petronilla met the visitors who came to their house. Papa always avoided them by staying indoors. Petronilla related to him the reason of their visit.

That first morning around eight, Papa came quietly to my room and was surprised to see me awake. He said that he had come to have a peep at me and to assure himself that I, his little Minnie, had really come to stay with him. We had our breakfast together. He was full of old memories of the past. He spoke of the poor untouchable people of India and the wonderful Indian food he missed. He asked me about the present plight of those people and I told him about the various changes in the last twenty years since India had become independent. We spent a lot of time talking about India and its people, but he was careful never to mention Mum. Sometimes I deliberately mentioned Mum or Violet and he would either listen without saying anything, or try to change the subject. Petronilla sat with us and listened to everything that was said. Once Papa asked me to sing a Hindi song and while I did so he taped my voice. I sang a very sad song about the loss of a dear one. It was meant to be an expression of my missing him. As days went past, I began getting more and more upset because I found I could not sit with my father alone and question him about his leaving us; as Petronilla always made sure she was with us. Every evening she took his blood pressure and fussed over him for his medications and rest. I wanted to rekindle his love and memories of Mum and Violet and get him back to India, but with Petronilla there it was impossible.

Papa enjoyed talking to me in Hindi, which we did frequently while Petronilla sat laughing. Every evening Papa gave me a small glass of red wine, something I had never known, to relax me and put me to sleep. I cooked Indian dishes for him and taught Petronilla some of them. I found she was very willing to learn Indian cookery.

One day Papa asked Petronilla to take me to the city and buy me a few dresses. So we drove in the big Buick. We went to a big department store where I chose two dresses, a maroon velvet with lace and a red and blue checked wool. They were both expensive and Petronilla seemed a bit annoyed at the cost, but did not refuse to buy them. I noticed that she signed the cheque as 'Mrs P Lyons'. I could not believe that the Church could give my father dispensation to marry and live as a lay person with an American woman in the USA, when he could not do so in India with the woman he loved and with whom he had two children.

One morning Petronilla was in the kitchen in a very revealing housecoat. She came to the table like that and stood beside Papa trying to butter his toast. I was disgusted at her walking around like that in full sight of my father. I could not help glancing at her in a way that displayed my repulsion. Papa caught my look and told her to change into more decent clothes, which she did at once. I could not help comparing Petronilla with my dear mother most of the time. My mother very gentle, simple, caring and loving, that woman was just the opposite; rough, exploitative and selfish, but intelligent enough to have hold over my father.

I spent two weeks with Papa, during which time he insisted daily that I should stay on with him in the USA and not return to India. He said that he would send me to the Boulder Denver

University for further studies and that I would be able to do more for both Mum and Violet from the USA than from India. It used to hurt me when he spoke like that, because he never once said that I could help them to America. I could not justify myself living in the lap of luxury, knowing what my dear Mum and sister would be going through in India. I had seen hungry children in the orphanage and on the streets. I had heard my sister being tormented about eating too much. So if I stayed, I would have them join us. But Papa only talked about me. There were times when I saw him sitting alone engrossed in deep thought. He shook his head from time to time as though he was talking to himself. Once I asked him what he was doing and he said to me that he was regretting what he could have done and did not do. He repeatedly said that my mother was very brave and good to have brought us up by herself.

There were days when I wanted to stay with Papa. I considered the idea of helping Mum and Violet from America. I did not wish to lose my father again. I was torn between my love for my Papa and that of my mother with the realisation of the struggle and poverty she had to endure.

One day a friend of Papa's dropped over and Petronilla introduced me to him as Papa's Indian friend's daughter who had come to stay for a few days. I was crushed. For the first time I knew I had to return to India to my mother who had openly accepted me as her daughter and had gone through a lot of embarrassment in doing so. I would stand by her. That evening the overseas news on the television reported that war between India and Pakistan had broken out. It showed scenes of bombing and heavy fighting at the India – China border, which strengthened my decision to return.. I told Papa that I was considering returning to India to Mum and Violet. Papa discouraged me and continued with his attempts to persuade me to stay with him. He said he had big plans to educate me in the USA. He had a small cottage in the mountains, he said, where he often went to hide and relax, where I could live and pursue my studies. I listened to his plans but in the end told him that Mum would be very upset if I did not return. Although I had craved to meet my father again, my plan included having him back in the same way as when we all lived together in Saharanpore. I never intended leaving Mum for him.

Eventually he accepted my decision because Petronilla made him realise I belonged to my mother, since she had raised me. He bought my ticket and planned my return trip through England, France and Rome to Bombay. He said I had two days stop-over in each country but could stay longer if I chose, as he would give me enough money in traveller's cheques to meet my expenses.

Suddenly I was not so committed to my decision. I loved my father and wanted to be with him, but at the same time I was concerned about Mum and Violet because the news on the television was frightening.

A few days before I left, Papa suggested that I should go out with him and learn to use his rifle in case I ever needed to defend myself in India. So we went into the backyard. I think this was to get me on my own without Petronilla. Papa set up cans as targets. He showed me how to aim and knock them over with bullets.

While he was loading the rifle he explained that he never really meant to leave us. He added that he never had a vocation. He was the eldest of the many children in his family. His mother was the only daughter of a very rich man in Detroit, a Senator. Papa's father, Patrick Lyons, did not have a stable job, which left them to face poverty often. He had drifted into alcoholism and violence. Papa said he had to work from the age of sixteen to help financially. He was idealistic and ambitious then.

His French mother was a staunch Catholic who had raised her children as such. At the time the Jesuit Mission in Chicago needed missionaries for India. He felt obligated to join the Jesuits and work for the conversion of the pagans in India. Since it was an honour for every Catholic family in the early twentieth century in USA to send their first son as a missionary, his mother was delighted. She encouraged him with the belief that it was God's plan and that they were blessed. His father was against it but eventually it was his mother's encouragement, which lead him to become a Jesuit Missionary. In turn the Jesuits promised to look after his parents and his younger brother and sisters.

He remained very close to his mother and the family, corresponding with them frequently but soon after Papa left for India his mother was found dead on the roadside. She had been mentally ill.

The Jesuits had not kept their promise.

The death of his mother upset him very much.

Papa said that about that time he started rebelling and was in conflict with the Jesuits in Patna Mission. He found my mother very comforting and affectionate. Papa had known her since she was a teenager and could not help loving her even when she joined the convent as a nun. He resigned from the Jesuits to live with her and take up the role of a father for Violet and me. Papa said Mum was very beautiful and petite, just like me. She was a very talented and capable woman and that he loved her very much and still did.

"Why did you leave her then?" I asked, cutting him short.

"I did not want to leave you all. I resigned from the Jesuits and tried to live with you all, but could not because both she and I were excommunicated. We were spied upon by the Jesuits wherever we went to live. I could not find a job of any sort in the British India as an ex-Jesuit priest. I tried everything, but failed. If I went to a petrol station for a job and the owner was a Protestant, he was told by the Catholic Church that I was a priest with a scandalous reputation and so I should not be employed. The Catholic employer would not help because it was a sin to encourage a priest to abandon his priestly duties. To them I was living in sin. In those days of the British Raj, every employer was either a Catholic or a Protestant.

Your mother and I had moved from place to place trying to find some way to support ourselves. At the time you were born in 1940, I had resigned from the Jesuits as a priest and was unemployed. I loved your mother and you, but did not know what to do. It was she who made me go back to the Church in 1944 after your sister Violet was born. Once we separated we were taken back by the Church and could both receive Holy Communion.

I worked with the different dioceses on contract as a priest. But I loved your mother very much and made her stay wherever

I was working as a priest. I made Natasha and Eddie stay with her and you. I could not write and explain all this to my brother and sisters as they had great hopes for me as a priest in India. It would have brought down the family honour and name, as we were all very respectable Catholics. Eventually I became frustrated at my failures and double life of a priest and a family man, so I decided to return to the USA in late 1945 to seek dispensation from the Chicago Mission and then return to India." He paused reflecting.

"Soon after my return to the USA, India got its independence and the country was engulfed in the war for the partition of India and Pakistan. I lost touch with you all, since you had moved from where I had left you. So I came to Denver, far from everyone. No one here knows that I was a priest once. I met Petronilla, a nurse, in Michigan, while I was collecting for the missions in India. She was of great help. We started this business together. But I have thought of you all often. I sent money to Bishop Wildermuth at the Patna Mission to give to your mother, but since I received no acknowledgment, I presumed she had married and that you two must have been looked after by the Church, as the other Anglo-Indian children abandoned in India were. I was later told by the bishop in Patna Mission that they were unable to locate you, so I stopped sending any money and instead helped the new seminarians and supported some missions around here. I still love Agnes, she was a wonderful woman. Convey my love to her and tell her that I will meet her in Heaven."

Papa spoke in a pleading way. I felt sorry for him, but at the same time I felt how easy it had been for him to make excuses, to forget us and to settle down with another woman. Surely he could have come to India after Independence and searched for us. It seemed to me he had forgotten us after he settled down with Petronilla in 1950, while we went through all our problems because of him. His earlier responsibilities had not weighed heavily enough with him and he had not thought of the sufferings he had caused us.

"I swear to you Minnie, I sent money, about ninety *rupees* each time, to the Bishop in Patna asking him to give it to Agnes.

He told me later that they did not know your whereabouts. So I stopped sending it, assuming you were all settled somewhere. Your mother is a wonderful person to have stayed by you two and given you both such a good education. You should be grateful to the good nuns at Allahabad for giving you a good English education which has helped you to reach the USA." Papa said to me in a desperate manner noticing my silence.

He was clearly feeling guilty and embarrassed but tried to cover it with his assuring but pleading voice. I knew that we had a good English education because of the efforts of Uncle Eddie and Aunt Natasha. It was Uncle who had embarrassed the Bishop of Allahabad and forced the nuns to take us free into the English School. I strongly felt that the Church had done nothing for my mother and us. She had struggled to bring us up alone without a man's support. Uncle Eddie had helped us to get into an English School and Aunt Natasha had stayed by my mother and us even though it was hard for her to accept us along with her own daughters. Mum was able to take up nursing and bring us up due to Aunt Natasha keeping us.

"Tell me if you had any other woman in India besides Mum. There have been rumours that you had children by other women in the village," I responded.

"I swear to you that you two are my only children and that Agnes is the only woman I have ever loved. People in India love to gossip about foreigners, but I could never have done so. I honestly loved your mother and had every good intention of rearing a family, but I was weakened by circumstances. I regret very much what I did. I wish I had come back to you and taken charge of my family." He sounded convincing then added, "Petronilla and I have no children. All this will be yours after she and I die. I would be happy if you stayed here and educated yourself at the University of Boulder. But I will have to tell everyone that you are the child of a friend in India, as people here are very conservative. Petronilla is a good woman, look after her when I am dead and all this will be yours after her. It would be enough to take care of you and Violet in your lifetime."

I was not interested in his wealth; I wanted his love and acceptance as a daughter. That was why I had been searching for him. I wanted the Papa who once gave me all his attention and made me feel all-important, for whom I would have done anything on earth. But this father stood in front of me offering me education and wealth for my future security but asking me to share him with Petronilla—not my mother. I had not changed, I had remained a daughter in search of her father's love. He had changed and could not claim me. I could see he was suffering mentally. He didn't realise that a child does not need money or education, just love and the feeling of belonging—education and wealth follows in its own time. He was my Papa and I was his daughter. What else mattered?

"What about Mum and Violet?" I asked angrily. "How can I leave them in India where they have to keep on struggling to exist while I am studying at the university here!"

"You can do more for them from here than in India," he replied.

I told him about Danny and how much he meant to me. Papa questioned me about him and then said to me thoughtfully:

"It will be best for you to stay single. Study hard, take up a profession and then do well for others. Do not put all your hopes on Danny; he might let you down. You should not depend on others for your happiness. You could do better for yourself as a single professional person."

He set up a tin can on a post and told me to knock it over with a bullet. My first shot missed. Papa told me to re-load and try again. Suddenly I had an almost uncontrollable desire to make him my target out of rage at the thought of the misery that he had caused us, by his weakness and selfishness since he had settled down with Petronilla and finally at his saying that if I stayed back with him I would have to take on a new identity as the daughter of a friend, thus having to live a lie day after day.

I loved him tremendously. It hurt me to realise that he did not understand my love for him.

I could not make a target of him and instead hit the tin, making him happy. He made me practise a few more times before going in for lunch.

As the day for my departure came closer, I saw Papa more

frequently sitting quietly and shaking his head, as though unsure of his decision to let me go. Once I asked him why he did so.

"I never realised till now what I was missing. I feel so upset thinking about the things I could have done and did not do. I have made a hash of my life and lost my most precious ones."

"You haven't lost anything. Everything will be all right if you return to India and live with us. Things have changed in India now," I said to him. But he just shook his head and sighed, saying that it was too late and that he was committed to Petronilla. He again pleaded that I not return to India but stay with him. My mind was made up. If my father could not acknowledge me publicly then I could not live with him under the guise of a daughter of one of his friends. I did not tell him this, as I did not think he would understand my feelings because at the time I was very idealistic and hated any kind of lies. Besides, I felt that my mother suffered but did not disown us, so my place was at her side. Papa was very disappointed at my decision.

On the day of my departure he drove me to the airport. He was very quiet and I was confused. Again I started doubting myself and wondering whether I had made the right decision. On the way to the airport, Papa spoke like a parent.

"Well, if you have decided to leave then you must. But I still wish for you to stay."

At the airport, while waiting for the plane, I stood looking at him. Somehow, I was waiting for him to say: "Minnie, don't go. I love you my dear daughter, stay back with me, I want you to be with me."

Perhaps if he had said those words I would have stayed because I was very sad at the idea of leaving him. But his refusal to recognise me as his daughter in public was rankling me. I wanted him so much to accept me with love in front of everyone. I hungered for his love and acceptance, not his wealth. But he stood in silence, looking very grim and thoughtful in his black suit, as though he was making a sacrifice of his will.

It was time to board the plane. He cradled me in his arms, hugged me and kissed me. He had a photograph taken of us together at the airport then handed me a letter claiming Violet and me as his natural daughters by Agnes. He asked me never to mention the letter to Petronilla and promised to get me American citizenship so I could return to the USA whenever I wanted. There were tears in his eyes.

"You have decided to return to India on your own. Do what I could not do there. Give my love to Agnes and tell her that I still love her as before and that we shall meet in Heaven." I heard my Papa say to me in a very sad voice for the last time before I boarded the plane.

I walked towards the plane hoping and wishing for him to call me back and say that he loved me and wanted me to stay as his daughter. But he did not. My seat was near the window and I could see him standing alone with one hand holding his chin and a finger over his lips. He looked very sad; tears rolled down my cheeks. Suddenly I felt I had made the wrong decision. The thought that I might never see him again made me forget my earlier demand that he should accept me in public and I felt the desire to be with my dear Papa in spite of everything. Immediately I got up sobbing, wanting to run back to him, but just then the plane moved and my final glimpse of him was in his black suit.

The plane stopped down at the next airport after about an hour. I hastily got off the plane and telephoned my father. Petronilla answered. I told her I wanted to talk to my father about my change of decision. I wanted to return to him and not go back to India. But she replied in a very calm voice that Papa was sleeping, as he was feeling unwell and tired and that she could not wake him up. She added that I had made the right decision to return to my mother in India who had brought me up and that 'Mike' would write to me. For the first time I realised that I should have told Papa how much I loved him, perhaps like me, he too was waiting for me to tell him so. Time and circumstances had made our love conditional between father and daughter. We could not express ourselves properly. Petronilla clearly did not want me to return to my Papa.

I could do nothing but get on the plane bound for London, en route to India. I had found it very difficult to make the important decision to leave my mother and stay with my father.

I needed time to think things over and perhaps discuss everything with my mother. I realised I could not suddenly leave her for my father, though I loved him so dearly, perhaps more than my mother, but I could not be disloyal to her. I thought it over again and decided that I would return to the USA soon after I met my mother and Violet.

I had written to Danny asking him to meet me at the airport in London. But he was not at Heathrow airport. I was given a visa valid for six months, but not seeing Danny, I felt dejected so caught a taxi to the other airport, from where I caught the Air-India plane to Bombay direct. I felt very upset and disappointed with myself on board the plane and slumped in a corner grieving over everything that had happened. I had cancelled the trip via France and Rome to reach India the fastest way. Nothing interested me more than my feelings for my parents. Eventually I reached Bombay and continued my trip to Jaipur. Papa had planned it that way because he was worried about me in the condition India was in because of the war.

29

Return to Motherland

Uncle David was at Jaipur Airport waiting for me, as I had sent him a telegram from Heathrow Airport in London. He took me to St Xavier's School Guest House where parents spent a few days while visiting their resident children. The school itself was run by Jesuit priests and brothers. It was large, accommodating three hundred boarders and six hundred day students. Most of the them were sons of very wealthy Indians, quite a number were descendants of rajahs and landowners of the state of Rajasthan.

I was mentally and physically exhausted after the long journey. I went to sleep as soon as Uncle left me. I do not know how long I slept, but I was awakened by Uncle David's passionate kisses on my lips. It made me sit up in surprise, as he had never kissed me like that before. I did not like it and moved my face away.

"You look so beautiful and grown up," he said to me.

"Yes; I am no longer the child you used to carry around with Mum in Darjeeling," I replied.

He smiled and asked me what I had brought for him. I fished out a pocket transistor from my handbag. He was delighted. I told him about my experiences in USA including my visit to Denver and my Papa. Finally, I asked him to arrange for my journey to Allahabad that evening. Uncle informed me that there was a curfew in force. Because of the border war with Pakistan the whole of northern India was subjected to blackout every evening: there were no street lights, none at the station or at the shopping areas. Somehow he managed to book me in the first-class compartment for the following night. Before I left Jaipur, he told me of his unhappiness in his religious life and his desire to leave the Jesuit Brotherhood. I smiled and said, "My dear Uncle, I never thought you had a vocation. It will do you good to get out and consider marriage with some good teacher." A year later that is what Uncle David did. He was able to leave the religious life because he was just a lay Jesuit Brother who did not have to take the vow of celibacy, I was told. He found himself an Indian teacher in Jaipur. Soon he and his wife opened their own Primary English School. They were soon blessed with two children, a boy and a girl and lived very happily together.

That was the first time I had travelled in a first-class train compartment where I had a berth to myself. Since I was booked into a Ladies' First Class Compartment, I slept well. In the morning I looked out of the window at the expanse of green fields covered with mustard-yellow flowers. Yes, I thought to myself, India was a beautiful country and I was glad to be back in the country of my birth, where I had a mother who accepted and loved me. I decided to study further and do great things to make my father want to accept me in public as his daughter. I would help the poor and needy, remembering what Papa had said at the airport before I left: "Do what I could not do in India!" I thought how good it was to live accepted and free instead of living a life pretending to be the daughter of my own father's friend! Soon Danny would return and we would marry. I would have a home of my own where I would help my husband fulfil his ambitions. After all, my life was my own, not my father's. I would forget the past and live my own life, as Aunt Trombley had suggested.

About ten in the morning the train reached New Delhi station. With the help of a porter I found the platform where the train to Allahabad was due at midday. I saw many security guards all over the station.

I was wearing a *sari* made of nylon curtain material that I had bought in Toledo. My suitcase and the hand luggage still had the airline tags, which suggested that I had come from overseas. I noticed the security guards hovering around me a couple of times and I thought that they were taken with my fine clothes.

While waiting for my train I thought it would be best if I went to Allahabad via Agra, since breaking my journey at Agra would enable me to enrol into the BA Part II as a regular full time student for 1966. I had already completed the BA Part I by correspondence before leaving for the States. Later in the evening I could catch a train to Allahabad from Agra. So I walked up to the guard at the platform and asked him what time the train to Agra left and whether I could go via Agra to Allahabad on the ticket I was holding. The guard looked at me suspiciously as he answered my question. I reconsidered the change in the light of the time I would have in Agra to visit the University. While I was thinking it over the guard asked me what I had decided and I replied that I thought it best to continue my journey as planned without any changes and walked back towards my luggage.

When the train eventually arrived, the porter saw that I was placed in the right compartment. I was the only occupant in the Ladies First Class Compartment. I locked the door from the inside and sat down near the window as the train started. It had just left the platform and was about to gather speed when it suddenly slowed down again, as if someone had pulled the emergency cord. As the train stopped I noticed a mass of faces peering through the closed glass window of my compartment. I thought they were looking in to find some place for themselves. Suddenly there was a loud banging on my door followed by an authoritative voice ordering me to open the door. When I did so, I found a guard in uniform with two policemen standing in front of me.

"We have been informed you are a spy, I am to search you and your luggage," the guard said in a high-handed way.

I was shocked. Never before had I ever been taken for a spy! I had travelled all over India without any problems in the past. I could not understand what suddenly made them think I was one. The crowd outside the window was growing noisy and banged on the window in rage and hatred. They had heard the guard at the platform inform the policemen of his suspicion and had followed the officials to my compartment when the train stopped. I allowed the guard to go through my luggage. While the guard was busy doing so, the two policemen stood at the door, perhaps to make sure that I did not bolt. The guard examined the contents of my suitcase after going through my handbags. Suddenly he straightened up with a triumphant gleam in his eyes, as though he had found what he had been looking for. He pounced on the pocket transistor I had brought for Mum.

"What is this?" he exclaimed as the two policemen stood alert. The crowd at the window sneered and chuckled. It was such a comical sight and I could not help a sarcastic laugh.

"Here! I will turn it on for you! It is just a pocket transistor, perhaps you have not seen one before!" I said.

A beautiful song by Lata Mangeskar, the famous singer of Indian films at the time, came from the radio. By coincidence it was a song about the ignorance of the human race and asked for wisdom from the Creator. The guard was embarrassed and apologised, explaining that he thought it was a bomb. He left, looking sheepish. Before doing so he instructed me to lock the door from the inside. The train moved once again. I was dazed by the incident and the true realisation of what could have happened if the mob had got me.

I was not over the shock when, about half an hour later; there was another loud knock at the door. I thought it was another passenger for the compartment, so I opened it. The compartment had two berths. I found a thin, insignificant-looking man in his thirties at the door, standing with his cloth bag. I was about to ask him what he was doing in front of a Ladies Compartment, when he walked in without hesitation, asking permission to leave his bag inside and explained that he was the first-class attendant on duty and that he would be back. He disappeared. I locked the door again, wondering why he left his bag in my compartment.

The train sped on. Night was falling fast and because of the India-Pakistan war everything was in darkness outside due to the blackout and curfew over Northern India. My compartment had a dim light on but the windows were shut and no light could penetrate outside.

After two hours and the train was speeding non-stop through small village-stations, the man returned. He knocked softly and whispered that it was the attendant to collect his bag.

I opened the door but instead of picking up his bag, he locked the door from the inside. He stood by the door. I asked him what he wanted and why he had locked the door, as I had begun to feel something evil about him.

"I heard that you were suspected of being a spy! A few days back another lady spy from Pakistan travelled in this train. She made me happy by obliging me and I let her go wherever she wanted to," he whispered and grinned in a most disgusting way. He started taking off his shirt. I was horrified and angry. I guessed that I was in a dangerous spot, but knew that I had to be calm and use my intelligence to keep myself safe. I shouted with confidence.

"Will you leave this compartment immediately or do I have to pull the emergency cord? I am not a spy and when we reach Allahabad, where everyone knows me, I shall report you to the stationmaster and the police. My parents are well known in Allahabad." I added, bluffing that the stationmaster was a relative of mine and that my father was a top-ranking officer in the police.

"You will be in the most serious trouble if you so much as lay a finger on me. Get out at once!" I pushed him and opened the door. He was so shocked at the sound of my authoritative voice that he left immediately without a word, his shirt in his hand. I threw his bag after him and locked the door yet again from the inside.

For the next few hours I sat impatiently waiting for Allahabad station. I felt all my former idealistic aims suddenly crumbling. I questioned my decision to return to India. After all, my father had offered me good further education and a comfortable American life. I had only to put up with a pretence about being his friend's daughter. He had even said that I could do more for Mum and Violet from the USA than in India. Perhaps he was right. I had decided on emotional grounds and Papa said that Indian people were prone to do this, whereas I should try to control my emotions and be more practical. I felt depressed. I realised my father's wisdom and decided to return to the USA as soon as I had seen Mum and Violet to convince them of my love and tell them about Papa,

At Allahabad station a porter helped me carry my luggage and I quickly left in a rickshaw. I was scared of further harassment by the attendant, or the guard, but nothing happened.

The rickshaw took me through dark roads to my house which was also in darkness. It was twelve midnight and the front door was locked. Mum opened the door when I called. Her eyes gleamed as she hugged me with joy. She had been ill since learning that I had stayed with Papa. Everyone was happy at my return. Violet told me how Mum had taken leave to welcome me at Delhi Airport. They searched for me among the arrivals and were desperate when I was not there. Then they had gone to Mrs Trevedi who had informed them that I had stayed back with my father. No one else saw them, not even Mr Dhawan, whom I had entrusted with the money for Mum. I was disgusted at their story. Mum had not been to work since she returned, as she was worried sick and looked very weak.

For a while I enjoyed their welcome and gave everyone the little gifts I had for them. I felt a change in my attitude towards Mum. I wondered who really was to blame for our miseries, she, Papa, or the Church. I wished my parents were together. I loved them both, but the way things were I could not see how their reunion could be brought about. I found it difficult to make my decision to live with one or the other. I made a wrong decision to return to India for Mum's sake, but in the USA it seemed to be the right one. A nagging doubt also returned: though Papa had said that she was a very good woman, why did she continue to have an affair with him, a priest and give birth to the two of us, when she must have known that the whole situation was an impossible one and sinful according to the church? Why did she not leave him and let him remain a priest if she really cared for him? Sudden bitterness came over me.

"You have changed, Minnie. You are not the same happy and loving daughter who left me for a visit to the USA," Mum said to me a few days later. I pretended that it was not true.

I had given her the white pocket transistor. The other nurses were jealous of it, because no one had even seen one like that in 1965 in Allahabad. Mum treasured it because she could hear her favourite songs on her own transistor in her little lonely room till late at night. She could not afford anything expensive like a transistor. I had bought her a cheap wristwatch and that is the only expensive thing she possessed other than bare necessities. All her earnings went into providing for us. The old clothes she still parcelled off to her brother's family in the village.

I told Mum that Papa had enquired of her and said that he would meet her in Heaven, but for the present he was living with another woman. Mum said nothing, just listened and changed the subject. I could not ask her the many questions that were burning in me, as I could not hurt her feelings. I felt sorry for her, even though I started blaming her for continuing her hopeless life with Papa. I knew the sacrifices she made for Violet and me. She consumed her whole life as a young woman working for us. She could not go back to her relatives in the village because of embarrassment over what was regarded as her disgraceful behaviour and she had to bear what everyone said about her as a single mother. Even if she had been at fault in bringing us into this world, I could not hate her because she had taken up the responsibility of a mother for us in the best way under the circumstances and given us more than Papa had. My love for her was there but somehow the bitterness kept me from being what I was before I had met my Papa.

I wrote to him and informed him of the incident on the train about my being suspected of being a spy. I thought it would amuse him too, but in reply he only said that I should not have changed my name from 'Anthony' to 'Lyons'. I could not understand what it had to do with being suspected as a spy. Just the same I could not have carried on with a false name when I came to know that my real surname was 'Lyons'. Truth was very important to me and I could not have lived telling lies and pretending for the remainder of my life.

1. *In mid-1945 my father visited us dressed in clerical attire. Introduced as a 'dost' (friend). I was confused because I recognised him as my father.*

1.

2.

3.

2. *My father, Rev. Michael D. Lyons, came to India from the United States in the early 1920s as a young Jesuit Seminarian.*
3. *My father in 1932, group photo in Patna with Bishop – front row second from right.*

1. *Grandmother Bertha Lyons.*
2. *Grandfather Michael Patrick Lyons.*

Great-grandfather Judge Peter Bienvenu Delisle -Bertha's father.

1. *My father's four sisters – left to right: Helen, Marie, Loretta and Margaret.*

2. *My grandmother and her four children – my father standing far right.*

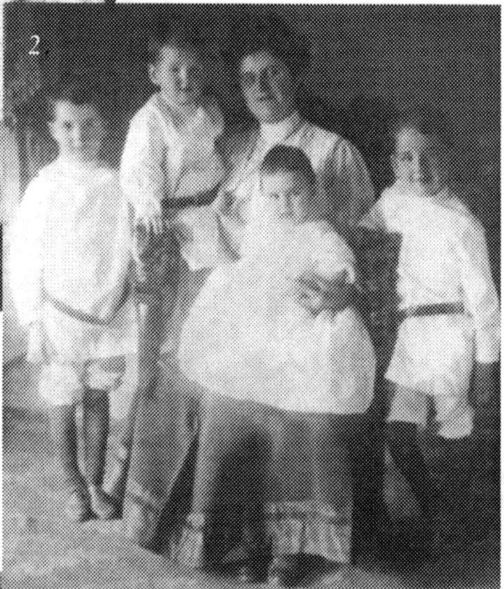

3. *Great-grandmother Adeline Piette (Paytte) Delisle – wife of judge Delisle, with my grandmother Bertha and my aunts.*

Aunt Margaret

1.

FATHER MICHAEL LYONS

2.

FATHER MICHAEL LYONS S. J.

The old cathedral of Patna, 1908 abandoned, which I have rebuilt for my headquarters.

Hundreds of baptisms in the old cathedral since last April. Last week 100 Passis (tree climbers) and 500 Lohars (blacksmiths) stood at my door begging instruction. Were you here to help me, dear missionary you could prepare them for baptism. A catechist will do this for us, if we support his family......and the cost is five dollars a month

3.

October 30, 1920

DETROIT RADIO NEWS

Published under the auspices of The Detroit Radio Association.
Cyrus C. Jenks, Chairman Publication Committee
433 Book Bldg. Cherry 2369.
MIKE → M. D. Lyons, Editor.
463 Green Ave. Cedar 3292-W.
FRANK → F. E. Lyons, Classified Ads. and Calls.
Ed. H. Boyes, Marine Editor. 170 Willis.
Theo. Schmalzriedt, Subscription Manager.
2410 West Fort Street
Cedar 98.
Subscription Rate, One Dollar a Year.

4.

5.

THE POOR MAN'S VOICE.

Vol. 1 No. 3 | MIRZAPUR, U. P., SEPTEMBER, 1941 | 2 Pice a copy 10 as yearly by post

THOUGHTS ON PRODUCTION.

We must keep insisting on increased Production.
Until there is enough to feed and clothe all.
It is not enough to say this, and then to forget.
We must keep on insisting.
Until all are able to get the necessities of life.

To have increased Production.
Obstacles must be removed
And incentives to Production must be given.

Antiquated regulations, red tape, class privileges, communalism,

THE CAUSE OF POVERTY

Four and five centuries ago Europeans risked life itself to find new ways of getting to the vast populated country of India with its great wealth including ivory, jewels and unsurpassed silk.

What has happened? The sight of crores of human beings acting and living as though they were practically animals, dwelling in unhealthy huts, trying to subsist on a starvation diet, unable except for a small fraction of the whole to read or to write, ignorant, superstitious, born today, married tomorrow and dead soon after,—with an average expectation of life at birth in many sections of less than twenty years,—remains a vivid ... that something terrible has happened.

I hope the "POOR MAN'S VOICE" which you are bringing out will serve to call attention of the public to the needs of the poor. That itself will be a service but I am sure your energies will not let you confine yourself to voicing the needs of the poor but will perforce lead to the removal of those needs.

—Rajendra Prasad

Sadakat Ashram, PATNA. 25—8—41

... It should be the duty of those who see the possibility of a true society, to open the eyes of all, and this will not be done if we simply

... to clothing, 40 per cent for food, and 20 per cent for amusement."

Jones; "But that adds up to 120 per cent"

Printed by M. L...

1. *My father, on a lecture tour in America, talking about his experiences in India.*
2. *The Old cathedral of Patna.*
3. *Detroit Radio news.*
4. *Cass Technical College Michigan – my father at 16 was instructor teaching radio.*
5. *Poor Man's Voice Mirzapur, India – Editor.*

30

Yet another rejection and suicide

Over the next few days I realised more and more that returning to India was a mistake. I missed the security my father had offered me, as well as him. I did not want to lose him again. I saw the wisdom of his advice that I could do more for Mum and others from the USA than from India. I wrote to him about my desire to return. I asked him to help me with an American citizenship to enable me to return. While I waited for his reply, I went to Agra and enrolled for the final year of the BA degree as a regular student at St John's College. I also went to Delhi and visited the US Embassy for a visa to USA. I was advised that I could have the visa only if my father or my stepmother sponsored me.

It is hard to get out of India even as a visitor, because every country requires a sponsor, since India does not allow enough money to be taken out for use overseas. Even though I had an American father, I could not prove it. I had no documents to say so, only my father could have done that, but he was taking his own time! I was disappointed and decided to return to the USA through another country. As months passed I became desperate and feared that if I did not hurry back I would lose my Papa again.

I visited the UK High Commission and the Australian Embassy applying for a visa. I had no success at the UK Embassy, but managed to obtain an interview at the Australian High Commission. Mr Dorsett, a middle-aged stout, short and very pleasant Australian gentleman interviewed me at the Australian High Commission. He showed me a map of Australia and told me about the country and its people. He said that Australia needed teachers and assured me that I would be accepted. At the time there was not much difficulty in migrating to Australia from India, if one could prove oneself to be an Anglo-Indian with a European background. Fortunately, Fr. Cyril George, President of the Anglo-Indian Association in Allahabad, had given me a letter stating that I was a member of the Anglo-Indian Association and that I had a European father.

The interview was over by noon, lunchtime in India. After the interview Mr Dorsett offered me a lift in his car to Connaught Place, which was on the way to Old Delhi where I was bound. I accepted the lift in his Holden Kingswood with delight. He invited me to have dinner with him that night. I refused saying that I was to leave for Allahabad late that evening. I was loyal to Danny.

I received my Australian Immigration visa which I renewed every six months. I received the Residence visa but had no money to buy my ticket, nor did I know anyone or anywhere to stay in Australia. Father De'Souza gave me the address of a Melbourne Catholic Immigration office which helped migrants with sponsorship and accommodation when they first arrived in Australia. I wrote to Father Rafter who was in charge of the Melbourne Catholic Immigration Centre. He replied immediately with a guarantee of accommodation in Melbourne. But I did not make use of my residence visa to Australia until 1970, because to buy the ticket I needed money, besides, I was still hopeful that my Papa would call me to USA. In one of his letters he promised he would but asked me to be patient as he did not wish Petronilla to know since she was not in favour of it. He said he would have to go to another state and send me the papers from there stating that I was his natural daughter.

Nothing happened.

I was shocked to realise that my father could not sponsor me without the permission of Petronilla! A man, who was so strong and determined, could not do, as he wanted for his own flesh and blood, his daughter whom he said he loved very much!

One day I booked a telephone call to Papa from Allahabad. I spent three days waiting at the telephone office to get through but could not. Eventually, I gave up the idea and began writing.

A few months after my return to Allahabad, Papa sent me a lot of books by seamail. He included two pieces of nylon each five metres long to be used as *saris*. I gave one of the *saris* to

Violet as a gift from her father. Aunt Natasha was very angry, because she said that I could not have disclosed to Papa how much she and Uncle Eddie had done for us. She said that if I had done, he would have sent gifts for her and her daughters also. In fact she was under the impression that Papa had actually sent gifts for them too and that I had not given them to her but instead sold them to the shops for money. I could not tell her that he did not even ask about her or Uncle Eddie, since we were so busy sorting out our feelings and the past. There was so much to talk about between a daughter and a father in those few days. Unfortunately, Aunt misunderstood me and I could feel a strain growing between Aunt, Enid, Helen and myself.

Their attitude made me feel that I had to help them by trying to find them a relative from Uncle Eddie's side, so I went through his old files again and found the address of Graham's Home in Kalimpong, where Uncle was brought up and wrote to them asking for any information on Uncle's relatives.

Two weeks later I received a letter stating that a *Nepali*-looking local man had once come to the Home with two Anglo-Indian looking children, a girl about five or six and a boy of about three. He had deposited the children with a bag of money at the Home saying that the children belonged to a white man and should be cared by the Home. No one in the Home saw the man again. The Home was being built in the early 1900s, so they kept the boy, Eddie and sent the girl to the convent on top of the hill run by the IBVM nuns. The money was paid to the nuns for the girl, Uncle Eddie's sister, whereas Uncle Eddie was brought up with the Anglo-Indian orphans the hard way, helping to build the Home, wearing little clothing and no shoes. His sister tried to meet him after she finished her education but he refused to have anything to do with her. Uncle said his sister should have insisted they stay together, since she was older and she should have at least come to see him at some stage of his school-life in the Home. So, after many efforts to befriend Uncle Eddie, the sister, Agnes, had eventually left for England as a married lady and no one had heard about her since then. The authorities could not tell me Uncle Eddie's sister's married name. I gave the reply to Aunt, as I thought they should know of it and my efforts on their behalf. But it did not change their attitude.

Since my return to India I corresponded with Danny regularly as before. In the beginning I received a letter from him every two weeks, long newsy ones about his studies and experiences at his college. Then his letters came less frequently, once a month, telling me about his new girlfriends, but it always finished saying that I was a good girl and it was nice to know someone like me. My letters to him were full of affection and professions of love as usual. No matter what he did to me he was my one and only in whom I put my hopes of a respectable life and the start of a good background for my children.

Danny's mother invited me to Bangalore that Christmas and I had a lovely time with the family being treated like a family member. His mother divulged that she was sincerely hoping Danny would marry me soon because she had grown very fond of me. She was worried about the girls he was seeing in England. Of course I had not told her about my parents and my background.

✣ ✣ ✣ ✣ ✣

It was 1966. Life at St John's College hostel was so different. I wore *saris* every day to attend the College for classes. The hostel was solely for girls. No boys were allowed on the hostel premises. Most of the girls were Indians, because Anglo-Indians hardly ever attended a College or University for a tertiary education as regular students. If they continued their studies, it was by correspondence while teaching.

We were served food on big steel plates and it was rationed. Our warden was Miss Wahid, a middle-aged Methodist Indian lady, whose attitude was similar to a jail warden. We returned to the hostel straight after the College ended and we had to obtain her permission before leaving the hostel at any time during the day. The hostel doors were locked at seven. The boys at the College often harassed the women-students verbally, although the principal of the College, Mr Chandi, a Methodist, was very strict about the students' discipline and behaviour. I entered the College just in time for classes and left immediately afterwards. Most of the time I spent in my room writing letters to Papa, Danny, or Mum.

I once took part in a play at the College and also performed an Indian dance at one of the functions. Since I had returned from the USA my self-confidence had grown, perhaps because I got to know my father and corresponded with him. All my friends and lecturers were very fond of me. I wrote to Papa of my experiences at the College and he would write back practically every week describing his past experience in India. He mostly typed his letters and signed off as 'M' for Michael. Once I questioned him why he did so: was he frightened to sign off as 'Your Papa'? He promptly replied by signing off in Hindi '*Tera Pita*' which means 'Your father'.

Papa continued sending me books by seamail. He seemed keen to educate me further. He had ambition for me, but kept ignoring my enquiries about the sponsorship or the citizenship he promised to obtain. By then Violet had also started to correspond with him on a regular basis. She said that in one of the letters to her, Papa had said that he would be leaving all his worldly possessions to Violet and me and that it would be sufficient to see us through our life-time.

I passed the Bachelor degree in the second division by the end of 1966 and returned to Allahabad in search of a job again. In India three major divisions were given depending on the marks. Those with 80% and above got First Division, between 60% and 79% got Second Division and between 59% to 40% got Third Division, below that was a failure. My subjects for BA were English Literature, Indian Medieval History, English Medieval History and Sociology. I also did Complementary Hindi as a subject. Since my medium of instruction was English I had to do a compulsory complementary Hindi to be able to get my degree. I was fluent in Hindi and English and enjoyed reading novels in both languages. My letters to my mother were always in Hindi. I wrote to everyone else, including Papa in English.

In 1967 I got a teaching position at St Joseph's Boys' School in Allahabad, where Aunt Natasha was also teaching. Most schools in India were single-sex schools. I taught Year 4 because in the boys' school they preferred male teachers above that level.

✣ ✣ ✣ ✣ ✣

Towards the middle of 1967 I became depressed, because I was losing hope of getting back to the USA. I wondered whether I would ever see my father again. The reality of my decision to return made very unhappy. Also, Danny's letters became very irregular. He began to find faults with me for being simple and too religious. In one letter he suggested I get myself a boyfriend who could teach me how to make love. But I thought once he returned to India he would change.

A few days after school closed in December I visited Mrs Macwan, a teacher friend of Aunt Natasha. Sarcastically, she informed me that Danny had returned from England. Mrs Macwan always seemed jealous of my friendship with Danny. I could not believe it. Danny wrote a month back and didn't mention his returning. I had replied to his letter and was waiting for a reply. His letter to me was normal and friendly as usual. When I returned home that afternoon I found a letter from his mother waiting. She wrote that I should forget Danny as he was not worthy of me: he had returned with a wife to her great disappointment.

The message pushed me to the last extremity and I decided to put an end to my life, because of rejection by both my father and Danny.

My hopes for a new beginning were shattered and I could not face the reality. I felt that no one wanted me, the Church, my father, then Danny, all of them rejected me so there was no point in my living on the earth where I was an unwanted daughter of a priest. I was considered a shame and no matter what I did no one ever appreciated me as an individual. I felt that I had no right to live amongst the respectable people.

I found some Midol tablets, which I had bought in the USA for period pain. The package said that no more than four a day should be taken, as they contained a large quantity of aspirin. I took twenty-four of them at once. After I swallowed them all I decided that I had to let Mrs Macwan know what I had done, so that Danny was informed and made to realise that I had killed myself as a result of his rejection. Aunt was home but I did not tell her anything. I took a rickshaw to Mrs Macwan's house. She was shocked when she heard what I had done. Immediately she forced me into a rickshaw and took me home. By then I felt hot and sick. Fortunately Mum arrived at the same time as we reached home; perhaps Mrs Macwan had sent a message to Mum. I was made to lie down and Mum and a nurse friend, Miss Gonsalves, who lived behind our house, gave me a stomach-wash while Aunt Natasha stood praying in tears. They called a doctor who refused to come at first, saying it was a police case, but later took pity on Mum and attended me. I was half-conscious and they did everything to keep me alive. When I came around I heard Mum saying a couple of times: "My dearest child how could you do this to yourself when I did everything to keep you alive all these years!" At that moment I felt I had to live for her sake and that she really cared and loved me.

The next morning my stomach was so bloated that I could not even do up my brassiere. That night I was heavily sedated. I received the Last Sacrament for the second time as I faced a critical twenty-four hours. I suffered severe gastric problems for a long time after the incident and my nerves were shattered. The following day, when I was declared out of danger, I realised the full meaning of what I had done. Owing to my disturbed stomach I suffered severe heart palpitations and developed a great fear of death. I no longer wanted to die. The fact that I had committed mortal sin by attempting suicide made me feel very guilty. For a couple of weeks I would not lie down to sleep. I was afraid of dying. Mum sedated me with an injection every night to help me sleep and I became very dependent on her treatment. Then, one night after a fortnight, Mum told me she was giving me just distilled water to deceive me into sleeping. She said I slept on my own. From then on, I slept without help. Every night I heard my heart beating fast and was afraid of having a heart attack and dying. Every night I slept with my head resting on three pillows, more or less in a sitting position, because I was afraid of choking to death and hated being alone. For over a year I was treated for a severe nervous breakdown.

Although I continued to casually teach at the Boys' School, I would often leave the class and run to Aunt or the Headmaster, feeling my pulse, complaining to them that I was not feeling well and was about to collapse with a heart attack. They would firmly tell me to go back to the class. They said there was nothing wrong with me and that I was imagining things. In class I never sat or relaxed for fear of collapsing and dying. I kept pacing about the room. By the evening I was exhausted from being on my feet all the time. Mum came home every evening to help me relax and sleep. She assured me that she was there should I become ill and would save me from dying. In her presence I felt confident of living.

In a letter to my Papa I informed him of what I did as a result of depression. I told him I wanted to return to him, but he had not done what was needed and Danny had let me down too. I expected Papa to immediately call me in the States, but instead I received a long letter from Petronilla telling me Papa was angry and upset with my actions. She lectured me at length about how I should consider myself lucky to be alive and that I should be grateful to the good people around me who helped me throughout my life. From then on I received very few letters from Papa. It was mostly Petronilla who replied. Her letters were very general – about the weather and American news. I never heard from Danny again.

I often visited many doctors in connection with my illness. Someone suggested that I visit a psychiatrist in a psychiatric hospital, Noor Manzil, in Lucknow. So I made a trip to Lucknow with Mum. The psychiatrist hypnotised me. He told me later that I lay there for two hours bitterly crying about my love for my father and how hurt I had been seeing him living with another woman. I kept repeating my desire to be with my father. I also spoke of how I felt about being the daughter of a priest and not being accepted by both the Church and the community at large. I said nothing about my rejection by Danny. When I regained consciousness my pillow was soaked with tears. I felt somewhat lighter after that and the times during which I feared I would die returned less frequently.

31

Days of the nervous breakdown

Towards the end of 1967, while I was still suffering a nervous breakdown and continuing with the medications, one of Violet's boyfriend's friend from the Air Force, Ralph, visited me. He said he heard about what had happened and was full of sympathy. He said he had often seen me in Church. He was also from Bangalore City like Danny. He was pleasant to talk to, especially when I was lonely and Aunt and Helen tried to keep to themselves. Mum was always at work. By then Aunt was convinced that I was on the verge of insanity. She and Helen treated me as if I was incapable of doing anything rational. So when Ralph came I found it good to talk to someone who understood me. Sometimes Ralph would take me to the movies.

In spite of all my medical complaints, one day Ralph professed that he had fallen in love with me since the first time he had seen me in the Church on a Sunday. Ralph said that it did not matter to him how ill I was, as he understood and was trying to cure me by being a good friend. He would help to develop my lost confidence.

He would often sit with me at the back of the house and we would talk and laugh about the things he found funny. To start with he was good company. I don't think I ever loved him but I needed a friend. At the time I was lonely and confused with my life. I was afraid to be alone in case my heart stopped beating!

About that time I suffered mild pain in my stomach. Mum took me to see Dr Tehliani. She knew Mrs Tehliani. She was a gynaecologist from the railway hospital. Dr Tehliani was a surgeon at the Allahabad Medical College. He and his wife ran private practices at home after hours.

Dr Tehliani, a short, well-built man with piercing eyes and his wife, a pretty woman with greenish eyes, were from the State of Punjab but had settled in Allahabad. He prescribed medicine and asked me to come back in three days. The medicines had not given me much relief. Mum was at the hospital working so I went to see him alone on the third day.

The doctor had me lie down as he felt my stomach, then his hand wandered into my panties for a few seconds, as if he was just performing part of the examination. He asked me to lie still and he left the room. I wondered if I had imagined what had taken place. He returned about five minutes later and again felt my stomach. This time his hand strayed under my brassiere and he muttered, "Beautiful!" while he felt my nipples. As I went to push his hand away, he removed it himself. "Well I think you have an inflamed appendix, so tell your mother to get in touch with me about a hospital booking." I was so confused I walked out hastily from the room.

Mum was upset about an appendectomy but she arranged a date. Aunt too was worried and shed a few tears. Ralph said very thoughtfully: "Perhaps all your illnesses have been real and we kept thinking that you were imagining them! "

I told Mum about the doctor's behaviour while examining me. She was very angry but said he was the top surgeon in Allahabad so there was nothing she could do. She promised to stay with me all the time I was with him in future to make sure it never occurred again.

A few days later I was admitted to the Allahabad Medical College. Mum took leave and stayed by my bedside. I was in the general ward. I remember the cry of one old woman while I was there. She had not been given a bed and lay on the floor. The whole day she cried with a most heart-wrenching sound. I was told she was a beggar woman of sixty and had been operated on for stomach cancer. The cancer was at a very advanced stage and the operation was bound to be unsuccessful, yet they operated on her to demonstrate the procedure for doctors and medical students. The woman had no relatives and no money. She was heavily sedated with free drugs the hospital could provide; yet she was in great pain and so kept on screaming and groaning. Every now and then nurses came to record her condition or do some test on her. Everyone said she was dying.

I felt sad for the old woman. She died during the night when I was asleep and her body was immediately removed from the ward for cremation.

The next day I was taken to the operating theatre. Mum was not allowed to accompany me. As I lay on the table I saw the piercing eyes of Dr Tehliani above his white mask. Once again he examined my stomach before allowing the anaesthetist to inject me. His hands again wandered under the white sheet covering me. The nurses, the other medical students and the student doctors stood around in silence, obviously thinking he was examining me before surgery.

When I regained consciousness I was happy to see Mum beside my bed. Aunt and Helen came to visit me in the afternoon with Ralph. Mum looked after me till I was strong enough to return home. She said that she was informed after the operation that the condition of my appendix was not very bad after all. Dr Tehliani saw me every day when he came on his rounds of the ward. On the third day he came to remove the stitches. Once again he managed to feel me as he had done on earlier occasions, even while Mum was standing nearby. Perhaps no one could see what he was doing under the cover!

Mum resumed her duties once I was home, she visited me every day after work. I had to stay in bed for some time. Aunt and Helen went out to teach while I stayed back with my two dogs, Rex and Bonzo.

Since I understood the problems my mother had undergone, she had loved my Papa but he had deserted her, leaving her with two children, I was taunted for what was considered the sins of my parents. I was therefore obsessed about being pure and chaste before marriage. I wanted my husband to be the only one to ever have sexual relations with me, for the purpose of having children. The nuns had also taught us that sex was important after marriage only to produce children. Besides, our household was made up of women and I had not known a relationship with any man except my father and Uncle Eddie.

When I recovered and started teaching again, Ralph continued visiting me often. Then one day he told me that he wanted to go steady with me and love me like a man should. That frightened me, I could not do so. I was obsessed with the idea of purity and chastity and we quarrelled for the first time. He left that evening saying that I was stupid and immature. It hurt me, because he used the words Danny had, before he left me, but I could not give up my values and my obsession with purity and respectability. I still went to Church on Sundays, even though the sight of the priest saying the Mass reminded me of my Papa and filled me with bitterness.

Soon Ralph began to see me only every now and then. He always said he was with another girlfriend when he returned to see me after an absence of a few days. He also insisted on my making love to him whenever he visited. I would never do so and we quarrelled. One day he left saying he was going home to Bangalore for a month's holiday and would write, which he did, just once telling me how much he loved me and how cruel I was for not understanding his needs. I had missed him and realised then how much I was used to his friendship. I looked forward to his return.

I remember the day he returned, very well. I was in the kitchen and very happy to see him again. He talked about his mother and sister and eventually told me his mother wanted him to meet a girl, Ann, whom she wanted him to marry, as she was the only daughter of a rich parent. Ann's father promised a car as a dowry to Ralph. The Anglo-Indians from Goa, who are supposedly descendants of Portuguese and Indians, believe in the dowry and caste systems.

At first I thought Ralph was joking, as he often did about other girls, to get me to do what he wanted, but when he kept talking about Ann, I became resentful. I tried to change the subject by telling him what was happening in Allahabad. Ralph listened in silence then asked me to go with him on his scooter to the post office as he had a telegram to send home. At the post office he wrote a telegram to Ann in front of me saying:

"I love you and miss you very much."

I said nothing then, but when we reached home and Ralph followed me to the kitchen still talking about Ann, I could tolerate it no further, so I slapped him hard across the face.

"Get out of my house. Go to Ann and sell yourself for a car. I am not rich. I cannot give you anything. Go and never come back to this house again."

He was so stunned he stood still, then left. I never saw him again. I felt better after slapping him. My anger at Danny and Papa had gone into that one slap.

The next day, a few of Ralph's friends from the Air Force visited and said they heard of the incident from Ralph. He was upset and too embarrassed to see me, so they decided they should visit. One of them was Sunderajan, a South Indian who was dark, tall, and sharp features which made him extremely handsome. He was the only one who owned an Indian Fiat car and seemed wealthy. His parents were against his working, as they said they had enough for him to live in luxury, but he joined the Air Force because he wanted to get away from his home town where he had been let down by a South Indian girlfriend he once loved. He had a violent temper and drank heavily. Like most rich people he was used to taking whatever he fancied. He spoke English with a distinct South Indian accent, was arrogant, shy and conservative. Sunderajan made sure I was aware of his dislike for Ralph. He and his friends visited me a couple of times and were extremely nice to me. It seemed they were trying to win my attention, since Ralph was not around and I had no one else courting me.

32

A recovery and a winner

I continued consulting different doctors, insisting that I feared a heart attack because of palpitations and feelings of faintness. One day Mum took me to Dr Burke, the same doctor who had cured me of meningitis years before. He examined me and then said in a firm voice, "Look, Esther, I am tired of being nice to you. I must tell you that there is nothing wrong. You will live longer than any of us. You have seen practically every doctor in Allahabad and everyone talks about your imaginary illnesses. It is a shame that a young, good-looking girl like you should behave like this. Think of what your poor mother is going through seeing you act in this crazy way. For her sake, if for nobody else's, pull yourself together and forget your illnesses. You are like my own daughter. I feel terrible when doctors at their meetings discuss your ailments and laugh at you."

That was the first time anyone spoke to me in such a way. There and then I decided not to visit another doctor and to overcome my nervous condition by my own devices. I had to do it myself as no one else could do it for me and I had to do it for Mum's sake.

"Yes, I want you to be my old Minnie; the one I was so proud of. There is really nothing wrong with you," Mum said gently on the way home.

That afternoon the Johnstones visited us. Mr Johnstone was in the railways. He had five daughters and a son. Mrs Johnstone told us about her eldest daughter taking part in a Miss Teen Princess, Beauty Contest. I looked at the Femina magazine they had brought along with them and discovered that the Miss Lucknow Beauty Contest was going to be held about the same time as the Miss Teen Princess. Immediately I decided to enter the contest, I had to divert my mind from myself and my illnesses. Mrs Johnstone encouraged me to do so. Immediately

I sent in the application with my photograph.

Every year the two leading magazines, Eve's Weekly and Femina, held beauty contests in the capital cities of the major states in India. From among these Miss India and Miss Universe contestants were later chosen to be sent overseas for the respective competitions. Both magazines were in English and contained short stories, cooking recipes and gossip, aimed at women from sophisticated and well-educated Indian families.

For the next few weeks I ignored all my familiar symptoms determined to be rid of them and become normal as before. Mrs Johnstone, her daughter Jennifer and I set out for Lucknow the evening before the contest was to be held. We had nowhere to spend the day except in the first-class waiting room of the railway station. I was not going to the La Martinere Girls' school where I had once taught, as I felt embarrassed; after going over to the USA here I was under the spell of a nervous breakdown!

We refreshed ourselves at the waiting room and then set out for the beauty parlour. The contest was to be held in the evening at Ravindralaya, a big hall with a stage constructed for the purpose of public entertainments. With the help of the photographs, which accompanied the applications, the organisers had selected twenty-five contestants for each competition. The applicants were among the few young Indian girls whose parents were modern and who had given their written permission for their daughters to enter the contest. Some middle-class Indian families, who could afford to send their daughters to English schools, looked upon contests as opportunities for their daughters to have a chance to make rich marriages. Educated and wealthy Indian men always advertise in the matrimonial columns of the major newspapers in India for fair, well-educated, beautiful girls for marriage.

At the beauty parlour I met a most beautiful girl, Nayara Mirza, a Muslim girl who I came to know was also entering the Famina Beauty Contest that evening. Her elder sister was with her and they were discussing a style for her hair that reached her ankles in a thick plait. The hairdresser thought it best to cut it shorter to set it up in a bun, but the girl and her sister were against it, so they could not come to a decision.

That evening at six the Femina Beauty Contest and the Fashion Show started. The hall was crowded with well to do Indians. There were also a few film directors and advertising agents looking for new faces. Many rich Indian families simply go to watch the fashion parade. They pay according to the seating arrangements. Mrs Johnstone had a pass, as her daughter was a contestant. My mother did not have leave nor train fare to accompany me.

Each contestant was given a number card to hold in front of her every time she walked on the stage. I wore a pink silk *sari* with silver work which my mother had bought for me on credit. The judges were seated in the front row of the audience. There was a fashion show between every round of the contest. The show started with all twenty-five Miss Lucknow contestants parading around the stage, holding their numbers in front. Then we all stood at the back in one line, while each one walked individually to the front of the stage, where the compere, Mr Amin Sayani, stood with the microphone and introduced them to the audience. Each contestant spoke about her interests and ambitions. When my turn came I was extremely nervous. My heart pounded, my legs trembled and my mouth went dry. I was almost paralysed with fear that I would have a heart attack and die. But I kept thinking of what Dr Burke said and was determined to hold to my recent resolution. I told myself if I was really sick I would rather die proudly on the stage than as a coward running to the doctors and someone who was a burden on a lonely mother. So I walked up and down the stage in spite of my feelings of sickness. Nothing happened to me.

Twelve of us were chosen from the twenty-five in the first round. Nayara Mirza was dressed in her rich pure white silk *sari* with gold border. Her hair was in a thick single plait trailing down her back to her ankles. I was one of the six selected from the twelve. After another display of the fashions, we six were again on the stage. The judges gave points on our dress, walk, posture, confidence and looks. In the semi-final round the compere, Mr Sayani, was to establish our wit and intelligence as well as our ability to speak fluently, so asked questions of us. I was unable to speak without a quiver in my voice and perhaps for this reason I was eliminated at that stage, but I gained my confidence and my fear of death disappeared which to me was more important. Nayara Mirza was crowned 'Miss Lucknow' that year and went to win the Miss India contest in Bombay then travelled overseas to the Miss Universe contest as the representative of India.

After the contest I decided to find a teaching position away from Allahabad, since I felt healthy again. I applied to my old school in Lucknow. The principal was happy to have me back. By then Aunt Clarke had retired and was headmistress at a private primary school run by a friend of hers in Lucknow. She lived on the school premises.

✣ ✣ ✣ ✣ ✣

While still waiting for the holidays to end, I had a surprise visit from Marvin, a young Anglo-Indian boy who lived near Mrs Macwan's house and was a second lieutenant in the Army. We had both grown up in Allahabad but had not had anything to do with each other. The boys in Allahabad had considered me too religious and thought I would be a nun one day. But since I had been to the USA and in the beauty contest and boyfriends, Danny and Ralph, they realised I could be approached and be friends. Marvin came to see me on the pretext of finding out about applying for immigration to Australia, as he was not happy in the Indian Army. He asked me to see a film one evening. After his holidays, he returned to Kashmir and we corresponded regularly for sometime. Marvin was very handsome, very fair in complexion, with dark brown hair. Both his parents were descendants of domiciled British, but since I was afraid of rejection and humiliation because of my background, I corresponded with him only as a friend, though his letters showed his feelings towards me.

✣ ✣ ✣ ✣ ✣

Flight Lieutenant Sundarajan informed me a week before the school was to open that he had been transferred to Lucknow and offered me a lift as I was to teach there in 1968. I was delighted and accepted the offer. I had never had the opportunity to travel long distance by road; besides, I was not looking forward to the train journey in a third-class compartment!

On the weekend, we drove along the Grand Trunk Road built by the great Emperor Ashoka two hundred years before the birth of Christ. On either side of the road, Emperor Ashok had planted huge Pipal (Banyan) trees with thick foliage, for the comforts of the pedestrian and the tourists. Resthouses were built beside the road, with free food and bed available to all travellers. The Grand Trunk Road ran from the North to the South of India. It remains as one of the central elements in the history of northern India. The British improved the road for modern vehicles as it runs through many important cities.

Not long after leaving Allahabad our car hit a bull as it suddenly lurched across the road. Fortunately, Sundarajan was able to stop quickly so it was not badly hurt and managed to get up and run off. But, seemingly out of nowhere, a crowd of men gathered, armed with large sticks of solid bamboo. They were all sturdy, well-built Indian farmers and herdsmen in dhotis (white loincloth wrapped around the waistline) and white turbans. They had been keeping an eye on the cattle from a distance and the accident made them run to the spot. Sundarajan knew they would chase and hit the car with the sticks and throw stones if he tried to leave, so we waited as they surrounded the car. He explained what happened, but they insisted the bull was injured and if we did not pay them compensation they would beat Sundarajan to death. So he gave them one hundred *rupees*. The men left mumbling and grumbling that the amount paid was too little. We continued the journey with no further adventures.

Sundarajan visited me quite often at the school. He took me to dances at the Defence Club, although he could not dance properly and would drink most of the time. He was very rude and abrupt when speaking to others, but to me he was polite, obliging and a good friend.

I decided to enter another beauty competition. Again I was in the finals, but not amongst the last three chosen. It was there I met Mr Nigam, a film director, who made documentaries for the Indian Film Division. A few days after the contest, Mr Nigam came to see me one evening at the school and offered me a role in his latest documentary film on family planning. I was overjoyed. I needed photographs taken to see if I was photogenic, so one Saturday morning Sundarajan took me to a photographer, a friend of Mr Nigam's who took several photographs of me in many different poses. I returned to the school with Sundarajan and inadvertently left my handbag in the car while I went upstairs to my room. When I returned I found one of Marvin's letters in Sundarajan's hand. He had gone through my handbag.

"You never told me you had a boyfriend with whom you have been corresponding!" he said with anger in his eyes.

"You have no business going through my bag and reading my letter. Besides, what is the harm! We are just friends, aren't we?" I said calmly to him.

He threw my bag and the letter out of the car and drove away in high dudgeon. I stood there feeling a mixture of guilt and sympathy. Sundarajan had never given me any indication of his feelings other than we were just good friends. Such extreme display of jealousy was not what I had imagined from him!

I spent that afternoon with Aunt Clarke. As previously planned, Sundarajan collected me in the evening. Throughout the journey we did not speak to each other. We had previously planned to attend a dance at the Defence Club. At the dance he kept drinking and saying he was very fond of me and desired to marry me. He repeatedly reproached me for writing to another boy while I was going out with him. Sundarajan looked sinister and drunk. His friends tried to stop him from drinking but could not. I was not going to bear his nonsense nor was I ready to commit to anyone, because of my experience with Danny. Sundarajan had given me no time to explain this. I became agitated with his dramatic behaviour and asked him to take me home. He walked towards his car carrying a glass of neat whisky and drove dangerously and I was frightened. I thought that it would not be good for my reputation as a teacher to be found injured or dead with a drunk at two in the morning! I summoned up my courage, pulled the glass out of his hand and then threw it out of the window onto the road. Then I commanded him to drive me home safely, as I was sick of his dramatics. I also said that if he continued the way he was I would not want to see him any more. My sudden change of attitude reduced him to total silence, as he had not anticipated my firmness and temper. He drove in silence to Aunt Clarke's house where I was going to spend the night. After leaving me, he drove off again at great speed, but returned several times that night, screaming in a drunken state about how much he loved me. I stayed inside with Aunt and did not open the door. Aunt Clarke was scared about what he might do to me in revenge as a wounded suitor, but that was the last I saw of him for some time.

✣ ✣ ✣ ✣ ✣

The photographs were impressive and Mr Nigam gave me a part in the documentary film on family planning.

The story was about two Indian farmers in a small village, one of whom had many children. After his death, his land was divided into necessarily small parts, making the family poorer as a result and unable to educate the children. But the other farmer had only one son, who was able to have a good education and even travel to the city to get a University education. He was able to marry an educated lady (me). The pair built a good brick house in the village and had two children whom they could educate and bring up properly. They had enough land to satisfy their needs.

I was busy with the role for a couple of weeks. Sundarajan had stopped seeing me and I stopped writing to Marvin. During the shooting Mr Nigam was a good friend and transported me to and from school. He saw me on some evenings during the weekdays to explain the requirements of the role. To start with, I was very proud to know a film director who had been to Bombay and knew some of my favourite film stars. A couple of times he invited me to his flat for dinner and cooked me my favourite meals. He was in his late thirties and lived by himself. I often wondered where his wife and family were, as he never spoke of them.

✣ ✣ ✣ ✣ ✣

At school, Allan Baker, a boy of about fourteen, visited me every Thursday from La Martiniere Boys' School. He was from Allahabad, the grandson of Mr Baker the old gentleman who had helped us when I had meningitis and collapsed. Allan and his younger brothers were boarders at the school. They were allowed out once a week to visit their local guardians. Allan had no local guardian, so when he came to know of my teaching at the Girls' School, he informed the authorities about my being his local guardian and managed to obtain permission to visit me. I did not mind, as he was a nice boy with very good manners; besides I did feel obliged to his grandfather.

One Thursday, Allan delivered me a message from one of his teachers, David, who was also from Allahabad and at the time was teaching in La Martiniere Boys' School. David wanted to meet me at the coming Founder's Day. I had seen David at the dances in Allahabad. He came from a very well to do Anglo-Indian family and was extremely handsome, like Dirk Bogarde, the famous film star of the English movies I had seen. Many Anglo-Indian girls fell in love with David for his looks. He seemed to prefer sophisticated Anglo-Indian girls. I could not believe he wanted to meet me. He was very fair and belonged to a domiciled European family.

I met David on the Founders' Day Ball held at La Martiniere Boys' School. The building of the Boys' School was like a castle and had the grave of the founder, Claude Martin, in the chapel, which was a part of the basement. La Martiniere Boys' School was once St Xaviers, run by the Roman Catholics and where Rudyard Kipling's character in the novel, Kim, went to study. Later the school was given to the Anglicans when it was renamed 'La Martiniere Boys' School'. It was meant for Anglo-Indian boys, but was available to all who could afford it. The medium of instruction was English. It had its own swimming pool, horse-riding grounds and stables for the horses.

The founder of both the Girls' and the Boys' La Martiniere Schools, Claude Martin, had come to India as a French soldier in the 17th century. He had gambled with the nawabs (Muslim noblemen and kings) over cockfights. The *nawabs* enjoyed gambling of any kind. Claude Martin won many buildings in the city of Lucknow from cockfights and lived a stately life thereafter. He never married but had many mistresses. One in particular was called the Blue Lady, a Muslim lady whose portrait still hangs in the Boys School. Around the Boys' School there are many graves of the women he loved. Claude Martin had many children from his mistresses and he saw to their education and maintenance. Before he died he left the two buildings in particular for use as an English Catholic School. Both the Anglican and Catholic churches claimed it and there was a court case which the Anglican Church won, as Claude Martin had not mentioned the word Roman Catholic in his will and he himself was not a practising Christian. The government took charge of his other buildings, as he left no will regarding them.

At the Founder's Day ceremony the teachers wore graduate gowns and walked in a long line of twos for the assembly and to the chapel before the Ball. I was in charge of the girls from the La Mariniere Girls' School and David and I danced amid the boys and the girls till ten at night.

I saw David practically every week after that. We walked around the school campus and talked about Allahabad and teaching. David didn't believe in going out to dinners or films. I realised he had fallen in love with me but he never told me so. It was Allan who informed me that David had confided in him of his love for me, but did not know how to tell his parents, because they wanted him to settle down with an Anglo-Indian of his own standard. I think I began to like him too, but again I was conscious that my background would not be acceptable. I knew his parents would prefer a girl from a good Anglo-Indian family having both parents wearing European clothes and following that culture.

My passport expired and when I went to renew it, I wrote truthfully without thinking that my father was an American. My application for an Indian passport was declined. I confided in Mr Nigam about this since I knew of his association with high-ranking Government authorities in Lucknow. He explained to me that I had to apply for Indian citizenship before I could get an Indian passport again and so I did. This meant that I had to go to Allahabad, the place of my residence. Mr Nigam asked me to dinner the night I was to leave for Allahabad. He was to take me to the station afterwards. He had cooked the dinner and I enjoyed it very much. Mr Nigam then took me for a long drive and by the time we reached the station, the train had already left. Since there was another train at 1 am, Mr Nigam suggested I spend the time at his flat. He said I could rest in his bed on the terrace while he did some work in his office and later he would see me off at the station when it was time.

I was very tired and dozed off to sleep. Around 11.30pm, I woke feeling that someone was watching me. Mr Nigam was peering at me through the net. I asked him what the matter was. He smiled and replied that he was just looking to see whether I was asleep. I could not go back to sleep after that and spent the time talking to him till it was time to leave for the station.

There were times when I thought that Mr Nigam was very fond of me. He was quite fair in complexion in comparison to other Indians and rather short and stout. He was not really handsome but had a very pleasant and friendly face with small, gleaming, expressive eyes. His smiles were full of encouragement and assurance. Once he told me of his love for an army officer's daughter, whom he was unable to marry, because his mother found her unsuitable. As a result, her parents arranged for her to marry someone else. He was very upset with his mother and walked out of her house, ever since living by himself. He said he did not believe in marriage any more. Although Mr Nigam drank a lot of alcohol when he was alone, he never drank in my company because he knew I did not approve of it. I could talk to him about any topic and he was always willing to listen and praise me when necessary, making me feel confident of myself. I began considering him a good friend and perhaps even started liking him a little. I know I was searching for someone who would accept me and give me the family background I did not have.

I wanted so much to belong to a family and be loved.

I wanted someone who would make me forget my past and the stigma which my scandalous birth had given me.

Towards the end of 1968 David informed me that Mrs

Carter and her husband had moved to La Martiniere School from Allahabad. She had taken up the position of a House Mistress and her husband that of the Physical Education teacher. They had to resign from their last job in Allahabad. I was not happy at the idea of her being in Lucknow. It reminded me of Allahabad when she publicly called us bastards and exposed our origins to the gossips. I became afraid of my involvements with David and Mr Nigam and felt that though they both loved me, neither of them spoke of marrying me because of some personal reason of their own, so I was not willing to accept them in any other way except as a husband. I was still determined to have a respectable home and a good background for my children. By the end of the year, I decided to leave Lucknow to a fresh start. I had been on move since childhood running from people and the past.

I applied for a teaching position at the Frank Anthony Public School in Delhi and was called for an interview. Danny's Aunt from his mother's side, Mrs Bains, was in Delhi. His mother once introduced me to Danny's Aunt and her husband Brigadier Bains. So I went to her place for two days. Brigadier Bains gave me a letter of recommendation, as he knew the principal of Frank Anthony, General Dunn, a retired army officer. His recommendations may have helped me, for I got the teaching position for the following year 1968 in Delhi.

Mr Nigam was happy to hear of my success in getting the position. He said he would get himself transferred to Delhi, as he too wanted to leave Lucknow.

David was upset, but did not stop me, nor did he make any promises. I felt I made the right choice before I faced another rejection. I was completely over my nervous breakdown by then.

33

A model and a teacher

I arrived in Delhi in January 1969. The English schools open in the second week of January, after the one-month winter holidays. Frank Anthony Public School provided accommodation for its teachers. I was given a small-elongated one-room flatette, attached to the landlord's accommodation. This was the first time I had to settle myself into a self-contained place. Mum came a week after I moved in and helped me establish myself. I did not know Delhi well at the time. Mum surprised me one day by saying that she had been to Delhi with Papa before I was born, but knew nothing about the place, as Papa had taken her around in his car. Many years later, after her death in Australia, I came to know that Papa had tried to live with Mum in Delhi as Mr and Mrs Lyons. At the time he found it very hard to find work and support a family as he had intended. The Jesuits spied upon his every move because they wanted him to return to the religious life as a priest. He and Mum then moved to Calcutta, where I was born and then to Mirzapur, Allahabad and Saharanpur. It was at Saharanpur that he was forced to return to the priesthood, with a promise to support the two of us.

While Mum was in Delhi we went sightseeing to some historic places. We travelled by bus most of the time and experienced the crowd and the rush. I had to hold on to mum's hands to ensure she was not lost. Mum left me a fortnight later after she had properly established me in my flat.

I had to wear dresses at school, as it was an Anglo-Indian institution. The main condition of employment in that school was to wear dresses and act like an Anglo-Indian following British ways. After school when shopping I usually wore a *sari*, as that way I was treated with respect by shopkeepers who considered that anyone wearing a dress could be expected to act like people in English films, that, to them, was behaving immorally by openly making love. There was no kissing in the Indian films at that time and even the relationship between a husband and a wife was always kept secret. No lovers dared to openly hold hands in public, as it was considered indecent.

✣ ✣ ✣ ✣ ✣

Frank Anthony Public School was a Co-educational school. Mr Frank Anthony, a Member of Parliament was the Founder of the school. He was the representative of Anglo-Indians in the Parliament. I became the class teacher of Year 5, teaching all the subjects except Hindi. I also taught English to Year 8. Since the school was not run by any religious organisation, I had to teach Moral Science instead of Religion to the students every morning, in the first period.

✣ ✣ ✣ ✣ ✣

I learned of agencies that took photographs for commercial modelling and visited one in Connaught Place with my folder of photographs taken by Mr Nigam's photographer. They liked them and I won many assignments for commercial modelling. I modelled in advertisements for suits, toothpaste, *saris*, temples, tourism, the Rajdoot motor-cycle, Fiat cars and many others. My pictures were on large billboards, in the magazines and newspapers and on the screen in the picture halls. Black and white commercials yielded two hundred *rupees* and coloured slides, five hundred *rupees*. My regular school salary was five hundred *rupees* per month. I also appeared in television programs. I found myself enjoying popularity. The money helped to pay some of Mum's debts.

I still wrote to Papa and informed him of all my activities. As usual he sometimes replied but most of the time Petronilla wrote to me in a very impersonal way. Papa's letters were mostly about his experiences in India. He made no comment or reference on my modelling. He was nearing sixty-eight years of age. At times I felt disgusted with his letters, they mostly contained news and lectures about how I must take life. I wanted him to write more personal letters displaying his affection for me, his daughter, so I started sending him letters complaining and asking why he did not write like other fathers, affectionately. I was still his little daughter full of love and eagerness. I wanted all his love and attention just like the little child he had left behind. Perhaps I had never grown out of that emotional stage towards him. Often his letters frustrated me, he did not understand the feelings of a daughter who loved him intensely. His letters were so impersonal. Perhaps, being a priest and committed, Papa felt he could not allow himself the freedom to express the feelings of a father to a daughter. He might have had the guilt embedded in him, being a priest, but I had nothing to restrict my love for him, my precious father. I ignored Petronilla's letters and wrote to him directly in reply to her letters. He ignored my reminders about his promise to obtain us the US citizenship. The letters from the USA came less frequently than before.

Although I was enjoying my new popularity as a commercial model and teaching in New Delhi, I was still waiting for my Papa to send me the citizenship papers to visit him again. Since the time I returned from Denver I had been wanting to go back so just carried on with my life aimlessly in the meantime. I was still confused at the way things turned out. I wasn't free to display my feelings like every other young woman could because I carried strict personal disciplinary and virtuous values in the light of my parents' scandalous act.

I also wanted to prove to Papa that even though he deserted us and I was born of an Indian mother, I was very much like him and could achieve a lot to make him proud. I wanted to claim my American father publicly but I could not, because everyone in India knew him to be a Catholic priest. I could not even talk about my American father to my friends. It really hurt when people asked me about my father. I avoided the topic or ignored them.

I could not tell a lie. I was unable to bluff my way in my life, it had to be truth, as bitter as it seemed, but no one was ready to accept the truth. Sometimes I wished I would find someone who would accept me as I was, someone who would either take me to my father or make me forget him and help me start a new life.

I wanted to live like everyone else but I needed an anchor to give me stability and security. I wanted someone to get me out of the disgrace other people and the church put me in so I felt that while my father was forgiven for breaking the vow he made to the church, I was punished for life.

Sometimes I wondered whether Papa received my letters. I wondered whether Petronilla opened the mail and did not tell my father what I wrote or told him what she wanted conveyed. But I could do nothing. I only hoped that one day soon I would be able to return to him.

34

An attempt to find a husband

I continued corresponding regularly with Mum in Allahabad. Although she was proud of my success in modelling and teaching she began bringing up the matter of marriage. She often wrote about Violet and my futures. She wanted us to marry and settle down before she died. I was nearing my twenty-eighth year. Papa also mentioned it in one of his letters, that since I wanted to marry and settle down, I should concentrate on getting myself a good Catholic husband, as I was getting beyond the marriageable age for a woman.

I liked modelling as it involved meeting all sorts of people. For many conservative Indians modelling was not a respectable profession. They paid the models well for advertising their products but considered the models as bad characters for exposing themselves to earn money. Rich industrialists thought they could make the models do anything for them by paying them well. I was very selective about my assignments and did not take any which would give me a bad name as a teacher, since that was my career.

Once I had done some modelling for a firm making woollen goods and was invited to a party involving drinking at Faridabad, some distance from Delhi, where the factory and the mansion of the industrialist was situated. I disliked the taste of alcohol and I was also of the opinion that most people got carried away after drinking and did things they would never have done otherwise. I refused the invitation. The photographer urged me to accept the invitation, as he said that going would open up more assignments. But I continued to refuse to protect my reputation.

I decided to make my mother happy by settling down to married life but I had found no one so far. I was jilted once by Danny and was frightened. I decided to answer advertisements in the matrimonial columns. I had a few replies from those in the Church newspaper, but they were from divorcees or widowers with grown-up children. In the Hindustan Times (a popular Indian newspaper), I saw one, which read: 'Wanted, fair convent-educated girl. Caste or religion no bar, for a fair Army officer'. Since it mentioned "convent-educated", I replied to the box number given assuming that the person advertising was a Christian. I gave the school telephone number for contact, as I had none of my own. There was a prompt response, a call to me a few days later. The very soft and pleasant voice introduced a Major Naresh Chauhan, a Punjabi, who asked me to meet him for lunch. I chose the Mikado Restaurant in Connaught Place and said that I would be wearing a green silk *sari*, while he said that he would be standing near his silver coloured Fiat car, the registration number he quoted. So that afternoon we met for coffee.

He was handsome, slim, of medium height, with a fair complexion and light-coloured eyes. He was wearing a khaki uniform that enhanced his looks. When he told me he was a Hindu I was taken aback. That first day I said nothing, I felt awkward at the arranged meeting with a stranger and left the restaurant soon after a cup of coffee. He rang the next day, wanting to see me again. I agreed to meet after school, but had decided that as he was not a Christian, I did not want to continue seeing him. I knew only what the good nuns had taught me at school. My Christian faith and religious values had helped me through my traumatic childhood and life so far and I was not willing to give up my faith for the sake of a man. From the window of my classroom I saw Naresh, waiting for me. In height and build he looked like Danny and like Papa as I remembered him from my childhood.

We drove to a restaurant in Connaught Place and I told him that I also did part-time commercial modelling. He seemed impressed. He told me how he felt about me from the first time he had seen me. He said he had received many responses to his advertisement for a bride. There were a couple from the south of India who were very rich but divorced. He felt that I was the one he would choose, as he had fallen in love with me at first sight. I promptly told him that I was sorry to disappoint him, as I had thought he was a Christian from his advertisement. I could not marry a non-Christian. However, he replied that religion was of no importance to him and that he was willing to convert to Christianity for my sake. That impressed me, but I firmly told him I needed time to think the matter over. He wanted us to be friends in the meantime. On leaving, he said he would wait for me and would eventually make me love him. I did not see him for the next few weeks.

I had a letter from Mr Nigam, short and formal, simply informing me that he was going to visit Delhi and would call on me. It was just his way of writing. He never displayed his emotions, which I found very annoying, since I certainly liked some of his ways especially his caring and considerate manner; in these respects he was like my father. He was so easy to talk to and I could tell him all my problems. But I could never have lived with him without getting married. I wanted a respectable family life which I had never had.

One day both Nigam and Naresh rang to say they were to visit me. About six that evening I waited, as they were to arrive about that time. I decided that if Nigam came before Naresh I would tell him I had a previous engagement, since he had not given me any prior notice. But Naresh was thirty minutes early so I got into his car for the drive to Connaught Place as planned. We turned the corner into the main road, when Mr Nigam's car approached and later when we were filling the petrol at a nearby station, I saw his car returning from my locked apartment. Although I felt sorry for him, I was glad I had been able to make clear to him he could not take me for granted, ignore my feelings and expect me to be his mistress waiting for him. Many years later I met him in Lucknow married to an Indian Christian girl who forced him marry her because she was pregnant with his child. He was a heavy drinker by then.

Naresh visited me quite often after that and we went to his Defence Club for dances or the discos. I kept my distance and was no more than a friend to him. He on the contrary always tried to impress me in order to win my attention and love by being very agreeable and emphasising his position.

Naresh promised to become a Christian for my sake. This, I thought was God's plan for me that if Naresh became a Catholic I would save a soul. I believed I had a purpose in life and even though I could not become a nun, I could still be a good Catholic, setting good example and saving souls for Jesus. It was very important for me to have a purpose in life, it made me feel wanted and accepted by Christ even though the Church had rejected my desire to become a nun. Although I had stopped going to Church as often as I had done before, I could not change my Christian views.

Audrey and Violet visited me during the short school break in October that year. I introduced them to Naresh. My first thought was that he would make a good husband for Violet who needed to settle down. Unfortunately, Naresh shattered my hopes by proclaiming to them over and over about how much he loved me and that I was the only woman for him. He said not accepting him was breaking his heart. Audrey and Violet praised him to me later and tried to make me understand the value of having someone as loving and faithful as Naresh.

35

A popular woman of the year 1969

Shortly after Violet and Audrey left for Allahabad, Naresh invited me to a cocktail party at the Defence Club. He said it was an official party, on the occasion of a change in the Chief of the Army. I did not want to go, but he urged me to attend, as I would never have the chance to see such a ceremony again. He said that he wanted me to witness the grandeur of army life. I eventually agreed. He asked me to dress in my best *sari*.

I wore a pink and silver *sari*. My dark brown hair was shoulder-length and I had worn make-up and the long silver earrings that I thought specially suited me. Naresh arrived in full uniform, looking very handsome, rather like Danny, I thought. We drove to the Army Club at Daula Kuah. From a distance I saw it was festively decorated. The Army band was blaring inside the building. The car park was full and soldiers in khaki were everywhere, attending to the cars and the gate. It all looked very formal.

Once we parked the car Naresh and I walked up the steps of the building. I noticed that the officer with his lady in front of us showed their invitation card at the door before entering. Just before showing his card Naresh whispered to me:

"You'll have to act as my wife, as no woman-friends are admitted. All the officers are Colonel or above in rank, except we four Majors who have been invited with our wives to cater to the other officers. I will not be with you. Mrs Prithviraj, the wife of one of my Major friends, will look after you."

I was shocked. I did not want to go in and act as his wife. It would be a lie. I could not do it. It made me angry that he had concealed that till the last moment.

"No, I cannot do that," I said angrily, "I wish to return home immediately. Please tell me where to catch the bus or taxi from."

"Don't be silly!" he hissed.

I turned towards the gate when I heard the officer at the door announce:

"Major and Mrs Chauhan!" Naresh had already handed the invitation card with the names printed on it. I felt Naresh's arm around me, gently pulling me inside the door. There was a couple behind us waiting to enter. I could do nothing but make an exhibition of my displeasure, but before I could say anything a middle-aged lady came up to us.

"Mrs Prithviraj, this is Minnie. Please take good care of her, as she is very nervous." Naresh said.

It seemed that Mrs Prithviraj was aware of his plan to bring me to the party as his wife. She was a short, plump lady wearing a black *sari* with gold border. She escorted me in, trying her best to make me feel at ease. Most Indian women like wearing black if they are fair-skinned as they considered it accentuates their complexion. (For Hindus, white is the colour of mourning, not black.)

Naresh disappeared through a glass door at the end of the passage which opened on to a verandah and a beautiful lawn, crowded with officers and women in superb *saris*, displaying their exquisite gold jewellery, mostly studded with diamonds. Most of the middle aged Indian women of the officers were drinking whisky, seemingly the fashion among the wives of higher-ranking officers. The officers were all smartly dressed in their medalled uniforms. There were many Sikhs with turbans amongst the officers.

"Don't look so shocked. Act normal," Naresh said, serving me a glass of orange juice, as he went around with a tray of drinks.

I stood in one corner dumbfound and angry with him for getting me into that situation. Mrs Prithviraj walked off every now and then to greet a senior officer's wife. I had no knowledge of army life, nor had I ever been to such a formal party. I was completely out of place.

"Hi there, I'm Sam. What's your name?"

I turned around, the words had been addressed to me by a tall, fair-skinned, middle-aged, handsome officer in uniform.

He was wearing numerous medals and ribbons. I thought he was being forward in speaking to me like that and was about to say to him, "Do I know you?" when I saw Mrs Prithiviraj scuttling back from the other officers' wives and her husband and Naresh striding back with their trays from different directions. Mrs Prithviraj reached us.

"This is Mrs Chauhan, wife of Major Chauhan, sir."

He ignored her and repeated his question to me about my name, adding one about the corps to which my husband belonged.

I looked at his twinkling eyes, with their touch of sarcasm and tried to say "Mrs Chauhan," then stuttered about the matter of the corps.

"You don't know what corps your husband is in!" He said laughing.

I saw Naresh freeze in the distance. Mrs Prithviraj could say nothing, as she had been ignored. For a moment I stood in an agony of dumb embarrassment. Then suddenly there was an announcement.

"The new commander-in-chief will now deliver his address."

"Excuse me." The officer who had been talking to me made his way to the microphone. He was the new commander-in-chief, General Manekshaw, who was also called 'Sam' by his friends!

"Thank God nothing went wrong," Naresh said, as he joined me. "I would have been court-martialled if he knew I brought a girlfriend to his official party."

We left the party shortly afterwards. Naresh said the new Chief liked young and beautiful women and that was why he had taken notice of me in preference to older wives of the senior officers. Naresh complimented me on my looks and dress, which had brought the Chief to speak to me.

✣ ✣ ✣ ✣ ✣

One day Naresh took me to a palatial house in the neighbouring suburb of Greater Kailash. He said that it belonged to his eldest sister who was married to an ex-prince from Punjab and the house was for sale, as his sister and her husband had not liked it after it had been built: The building had eight rooms, which were all locked except for the drawing room. It was huge with a large fireplace. I was impressed with the building. Naresh took me on to the terrace upstairs and for the first time tried to kiss me. I strongly objected and pushing his face away, started walking towards the door, saying I wanted to return to the car. Naresh was very apologetic for upsetting me and before I could say anything else, he bit the tip of the index finger of his left hand, making it bleed and swore saying, that, by the blood of a Rajput, he loved me very much and was going to marry me at any cost.

I was stunned and as I had never witnessed such behaviour, except in Indian films. He was in his mid-thirties then. All the way back he kept apologising for his behaviour and swearing his love for me. After that day he started obliging me with lifts in his car to and from modelling assignments. It was as though he was trying to win my confidence and make me dependent on him. I hated to travel by crowded bus and the auto-rickshaws cost too much, so I was happy to have a good friend who was kind and caring and at the same time a great help in a big city like Delhi.

I decided to enter another beauty contest. Naresh presented me with a sky-blue chiffon *sari* and a pair of black high-heeled sandals. He even helped me do my make-up with eyeliner and encouraged me to wear dark lipstick, which suited me. I walked and talked with more confidence, since I knew that Naresh was sitting amongst the audience and watching me with anticipation. I felt encouraged by his devotion and expectations.

I placed first among the runners-up in Delhi and was presented with five hundred *rupees* and a beauty set. I was one of the few selected to compete in the Miss India contest later in Bombay. The winner would be sent overseas for the Miss Universe Competition.

Naresh was overjoyed at my success and took me to the Oberoi five-star hotel to celebrate. He boasted to everyone about how he had given me guidance on make-up and dressing, which had helped me to win the contest as the first runner-up. He also boasted to all his friends that his girlfriend was one of the beauty contest winners.

The day after the competition my photograph was in the leading newspapers and women's magazines of India. I was interviewed by the fashion press and featured on the front page of, Femina. That year I won many contests; the "May Queen 1969" competition held at the Anglo-Indian Club in Delhi, "Lady Shree Ram Queen '69", organised by the Shree Ram cloth mills for suiting materials and the "the Lakme Queen 1969", organised by Lakme cosmetics for women. Those successes led to more modelling assignments.

The child who was once placed into various orphanages, who had walked the streets of Allahabad homeless in the heat of mid-summer in India, was rejected by the Church and could not become a nun and who had sunk to suicidal depression, was in the leading papers and magazines of India with the name of her father reluctantly given to her and published for anyone to read, was socially accepted.

I wrote to Papa about my successes with mixed feelings of information and exhilaration. I told him about Naresh, who was from a wealthy and respectable family and had proposed marriage with a promise to become a Christian. A few weeks later, I had a reply from him, advising me to marry a poor Anglo-Indian teacher rather than a Hindu. He said that mixed religion marriages never worked. He further advised me to live purposefully, doing good for the many unfortunates in India, rather than marry at the late age of almost twenty-nine. At the time his letter annoyed me, especially as he did not even congratulate me on my successes. I felt that my father never cared to understand me. He was always looking at me from the point of a missionary and not that of a father. All my life I had craved for his love as a father. It was easy for him to forget a child he had helped to create, whereas, I, his daughter, could not forget the man who was partly responsible for bringing me into this world, whose flesh and blood I was. I believed he had the responsibility of giving me emotional and physical security by providing me with a home and a respectable family life and had not done so, instead he himself had settled down to one leaving us to face the consequences of his wrongdoing. His other commitments were not important to me because I felt that I mattered more than all of them, since he had brought me into this world. At that time I was very upset with his letter, as I had hoped for his recognition and appreciation. He had not kept his promise to obtain citizenship for me to enable me to return to the USA. I had been patiently overlooking all his letters which mainly related his past experiences in India and few pieces of advice. I felt confident to write and tell him my feelings about him. I wrote that he had no right to lay down the law to me about what I should or should not do, because when I had needed his guidance throughout my childhood, he had never been there and since I was an adult I knew my mind and could make my own choices. I told him that if I married a Hindu at least I would have a home, which was more than he ever gave me. An Anglo-Indian or a Christian would always taunt me for my background, whereas a Hindu may never discover it. I told him he was to blame for the sufferings we had undergone, while he sat in the USA making another home for himself and that, in the circumstances it was best for him to consider two options, one to return to the Church as a priest and the other, to return to India and marry my mother, giving her a respectable home in her old age.

I had never told my father of the treatment we had received from everyone as a result of being the daughters of a priest, since we had limited time together when in Denver, USA; besides I was too shocked with the whole thing while I was with him. I could not bring myself to hurt a father, whom I found after so many years of separation. I could not tell him what we underwent because of his desertion. I was afraid to lose him again and I needed to develop a relationship with a father whose image I carried in my heart, but did not know as a person. It was my first letter telling him some of my thoughts. I never heard from Papa or Petronilla after that, though he continued writing to Violet for some time. After a year Petronilla continued the correspondence with Violet saying that 'Mike' was too busy to write. Sometimes she sent Violet and later, her children, gifts of clothes and food, but I was forgotten.

36

A desire for a respectable marriage

I had to leave for Bombay to participate in the final round of the Miss India Competition. The three contestants from every State in India were going to compete to be Miss India. Next was a trip for the winner to the USA for the Miss Universe Competition.

Naresh offered to accompany me to Bombay and to help me with the make-up, as well as give me moral support. I thought it was a good idea. He obtained two return tickets on the internal flight to Bombay on an Army concession. At Bombay I was given a room along with other contestants in a hotel organised by the contest authorities. Naresh stayed at an Army guesthouse nearby.

We stayed in Bombay for four days. On the first day Naresh took me to visit a friend of his, Dinaz, whom he had met during a posting in Bombay. She was a Parsee by religion. Naresh said that she was a good friend of his and had been a great comfort when his younger brother, Surinder, had been murdered. As a result of the tragedy, Naresh had himself transferred to Delhi, to support his parents. Dinaz had written many consoling letters to him, even after he had left Bombay.

We found Dinaz at home. She was in her early twenties and seemed very happy to see Naresh as she opened the door, but her expression changed when she saw me. Naresh greeted her casually and introduced me to her with a note of pride in his voice and gestures.

"I would like you to meet Minnie. She is a beauty queen from Delhi and has come here to take part in the Miss India competition. I would like you to guide her to the best cosmetic shops in Bombay and help her select everything that would make her a winner this evening."

I thought Naresh was rather presumptuous in making the requests, which sounded more like orders.

"All right, but it will have to wait till the afternoon because I am just about to take my younger brother to a swimming pool," she said looking rather hurt and angry at his manner.

"Okay. We'll be here at 4 o'clock. Make sure you are not late," Naresh said, turning to the door and giving no sign of friendliness or politeness, even though they had met after a long while and had been good friends once. I told him as we walked through gate that he had been rather abrupt with her and that I would be very surprised if she were there at the set time.

"Oh, we understand each other and she knows me well enough. She'll be there you will see," he said.

But, as I expected, she was not. Her servant said she had not returned from the pool and left a message before leaving that she would not be back till late that evening. I reminded Naresh of his abrupt manner towards her, but he was not ready to accept his fault.

That evening Naresh was determined I use heavy make-up and have my hair up in a bun for the Beauty Contest. He insisted on my buying a black and gold *sari* for the occasion, since he said the black would go very well with my fair complexion. I hated dull colours like black and brown, as they made me look old and morbid, but I did as Naresh advised, because I could not win an argument with him.

This time I made the semi-finals in Bombay, but was not among the first three. Perhaps the black *sari* had decreased my confidence.

The next day I met the compere, Mr Sayani. He had come to the hotel with some film directors looking for new faces for a film. Many contestants often became film actresses or models after the contests. Mr Sayani introduced me to a film director who offered me a role in his new film, in spite of the fact that I spoke Hindi with a foreign accent, like all Anglo-Indians, he said. The director said he would have my voice dubbed. I was delighted and told Naresh about it when he came to visit me later. To my surprise, Naresh was disappointed at the news. He discouraged me by saying that a film career was not an ideal one for women, as actresses never make a home and settle down to the role of wife and mother. I assumed that he was jealous.

But later I thought over the whole thing again. By morning I had decided against taking the role in the film, since I wanted to be married and have a good home rather than only popularity as an actress. That afternoon Mr Sayani tried to talk me out of my decision, saying I should think very carefully about turning down the opportunity. He added that, in his opinion, Naresh would never make a good husband and that I should pursue my career as a film actress. But I was at the time obsessed with a desire to have a home and a respectable family of my own and so I turned down the offer to become an actress in the Indian film industry!

Naresh did not visit me for a few days after our return from Bombay. Then one day he came to see me with a proposal to visit the small town of Sardhana, about two hours' drive from Delhi. He said he had a friend there who would put us up for the night, as it would be difficult to return the same day. His friend was in the Army and had informed him that Sardhana had a shrine of Our Lady. The Muslim wife of a nawab, who had died in the Mutiny, built the shrine. The wife had later married a Frenchman and become a Catholic. Unfortunately her French husband also died a few months after the marriage and she became a widow the second time. After her husband's death she built the shrine of Our Lady in Sardhana and donated her palatial house to the Catholic Mission. Many people, both Catholics and the non-Catholics, went there daily with their ailments, from which many of them claimed to be cured. I was still suffering with occasional ear trouble and had to take antibiotics frequently. I jumped at the opportunity and agreed to go with him.

The following Saturday we set out in the evening since we were going to spend the night in his friend's house. It was a long drive on the dusty road. Naresh did not speak much and seemed preoccupied. He even ran over a dog without showing any regret. When we reached Sardhana about eight in the evening, he drove to a house, which was in complete darkness. Naresh said that perhaps his friend had gone to sleep and forgotten about him, suggesting that it would be best to spend the night at the Army guest-house which was close by. At the guesthouse, I was informed that there was only one room available, with just one double bed. It made me furious and I refused to sleep in the same bed with him, since we were not married. I said I was insulted for him to even make the suggestion and that he would never have suggested it to a girl of his religion and caste.

"I am sorry this has happened. I have no intention of hurting you in any way but there is no alternative. We cannot go back now as I am too tired and the road is not safe at this time of the night. Besides, it would be a pity not to see the shrine. So we'd better stay the night here. I had to tell the guesthouse authority that we were husband and wife to get the room. So it would be best if you do not make much noise or else I will be in trouble for telling lies," Naresh said very calmly to me.

I threatened to leave the room and walk home alone if he made any advances during the night. We shared the same bed that night, but I kept on one end, still dressed in the *sari* in which I had travelled. I found it difficult to sleep. Throughout the night I was haunted with the idea of deceit and sin and the thought of the bad name I would get if anyone found out where and how I had spent that night. Naresh seemed to be tired from the drive and was snoring in a short while, but I lay in confusion.

Next morning Naresh was polite as usual and I believed that his friend was to be blamed for the poor arrangements. We went to the Shrine as planned. It was a long time since I had been to a church. I felt the urge to pray to Jesus and Mary once again, as I did when I was a child, ignorant that I was the daughter of a priest. I prayed that Naresh would soon become converted to Christianity so that I would be able to marry him. Afterwards, Naresh told me that he had prayed for the strength to make me happy and that Mother Mary should take away his sight if he ever made me feel otherwise. He was always so dramatic, but all the same I was impressed with his faith and felt certain I had found my partner in life.

I saw more of Naresh from then on and we spent many evenings together at dances and discos. He was always obliging and considerate and made me believe that he loved me very much. I began to enjoy the attention he gave me and the comforts of an upper-class Indian, moving in cars and experiencing the luxury of eating in expensive restaurants. I forgot my past and even my dear Papa and the absence of his letters.

Unfortunately, my happiness was short-lived, because one day after a dance at the Anglo-Indian Club, my friend Jenny Walker advised me to break off with Naresh, as she had heard something bad about him. After much persuasion, she confided that she had been informed that Naresh was married and that his wife had left him. The divorce case on grounds of mental cruelty was in the courts awaiting decision. It shocked me.

When Naresh came to see me the following evening I told him what I had heard. At first his face changed colour, then he burst into tears, saying that he had married a Hindu girl, Shobha, the daughter of an Air Force officer, whom he had seen once as a result of his parents' moves to arrange a marriage. He liked her when they were made to see each other after the parents had accepted the match. But later his parents changed their minds, since Shobha's parents could not offer a large dowry. Naresh did not like the way his parents treated the whole affair and decided to marry Shobha against his parents' wishes. He didn't think the matter of a dowry was import since he earned good money. But after marriage he found that Shobha was flirtatious and humiliated him by her conduct with other officers. It ended up in their having daily quarrels. She used to hit him with slippers and so on and he used to retaliate in defence, which led to their deciding on a separation. Naresh swore to me that it was not his fault and that he meant to tell me about it, but since I seemed such a puritan, he was afraid of losing me. He left the house, but an hour later returned with a file and asked me to read his case and decide for myself who was at fault. He looked very sad and I felt sorry to see him like that. I did not think it necessary to go through the file instead told him that I believed in him, yet needed time to think things over, since it had been a shock to learn of it from someone other than him.

Later Jenny said Naresh's wife worked as a receptionist at a firm and was keen to meet me. She wanted to inform me about Naresh and his treatment of her, but she never kept the appointments we made to meet each other. We spoke on the phone only once.

After learning of Naresh's first marriage I became somewhat indifferent towards him and intended to stop seeing him, even though I had developed great hopes in his promises to marry me and to have a home of my own. Naresh noticed my change in behaviour and one day asked me to visit his home and his parents. I accepted it reluctantly. His father, a north Indian Punjabi, was tall and fair with blue-grey eyes like Naresh's. He was confined to a chair as a result of a stroke. He had once been an engineer working for a British company in Lahore before the partition of India and Pakistan. His father, Milkhi Ram Chauhan, was the eldest son of a wealthy landlord. He was able to go overseas for his degree in engineering. His wife was dark and almost illiterate, as girls were not educated in her time. However, she seemed very smart and had managed to learn to read the Ramayan and the Gita, the two religious books of the Hindus, by herself. She could speak neither English nor Hindi and spoke only in Punjabi, which I could not understand. She sat in the drawing room admiring my looks and complexion and then shed tears.

Naresh translated what she was saying. He said that she was crying at his fate, because his wife, Shobha, had made a mess of his life. Naresh's elder brother, Roshan, was also present with his wife. He too had been educated in London as an electronics engineer, but his wife, the daughter of a doctor was not very well educated. She could not speak English. Roshan, spoke to me in English and told me that Shobha was a bad woman. He said she had ruined his brother's life and that they were happy that Naresh had found a good girl like me for his life-partner.

Naresh took me to his flat and showed me the photographs of the many women who had replied to his newspaper advertisement. He claimed they were all wealthy Indian women, but he preferred me because he had fallen in love with me at first sight since I looked so pure and sincere. He repeated that he had been afraid to tell me about his previous marriage because I was so religious and idealistic and he feared I would reject him. In India the community does not approve divorce, even though it is legal. Divorced men and women are not looked upon with respect. They find it hard to find a partner for a second marriage.

I returned home confused, but much taken by Naresh's behaviour. I was sorry for him. There were stories from both sides that conflicted and I had to make up my own mind. After all, I had been with him a lot and he had been good to me. What happened between him and Shobha was their business, I thought. I could not overlook Naresh's sincerity and respect towards me. Besides I was aware I was not getting any younger, that, since he was not a Catholic, he would never know about my origins and I would have no embarrassment to face from him. But I did intend marrying in the Church as a good Catholic and also convert Naresh to Catholicism. I had no idea the Catholic Church would frown upon a divorced person.

A few weeks later I discovered, through my friend, Jenny, that Naresh had a daughter by his first wife. I thought it did not matter to me, as I was willing to take over his child if necessary, since I loved children. Naresh told me his wife would not part with the child and would not allow him to have custody. Naresh and his family said that his wife was flirtatious and they quarrelled, I believed him, since to me, he was loving, caring and devoted. I did not think the accusations of his wife Shobha, were true. I gave no importance to the stories about Naresh's past, but judged him according to his attitude towards me and continued our relationship with a view to marriage.

Not long after my discovery that he had a daughter, he asked me to meet his niece, Priya, daughter of the sister who owned the mansion in Greater Kailash. She was a radiologist and her husband was a skin specialist in the Indian Medical Institute, New Delhi. It seemed he had confided in them about his feelings for me and of my discovery of his previous marriage. They repeatedly told me about being very pleased to see their favourite and handsome Uncle happy with me. They said that Naresh had not been treated well by his wife and that Shobha's and Naresh's blood didn't match. She was RH negative, he was RH positive. The incompatibility of blood made a lot of difference and they quarrelled. They took a sample of my blood for testing and later informed me that my blood was normal and matched Naresh's and so we would have no problems. I knew nothing of what they were talking about in medical terms. All I knew was that they seemed to like me and were of a very respectable and highly educated family.

I did not think it necessary to discuss Naresh's previous marriage with Mum or anyone at home. Mum was keen only for me to be married and settled.

✣ ✣ ✣ ✣ ✣

Towards the end of the year Naresh suggested I change my school and take up a teaching position closer to where I usually went for modelling assignments. I did not realise then that he was actually trying to get me away from those Anglo-Indian friends of mine who had informed me of his previous marriage. I was successful in securing a teaching position at the Convent of Jesus and Mary in Connaught Place for 1970.

Since I had resigned from Frank Anthony I had to find accommodation. The convent school offered no accommodation to their teachers. Instead, were given an allowance. I obtained a place in the YWCA house, which was within walking distance of the convent. Helen was to share a room with me as she was also teaching in Delhi by then.

A month before the school closed for the winter holidays Violet came to see me. She spent a few days during which she went out every day with boyfriends from Frank Anthony School. Most of them were ex-students of the Teachers' Training College in Allahabad and she had known them before. She told me that she had a fight with her fiance, Russell. She was engaged to be married for the third time but Russell had not fixed the date for marriage. He was an Anglican teacher with no parents and was two years younger than her. Violet was determined to get married that year and had warned him that she would flirt till he made up his mind to marry her within that year.

Russell sent her letters every few days since she came to Delhi and begged in every letter to return to Allahabad, as he was missing her, but Violet ignored them. I took it upon myself to write to Russell and advised him to decide upon a marriage with Violet quickly, before he lost her. Within a week Russell was at the doorstep proposing marriage. Violet was delighted and promised to return. She intended helping me shift from the Frank Anthony's accommodation before we returned to Allahabad together.

37

Another superstition and yet another rejection

Violet and Russell were married during the holidays. Mum attended the wedding with pride and took a few of her nurse friends. She went for only a few hours during the time she was off-duty, as Violet did not seem to need her help. She had organised everything for the wedding with Russell. It was a grand wedding with many of Russell's relatives present. Russell had a big family. Aunt Natasha felt neglected, as Russell's relatives tried to make themselves more important. I was the maid of honour and was very proud that my sister was respectably married and would have a home of her very own at last. I felt that my duty towards her was completed. I invited Naresh for the wedding, partly because I wanted him to witness my flirtatious sister respectably married. He was introduced to everyone at home as my fiancee. I told Mum and Aunt that he was going to become a Christian before our marriage. His looks and his position as a Major in the Indian Army impressed Aunt and Mum. Naresh was very polite and everyone considered him a thorough gentleman.

In the month of March, Naresh went to Singapore for six weeks. He presented me with a few expensive chiffon *saris* and a gold engagement ring on his return. I was thrilled with the presents, as I had never received such expensive gifts from anyone before. I was teaching in a convent school so I was free to wear whatever I preferred, dress or saris and since Naresh liked me to wear *saris* all the time, I did so. From then onwards I considered myself Naresh's fiancee with the gold ring on my finger, waiting patiently for him to decide the date of our marriage. I spoke to him about the Christian religion and made him accompany me to Sunday Services in the Church, which he did without complaint.

A month after his return from Singapore, he took me to his home in the evening as usual. That day I found his father very sick in bed with severe diarrhoea and dehydration as a result of having had fatty bone soup. I advised Naresh to take him immediately to the hospital, but he laughed and put it off, saying his father was not that bad and if necessary, he would take him to the Army Hospital on Monday, as he did not wish to have a private doctor or hospital. The Army Hospital was free to his parents and it was the best, he said. That was on a Saturday.

Unfortunately, on Monday when his father was finally admitted to the hospital, he was beyond help and died within the week. I went to pay my respects to the dead body, which was brought home from the hospital before cremation, as is the Indian custom. Everyone sat mourning in white clothes, crying loudly around the dead body. It is considered appropriate to beat the head and the chest in grief and cry out loudly when someone has died and that is what many were doing before the body was taken by the men only, for cremation that day according to the law. There are no funeral homes in India and the dead have to be disposed off within twelve hours according to the individual religious customs.

Naresh did not see me for a couple of weeks after his father's death. He moved into his parent's home for some time. The Hindus mourn for many weeks for the dead and have many death ceremonies to perform for the salvation of the soul of the dead.

Since he had not visited me for some time I went to visit him at his home and found him behaving indifferently. I thought perhaps he was still upset about his father's death. One evening after my visit to his house, he came to see me and informed me of his wish to discontinue our relationship. He gave me the excuse that his mother and sisters felt I brought bad luck to the family and in particular, since he had given me the gold ring for our engagement, I had caused the death of his father. I could not believe my ears and sat there too shocked to say a word. I had never known Naresh to be superstitious and irrational. The old man had died as a result of their neglect and I had warned them about his condition when he could have been saved. The sense of being a failure and of being rejected, which I had felt so many times before once again made me very depressed. I left for Allahabad that weekend feeling very hurt. I needed a change and home in Allahabad was the only place I could go.

It was while I was in Allahabad that I remembered I had a valid Australian Residence Visa. I had been scared to migrate to a country where I knew no one, but Naresh's rejection made me want to leave India and I seriously contemplated migrating and starting a life away from everyone. Again I decided on a move to solve my problems. It seemed impossible to go back to the USA. Both Papa and Petronilla had evaded my request for sponsorship and by then even stopped corresponding with me. I had written several letters to Papa, apologising for my letter to him earlier and explaining my disappointment at his not calling me back to the USA, but to no effect. Violet was preparing for the birth of her first baby and had become too engrossed in her married life.

I had also started getting fewer and fewer modelling assignments, as new faces were constantly appearing; besides I did not take the ones which exposed me too much or were too suggestive. I had continued with a few television appearances until the person who gave me the roles wanted me to go out with him. My refusal to do so cost me my job there.

Aunt Natasha developed high blood pressure which made her ill and she had to take time off from school often. The new principal asked her to resign as he did not consider her medically fit to teach. Helen decided to take up her case against the principal but was unsuccessful. She failed to restore her back to work. Aunt had to resign. Helen began supporting her as she had no savings or funds of her own. There are no old age pensions given in India. Mum was of the same age but she was in better health. She was able to visit Aunt regularly from the hospital and looked after her with medicines and her company. Later, Aunt helped Violet with her baby, Michelle. It kept her busy and occupied. All Aunt's other relatives were busy in their own families and stopped visiting her, although they did correspond with each other from time to time. Enid and Helen settled down to the Anglo-Indian way of life like their father and did not consider it necessary to visit Bettiah. The four of us looked upon each other as cousins and had established a better understanding and relationship.

38

Arrangements for immigration

When I returned to Delhi I informed Naresh about my decision to migrate to Australia. This brought an immediate change in him. He displayed surprise at my possessing an Australian residence visa. He never believed in my having an American father. At the mention of an Australian visa he changed his attitude towards me and said he was equally upset at his family's attitude towards me. He said he loved me tremendously and if I migrated to Australia, he would join me and marry me in the Church as promised, converting to the Catholic religion. He visited me as before. Every day he made plans for our move to Australia. He said that in Australia we would be able to bring up our children in peace and prosperity, without any further problems from his family and their superstitions. We would have a big and happy family.

One day Naresh took me to the house of another of his sisters, Nirmala. She was a schoolteacher and her husband was a qualified lawyer, but he worked as a clerk. Nirmala took Naresh and me to an astrologer and had our horoscopes matched. Since the Christians in India generally do not believe in horoscopes unlike the Hindus, Nirmala had mine made according to my date of birth and the actual time of birth. Naresh had his already with her. It was made at the time of his birth according to the Hindu custom. After looking at both the births charts, the astrologer told her that our horoscopes matched and that our marriage would be a success.

* * * * *

Although I had made the decision to migrate to Australia, I was not really happy about it. I was worried about Mum who was getting old and had no one to take care of her. Although I wanted to settle down to a married life, I had always thought that I would keep my mother with me and take care of her. I was confident that the man I married would let me do so. I never wanted to leave her alone. Violet was too involved with her own family. I hoped that Naresh might decide to marry me instead of letting me migrate, but, on the contrary, he had surprised me. In fact, he more or less pushed me into migration and constantly promised to join me later. I was then nearing my thirtieth year.

While I sat thinking over my failures to achieve a home and a loving family, I decided to visit Mother Teresa's Home for the Orphans on day, thinking that perhaps the place may help my state of mind.

The orphanage, 'Shishu Bhawan', had three rooms full of babies, mostly female, aged from one day onwards. There were few foreign girls helping the nuns on a voluntary basis. I helped with the changing and feeding of the babies till about five in the evening. Three months old babies were fed on freshly mashed bananas, since bananas are cheaper in India than milk and there are hardly any canned baby foods available. The babies were introduced to solids with soft rice, lentil soup and mashed fruits, freshly prepared at home. Fruits, apart from bananas and mangoes in summer, were very expensive.

I thought I would find peace and a feeling of usefulness at Mother Teresa's Home, but I did not. Instead, I felt more depressed than ever, because I kept remembering my origin and the thought that this was the sort of place where I might have been if Mum and Aunt Natasha had not decided to keep me. Even though I was full of sympathy for the children at the Shishu Bhawan and felt a great regard for the nuns and the volunteers, I could not go back to help again as it made me more depressed and drove me back on myself and the past even more.

I was used to planning things for myself, without burdening Mum with my problems, that I never considered it necessary to sit and talk things out with her. I always told her my decisions and she would calmly accept them. She had great trust in me and seldom displayed her emotions. Even when we were very young, I hardly ever remember mum hugging and cuddling us. I only remember that she was always there to see that our needs were met. Once she started working as a nurse she was mostly away from us. The absence made Violet become indifferent towards her needs. Violet remembered to respect her as a mother only. I still showed my affection to Mum and kept my hurt to myself.

Although, at times I thought Mum observed everything and understood my plight, but did not wish to talk about it. Perhaps she felt guilty with her inability, so we got into the habit of never discussing our feelings with each other. When I told her my decision to immigrate to Australia, she did not try to stop me, only asked when I would return. I told her that I would eventually take her over and we would have a better life in Australia. She asked about my marriage to Naresh and of his becoming a Catholic. I told Mum that Naresh would join me in Australia where we would marry in the Church. I think she was satisfied though not happy that I was going so far away. Yet she was confident I would return as I had done from the USA.

✣ ✣ ✣ ✣ ✣

I discovered that a brother of Pam Brown, an old friend of mine, was settled in Perth. Pam gave me his address and said he would be delighted to put me up at their place till I found a job and accommodation. The Browns were an old Anglo-Indian family from Allahabad. Old Mr Brown was in the Air Force and his three sons and a daughter, Pam, were all teachers who trained at the same Teachers' College as me.

With the accommodation in Perth arranged, I told Naresh my plan to resign from school in December. He was transferred from Delhi to the India – Pakistan border. He said it was good that I had decided to emigrate, because if I had married him I would have had to stay with his mother and live like other Hindu daughters-in-law, under her domination. He said she was not easy to get along with. He insisted on buying my ticket to Australia, because then he knew that I would not leave him. At first I did not want to accept his offer, but since I did not have enough money of my own and it would have meant borrowing it from somewhere, I did so, promising to return it to him soon. He laughed and said that his money was mine too, as we were engaged to be married and he was going to join me in Perth to settle down.

In December 1970 he bought me a return ticket to Perth. He made sure that I had a free stopover each way at Hong Kong, where I could buy myself a duty-free portable television, which was very expensive in India then, to take to Perth. He said I should sit and watch the colour television when I was lonely and if I did not like the place then I could return to India and bring the television. The sale of the television in India would cover the cost of the ticket both ways.

✣ ✣ ✣ ✣ ✣

He packed my things in his very old suitcase, which could not be locked, but had to be tied with string and sticky tape. He said I should get rid of the old case in Australia and buy a new one to bring back, if I had to return. He arranged the passport renewal and all other formalities. Finally, I was ready to leave at the end of January 1971. Throughout I was very upset. I could neither discuss nor confide in anyone. I watched Naresh enthusiastically doing everything to get rid of me and, at the same time making promises and swearing his love for me. I was worried about Mum, as she was not in good health: she had collapsed with severe pain in her ribs a couple of times, although tests did not show that there was anything wrong with her. She was fifty-eight years old.

On the day of the departure Naresh gave me a box full of clothes and costume jewellery with which to start a business for him in Perth. It was a very cold January night when I left Delhi. Both Aunt and Mum came to see me off at the airport and both cried when I was leaving. I felt terribly sad to leave them behind, but I felt that I could do nothing else and that it was for the best.

I consoled myself with the idea that perhaps I could do more for them from Australia.

39

Challenges of a new country, Australia – 1971

My luggage was checked in Hong Kong where I had a day's stopover. Getting the sticky tape off the suitcase and then putting it on again was a problem. As Naresh had asked me, I bought a small portable television of the brand he had recommended. Unfortunately I was not allowed to take it with me on the plane, so I had to send it separately to Australia at the cheapest rate.

Perth Airport was warm and humid where Victor Brown, his wife and seven-year-old daughter, Trisha met me at the airport. They had a house with three bedrooms, but only two were furnished, the third being used as a storeroom and for ironing clothes. They suggested that I leave my things in that room and sleep in the lounge-room on the sofa. I was to pay them ten dollars per week for board and lodging.

Next day they advised me to visit the Social Security office and list myself there as a migrant in order to receive ten dollars per week Social Security. This I did. The next few days I spent trying to find buyers for Naresh's wares and to establish a business for him. I had to walk everywhere, as I had no transport and no extra money. However, at that time the unemployed were issued with free passes for travelling to look for a job, so I took buses seeking a teaching position. Victor was working in the public school system as an English teacher, so he directed me to the West Australian Education Department. I applied for a position and was assessed as two-year trained at the top of the scale. But they said that no jobs were available and, in addition, they found that the Indian teachers had problems with discipline. I begged them to try me, as not everybody from India was the same. I haunted them, telling them that they had to try me out to know my abilities and that I was willing to take up a teaching position anywhere.

Mr Louden, who was in charge of the secondary appointments, seemed to be sympathetic. At the same time I made every effort on Naresh's behalf, trying to get him some business contacts with the things he had sent along with me; but I did not have much success. Naresh's letters started coming frequently from the border area where he had been posted as soon as I left India. His first letter said that he cried after he saw me off at the airport in Delhi. He suddenly realised what he had done after I had left and felt terribly guilty about allowing me to leave for Perth all alone and that he wanted me back in India if I found it difficult to settle down in a new country. His letters were so affectionate and sounded so sincere that I decided to make every effort to sell his things and establish a business for him as a sign of my love and gratitude for all he had done for me. I felt obliged to him and could not let myself return immediately, although I had the return ticket, because I did not want to betray his trust in me. However, I was very lonely and homesick. My mother wrote to me regularly too. I wrote to Papa in the USA once again and asked him to make it possible for me to go to Denver, because I found Australians very rough, unlike Americans. But he did not reply. Pet did though, telling me that since I had migrated to Australia, I should make the best of it and that maybe she and 'Mike', would visit me some time in the future.

My life at the Browns was becoming increasingly upsetting. It soon became clear that Victor drank heavily and abused his wife verbally. His wife was very quiet and tolerated his bad treatment. Once a day she cooked enough for both lunch and dinner, because she was used to servants at home in India and found cooking and other domestic chores very hard. Victor never lent a hand in any housework as he would in India. He taunted her, saying she was lazy and useless as a bearer of children, as she could only give him one daughter, when he wanted a son to carry his name. Mitzi never retaliated. Things worsened when she lost her job at the Catholic primary school in the neighbourhood. He would humiliate her in front of his Indian friends whenever we went visiting.

The situation made me write very romantic and passionate

letters to Naresh, swearing my love for him and confessing how much I missed him. I did not want to lose him. I thought he was the one who could give me the home I desired. I knew no one else, nor did I want to start looking for another person to marry at my age.

Victor's drinking and abuse worsened and once gave him a dressing-down for abusing his wife in front of me. I slept on the floor of the lounge because the sofa was uncomfortable. One night, not long after I had told him off, I felt someone lying next to me and trying to kiss me. I jumped up with a start.

"Esther, it's me. Move over and let us have some sex." It was Victor's voice.

"Victor!" I exclaimed with horror, "Get out of here."

"All right, all right, don't make so much noise," he said and left the room at once, leaving me shaking with fear and anger. I felt insulted that he should have considered taking advantage of me because I was indebted to them for their kindness. After that I barred the door with chairs and table every night before I went to sleep. So nothing like that ever occurred again. I could not tell Mitzi what happened then, but I did so once I moved out of the house. She seemed to know her husband, yet she did not want to leave him.

"He is bad when he is drunk, otherwise, he is a perfect husband and a wonderful father to his daughter." She said. Many years later Mitzi developed a brain tumour and Victor nursed her very devotedly till she died and then became a very dedicated father to his daughter, Trisha.

While I was at the Browns' place the portable television arrived from Hong Kong. The duty on it was 100% so I could not take possession of it. Instead I advertised it for sale, as instructed by Victor. I was not successful, after adding the duty, it was the same price as the local shops in India. I asked for it to be kept in the warehouse until I could take it back to India.

I received nine dresses from Naresh as samples to start his business. Customs would not release them until I paid duty, because they were classified as new and had price tags indicating they were for sale. I did not have enough money to claim them, so the custom's man took scissors to them, making a small hole in each, so they were unfit for sale. I ended up wearing them after making the repairs.

Owing to the situation at Victor's house, I visited the Education Department daily, begging for any teaching position anywhere at all. I knew no other sort of work. In India, teaching, nursing and secretarial work were the only professions open to me, the rest being done by people with little or no education.

My perseverance paid off. One day I was offered a casual position for six weeks at Kalgoorlie High School. They said that if I helped them out there, they would help me later to find a permanent position. I was overjoyed and accepted the position on the spot, but when I returned home and informed Mitzi and Victor, they gave me a horrible picture of Kalgoorlie, as a mining town with a red-light district and much violence and drunkenness. I was upset and rang the department the next day to ask if they could change the place for me. They were very understanding and gave me Southern Cross High School instead, not far from Kalgoorlie. I prepared to leave that weekend.

I met a friend from India, Jillian, working at the ANZ Bank. She and her boyfriend helped me take my luggage to the station. Jillian asked me to share her room the next time I was in Perth, which was a relief.

I felt very pleased with myself as I stepped into the train bound for Southern Cross. It was nothing like the ones in India; no crowd, no noise and the station was immaculately clean and tidy. The conductor asked me if it was my first trip to rural Australia and I told him it was. With a mischievous look in his eyes, he told me to watch out for the kangaroos, as they were just as bad as the tigers and lions in India. I had heard of the kangaroos but was not sure whether they were ferocious or gentle. He said they were ferocious. He told me we were due in Southern Cross at 12.45 at night and suggested that I sleep, assuring me that he would wake me at 12.30. I did, everything was so comfortable and peaceful. The attendant was as good as his word and helped me alight at the station, which was very quiet. I was the only passenger to get off the train. The attendant handed me to the stationmaster, who seemed to know of my coming from the principal of the school. Before leaving on the train the attendant once again called out to me and warned me about the kangaroos. The stationmaster laughed at him and told me that the kangaroos were very mild and I should not worry about them. He turned off the station lights, locked the doors and drove me to the principal's house. The principal was a tall, strapping man. He drove me to a nearby duplex where three Australian women were living. I had a room to myself at last.

I was soon familiar with the school routine and was able to teach successfully. The principal's wife was very pleasant and involved me in the Annual Day of the Kindergarten Association. I set up a 'Brides of India' item, dressing the young teachers in the *saris* given to me by Naresh to sell. We paraded round the hall and the audience enjoyed the display.

Women teachers on one side and male teachers on the other occupied the duplex I lived in. On our side we took it in turns to do the cooking, washing and cleaning and it worked well. They were happy to try my Indian dishes so long as they were not hot. I met John, a twenty-six-year old teacher. No one liked him and on weekends he was often left by himself. The women teachers said that he was lazy, boring and sloppy. I felt sorry for him and would always greet him and exchange a few words. One weekend he asked me to a drive-in. I found both it and John's company very interesting. He told me that he found it difficult to communicate with others because he had come to Australia at the age of six, as an orphan. He knew nothing about his parents. He had always been in a Home and found it difficult to relate to people who had a family background. I liked him and we went to the drive-in movie a couple of times. I also helped him clean up his room so the others would not think him a slovenly person. Whenever it was my turn to cook, I offered him food. The others started talking to him too.

Naresh's letters were very regular, always swearing love and telling me how much he missed me. He insisted that I hang on in Australia till he came to join me. In the meantime my six weeks at Southern Cross ended happily and I returned to Perth. I lived with Jillian while waiting for another appointment with the Department, it was a permanent position at Carnarvon, in the north and I was provided with a plane ticket to get there.

At Carnarvon I was placed in a house with some other teachers, sharing a room with another young teacher. Everyone seemed to have boyfriends, most of whom were local miners. I was introduced to a pleasant young man from Mauritius, settled in Australia. He asked me out for dinner one evening. He seemed to have taken a fancy to me, but before he could get serious, I told him about my engagement to Naresh.

I was at Carnarvon for only three weeks, as the school closed for a two-week break at the end of that time. I did not find it a pleasant place because I felt isolated. The people were busy with their own lives, no one had time for newcomers. I found myself often alone in the house. My room-mate was out till late at night trying to get her boyfriend, a miner, to propose to her.

One evening before the school broke up there was a dance party at the cottage where the male teachers lived. Everyone was invited and asked to bring a plate. At the urging of some of my cottage mates, I decided to go. I dressed in the blue *sari* which I had worn for the Beauty Contest in Delhi. I wore the long silver earrings and expected that it would be like a dance party in India, where people wore their best clothes. It was a shock to find there was only one dim light on in the cottage. Soft waltz music was playing, but no one was dancing. Instead there were couples everywhere in the corners or on the sofa kissing or making love. It was the first time I had seen women sitting on the laps of men and kissing. I felt completely out of place, no one greeted me. I stood in one corner for a few minutes awkwardly and then decided to return to my empty room, where I went to sleep.

Next day was Sunday and everyone slept till late. I woke around six o'clock to find two pairs of feet on the other bed where my room-mate slept. I sat up quietly to make sure I was not dreaming and found that the owners of the feet were nude, with a small sheet barely covering them. Their clothes and underwear were all over the place. My room-mate was lying under her boyfriend whose lower body was moving vigorously up and down over her. I was thunderstruck with shock and repulsion. Hurriedly, but quietly, I walked out of the room in my nightgown. I was too embarrassed to think of getting my house-coat. For the next three hours I sat in the lounge-room wondering what to do. I could not bring myself to return to the bedroom, even for my own clothes. I had never seen a sight like that before and could not believe that I had slept the whole night through with two people making love beside me. I considered it sinful even to see a thing like that before marriage. My room-mate and her boyfriend left the room fully dressed about ten o'clock. They passed me sitting in the lounge-room, ignoring me completely and walked out. I decided there and then to return to India. I could never fit into the culture of Australia there was no reticence in behaviour. I thought of Naresh and decided to make a home in the country where I was born and brought up. I thought even if I live with his mother and try to adjust to their way of living, may be they would also allow my mother to live with us.

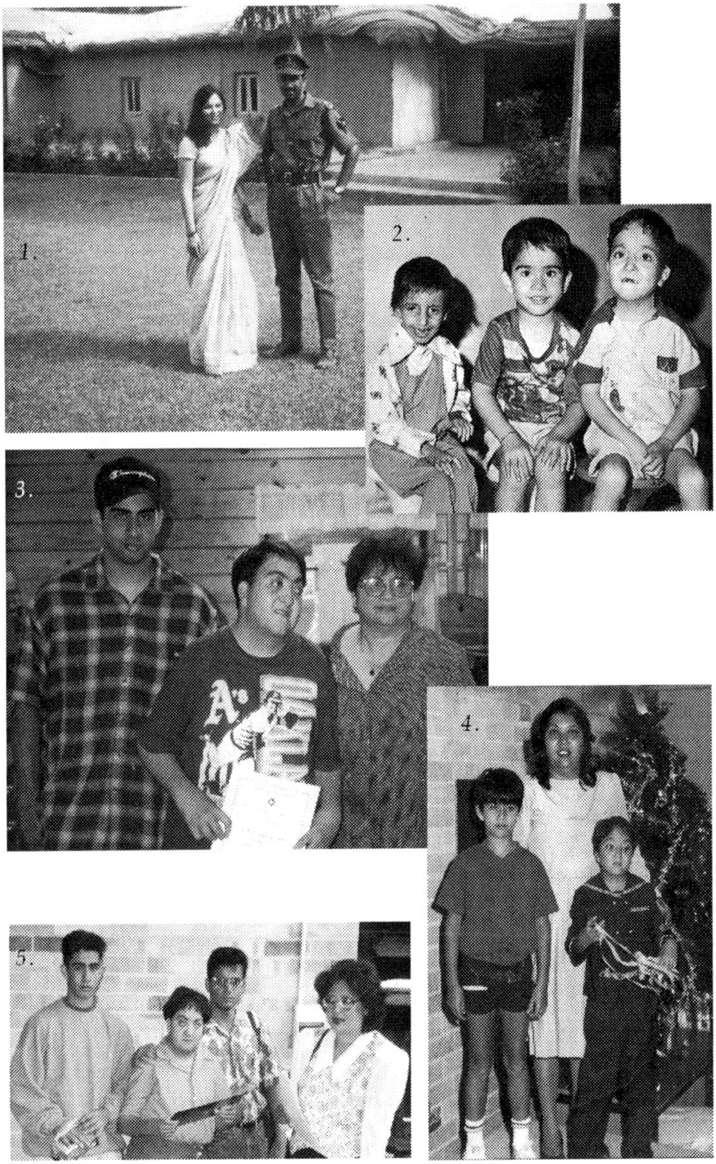

1. *My husband and me.*
2. *Our three sons – Aman, Mario and Fabian (Tinku).*
3. *Mario, Tinku and me – Australia 1994.*
4. *Mario, Tinku, Felix (mum's relative) and Enid*
5. *Mario, Tinku and Helen*

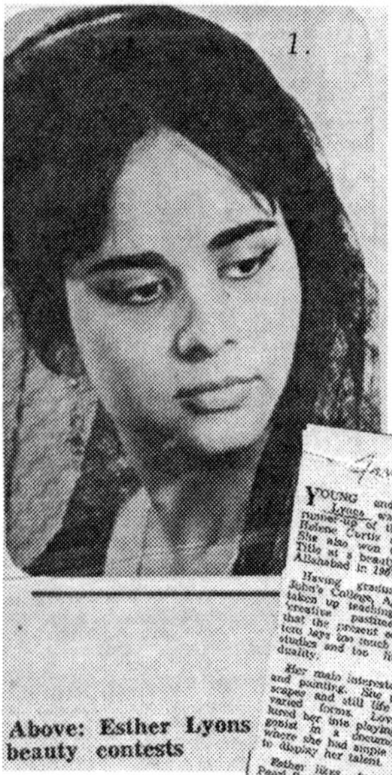
Above: Esther Lyons
beauty contests

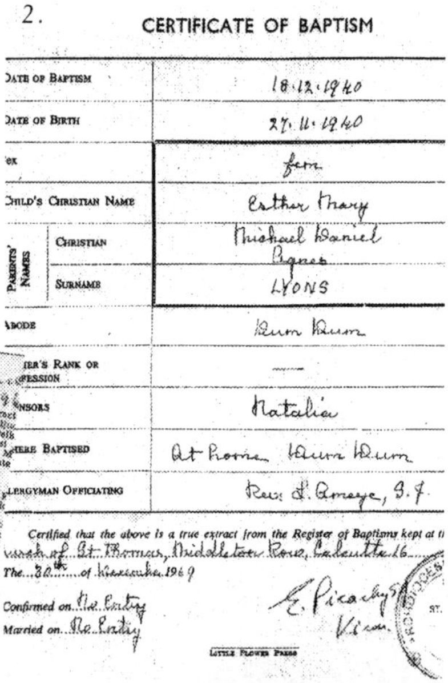

CERTIFICATE OF BAPTISM

Date of Baptism		18.12.1940
Date of Birth		27.11.1940
ex		fem
Child's Christian Name		Esther Mary
Parents' Names	Christian	Michael Daniel / Agnes
	Surname	LYONS
Abode		Dum Dum
…er's Rank or …fession		—
…nsors		Natalia
…here Baptised		At home Dum Dum
…lergyman Officiating		Rev. L. Ameye, S.J.

Certified that the above is a true extract from the Register of Baptisms kept at t… …urch of St. Thomas, Middleton Row, Calcutta 16
The 30th of November 1969

Confirmed on No Entry
Married on No Entry

E. Picachy S.J.
Vicar

Little Flower Press

1. Beauty contest article.
2. Certificate of Baptism.
3. With my father at Denver Airport after visiting the US in 1965.

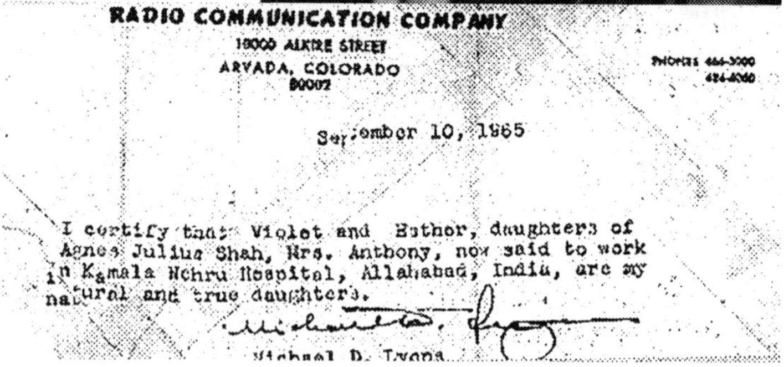

RADIO COMMUNICATION COMPANY
15000 ALKIRE STREET
ARVADA, COLORADO
80007

PHONES 464-3200
424-4060

September 10, 1965

I certify that Violet and Esther, daughters of Agnes Julius Shah, Mrs. Anthony, now said to work in Kamala Nehru Hospital, Allahabad, India, are my natural and true daughters.

Michael D. Lyons

4. *My father gave me the above paper at Denver Airport before I returned to India.*

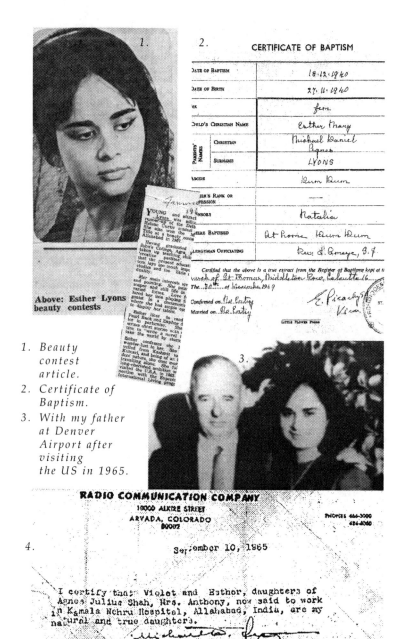

1.

2.

3.

4.

5.

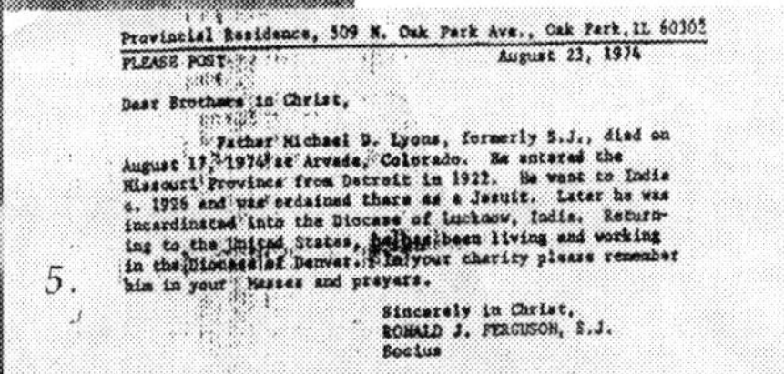

Provincial Residence, 509 N. Oak Park Ave., Oak Park, IL 60302
PLEASE POST August 23, 1974

Dear Brothers in Christ,

Father Michael D. Lyons, formerly S.J., died on August 17, 1974 at Arvada, Colorado. He entered the Missouri Province from Detroit in 1922. He went to India c. 1926 and was ordained there as a Jesuit. Later he was incardinated into the Diocese of Lucknow, India. Returning to the United States, he has been living and working in the Diocese of Denver. In your charity please remember him in your Masses and prayers.

Sincerely in Christ,
RONALD J. FERGUSON, S.J.
Socius

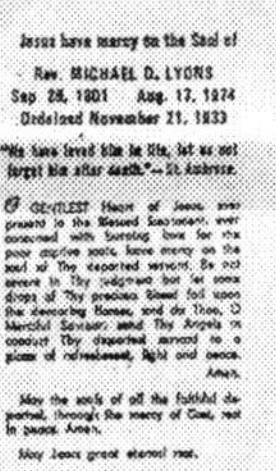

Jesus have mercy on the Soul of

Rev. MICHAEL D. LYONS
Sep 26, 1901 Aug. 17, 1974
Ordained November 21, 1933

"We have loved him in life, let us not forget him after death."—St. Ambrose.

O GENTLEST Heart of Jesus, ever present in the Blessed Sacrament, ever consumed with burning love for the poor captive souls, have mercy on the soul of Thy departed servant. Be not severe in Thy judgment but let some drops of Thy precious Blood fall upon the devouring flames, and do Thou, O Merciful Saviour, send Thy Angels to conduct Thy departed servant to a place of refreshment, light and peace. Amen.

May the souls of all the faithful departed, through the mercy of God, rest in peace. Amen.

May Jesus grant eternal rest.

6.

7.

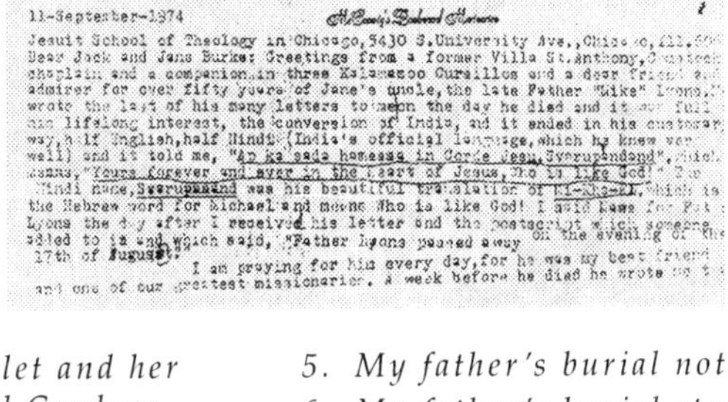

11-September-1974

Jesuit School of Theology in Chicago, 5430 S. University Ave., Chicago, Ill. [illegible]
Dear Jack and Jane Burke: Greetings from a former Villa St. Anthony, [illegible] chaplain and a companion in three Kalamazoo Cursillos and a dear friend and admirer for over fifty years of Jane's uncle, the late Father "Mike" Lyons. [illegible] wrote the last of his many letters to me on the day he died and it [illegible] full [illegible] lifelong interest, the conversion of India, and it ended in his customary way, half English, half Hindi (India's official language, which he knew very well) and it told me, "Ap ka sada hamesha in Corde Jesu, Swarupanand", which means, "Yours forever and ever in the Heart of Jesus, Who is like God!" The Hindi name, Swarupanand was his beautiful translation of Mi-cha-el, which is the Hebrew word for Michael and means Who is like God! I said Mass for Fat[illegible] Lyons the day after I received his letter and the postscript which someone added to it and which said, "Father Lyons passed away on the evening of the 17th of August."

I am praying for him every day, for he was my best friend and one of our greatest missionaries. A week before he died he wrote [illegible]

1. *My sister – Violet and her husband Russell Gardner.*
2. *Dr Wal Suchting in Australia.*
3. *La Porte – Delile France.*
4. *Christian Soulard, Paris, France, 2000.*
5. *My father's burial notice*
6. *My father's burial stone*
7. *My great-great-grandmother Catherine Solo*

1. *Mrs Trombley – 1997.*
2. *Aunt Marie – 1997.*
3. *Aunt Loretta – 1997.*
4. *Uncle Frank's family – 1997.*
5. *Uncle Frank – 1965.*
6. *My father's nephews and niece with me – 1997.*

1. *Aunt Loretta's third daughter, Jane, graduating.*
2. *Aunt Loretta with two of her daughters, Kay and Pat.*
3. *Jeff McQueen.*
4. *Violet's grandchildren, Jessica and Jonathon Gardner.*
5. *Violet's grandson, Sean Khanna.*

1.

2.

3.

4.

5.

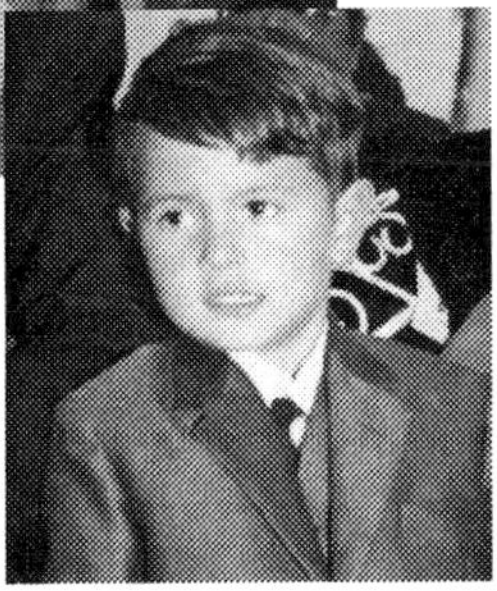

6

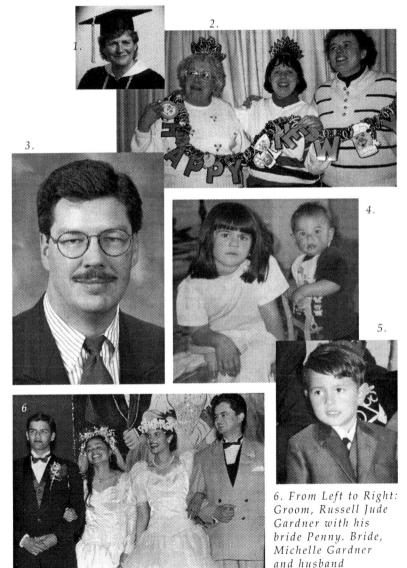

6. From Left to Right: Groom, Russell Jude Gardner with his bride Penny. Bride, Michelle Gardner and husband Reggie Khanna.

1.

BT 116-24,503

Mr. LYONS. They entered the office located in the LYONS residence and [redacted] observed an expensive short wave transmitter. During their conversations Mrs. LYONS indicated they, the LYONS, had radio contact throughout the world. b7c

BT 116-24,503

Mr. LYONS. They entered the office located in the LYONS residence and [redacted] observed an expensive short wave transmitter. During their conversations Mrs. LYONS indicated they, the LYONS, had radio contact throughout the world. b7c

...and tell ... to cooperate, and full particulars concerning the situation and ...ch I referred.

...of his letters are enclosed with this

...rmation refers to matters of section ... y after you receive this ... d give you the information ... really do not want to ... and I shall greatly ... it, you make note of it ... It has no conceivable co... orm has been filled out ... t as I could make it.

...er which means a great ... s matter will be very ... be most grateful to you

This file contained a note which indicated the Applicant had telephonically contacted [redacted] There was no date recorded. This note stated the Applicant reported he had two illigitimate children in India. There were no particulars given. b7

There was also a letter directed to the ... Energy Commission regarding the Applicant's ... follows:

"I am informe... Brush Beryll... Ohio

2.

Office Memorandum • UNITED STATES GOVERNMENT

DATE: October 30, 1947 [redacted] b7C

TO: Director, FBI

FROM: [redacted] SAC, Detroit

SUBJECT: MICHAEL DELISLE LYONS - ... 56060 aka Anthony Delisle. ATOMIC ENERGY ACT - APPLICANT

Reference made to report of SA [redacted] dated October 30, 1947, in the above captioned matter. b7c

[redacted] University of Detroit High School, Detroit, Michigan, advised that above individual has held himself out as a priest of the Roman Catholic church, and has performed priestly duties while visiting in the Detroit area since his return from India. [redacted] also stated that to his knowledge, no priest is ever granted permission by the church to act as a layman for a temporary period. b7c

This is being called to the attention of the Bureau in the event investigation is deemed desirable to ascertain whether or not Applicant ... why he laicized himself. b7c [redacted]

RECORDED 32 DEC 16 1947

116-2125

Filed in the District Court of Jefferson County, Colorado

IN THE MATTER OF THE ESTATE OF MICHAEL D. LYONS, Deceased

APPLICATION FOR INFORMAL PROBATE OF WILL AND INFORMAL APPOINTMENT OF PERSONAL REPRESENTATIVE

Dr. John C. Patterson,
U.S. Office of Education,
Federal Security Agency,
Washington, D.C.

Dear John,

I wish to introduce my friend and recent colleague, Father Michael D. Lyons, who has returned to the United States for a short time from India. Father Lyons, a pupil in his school days 25 years ago under Father MacIlwain, the seismologist of St. Louis University, under whom he learned the elements of geology and established the foundations of an interest in the science and an eye for its practical applications which our organization here in India has found extremely valuable, has worked with me as a Consultant during the last 19 or 20 months. During this time, with the permission of his old friend the Bishop of Allahabad to absent himself from his Mission work in the interests of assisting us in scouting for strategic and critical minerals in India, Father Lyons has made field studies for us in Bihar, Bengal, Kashmir, the United Provinces, Rajputana, and the whole of South India.

I know you will enjoy becoming acquainted with him.

Ever sincerely yours,

Andy

Andrew V. Corry
Mineral Specialist

3.

1. *Various FBI letters referring to my father.*
2. *Core samples found near the house.*
3. *Rock grinders, Denver.*

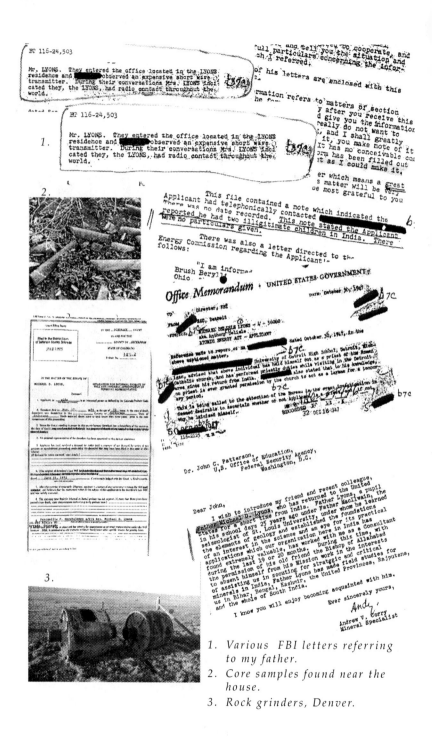

40

A marriage to remember

I informed Naresh of my decision and he seemed happy. He had changed his mind about immigrating too and wanted me to return. He said he missed me and asked me to bring back various things that he could sell in India to recover the money he spent on my ticket. One was a Webley and Scott pistol in Hong Kong; he said I was to make sure that it was registered as a gift for him in order to avoid Indian customs charges. He asked me to change the TV, which was still at the Customs warehouse in Perth into a 22-inch model and also buy a Canon 35 mm camera. I did as he told me.

Naresh met me at the airport in Delhi at three in the morning. He was thrilled with the things I had brought for him and drove me to his mother's where he was staying on two days' leave from his station at Abohar, a small town on the border with Pakistan. Everyone was fast asleep when we reached the house. He took me to his bedroom where I found two single beds put together. As soon as I was in the room he locked it quietly from the inside. "What are you doing? Why are you closing the door?" I asked worried.

"Shoo, don't speak loudly. My mother will wake up." He whispered, "I had to tell them that we married before you left for Australia and that they had to accept you as my wife."

"But we are not married and we cannot live together as husband and wife in this room." I said firmly.

He ignored what I said and instead put his hand firmly on my mouth, pleading, "Please do not make a scene and disgrace me in front of my family. We have to keep up the pretence of being married otherwise my lie to them would be revealed. It would be very embarrassing for both of us. I did it only because I love you and this seemed to be the only way to get married and have their permission." He then swore that the next day he would take me to the parish priest and arrange a church marriage.

The next morning, as promised, Naresh went with me to the Catholic Church and the parish priest I knew.

"Well," said Father De Souza "There will have to be the banns proclaimed for three Sundays before the day of the marriage. Naresh will have to get his divorce papers before he could even consider proclaiming the banns."

I did not wish to wait that long, so I asked Naresh about a Court marriage in order to hurry it up. Naresh was happy to take me to the Court. There we were informed that no court marriage could take place between us until two years had passed after the legal divorce. Naresh's divorce proceedings had only just been finalised. He looked apologetic and said that he was not aware of such conditions and that in the meantime he would marry me in the temple. He said that would be accepted in his community and we could have a church marriage later. He took me home for lunch first. During lunch, he, his mother and his second eldest sister, Satya, had a discussion in Punjabi which I did not understand. Later his mother gave me an old red and gold silk *sari* and a gold bracelet. Naresh asked me to wear them before we went to the temple nearby in Connaught Place. On the way to the temple he asked why we two could not live like one of their tenants who were never married but lived together as husband and wife. The man was a Hindu Punjabi and the woman was an Indian Christian. I looked sharply at Naresh and firmly told him that I wanted to live a respectable and honest life as a wife and that marriage was very important to me.

At the temple of Shiva, Naresh made me walk alongside him, seven times, around the temple and then declared that we were married. I kept saying my prayers to Jesus while we walked around the temple and begged of His understanding and mercy, because I felt rejected by his Church and had to find a husband in order to have a home and a respectable married life. Circumstances forced me into marrying in the temple, but I felt that God was everywhere and the same for all but named differently according to the worshippers and the religions. I firmly believed that Jesus knew my intentions to be pure and that He blessed my marriage even though it was in the temple.

When we returned to his mother's house, Satya brought a steel plate full of rice and a whole coconut. She broke the coconut on the steps in front of me and then placed the plate of rice on the floor and made me walk over it – a rite to ensure fertility, Naresh informed me later.

I could not help feeling a pang of jealousy regarding Violet. She had a wonderful wedding. I had seen to her happiness but there was no one to guide me. I always felt sad that my sister had never known the love of a father and therefore saw to it that she received the best from me as a sister, forgetting my own needs. While I sat in silence in Naresh's house on the first day of the marriage I felt sudden self-pity and sadness. That night Naresh took me on the train bound for Abohar as his leave was over.

We reached the Rajasthan border in the morning. I was still in a daze after all that had taken place in such a short time. The train was full of soldiers and officers, all in khaki uniforms. I was referred to as Mrs Chauhan, wife of Major Chauhan. There had been no ceremony to mark the change that had taken place: everything had happened so suddenly and without my will.

The army jeep took us to the battalion, which was camped, on both sides of a canal. Everyone lived in tents and improvised mud huts with thatched roofs. There was just one other lady in the whole of the unit. She was the wife of an army captain, a doctor to the battalion.

We had barely reached the unit when Naresh received orders from his commanding officer to join a twenty-four hour exercise immediately. I was left alone in Naresh's primitive quarters with his batman to look after me. The water was drawn from the canal and was filthy. I had to bathe with that water which was green and had algae in it. The batman brought the water in metal buckets for cleaning and bathing purposes. Everyone around washed clothes beside the canal and the animals drank from it. Once a day drinking water was brought in trucks from a nearby city for the battalion. It was then stored in huge mud pots for use in every house. The batman who attended Naresh informed me that they had seen dead bodies floating in the canal very frequently, the last one having been that of a woman, gagged and tied up with a rope. I believe that the woman's body remained unidentified, probably because the police had been bribed not to enquire too closely into the matter. The area belonged to rich landlords who used camels for ploughing instead of bullocks and had many poor labourers working for them. The landowners walked about with rifles on their shoulders and belts studded with bullets around their waist. They daily fought to the death with their enemies and womanised with the poor women of the labourers, raping them and murdering them if necessary without any sense of guilt. This was the area where *dacoits* (outlaws) found it easy to hide and be active. During the day everything was dusty and gritty from sand blown by the wind, as the area was near the great Thar desert of northern India.

Naresh returned after twenty-four hours. He was very angry with his commander. He said the latter asked him whether he brought a girl-friend or a wife. When Naresh said he had a newly wedded wife with him, the commander, Cl. Suri who happened to know his first wife, Shobha, from military academy days, insisted that Naresh should have a marriage ceremony performed in front of the battalion. The *pundit* (a Hindu priest) of the battalion fortunately refused to perform the ceremony, saying that it could only be done if some of Naresh's relatives were present. So the commander had ended the matter by making Naresh declare his marriage to me in a written statement. This declaration was sent to the Army Headquarters and made me the heir to all his army benefits as his legal wife. The alternative was a court-martial because army personnel were not allowed to bring girl-friends to the border area. Naresh was not happy about it all and openly condemned it.

"The commander has always hated me for leaving Shobha, because he himself had flirted with her and was one of her lovers. Anyway, he has seen that you are my legal wife and an heir to all I possess."

I could not understand his attitude, because I thought that what the commander had done was perfectly reasonable. Much later I realised that Naresh had gone through the pretence of the marriage in Delhi only to persuade me to follow him to his battalion with the articles I had brought from Australia, as he did not want his sister and mother to see them, since he owed them money. Naresh's sister Satya was married to an engineer. Her husband was working for the Indian Government and had a lot of money. He had lent Naresh enough to pay Sobha a divorce settlement and for the maintenance of their daughter. Satya would have wanted to take some of the things I brought to pay off part of the loan.

Naresh had not planned to declare his marriage officially, but luck was on my side and his commander was an honest and strict man of discipline who knew Naresh only too well.

Later I came to know that Naresh's mother was an orphan daughter of a landlord, whose father had been poisoned by her father's only brother over a land seizure. Her uncle had then brought up *Mataji* (Naresh's mother) and her elder brother as orphans. Since *Mataji* was betrothed for marriage to another landlord's son soon after birth, as was the custom then, she was married off and sent to her husband's family at the age of eleven. *Pitaji's* (Naresh's father) family treated her very badly, making her do all the housework, since she had not brought any dowry with her and also because they did not consider her suitable for their eldest son any more, since he was studying to be an engineer and they were planning to send him overseas to further his education. *Mataji's* life was further made unbearable when for many years she proved to be incapable in giving birth to a son. The family seriously considered having a second marriage for their eldest son. *Mataji* was illiterate, as it was thought to be inappropriate to educate Indian girls in those days. But *Mataji* learned to read the Hindu religious books The Ramayan and The Gita. In desperation over her fate, she spent a lot of her time in prayers. She never heard from her Uncle and her only brother ran away to become a singer and a herbalist in some faraway town. Fortunately, before the family managed to get her husband married a second time, she gave birth to Roshan and then Naresh and two other younger sons.

After *Mataji* had sons born to her, she realised she could win her husband's love and confidence. She saw that he ultimately left the family, demanding his share of the property, being the eldest son and settling down with her and the seven children they had together. *Mataji* never forgot her childhood and the treatment she received from her in-laws. She developed asthma after the birth of Roshan and used it to get everyone's attention. Her husband and the children attended on her with devotion and she took charge of the income.

During the partition of India and Pakistan, *Mataji* was forced to migrate with her family to India from Lahore in Pakistan where they were born and brought up. She took with her a great deal of gold jewellery, in which she had invested all her savings from her husband's salary. She had also been taking rich gifts of gold from her husband's clients. These bought plots of land in different parts of Delhi.

Naresh had borrowed money from his mother to buy a car. He was sure she would want some of it returned if she saw some of the goods I had brought from Australia as these were very expensive in 1971.

The commander, Colonel Suri, later made Naresh take me back to Delhi, granting him two days leave to do so. He said that the unit at the border was no place for a lady and that it was against army regulation to have a family of the army personnel living there. While we travelled back to Delhi Naresh asked me to return to Australia again. He said he was certain I would find it difficult to live with his orthodox mother like a Hindu daughter-in-law, obediently attending to her needs, becoming a vegetarian as were all the women in the family, doing all the housework and cooking in the kitchen barefoot. I would also be expected to clean her spittoons and her soiled clothes daily as she had no control over her bowels when she had an attack of asthma every morning around four or five. It was then she would need me to attend to her with *Dhatura* (a strong and poisonous herb) inhalation to help her breathe freely again. She used both herbal and allopathic medications. I would also have to touch the feet of every relative who was senior in relationship. The picture Naresh painted of his mother and sisters made me want to return to Australia. Naresh's promise to join me at the end of the year during his annual leave and to marry me in the church before settling down to a happy married life helped me decide.

I visited Allahabad for a week before returning and informed Mum and Aunt I had married Naresh in the Court and he was going to join me in Australia, where we would again marry in the Church with proper banns as there was not enough time to do so in India, since I had to return to rejoin my work in a week's time. I assured Mum and Aunt that I would return again and promised to call them to Australia if I decided to make a home there with Naresh.

When I arrived in Delhi a day before I was to leave for Australia, I found Naresh waiting for me with a new passport in my new name of Mrs Chauhan. He said he had done so because he wanted to make sure that I considered myself his wife. Later I realised he had done it so that I could bring in the same articles again under my new name, as the custom regulations in India allowed some of the articles to be brought in by the same person only once in two or three years.

I found *Mataji* and Satya *Bahen*ji (sister, a term used out of respect as Indians do not take the names of people older than them) very angry with me. They said that they had expected me to stay with *Mataji* and attend to her as a good dutiful daughter-in-law, as was the Hindu custom. Since I came from a poor home and brought them no dowry, they had considered that I would be dependent on them and in gratitude for accepting me into the family, would serve them well throughout life. In her temper Satya said she considered all Christian women to be of loose character and out to lure respectable Hindu men for their money and that they never could make a responsible and respectable wife or daughter-in-law. I was shocked to hear her speak like that and wept with self-pity and confusion. I tried to explain to them that it was Naresh's idea that I leave for Australia, but they would not listen to me. Naresh sat in one corner interpreting for us and remarking to me that this was an example of why I could never live with them. He said he could not intervene as they were his elder sister and mother and it would not be appropriate for him to speak to them in any way except to agree with them and that I had to put my foot down and leave as planned. He only spoke to them in Punjabi so I could not understand what he said unless he interpreted for me. He made me return the old red *sari* and the gold bracelet they had given me, telling me to say I could afford better myself and did not need their cast-offs.

In my obsession to make my life a success as a good wife and mother and to acquire respectability and an identity, I married a person from a different religion. I thought this would help me forget the past. I thought Naresh would never come to know of my father being a Catholic priest. I was hopeful that Naresh would allow my mother to live with us eventually and I would be able to give her a happy homelife before she died.

Perhaps I was trying to change the destiny of being the daughter of a Catholic priest.

I was running away from the bitter truth of my origin and was anxious to start my life afresh as an individual, with full confidence and trust in Naresh.

I was confidant the Good Lord who had taken care of me in the absence of my natural father throughout my childhood, would change Naresh into a faithful and honest husband who would give me the respectability I desired and a home full of healthy happy children.

I did not know that, Naresh, on the other hand had realised my weakness for a secure home and family and had taken advantage of it. He assumed that a poor girl with no father or background could be easily exploited for his material benefit.

41

A mother with a family to care

I returned to Perth and was lucky to rejoin the Department of Education. This time I was offered a permanent job at Narembeen High School, a few hours by car from Perth. Naresh visited me that year as he had promised and we were married in the Catholic Church with my school principal and Mrs Miller, a teacher, as witnesses. At last my desire to be married was fulfilled at the age of thirty-one. But although Naresh signed the marriage documents and gave his consent for the children to be baptised Catholics after birth, he did not become one himself, as he had promised. Neither did he want to stay and settle in Australia. He said he could not assimilate into the culture of the country and therefore he wanted me to return as well at the end of the year. During the two months that he lived with me in Perth, he made sure he selected the best second hand car, a Toyota Crown, for himself and instructed me to purchase it before returning to India, as the sale of the car would get us enough money to buy a house and start a home for our children.

I trusted him and did as he wanted. I spent my entire savings on the car of his choice, as well as other articles, including another Webley and Scott pistol and a colour television. In December 1972, I returned to India with all the purchases. The good thing I did for myself was to take up an Australian citizenship so that I could return if necessary. My intuition guided me to keep this option open.

Once back in India, I found Naresh a changed man. He took charge of the car and all the articles as before, stating he had to sell them all in order to repay his loans and I had to live as he wanted me to. Soon we started having many arguments, mainly about money. After one argument he said that perhaps it was best for us to separate, since he realised our religious and cultural differences made it impossible for us to live together. I discovered that the Indian law had a clause permitting divorce on grounds of difference of religion. But by then I was pregnant with his first child. He was still posted to the border area, so he made me return to Allahabad and live with Aunt and Mum. Nine months later when I gave birth by caesarean operation, to a stillborn eight pounds baby girl, Naresh told me for the first time that his child from Shobha was intellectually and physically handicapped and that the couple had two other children, both boys, who were severely retarded and had died soon after birth. This led to their divorce and at the time he blamed his wife for being RH negative. He also recalled being warned once by an army doctor about the possibility of abnormal children since he had a defective genetic condition. Naresh gave me the freedom to choose a marriage annulment. I was shocked and very upset. I felt cheated. All my dreams of a big home and happy children came crashing down. Yet, as I watched Naresh crying bitterly, I said, "Naresh, I cannot do that. I am a Catholic, I married you in the church. I cannot leave you just because you cannot give normal children! It is not your fault, although you should have told me about it. Anyway, it is all God's plan and I have to remain by your side as a good, faithful wife even though you are incapable of producing a normal child. We shall adopt a child from an orphanage."

On the 11th of May 1974, I was given a five days old baby from the Pratapgarh Mission Hospital, a suburb of Allahabad. I loved the child as my own but he was always sick. In the meantime, ten months after my first stillborn child, I gave birth to another child by Naresh and I baptised him Mario. Naresh had never taken any precautions against making me pregnant in spite of his knowledge of his abnormal genes. I was brought up with strict Catholic principles and did not know anything about birth control devices; besides, even if I had, I would never have used them, knowing the Catholic Church view on conception. Mario was physically and intellectually handicapped at birth and about the same time I also discovered that the child I had adopted, Aman, was allergic to sunlight. My entire time was spent attending to the two invalid children, Aman and Mario. My mother came to help me frequently. I loved my adopted son, Aman, very much. Perhaps I identified with him. I felt terrible to see him suffer and while I attended him like a devoted mother, I developed a strong faith that God would either cure him of his ailments, or give me a normal son one day if Aman were to die. I could not believe that God would be so cruel as to take away the child I loved so much, after making him suffer at such an early age for no reason.

In 1975, Violet told me that my father had died and that Petronilla had informed her in December 1974, just before Christmas. She said my father had died in the month of August 1974. Later, after the death of my mother in 1991, I discovered that two years before he died he went back to being an active priest. He said the Mass in his own home with the permission of Bishop Sullivan, who was then living in Denver. Petronilla went back to being his housekeeper and brought her mother to live with them in the same house till the day he died. My father was a very sick man by then and had to stay on oxygen most of the time. We were never informed of his illness nor death when it happened, although, Petronilla was in continual correspondence with Violet.

My third pregnancy in 1976 was a miscarriage, but my fourth arrived on the 3rd October 1977, a healthy and normal eight pounds baby boy in Allahabad. Tinku was my third caesarean birth within four years and a very painful one. He was my fourth child. I thought the birth of a normal son would make Naresh happy and change him back to what he was towards me before we married. But to my disappointment he still was not happy. Over the years he grew more materialistic and mean. Throughout every pregnancy, he behaved more aggressively and was extremely cruel to me. I always forgave him, thinking that it was due to his fear of another abnormal child.

A few months after the birth of Tinku, Naresh disclosed that the reason for not being happy was that he thought the child was not his, suggesting that I must have been unfaithful to him and the child was by one of the soldiers working in the house, since his doctor had warned him that he would never father a normal child. That was the last straw and I lost all hopes of ever making him happy and a responsible husband. I decided to leave him and return to Australia with my own family of infant children and my old mother. I didn't need a husband any more, I had my children to take care of. Unfortunately I could not take the step to do so immediately, as Aman was very sick and needed a big house with protection from the sun.

Naresh never wanted Aman or Mario with us whenever we went out on social calls to his fellow officers. Very often he suggest I put them both in an orphanage. I would not. I considered them my responsibility and not that of an orphanage. I loved both the children very much. Aman could never face the sunlight. It became worse as he grew up. He remained only six kilograms at the age of six years. His teeth started turning to powder and his hair began falling out. He was shrivelled and dark due to frequent diarrhoea as a result of the allergic condition to the slightest sun exposure. I tried to give him the best of food and even learnt homoeopathic medicine to be able to attend to him myself, as the doctors were not hopeful and cooperative. They said that he had Xero Derma Pigmentation, for which there was no cure. I had to go back to teaching to support him financially while my mother resigned from her nursing position to help me with the three infants. Aman looked a sight and everyone, including Naresh and his mother, thought I was mad to give him love and care; but I could not leave him. Only my mother remained sympathetic and understanding towards Aman and me; she loved and cared for both Aman and Mario alike. When Tinku was born, Mum took full charge of him while I attended to the other two.

Aman died a most painful death at the age of six years and twenty-three days in Delhi Army hospital as a result of Serum Hepatitis due to a transfusion of infected blood, something I had predicted, though no one took notice of me when he was given the blood. Tinku, was just two and half when Aman died.

Violet was living happily with her husband. She had settled in the Anglo-Indian background with the help of her Anglican husband who was very much in love with her and gave her the security of a happy family life. He knew all about our origin but it did not seem to matter to him. He said he knew his wife as an individual and loved her for what she was to him. Although Violet kept in contact with Mum and me while we were in India, she never thought it necessary to get involved in my misfortunes. Enid and Helen helped me financially while we were posted to Delhi, since they had good teaching jobs with contacts among rich Indian parents. Naresh refused to give me extra for the medical treatment of the children, as he said he needed money to pay the flat he was buying. He sold the car I bought and used the money to buy the three bed-roomed flat. He intended renting it out rather than living in it with us as a family.

A year after Aman's death I decided to return to Australia permanently with my remaining two children and mother who was sixty-nine years old. Violet saw us off and said that she was happy that I was returning to Australia, because she too had hopes of immigrating with her family. She asked me to sponsor them as soon as I could and promised to do all she could to help me once we were reunited as a family in Australia. She was happy that I was taking my old mother with me. Enid and Helen said the same. Only Aunt Natasha cried, she was very sick and felt that we would never meet again. She died a few months after I left India.

Mum had no knowledge of the new country, Australia. She had nowhere to go, all the years she had struggled to keep the two of us alive and saved nothing for herself. In a country where there is no social security or financial help for the aged and the poor, my mother, who had also served the rich as a nurse, had nothing to look forward to. She could not allow me to battle life alone with a severely intellectually and physically disabled child of only five. He could not even walk or talk properly and had to be carried most of the time. Tinku was just three and needed care. My mother took upon herself to join me in our adventurous journey for a better life to an unknown country.

As I boarded the plane in July 1981, carrying Mario, I noticed my younger son Tinku, was leading my old mother by the hand rather than her leading him. I thought that it was a good omen for the future, that we were starting, the little group of us, standing by one another and I had a family of my own to love and take care of in the new country where no one knew us. I was then forty years of age and still searching for my identity while trying to find security and stability in my life with added responsibilities. Life had been a challenge from the time of my birth and I was ready to take on another challenge. I had not given up my determination and independence to win myself the right to live with dignity.

42

1981 – Living in Australia

It was difficult to begin a new life in Australia as a single mother, especially when one of the children was severely handicapped. I could never have managed without my mother. Fortunately, we were able to get a three-bedroom flat from the Housing Commission in Perth, Western Australia a month after our arrival.

Although the accommodation was good, it was on the second floor in a block of units. We had to climb up every day carrying Mario, then nearing his sixth year. He found it a struggle to climb the steps. Six weeks after we settled in that flat, I returned home from the employment office one day to find Mario in great pain with swelling in his right thigh. Somehow, while climbing the steps with Mum, he had dislocated his hip joint. I rushed him to the children's hospital where he underwent immediate surgery. For a while I lived between the hospital and the flat, taking care of both the children and my mother, using public transport.

Since the Education Department's policy for foreign teachers had changed and no one wanted two years trained Secondary teachers, I remained on the Social Security with limited income. I decided to move to Sydney in the state of New South Wales with my family, as soon as Mario was released from the hospital. There were more chances of employment I was told by the doctor who attended to Mario at the hospital. We travelled for three days and nights, across the vast expanse of the Simpson Desert in the centre of Australia and reached Sydney in October 1981. I found Sydney crowded compared to Perth. Suddenly, I felt the pang of depression and frustration in my effort to establish a home for my little family and myself. My one thought was to return to India and for the sake of the children, live with Naresh and bear whatever treatment he offered. I even wrote to him and he visited us a month after we arrived in Sydney. He introduced me to his elder sister and brother-in-law who lived in Sydney. His brother-in-law was a doctor. Their daughter, the one who had once tested my blood in Delhi and said that it matched with Naresh's, was now established in Sydney along with her doctor husband. Both were leading medical specialists.

"Well," Naresh said, "You could not do without me? Anyway, my sister is willing to let you stay in her garage, till you find a job and take care of the family yourself. I cannot stay, I prefer my army life in India where I have all my relatives. If you want to return to India and live with me, save money and buy tickets for yourself and the children. Leave your mother in Australia, or tell your sister to take care of her. Your sister should send the money for her return. I don't want her in my house any more. You have to do as I tell you, I have to obey my family even when I dislike it. You have to learn to be submissive and obedient like the Indian women are."

"You should have found yourself an illiterate Indian woman. No educated woman from India would tolerate total dictatorship as you are proposing. Times have changed Naresh. Besides how do you think I will be able to save money for our tickets. I don't have a job. It will take me years to save for the three tickets!" I replied in tears.

"Well I have no money to spare for your return. You can send Tinku with me. My sister in India will give him a good life. He will be able to eat and live well in her house. After all she only has two daughters and wants a son very badly. She is rich, her husband is an Engineer, Tinku will do well with them, better than with you. He will rot with you over here." Replied Naresh with arrogance.

I was horrified at the thought of parting with my son.

"No. Never," I replied, "I will never do that, I will never give my son away, nor will I leave my mother over here. I prefer to rot here with them than do as you are saying."

"Well then, do as you like. I knew that a woman like you, with your background of Christian and Anglo-Indian, would never be able to understand the priorities of life. You people just eat and live. You are the curse of my life," Naresh said, "If you want to return, save money and return, I have no money to give you." He repeated again.

I cried in desperation, but after many sleepless nights decided to take up the challenge of living in Australia and supporting my family independently. I did not need Naresh's help, I said to myself.

"My sister can get you some work. She knows someone who wants labels to be stitched on garments. You will get good money depending on your speed and the number of labels you can stitch per day." Naresh said again.

"I cannot stitch labels," I replied. "I have always been a teacher and I am going to find a teaching position soon, I know. I like teaching. I enjoy being with children rather than making money with machines, it is so boring!"

"You are stupid. We cannot agree on anything! What is wrong with making money, can't you see you are penniless? You need to take up whatever comes your way."

Eventually I took up a position at Kentucky Fried Chicken Restaurant, while I sent out many applications for teaching positions advertised in the newspapers. For a long time I only received negative replies till one day, I had a letter inviting me to an interview for a History and English teacher in a Catholic School in Glebe. I was desperate for a teaching position. Unfortunately, I was not successful at the interview. I had become very emotional and teary partly because of my frustration and failures. I wanted to be independent of Naresh but I found that I still looked for help from him. Though I considered myself a Christian and a part European, I found I was not being accepted as such. I was always considered an Indian by virtue of my country of birth and my accent.

At the interview in Glebe, Catholic school, when I was given a negative answer, I could not help saying, " Please sir, give me a chance to teach. I need the job. I love teaching and to me it is a vocation. It gives me great satisfaction and a sense of achievement." I then told him how hard it had been for me to live in Australia and start a new life as a single mother. I also told him my background and how I had tried my best to live independently with my background.

The man listened in silence and then said that he would inform me of his decision through the mail as he had many more to interview, "Just the same," he said, "you should make an appointment with the Centre Care in the City and see a counsellor."

I did not get the position. I felt very sad. I realised that in a cruel and competitive world, there was no place for tears and a sad story. No one had the time or patience to help and guide.

One day Naresh took me to see a vacant flat on top of a shop, at the side of a very busy road and said, "Well, here is a flat you must consider to rent. You and your mother can live upstairs with the children and have an Indian restaurant downstairs. I shall send Indian things to sell from India."

"How do you think my mother and Mario would climb those spiral steps? I don't know business, why can't you live with us and run the shop?" I said in disgust.

"You stupid woman, your mother can carry Mario. She is here to help you with the children and the home. You pamper that old woman. I have no time to do business, I have my own officer's position in India. Your blessed children will not die if you leave them to work in the restaurant," Naresh replied.

"How dare you talk like that about my mother. I brought her here to take care of her and not to burden her with my responsibilities. My children are also your responsibility. They are yours too." I replied, but I knew it was all useless. I had to take up the responsibility of a single mother myself.

Naresh and I argued every day he lived in Sydney on his holiday. I felt deserted and abandoned again the day my husband left for India. I had to take the challenge of supporting my children, the same as my mother had done years back. Like her, I had two sons instead of two daughters, but mine was harder because of Mario and I was in a country where I knew no one. The new country had all the facilities and the support but I had to find where and how to get them. I wanted to bring up my children with dignity and so I had to find a job of a teacher for myself. That was very important for me.

One day I met a Christian Brother whom I happened to know from Delhi, while teaching in an Irish Christian Brothers' School, St Columbus, in New Delhi. He was very kind and helped me with an application for a temporary position at Christian Brothers School in Lewisham. With his recommendation, I was able to get a temporary teaching position at the school. For three months I worked at the school with peace and satisfaction. Tinku was admitted to a Kindergarten school close to mine, while Mario went to the Special School. He travelled to and from school in the taxi for the children with disabilities. For a while I was happy and assumed we were settled, but at the end of the three months the Principal asked me to look for a teaching position elsewhere since his permanent staff was returning.

"Besides, I really think you are very quiet for the Australian schools. I have watched you in the playground when on duty. You do not talk to the boys and you are very reserved. It would do you good to enrol yourself into a Teachers College to upgrade your qualifications in Australia," the Principal said.

I could not help my tears while I told him how much I had enjoyed teaching. I thought of my past rejections and this added to it. I did not talk much to the students, because that was what was expected of a teacher in India, I told him. The teachers in India did not develop friendships with the students, because they wished to maintain distance from them in order to get their respect. In India the teachers were looked upon as having the wisdom and knowledge and the students had to give them that respect. Some traditional Hindu families expect their children to touch the feet of the elders and the teachers, as a mark of great respect.

"But it is not that way over here, in the western world. We believe in teaching the students in a friendly atmosphere, that is why I am asking you to consider upgrading your qualifications. This is not India, this is Australia, if you want to teach here, you must learn our way of teaching," Brother said.

There had never been any such comments when I was teaching in Western Australia. My Principals had always been happy with my teaching throughout. I could not understand why this had become an issue for me when I have decided to settle in the country with my family and as a single mother. Perhaps times had changed, this was 1983 and not 1971. Besides, I was in the city, not in a remote country town of Western Australia! Tears rolled down my cheeks again at the thought of being without a teaching job and an unemployed on the dole again. I thought of all the hardships I had endured. How easy it was for the Principal to ask me to consider upgrading my qualifications at my age, when I had so much commitments.

Amidst my tears I told him how hard I was trying with the challenges of my life, especially as a single mother and in a new country. All I needed was his guidance and I would do my best to improve the relationship, as expected, with the students. I did not have any problems while teaching in the class. At this point I could not help telling him about my past and as the daughter of an American Jesuit priest. I hoped he would understand and help, but unfortunately it had an adverse effect. He thought that I was using that as an excuse to get his sympathy. At the end of the year I was again without a job and back on the dole.

"Well, upgrade your qualifications and then you will be able to teach in any schools in Australia," said Professor Wallace Suchting whom I met at Naresh's sister's house, earlier in the year. He had become a good friend ever since.

The New South Wales Department of Education could not offer me a teaching position till I had upgraded my two years Teachers Certificate to the four years. In 1971, the same two years Teachers Certificate was recognised in Western Australia, as well as in the other parts of Australia. I had applied to the Education Departments of New South Wales and Victoria, before taking up the position in Western Australia. All the States in Australia had given me two-year standing because of my training at the English Catholic Teachers College in Allahabad, India. Unfortunately, over the years the requirements had changed and the Education Departments everywhere in Australia accepted only four years trained teachers. I was asked to do two years full-time studies at Sydney University Teachers College for *Diploma in Teaching and, Bachelor of Education.*

I could neither drive nor afford to learn driving being on the dole. Every day I caught a bus to the college and during the free period, I returned home, just to give my mother a helping hand and to see to her and the children's wellbeing. I did all my studies and assignments late at nights. The first year was very tough. My mother was seventy by then. We had a limited amount to run the house with. I was also forced to take up a waitress' job at the Mayur Indian Restaurant in the city on the weekends and on Thursday nights, while I was upgrading my qualifications. Fortunately, in the second year of my studies at the college, I was offered a full-time teaching position by Brother Mark, Principal of Marist High School, Benedict Senior College, in Auburn. The Principal had selected me from out of the list of casual teachers at the Catholic Education Office. I was given permission to study part-time by the Teachers College when I got the full-time teaching position. The English and Social Science position offered to me was point eight only. At the end of the year, I was informed that a full-time teaching position was going to be available in a Special Education the following year. I had to enrol myself in Special Education course at Bathurst University to qualify for the position.

"You can do it by correspondence if you like," Brother Mark, my Principal said. And so I did. This meant that the following year, while I was still doing part-time Bachelor in Education, second year, at the College in Sydney University, I also was enrolled for a correspondence course at Bathurst University for *Graduate Diploma in Special Education.* During the holidays, I had to drive down to Bathurst for the holiday courses. By then I had learned to drive after many adventurous experiences and become independent and mobile. I took my family to Bathurst every holiday when I went for the course. They lived in the nearby caravan park while I attended the course. I could not burden my mother with the care of my children alone while I was away and therefore, they came with me everywhere I went. In my free periods I visited my family and was there to shoulder my responsibilities alongside my dear mother. After completing both Bachelor in Education and, Graduate Diploma in Special Education, I decided to do my

Masters in Pastoral Care in the hopes of teaching religion as well and expanding my areas of teaching subjects.

I taught at Benedict High School for eight years before moving to the State School in 1990. I made the change only because my mother became blind as a result of diabetes and aging. I had completed all the required upgrading by the age of forty-nine. I had always wanted to study further in India but could not because of lack of financial resources. We were always living hand to mouth. Life always been a struggle for survival so far. As a child I loved music and dancing. But could never afford the luxury of learning it. Once I enrolled myself for a course in French language at Allahabad University. I was interested in the French as a language just out of interest, but had to drop it because of my financial status. In Australia, I was able to satisfy my desire for further education at a very late age because of the need of survival and commitments. I felt I had to give my children the best, which I could not do while I was on the dole.

There was no one to question my background or caste in Australia, but I had to face a different type of discrimination. In spite of all my qualifications and the stress of successfully taking charge of my children as a single mother, I found myself continually facing the challenges of discrimination and prejudices at the few State Schools I taught, because of my Anglo-Indian accent and the fact that I was born in India. It did not seem to matter to the parents and the students. They respected and loved me, but it did matter to the few staff who were not willing to accept me teach English with my typical accent! It seemed that my accent was not good enough for teaching English to the children with learning difficulties. Also I was too committed as a single mother so I could never reach the schools earlier than 8.45 am and had to leave as soon as the afternoon bell went at 3.15 pm., another issue for some schools.

A film director in India once told me, that I did not speak Hindi with a proper Indian accent. He said that I had an Anglo-Indian accent, even though my first language was Hindi since my mother spoke Hindi all the time and I learnt to speak in her language first. I was criticised for the same accent in Australia.

They said I spoke English with an Indian accent! Being of fairer complexion than average Indians, I felt I was picked upon by the many in India for being the child of a European man and a half-caste. In Australia I felt discriminated because I am darker than the average Australians, while all the time I was aware that I am part European, although born and brought up in India, where I acquired my accent. Having faced the discrimination and prejudices throughout my childhood and youth, I tried to face all the challenges the same way as I did in India. My age and my commitments made me depressed with life at times. There seemed to be no end of testing for me. It occurred to me very often that, perhaps this would not have been the case had my father lived with us.

If my father had been allowed to take up his responsibility as a parent and I was brought up in a family, I would have grown up with more confidence, with a good education in a better environment. No one would have criticised me in India, or in Australia, or anywhere in the world. No one would have mortified me for my background, or accent and lack of communication skills, if I had an American father living with us! Life would have been different and perhaps I would never have struggled so much to survive and developed the psychological side of me, of inferiority complex.

With all the challenges and struggles in life I successfully qualified to the highest standard, which did not seem to be of any consideration to anyone. With all my experience in life I came to the conclusion that people all over the world are the same, the people in power control the weak, perhaps that way they satisfied their ego of superiority and of having the power and the authority. No matter where one is born, or how one is born; in the third world, or in the most cultured and civilised society, the human nature of putting down the weak has not changed. People are people, no matter what race or nationality, educated or uneducated.

The good side and the bad side of the people remain with them in every race, country and nation. Just like the death and birth of every living being. I realised through my experiences, that no matter how much I achieved in life, I still had no power and I was no one. I could never win in the world where power and might was the only right thing it seemed. So ultimately, I realised that it was not the church my problem started with, but the people who are the church. It was not the founder of Christianity, Jesus Christ, but the people who made the laws for the Catholic Church that discriminated me for being the child of a Catholic priest. My faith in Jesus never wavered, in fact, I felt strengthened by having trust in Him, my Creator. I realised that Jesus took care of me throughout my childhood as a father, in the absence of my natural one.

The rejection of not being accepted as a nun because of my parents' had a very lasting psychological imprint on me and I completely changed from a quiet, humble and innocent child into a person whose one aim in life became that of establishing my rights as an individual searching for identity and freedom of choice. I wanted to establish that I had the right to be accepted as a respectable person like every child born. Every child is born with its own individuality and is innocent, it is the environment which makes the child into what it become as an adult. I did not think that a child should be labelled from birth and made a victim because of the parents. The child has no choice in selecting parents and background. I had no choice in my being born and from whom I was born, then why was I excluded from joining the convent as a Catholic nun? That rejection made me antagonistic and I became my own enemy. The rejection led me away from the path I had wanted to follow as a child, that of a caring, loving and trusting person, with so much to share and give. It made me blind to the world around me and I became the person who egoistically struggled to get what seemed to me most important, my identity.

My one mission in life was to prove my worth to the church and the community that rejected me and limited my choices. I failed to see that throughout, my heavenly Father had taken care of me and also reminded me of my vocation in life by giving me many responsibilities and commitments. I could not become a nun, but I ended up having to take care of children with disabilities throughout and ultimately became a Special Education teacher. The Creator without whose Will nothing is born or dies, allowed my birth on this earth for a purpose and gave me the strength throughout, while the church that preached Creation through the Will of God, forgot its preaching when I was born! That one rejection left such an everlasting scar on my mental state that every time I was rejected after that, I could not help breaking down into tears and link it to my birth and origin. I could not forget that I was not even given the rights of having a father and a mother and a family to start with. I could never forget the taunting and hurtful words of having no background, spoken to me as a child when I hardly knew my parents! I found it hard to forgive because I was being punished without any fault of mine. A part of me remained a child asking for justice throughout, as a result of my suffering and mental trauma at an early age. Unfortunately, while I suffered throughout psychologically, no one had the time to listen, or understand me. Of course, changing a country and place could not change my psychological laceration. I only learnt that people are people the same in every place and race, some good and helpful while others too involved in their own egoism and have no time for the weak and suffering, no time to understand and accept another human being. Education technology and civilisation has not changed the false self prestige and egoism in the few. A sense of superiority came to those in power and the weak always suffered anywhere in the world.

I always considered my father to be the victim of circumstances and time, forgiving him for all his part in my miseries. I forgave him because I loved him blindly as his daughter, although, I suffered extensively because of his big part in my being born and so did my mother suffer. My mother could forgive and accepted her fate, whereas I found it hard to forgive, because I was innocent and still punished. I had no part in being born of a priest who took the vow of celibacy. I struggled throughout to prove myself innocent, with equal rights of every other child born to the human race. I struggled my whole lifetime in search of love, identity and acceptance.

I was able to sponsor Enid and Helen. They managed to immigrate to Australia after their mother died in 1983. They were a great help and support to me since they took charge of

Mario when Mum found it difficult. Once Helen secured a teaching position, we took up a house together and shared the mortgage. Violet also migrated with her children on a family reunion immigration policy once I was able to sponsor them. She was happy with her life because she did not give importance to her identity or background, besides she never wanted to be a nun and had not faced rejection as I did. She wanted to marry. Violet was lucky to find a husband who loved her tremendously. He gave her a loving home and family. She made her home both in India as well as in Australia. Her husband refused to give up his prestigious job as a principal of a large High School, St Thomas College, in Dehra Dun, India, but saw both his children settled in Australia. After the children grew up, Violet returned to India and became the principal of her own private school, St. Jude High School, with the help of her husband.

Naresh visited Australia every year during his annual leave. He soon realised his mistake about Tinku, who grew up resembling him in physical appearance. The specialist at Children's Hospital, Camperdown, New South Wales, explained to him that with the genetic condition he had, there was a one in four chance of his having a normal child, depending on the genes of his wife. Unfortunately, we had drifted very far from each other emotionally. He never relinquished his materialistic outlook and saw that he carried back to India enough things every visit to make up for his airfare and more. He could never be a father to his children nor make a good husband for me, yet, I was able to successfully provide for my children as a single working mother in Australia, the same as my mother had done in India under terrible conditions of poverty and shame.

EPILOGUE –

American relatives with French and Irish ancestors!

On the 9th of May 1991 my mother died at the age of seventy-seven years and ten months. She was the only one who stood by me throughout my life. After her death I felt very lonely and bitterly regretted that, during all those years I did not tell her how much I loved her and how grateful I was for all she had done for me and my children. I thought I would take care of her in Australia, but since it was hard to start a life in the new country, I found instead that I depended on her support all the more. She remained the religious and caring person she had always been. She was a devoted mother and a loving grandmother. She always had the Rosary in her hand ready to say the prayers whenever she had a few moments.

Her sudden death from a stroke caused me great sorrow. Memories came flooding back of the sad years we shared together. I started writing my autobiography while she was still alive. Dr. Wallace Suchting, the Australian friend who had retired as a Reader in Philosophy from the University of Sydney, inspired and encouraged me to begin it in 1991. I visited him nearly every weekend from 1983, for a few hours in the evening. That was the only time I gave to myself as a single working mother. We went out to dinner and movies together. My mother looked after the children while I was away. I left them after they all had their dinner and were ready for bed.

Wallace was fascinated by India after he visited there in 1981. We spent many hours discussing different issues in the Indian and Australian cultures and he enjoyed my stories of my experiences in India. While it was a fascinating story for him, it became my reminder of the conditions under which I lived. The philosopher who had no experience, did not understand what I went through while I wrote for his pleasure.

Wallace did extensive editing of my writings.

"Go as far as you can into your childhood and as far as you can remember," he'd said. "We will see how the story turns out."

At first I wrote by hand and Wal typed the 580 pages. Next, he insisted that I learn word processing and type out the edited work onto a computer under the working title of *Unwanted*.

In 1990, a year before his retirement, Wallace surprised me one day.

"Let us get married. You will need my superannuation for Tinku's education."

I was hurt at the way he proposed. It reminded me of my father and the way he asked me to stay in Denver in 1965.

"Stay here with me," he had said, "I shall send you to Denver Boulder University for further education. The money I leave for both of you will be enough to last you through your life-time," then added, "but you will have to stay here with me as my friend's daughter and not mine."

Money was all they both knew to offer, as though they could buy me with their money! They did not consider my feelings and my desire to be accepted. I only wanted love and acceptance as a family member. I had deep seated desires and values on all that I missed out on from the time I was born. Although I needed money very much, my values in life were more important to me than money or any material goods. I could never accept the proposal of marriage for the sake of money!

"What a way to propose, Wal," I replied, "If you said that you love me and that is why you asked me to marry you, I would immediately accept it. Invalidate or divorce my husband and be your wife. But I would never marry for material benefit. Money does not have any importance to me in place of love, family, commitment and acceptance. You know that, don't you? Then why don't you say that you love me and that is why you want us to get married?"

Wal, a man of few words only said, "Oh-well!" I later discovered that he found it hard to express his feelings. He was the philosopher who read and wrote many books; *Marx, An Introduction and, Marx and Philosophy, published by The Harvester*

Press Limited in Great Britain. Marx and Philosophy and GWF Hegel – The Encyclopaedia Logic. As an academic, he lived in the solitary world of books, forgetting the real world. He was so buried in his thoughts originated from the books he read, that he began to act and think according to them. He forgot to be himself.

He never talked of marriage again, nor that he loved me, but always encouraged and advised me as a true friend. Wallace took his life in January 1997. He did not disclose to me about his oncoming blindness with glaucoma and cataract. He pretended that he had no difficulty reading or writing and I was unaware of his medical condition. Very often he enquired about my handicapped son, Mario indicating that I was too committed. I would reply simply that I am a mother. Wallace left a letter for me beside his dead body, on the table. He thanked me for my company throughout the fourteen years we knew each other. He ended the letter with his 'love.' I knew him all those years, yet, because I was so committed to my own children and my mother, I did not have time to know and understand Wallace.

He encouraged me to write the stories I told him, in diary form and later as an autobiography.

"You are a born writer, my dear," he said one day. "I like your style, it is superb." My book was first published in 1996. Wallace was delighted, "Now, my dear you are an author too. You are the only woman I have met who does not like money," he said, " Well here is a hobby for you. It will keep you busy should anything happen to me. I have taught you a skill which you should never forget." Wal died on 12th January 1997 after he had read the first copy of *Unwanted* the book he helped me write.

Bro. Raymond, ex-principal of Marist Brothers Benedict High School, Auburn where I taught was in the USA in 1991. I found the courage to tell Bro. Raymond about my father and my origin as the daughter of a Jesuit priest. I requested him to obtain his birth and death certificate for me from USA. After my Mother died, I felt compelled to find out more about my father and his relatives, just as much as I did about my mother's in India.

Bro. Raymond directed me to the Jesuit Provincial House

in Chicago. Fortunately the Priest in charge, Rev. Fr. Harland, had once been working under the Patna diocese, in India. He had heard of my father and was fully aware of the circumstances. It was a great surprise for him to hear from late Fr Lyons' daughter. He sent me a lot of information from the archives about the good work my father had once done as a Jesuit priest in India. He sent me copies from the "Patna Mission Letters", a Jesuit Magazine, of which my father was the editor while he was in India. No one had ever told me about the great things my father did while he was in India or when he was young in America.

For the first time, at the age of fifty-one, I came to know about his good work. I was hurt, as well as happy, to know of my father through those old papers sent to me many years after his death. I developed a sense of identity and a desire to be accepted as an American citizen, being the natural daughter of an American. I wrote to the president of USA at the time, George Bush and told him my story. He was very prompt in cabling my letter to the US Consulate, Canberra, asking them to look into it. One fine day I was called to the US Consulate in Sydney, where they asked me for the Birth Certificate of my father, or a letter from a Jesuit priest saying I was the daughter of a Father Lyons. I was also asked to provide them with the death certificate of my father. I wrote and asked Father Harland for them.

He helped me get the death certificate. One of his letters to me clearly said, "I know about your father, Fr. Michael Lyons and the problems he had. I know that he had children from an Indian lady. But I never thought that one day I would come to know you, his daughter." I showed the letter at the US High Commission. Immediately, both my sister and I received our American Passport as American Citizens. At last in our fifties we received what was our birth right being the daughters of an American born.

Fr. Harland also informed me that a grand-nephew of my father's, Jeff McQueen, was doing research on my father with the view of writing his uncle's biography. Jeff's grandmother, Helen, my father's sister, had told him about her genius and beloved elder brother Michael. I requested Fr. Harland to get me in touch with Jeff. I also sent Fr Harland a letter including one for Jeff McQueen. For a long time there was no reply from Fr. Harland. I wrote another letter begging him to please give me Jeff McQueen's address. Suddenly one morning in 1993, my telephone rang and to my great surprise, it was the voice of Jeff McQueen from Michigan!

"I am Jeff, your father's sister, Helen's grandson. I received your letter just yesterday. I am so happy to have found you. My father is also very excited. We love you as our cousin and, accept you as our family member. My grandmother would have been so happy to know you. She knew nothing about the two of you, nor did anyone else in the family. Everyone thought that your father had returned to India in 1947 as a Jesuit missionary and lived there. Your father's brother, Frank Lyons, corresponded with your father regularly, he may have known about his living in Colorado, instead of India. I just want to say that we welcome you into a big family where you belong. This family is connected to the French Pioneers who helped the settlement around the Detroit River Region in the 1700s. Your great grandfather was a judge and a state representative. There are roads named after some of your ancestors..." Jeff went on and on for over an hour.

I could not believe my ears. For days after that I kept phoning him to make sure I was not dreaming. Through him I managed to contact most of my "Lyons" relatives in the state of Michigan in USA. All the years of my life so far, I had no relatives, no one to call my own. Everyone boasted of a big family and great background, but I had neither. I was humiliated and treated as inferior throughout by all, including my husband and now I was told I had a great family and ancestors. For some time I walked as though my head was touching the sky, a feeling I cannot describe, nor anyone would understand.

I came to know that after my father's brother, Frank, died in 1974 leaving a box of old letters to his two daughters. They found many old letters written by my father to Uncle Frank from all over the world. Among them were letters written in the 1940s, disclosing the existence of his family in India. The relatives had high expectations of my father and so Uncle Frank did not tell anyone. He kept quiet until 1965 when I visited my father in

Denver. My father sent a photograph of my sister and me to Uncle Frank. But he only disclosed this to his sons and daughters and bound them to secrecy, just as my father had requested him.

My father was afraid of a scandal in the church and the family.

It was then in 1965 that Frank requested his eldest daughter, Jane, to correspond with me, which, unfortunately never took place. Jane was shocked with the fact that her Jesuit priest uncle had a child. Besides she did not know how to start a correspondence with someone she knew nothing about. She could not decide upon a communication with someone who belonged to a different country and culture. In the meantime I had decided to return to India. I was never informed of Frank's whereabouts. I remember my father once wrote to me in 1966, saying:

"My brother Frank is quite disappointed with me. He does not want to tell my sisters I was unfaithful to the Church that sent me to India and trusted me. He does not want to believe the truth."

Jeff McQueen sent me a packet by mail with papers and articles about my father. Amongst the papers I found one which said that my father and his brother Frank assembled an 9MK radio station (the predecessor of WWJ). They had come to the attention of the Scripps family through their amateur station, 8AM, built in the backyard of the Lyons' house at 825 Green Avenue, in Delray, Detroit. The Scripps family of the Detroit News paid my father, my uncle Frank and the other radio operators for their work. WWJ and KDKA of Pittsburgh, Pennsylvania both claim to be the first commercial radio stations in the world. The Scripps family of Detroit originally insisted that 8MK be licensed in my father's name; they feared people would laugh if they knew they had invested in radio. My father installed the transmitter in the Detroit News Building from which the first commercial radio broadcast was heard on the 20th August 1920. He later joined the Jesuit order and left for India. Radio 8MK later became WWJ.

In a letter addressed to the Fr Provincial, St Xavier's, Patna, India, on 15th July 1945, Rev Fr Loesch, SJ said:

'About fifteen months ago Padri Lyons engaged as teachers for his school at Gaya the services of Misses A and B, two ex-nuns from Bettiah. He had to be reprimanded more than once for his too easy and imprudent ways with them and to be given orders to have their dwelling removed farther away from his own bungalow. It was with these two ex-nuns, A and B, that Padri Lyons recently himself guilty of 'fuga' and 'apostasia' (flight). For Padri Lyons made no secret of it in Gaya that he was going to leave in a short time, on a long holiday without permission. A few days previously A and B resigned as teachers, saying they were leaving Gaya and would not come back again to that place, nor would Padri Lyons come back, they said. Towards the end of May, therefore, Padri Lyons without any justification for presuming the permission, left the very presence of his superior and started for an unspecified destination and from some station on the way took along in the same train both Misses A and B. They said they were going to Calcutta. Later they left for Delhi where Padri Lyons was presumably in lay dress and called himself Mr Lyons. He rented a flat which was to be occupied by himself, Mrs Lyons and her sister Natasha, his sister-in-law.'

In another letter written on 9th Sept. 1945, Rev Fr Loesch writes:-

'Sometime ago I sent you a "declaratio facti (statement of the fact) dequo Can.646/1, n.2) for Father Lyons...... He signed the litterae dimissionis, (letters of dismissal) which he asked for, on Sept 2nd. Canonists who examined the case stated that I was justified in making the declaration facti on the information I had.'

My father's letter dated 1944, written from Catholic Church, Indore, Central India, to one of his classmates in the Patna Mission Service, St Ignatius High School, 1076 West Roosevelt Road, Chicago, Illinois states:

'I asked for and got my release from the Jesuit Order. That is the news... ... Why and for what reason, I would prefer that the troubles of this side of the world remain on the side. I am rather annoyed and all that and often look back and think that things could have been otherwise if...' But I still do not blame the Jesuit Order, that is, the organisation not the ideals. For a long time I saw that the step had to be taken and I hated to hurt the feelings of good friends I had here and back in the States, I think for America I should say, only this-left and has no hard feelings... The Superior out here offered and even urged me to accept a passage to the States. The Bishop of Patna and Calcutta Jesuit headquarters, now in full charge of all Jesuits in India, offered to help me find a bishop in the States or elsewhere. They did not care to see a foreign secular priest established in a mission diocese like Patna. I understand their attitude: there are different ways of looking at it. Anyhow, I am now at the above address and doing a little to help out in a Prefecture Apostolic (a mission not yet raised to the status of a diocese with a bishop under the SVD Father) where a number of the missionaries were interned for being Germans and where the Prefect, Msgr. Janser, SVD formerly Provincial at Technology, Illinois, in charge, is an American. I have not decided whether to settle down eventually in some Indian diocese under the Indian bishop or take up work for the missions elsewhere. War time is hardly the time to decide, for so many reasons. For one, I think it just as well to give a hand here for the time being... In the time I have free to myself, I am doing a little writing and if you are interested in social problems of India I shall send you what is published. This line has interested me a great deal and had something to do with my troubles. I hope to get a few pennies by writing for publication."

I found a copy of a letter written on the 2nd of January 1945, by Westmore Willcox, Special Representative, Foreign Procurement and Development Branch, Foreign Economic Administration, Washington:

'I wish to take this occasion to express officially the appreciation which this office has for the work of (Rev) M D Lyons. Father Lyons is a missionary, whose college training included some work in geology under professor at St. Louis University. Maintaining his interest in his scientific hobby and desiring to be of assistance in the war effort, Father Lyons secured permission of his ecclesiastical superiors to place his services temporarily at our disposal. We have found him uniquely useful in carrying out our field investigations, because he has been able to "translate" his geological language into terms comprehensible to the villagers whose sometimes amazingly extensive information about the occurrences of various kinds of rocks and minerals in their own localities could thus in turn become available to us.'

Jeff and I had a long conversation on the phone another day. We came to the conclusion with the help of some written articles and letters, that after I was born on the 27th November, 1940, my parents left for Delhi, where my father worked as a journalist. In 1941 he officially resigned from the Society of Jesus. Later my father met Mahatma Gandhi and worked with him for sometime. He also met Jawaharlal Nehru and Dr Rajendra Prasad, the first prime minister and the president of India. They were all impressed with his paper, *The voice of the Poor* which my father edited and published in Mirzapur. The paper voiced the suffering people under the British rule.

In March 1943, my father was re-assigned by church authorities to St Xavier's Mission of Robertsganj in Mirzapur, as a secular priest. From there he moved to Meerut where he made Aunt Natasha marry Uncle Eddie, a young Anglo-Indian in search of employment. He thrust upon them the responsibilities of Mum and myself. He visited us only from time to time. In 1944 he contacted the American soldiers stationed in Allahabad and was appointed army chaplain. On 23rd February, 1944, my sister, Violet, was born. By then we had moved to Saharanpore and I saw very little of my father. He was given dispensation by the Bishop of Allahabad to work for the Federal Economic Administration (FEA) to locate strategic minerals in India, especially Beryllium, a key element for detonating atom bombs. The neutrons in Beryllium split the atom. He began travelling throughout India in a jeep, mapping the whereabouts of these minerals for the US Government.

In a letter dated 2nd January 1945 and marked "confidential" a Mr H.W. Witt, Procurement Officer of the FEA wrote the following to Mr. Arthur Z .Gardiner, of the Foreign Procurement and Development Branch in Washington, DC:

'Lyons is particularly well fitted for this type of work. He is an indefatigable worker with rarely found knowledge of India and her peoples. He has been 17 years in the villages, knows many of the native languages and obtains information that I doubt could be obtained by anyone else in India, including the British. Lyons spent some time in Bihar. He reported on the occurrences of beryl and other minerals. At present Lyons is in South India. His reports to date on this area comprise about 100 pages. They *cover* a wide range of interests, including general geological information, mineral occurrences (not limited to beryl and tantalite)...'

According to Clyde McQueen, Jeff's uncle and the second eldest son of Aunt Helen, my father was in the US briefly in 1945 to participate in the first A-bomb test at Los Alamos, New Mexico.

Jeff told me that in 1947, the US Government sent my father to the United States on official business. He was refused re-entry to the British India after and his visa was cancelled at Liverpool in England while he was on his way to India in a ship, because he was working for the US Government. It seems that he cabled to the new Bishop Wildermuth in Patna for help in returning to India but was told to go back to being a priest in the USA and that Jesuits in India were under strict orders to avoid contact with him. This made it impossible for him to contact us through the church. There was no other way he could get in touch with us as India was engulfed in a bloody war of independence and partition and we had moved from where he left us in Saharanpore. About this time we moved to Kalimpong from Saharanpore where Papa had left us.

While in the US in 1947, my father spent two weeks with his elder sister, Helen. Clyde, her eldest son, was very young then, but could recall his visit. He remembered my father spending most of his time at the typewriter, or on solitary walks. He seemed preoccupied and somewhat distant. While in India he had received assurances from the then Bishop of Patna, Bishop Sullivan, his mentor and friend, that we would be taken care of if he returned to the US and remained a priest.

My father wrote several articles on India which appeared in the New York Times on 22nd December 1946 and in the January and February 1947 issues of the Columbia Magazine.

From the time he returned to the USA in early 1947, he worked as a priest writing articles on India and collecting funds for the missions in Lucknow, Allahabad and Patna in India. While he was collecting money, he met Petronilla, a nurse, who helped him with the mission work and later, became his mistress. In 1949 Petronilla moved with my father as a secretary and a housekeeper 3,200 kilometres away from Michigan, to Denver. From a hill facing the mountains and Boulder to the west, my father began The Radio Communications Company and The Beryl Ores Company. This was the business that most people in the area knew my father owned. The townspeople of Arvada made him the President of the Chamber of Commerce without knowing he was a Catholic priest.

Once again he resigned from the priesthood and this time he received the dispensation. He lived as a married man with a wife and worked for the US Government. He started the *Beryl Ores Company"* to extract Beryllium for the US Government. He had a mine in his backyard where he employed a few black Americans to work for him. He was one of the two men in the world who knew how to extract Beryllium and Plutonium which were used in triggered mechanisms for nuclear weapons. My father had security guards to look after him. He was able to get two Government Officers in New York to get me on the plane bound for Denver instead of India in 1965 to visit him.

While maintaining his work with the beryl for the Government he kept up missionary work, raising money and sending it to the missions in India anonymously. He also helped financially with the education of the new seminarians in the USA. Petronilla and my father were known as, Mr and Mrs Lyons to the neighbours. None of his relatives in the USA knew of this relationship with Petronilla until he died in August, 1974. His brother, Frank found him and visited a few years before he died but did not learn of his relationship with Petronilla. I was the only other person permitted to visit and spend a few days in his house in 10,000 Alkire St., Arvada. It seems that the Italian Bishop of Allahabad and Lucknow and the Jesuit American Bishop of Patna Diocese knew of his whereabouts, but did never think it necessary to put us in contact.

In 1970 he officially returned to the priesthood. He was a sick man by then and was on oxygen frequently; his lungs had been affected by the Beryllium. After he returned to the priesthood, Bishop Sullivan, who had retired from Patna Mission in India and settled down in the nearby Jesuit mission in Denver, allowed him to say Mass in his own house. Petronilla brought her mother to live with them, and went back to living as his housekeeper in the same house till the day he died.

The History of the Patna Jesuits, 1921 -1981, called "Blessed by the Lord" by Henry Pascual Oiz, S.J., printed in Patna, India, page 73 reads:

'Of the 15 scholastics only two left the Society: Fr Michael Lyons and Fr Peter Angelo. Both ended their lives well. Fr. Lyons, who had started his missionary career with the Santhals and the depressed classes of people, left the Society and was laicised. Towards the end of his life he had received authorised dispensation and was reinstated as a priest and was incardinated in the diocese of Denver, Colorado, USA. The day he died, August 17th, 1974, he had celebrated Mass, as he did daily during the period of reinstatement into the priestly life.'

As 1974 approached, my father knew he was dying. He contacted the local bishop and asked if he could be buried with the Jesuits near Bishop Sullivan (who had died by then) at Mount Oliveti Cemetery. The death certificate indicates that he died of "acute respiratory failure." He was on oxygen for most of his last two years and had to carry oxygen wherever he went. He died because accidentally the oxygen was cut off and forgotten to be switched on.

A publication by the Rocky Flats Plant states:

'chronic Beryllium disease (similar to asbestosis) ...'

He was buried with all honours as a priest at the foot of Bishop Sullivan with the other Jesuits. The inscription on his headstone reads: *Michael D. Lyons, Sacerdos, (a priest).*

Fr. Paul Dent, S.J., from the Jesuit School of Theology in Chicago, Illinois, who had been in correspondence with him for over fifty years, wrote in one of his letters, dated. 11th Sept '74, to Uncle Frank's eldest daughter:

'Father Lyons was my best friend and one of our greatest

missionaries. He wrote the last of his letters to me on the day he died and it was full of his lifelong interest, the conversion of India. He said his daily Masses privately as a retired priest and kept up an intelligent interest in the Church in India and America. I hope I shall be able to do as much priestly work as he kept on doing until the good Lord called him. I have sent cards about his death to Mike's friends in the Society of Jesus in the places east and west of Patna, India, where Mike and I were missionaries together in the nineteen thirties.'

When my father died, his relatives were informed of his wish that only a representative of the family was to attend his funeral. Uncle Frank had died of cancer a few months earlier so his eldest son, Michael and his sister Helen's eldest son, Clyde McQueen, attended the funeral. Petronilla had not thought it necessary to inform Violet and me even though she was in regular correspondence with my sister. She had not even informed Violet of his illness and his return to the church as an active priest. It was at the funeral that Michael and Clyde discovered his relationship with Petronilla.

Michael and Clyde tried unsuccessfully to see Petronilla after the funeral to question her about my father. She avoided them till they boarded the plane back to Michigan. On the way back Michael Lyons, Uncle Frank's son, informed Clyde McQueen about their uncle, Rev. Fr. Michael Lyons having a family in India. Uncle Frank had thought it necessary to inform all his children, before he died of long illness. Cousin Clyde carried the news to his mother, Helen McQueen and she made every attempt to find us. She rang Petronilla on several occasions to find out about us, but was unsuccessful. She died without knowing our whereabouts. Petronilla continued to correspond with Violet till a few months before her death in Dec.1990. My father's superiors shut their eyes to the way my father and Petronilla lived, yet could not allow me to become a nun because my father was a priest. He was given a great missionary's burial because he financially supported new Seminarians and gave a lot of money to the various missions both in the USA and in India throughout his life time. Whereas my mother, who heroically took up the responsibility of mothering and bringing up, his children, suffered great poverty and humiliations throughout her life time.

According to Jeff McQueen, my father was Chief Radio Operator on the steamer named City of Mackinac before he joined the Jesuits. It was owned by the Detroit and Cleveland (D&C) Navigation Company. In the Summer of 1987, an old trunk was found at the bottom of the old steamer in Grayling, Michigan, containing letters, documents and photos. It led to an eight year quest to unravel and unusual story about Father Michael D. Lyons. The discovery led Jeff McQueen to start research on his dear grand-uncle. His grandmother, Helen had always told him interesting stories about her clever brother who had left them very early in age and joined the Jesuits Mission in Patna, India, through Chicago Jesuits. This research had led him to find me in Australia.

Jeff McQueen sent me a copy of my father's Will in which he had left all his large fortune in cash and property to Petronilla listed as a "wife". In other documents with the Will she claimed to be his wife, Mrs. Lyons. He willed nothing to my sister and me. Petronilla, before she died in 1990, willed the money, over a million dollars in cash, to the various Catholic missions, including Mother Teresa, the Patna and Allahabad-Lucknow missions in India. She also left one hundred dollars each to about twenty churches in the USA asking them to pray for her and her 'friend's' soul. She left considerable money to her attorney and her own brother, but ignored the existence of Fr. Lyons' daughters with whom she had been corresponding. The property in Washington was gifted to the missionaries who were renting it and the forty acres of land containing the mine at 10,000 Alkire Street, Arvada, was donated to the Franciscan Sisters of the New Covenant, who renamed it 'Charis Christi (Gift of Christ)'.

The leaflet, *And you shall be MY WITNESSES* reports the message from the co-foundress, Sister Angeline Bukowiecki SNC, in 1985 stating: *'Much to our surprise 40 acres of land was given to us by our friend Petronilla Marchulones. What a generous gift!'*

In 1995 I learnt from Jeff that the probate was not settled

on the Estate of Petronilla. Her solicitor, Mr Gerdis, had disappeared with about $400,000. I therefore, looked up the list of solicitors in Denver at the State Library in Sydney and chose a solicitor, Mr Gaddis, from Grant, Bernard, Lyons and Gaddis Solicitors, to represent me and contest the Will.

Sister Angeline Bukowiecki was the self-appointed Successor Personal Representative of Petronilla's Estate. Before I contested the Will of Petronilla I pleaded with Sister for financial help for my handicapped son and requested her to kindly undertake the care of my severely handicap son after my death, on my father's property till his death. But she refused. A very small amount of the money left by my father to Petronilla was offered to us as an out-of-court settlement when it was brought to their notice that I had written my autobiography *Unwanted*. Mother Teresa from India and the other beneficiaries decided to give my sister, Violet and me the small amount recognising our existence as the daughters of Father Michael D. Lyons.

Jeff later sent me tickets to visit the USA. On the 3rd April 1996 I flew to Detroit with my two sons and met my father's family for the first time in my life at the age of fifty-five. They had gathered from all parts of the United States in Detroit to meet me. Everyone happily accepted us and made us a part of the "Lyons" family. We stayed at Jeff's house just as my father had done in 1947 when he had returned from India. Later in the year he had visited Mrs Trembly and stayed with her in Toledo for a few weeks. He had taken his priestly habit off in her house and then proceeded to Denver with Petronilla.

I was invited by Jane Lyons, the elder daughter of Uncle Frank, to meet all her brothers and sisters and their children at her home. At the reunion I met my father's sister, Marie Fitzpatrick and her husband, Dan. Aunt Marie was surprised, but happy to accept me as her priest brother's daughter. She had not met him since he left for India seventy years earlier although, she had been in correspondence with him till he settled back in Denver working for the Government and stopped writing to her directly. He continued corresponding with all his sisters through Frank. Everyone, except Frank, were under the impression that he was doing great work as a priest in India.

One morning, Jeff's father Jim McQueen and his brother Clyde, took me to visit Loretta Williams, the other sister of my father. She had lost her memory and could not talk but when her youngest daughter, Peggy Scott tried to tell her that I was the daughter of her brother, Mike. She cried at the mention of his name and looked at me.

Aunt Loretta's daughter, Peggy Scott, informed me that her mother Loretta and Aunt Marie had not spoken to each other for years. That they had a misunderstanding after the death of their beloved sister, Margaret. Over the next few months while I continually communicated with Aunt Marie, telephonically from Australia, I told her of Aunt Loretta's health condition. She did not know of it. No one had told her. As a result of my conversation, after years Aunt Marie and Uncle Dan visited Aunt Loretta. It was a great shock to Aunt Marie to find her only surviving sister in that condition. They kept up their communication from then on through Aunt Loretta's husband. Soon after that day Aunt Marie died. I am still in communication with her husband Uncle Dan.

I also met the other daughters of Aunt Loretta, Kay Cox and Jane Karalafh. One of Jane Lyons' brothers, Bob Lyons, told me how one day, when he was only a young boy in school in early 1950, he had returned home to find the FBI at his house, investigating the whereabouts of their Uncle Michael, whom they thought had returned to India. The FBI wanted him regarding some employment with the US Government. He said that his friends and neighbours were very inquisitive as to why the FBI police visited them and whether their uncle was involved in criminal activities.

"It is a great shame that you have suffered, Esther, due to the two villains in our family, your father and my father," Uncle Frank's eldest son, Michael, said at the Lyons family reunion, "they kept the secret and did not allow us to know you two. But now that we have found you, I want you to know that we accept you as a member of our Lyons family and we love you as our dear long lost cousin." I was presented with a framed photograph of my grandmother, Bertha Ida DeLisle with her young family of sons, the eldest being my father at the age of ten.

In early 1996, I obtained my father's employment report of The Beryllium Corporation through the Freedom of Information Act, from the United States Office of Personnel Management, which said:

'As I understand his background, he had formerly operated a mission in Allahabad, India, where he taught Indians how to hand-pick Beryl Ore and through the sale of this ore, he was able to support his mission school. He took one year's leave and came to the United States with the idea of engaging in work related to Beryl Ore mining and through this connection, realise profit for his mission in India... From December 1946 until the spring and early summer of 1947, Mr Lyons was travelling throughout the New England Area contacting miners and farmers and trying to reach an agreement with them whereby they would collect Beryl Ore , store it and eventually, when there was sufficient ore to warrant a bulk shipment, ship the ore to Reading...... During all of his time, rumours were being circulated throughout the personnel concerning his actual status. The question was whether or not he was actually a priest and if not who was he. Whenever he was in Reading on business trips, he continued to wear the clerical garb and called himself Father Lyons.'

An FBI Report I received through the Freedom of Information Act stated:

'Neighbour: I have known Michael Lyons a neighbour since 1950. Throughout the years that we have been neighbours I have had practically no contact with him as he does not impress me as being a very sociable or neighbourly individual. He stays pretty much to himself and does not mix with others in this rural community. I regard him as an abnormally secretive individual.'

Through the Freedom of Information I learnt that my father used many aliases. One being 'Anthony'. It is clearly stated on one of the FBI Reports that they could find no record of his marriage to Petronilla. It also said that my father purchased property and put it in his wife's maiden name, causing the neighbours to be even more suspicious. Some thought he was a Russian and a Communist spy because of his powerful radio equipment.

Report of investigation by United States Civil Services Commission, Reading Pennsylvania, on 25th March, 1959. Agency, Atomic Energy Commission, csc.-case serial no 3.21.59.10912. Type of case- Full Field:

'SYNOPSIS OF FACTS

This report contains the results of an interview with......... who refused to recommend the subject for national security work. Employment: THE BERYLLIUM CORPORATION, Tuckerton Road.

"I first came to into contact with Michael Lyons or Father Lyons, by which he was more popularly known. I believe that this time he was just getting acquainted with our company and he was engaged by our company to contact people in the New England Area who might be able to supply us with Beryl Ore... ... ... As I understand his background, he had formerly operated a mission in Allahabad, India, where he taught Indians how to hand-pick Beryl Ore and through the sale of this ore, he was able to support his mission school. He took one year leave and came to the United States with the idea of engaging in work related to Beryl Ore mining and through this connection, realise a profit for his mission in India. Beryl Ore, then as now, was very scarce and had to be hand-picked by miners, farmers and others who happened to live in areas where this ore could be found.

From December 1946 until the spring and early summer of 1947, Mr Lyons was travelling throughout the New England Area of this country contacting miners and farmers and trying to reach an agreement with them whereby they would collect this scarce ore, store it and eventually, when there was sufficient ore to warrant a bulk shipment, ship this ore to us here in Reading. He would then be compensated for this amount he paid for the ore plus a profit. During this time, he was in and out of Reading several times on business trips, but most of the time was spent in the New England area on a constant itinerary.

During all of this time, rumours were being circulated throughout our personnel concerning his actual status. The question was whether or not he was actually a priest and if not, who was he. Someone of our personnel inquired of a local clergyman as to his status and an investigation was initiated by this religious organisation to determine Lyons' status. The result was that he was a duly ordained priest. Whenever I saw him here in Reading on business trips, he continued to wear his clerical garb, but I noticed that when the summer months came, he changed to informal street wear, consisting of a sports shirt and slacks. Then some question came up as to how he should be addressed. He stated that it was all right if he were addressed as Mister or Father.......... As time went on, he gradually shipped in less and less ore and eventually we lost contact with him altogether. I could not say now just when our last contact with him was, but I believe he disassociated himself from us soon after 1947... ... I never heard or saw anything unfavourable about the man that would reflect on his habits, use or intoxicants or moral conduct while he was connected with our firm. However, in 1957, one of our consultants reported that he met Lyons out in the far West and this man reported that Lyons had acquired a common law wife and that he had shed his clerical title.........

I personally have nothing against the man and I am sure he is a loyal American citizen. I never knew him to do anything or say anything out of the way that would possibly reflect upon his reputation or loyalty. The only thing that disturbs me is that he has demonstrated instability in that he never said definitely that he was or was not a priest. If he was a priest, why did he give it up? And if he was not a priest, why did he wear the clothes of a cleric, invent the story of his mission and come to us with the explanation that the only reason he engaged in Beryl Ore procurement was in order to realise a profit for his mission school. I think that all of this indicates a certain level or instability and for these reasons, I would not recommend him for important work involving the safety and security of the country".

READING POLICE DEPARTMENT, 6th and Washington Streets.'

In one of the declaration forms in 1949 for the FBI, he had clearly stated that he had two *'illegitimate daughters'* in India. He had not written the whereabouts of the children and no one made further enquiries into it.

Later I managed to obtain 30 pages of research work done by my father, from Washington, on the mineral findings in India.

"Your grandfather, Michael Patrick Lyons was an Irishman who was born in Springfield, Ohio. His father Daniel, with his mother Ellen, his brother Michael, who married Mary Ryan, and sisters Joanne and Catherine, came to Springfield, Ohio from Cork in Ireland, during the height of the Potato Famine around 1847." Jeff said on the phone one morning.

"One of your uncles, Daniel Lyons junior, became the editor of the Collier's Magazine. He is supposed to have written a dictionary which was used in schools for many years in New York."

Later, Jeff McQueen sent me a copy of the family tree he had made. My grandmother, Bertha Ida DeLisle, (my father's mother) was the daughter of Peter Bienvenu dit DeLisle, a Judge and the State Representative of Delray. He was the descendant of Francois Bienvenu "dit" DeLisle, a Lieutenant and Detroit's first tavern keeper, who travelled with Monsieur Cadillac on his founding voyage to Detroit in 1701.

Genealogy of the French Families of the Detroit River Region, Volume 1 and 11, by Denissen, helped me with the research on my father's French line of ancestry, through his French mother, Bertha Ida DeLisle. My grandmother's ancestors came from a very wealthy and affluent family in France. Through marriage, my grandmother was related to royalist as Monsr Francois De'Chavigy and Madam Elenora Grandmiere and also Premier DuPlessis of Canada. They first settled in Montreal, Canada and then came to Detroit.

Early in 1998, I started further research on my ancestors through the internet. I came in contact with Phil Campeau from New York. He was one of the Program Coordinators at The North County Transitional Living Services in Watertown, New York. Phil Campeau worked with the programs that served seriously emotionally disturbed children and was in charge of the two programs, one being in a community residence for adolescent boys and the other being home and community based services. We soon discovered that we were eighth cousins once removed. Our common ancestor being Stephen (Etienne)

Campau, son of Leonard Campau.

While my line of Campeaus came down with Leonard Campau, Stephen (Etienne) Campau, Jacques (James) Campau, Nicholas Campeau dit Niagara, Marie-Anne Campeau, Bienvenu DeLisle, Peter Bienvenu DeLisle, Michael DeLisle Lyons and then myself, Esther Lyons.

Phil's line came down from Leonard Campau, Stephen (Etienne) Campau, Francois Campau, Joseph Campau, Jean Baptiste Campau, Jean Baptiste Campau, Prosper Campau, Prosper Compo, Benjamin Compo, Paul Compeau, Phil Compeau.

I also met another cousin through Phil Compeau, Suzanne Bojolie. Her line of Campeau were, Leonard Campau, Stephen (Etienne) Campau, Francois Campau, Francois Campau, Pierre Campau, Benjamin-Amable Campau, Pierre Campau, Jean Baptiste Campau, Luc Campau, Euclide Campau, Henri Campeau, Suzanne Bojolie.

They were thrilled to know me and bought my book, UNWANTED, to keep as the work of a family member. We have remained in contact ever since.

Later I was contacted by a Betty L. Goniea, whose husband also descended from Leonard Campau, Stephen (Etienne) Campau and Catherine Paulo, James (Jacques) Campau, Nicholas "Niagra" Campau, Barnard Campau (brother of Ann Marie Campau), Claude Campaeu, Claude Campeau, Mary Ann Campeau, George Goniea, Emery Louis Goniea, Larry Goniea, the husband of Betty.

I also found Don and Chris Riopelle and their aunt, Ruth Bolla, who were the descendants of Ambrose and Teresa Riopel. Their daughter, Zoe Riopel married my ancestor Bienvenu DeLisle. Through the Michigan's Habitant Heritage Magazine I was able to know Gail Moreau, the Editor. I became a member of the French-Canadian Heritage Society of Michigan and was able to find Yvonne Latta. She was the descendant of my great grandmother, Adeline Piette's mother, Catherine Solo. Catherine, a widow of John Baptist Piette had remarried Peter Drouillard in 1857. Yvonne Latta was the grand daughter of Catherine Solo and Peter Drouillard. She informed me that all the French families from Acadia were all related and that I was a cousin of hers. In mid June 1999 I received an email from Christian Soulard in Paris, France. He introduced himself as the descendant of Francois Beinvenu "dit" DeLisle through his sister, Catherine DeLisle. He had seen my book, UNWANTED advertised in the internet and contacted me about his great grand Uncle, Francois Beinvenu "dit" DeLisle, a French man who migrated to Montreal and then to Detroit. He was amongst the first French pioneers who helped establish French settlement around River Detroit. Ever since Christian Soulard and myself have been in contact as distant cousins.

I have kept in touch with all the Lyons cousins, their children and their grandchildren. The great grand children of Uncle Frank, Zach and Alec Soles, the children of Threse Soles, communicate with me practically every week on the America On Line, Instant Messenger. The daughter of my Aunt Loretta, Kay Cox emails me every week, as do the children of Aunt Helen, Patrick McQueen, Jim McQueen, William McQueen and Clyde McQueen. Everyone has now accepted me in the family without any prejudice. Unfortunately we are just getting to know each other. All my life passed through struggling for acceptance and for identity. My father's two sisters, Margaret and Marie, never had any children. Marie adopted children. Margaret died without having any, while we struggled without a father and without a proper name and identity. The family members of my father were kept in the dark about our existence throughout.

"You would have loved your Aunt Margaret," Uncle Dan, the husband of Aunt Marie said, "She was such a kind person. Such a loving and caring, gentle person. She played music and played the piano very well."

Although all of my father's sisters are dead and his brother Frank is also dead and so is my father, at fifty-nine years old I have found and been accepted by all the wonderful family members in the USA and France. Due to this acceptance, my sister's and my children, can finally speak with pride about their American grandfather and his relatives in the USA, without shame. They will not have to tell lies to cover up a family scandal and a shame any more.

Unfortunately, I cannot find anything about my mother's parents in India. There are no records of their parents in the orphanage where they were brought up, in the village of Latonah, Bihar, India.

I have also made many friends in Ohio and Michigan, who have helped me research my family tree from Detroit River Region and Toledo. Jo Hubbard and Ken Mills are the two who have been of great help to me. I later found out that Ken Mills is also distantly related to me through the DeLisle family. Jo helped to set up a family tree website for me. I also came in contact with a Frank Nadean who was also related to me distantly through the DeLisle family, the same as Dr Michael Geron from Springfield, Ohio, a relative from the Lyons side of the family. Everyone accepted me and there never has been any kind of prejudice against me. "You are just like us. You resemble us," Kay Cox, the daughter of my father's sister, Loretta told me once.

"I am so happy to meet you and I don't know why I cannot help crying," said Pat, Kay's Sister when she met me in Detroit, the time I visited them in 1996.

"You are a bit darker than us in complexion, but you are our beloved cousin and we love you. We accept you in our family being our grand Uncle's daughter," Jeff McQueen said when I went to stay at his house in 1996 and met him for the first time in my life. I met Rita McQueen the other daughter of Aunt Helen, who came a long distance just to welcome me into the family.

"I have come all the way to meet you, because I wanted to see you and accept you," said Jane Karalafh, the daughter of my Aunt Loretta. Virginia Lyons, the daughter of Uncle Frank, also came from California to Detroit specially to meet me on the day of the reunion.

✣ ✣ ✣ ✣ ✣

In those years of my childhood and youth I shed bitter tears whenever anyone spoke sarcastically about my background. I had no a father and no relatives. While everyone boasted of relatives, grandparents and backgrounds, I had no one and nothing to speak about. I spent all my time in the backyard of the house, confused and in tears of hurt and pain, praying and asking Jesus for answers to my many questions. I never got any answers, but I trusted in His love and mercy. I wanted to belong to a family and was very family oriented but I could not have any, except when I had my own children born to me. But, in my late fifties I shed sweet tears as I found myself belonging to a large and respectable family. A family with ancestors who were important and successful people, after whom some of the streets are named in Detroit. At last I have found my identity. I now have the right of every human being, to belong. It was not given to me like every other child, I had to search for it. My sister and I were made orphans when our parents were alive.

We lived in great poverty while he lived making a lot of money for the church, which chose to ignore our existence. I am still a Christian since it was my love for Jesus and my faith in Him, which helped me survive those years of my troubled and painful childhood and youth. The discovery of the truth about my father and the injustice done to us and my dear mother, had drifted me far from the Catholic Church.

When I was writing my manuscript for my book, I informed the provincial of the Jesuits in Sydney about it.

"If you feel like writing your autobiography then write it. It will do you good." he said.

I also wrote to the Pope regarding the manuscript and received a letter from his representative in Canberra, saying, that the Pope sends me his blessings and his prayers.

Later I sent a copy of the book to Cardinal Clancy in Sydney and told him of my rejections which had turned me against the church. I also received a reply from him.

Suddenly as a result I felt I was not rejected any more, that I was at last accepted as Father Michael Lyons' daughter by all. While I lived with the pain of continual rejection and of being the unwanted daughter of a Catholic priest, I had moved from the place of my birth into a different country and culture and have become a highly qualified adult. People started judging me according to what I was as an individual, many did not know my background. Yet I could never forget my origin nor the bitter experience of rejections as an innocent child. Although, I had moulded myself into an accepted person from a non-person, I lived bound to my tormenting childhood memories of being illegitimate and abandoned. Suddenly, now I have woken up, in my late fifties, to the fact that while I was rejected due to the Canon Law of the Church, there were many amongst the religious in the Catholic Church itself who helped me with good education and with my identity, in spite of the existing rule of celibacy, which had caused all the misery to me.

At the beginning of Year 2000, I was offered a position as a Support Teacher by Brother Michael, a Marist Brother, in his school at Berne Education Centre, Lewisham, New South Wales, Australia. I am now back teaching in the Catholic School where I feel I am accepted with all my qualifications and as an individual. Particularly being the great grand-daughter of Judge Peter Bienvenu "dit" DeLisle of Delray, Michigan, USA, truth and justice had always been important to me. It did not matter where I was born, the genes of my ancestors made me determined and stubborn into finding my identity.

I often wonder why my mother could not have been given the honour of being buried as a nun when my father could be buried as a priest after all. Was it because she was a woman? She was a great mother and a woman who took all the responsibilities in the face of great poverty. She struggled throughout her life to survive and keep us alive. I love her for her courage. My sister and I grew up in shame, without a father and with the stigma of being unwanted and my mother suffered humiliation while she courageously carried out the responsibility of a single mother throughout her one lifetime on this earth! She had all the love of a mother to give which encouraged us to carry on living.

My father was also responsible for bringing my sister and me into this world and we needed him as a Papa alongside our dear Mother.

To me that was more important than the priesthood he belonged to!

✢ ✢ ✢ ✢ ✢

I have at last found my identity and am proud to belong to a family with a great background! I can now die in peace knowing that I and my sister are accepted by all, in the Church and the world. Yet, when I think of the many years of my life's journey spent in search of something which was my birth right, I shed bitter tears. I became a prisoner of those terrifying experiences of childhood which had a great psychological effect for my entire life. Only now when I am nearly 60 years of age, I can shed sweet tears. Unfortunately my mother died knowing nothing and with guilt and shame, but I am free of all stigma and blame. I am a person like everyone else with name and identity with a confidence of one who has a great family background.

BIBLIOGRAPHY:

1. Information given by Jeffrey McQueen (Michigan).
2. Jo Hubbard (Springfield, Ohio).
3. Information given by Christian Soulard (France).
4. Rev. Fr. Christian Denissen, Genealogy of the French Families of the Detroit River Region 1701-1936 – Vol. 1 and Vol. 2 (Published by Detroit Society for Genealogical Research).
5. Newspaper announcement.
6. Interview with Direct Relative (Parent, Child, Spouse or Actual Person).
7. Gail Moreau from Historical Society of French Pioneers to Detroit.
8. Ken Mills (Ohio).
9. Phil Campeau (New York).

FAMILY CHART NO. 1 – Descendants of Michael Bienvenu

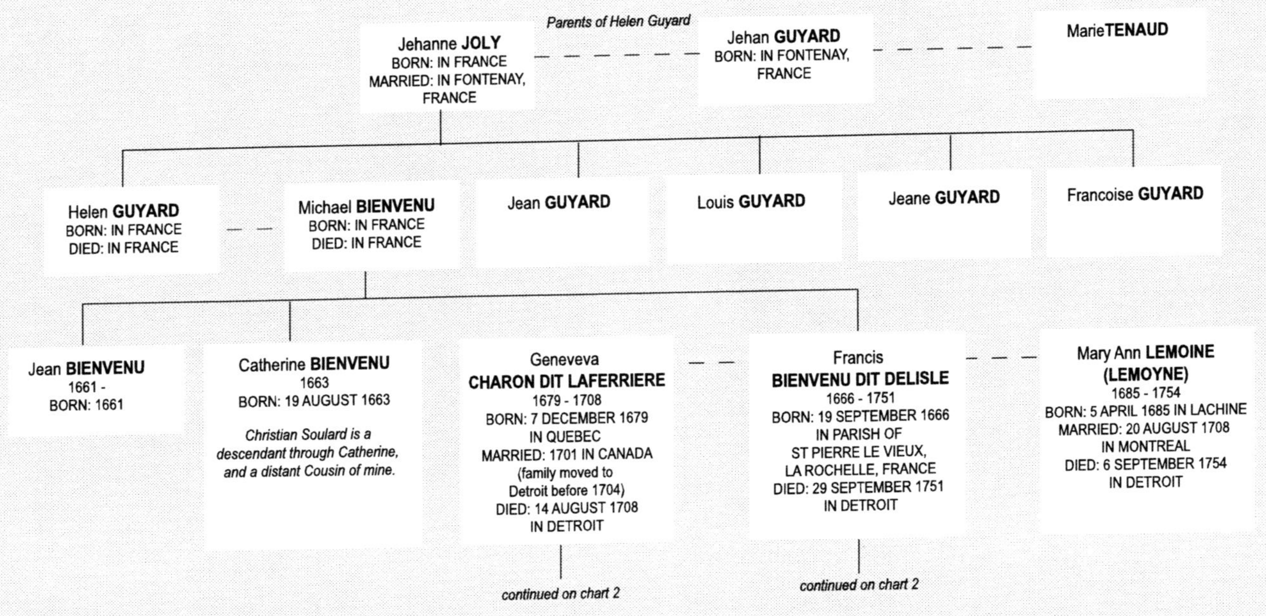

Parents of Helen Guyard
Jehanne JOLY
BORN: IN FRANCE
MARRIED: IN FONTENAY, FRANCE
Jehan GUYARD
BORN: IN FONTENAY, FRANCE
MarieTENAUD
Helen GUYARD
BORN: IN FRANCE
DIED: IN FRANCE
Michael BIENVENU
BORN: IN FRANCE
DIED: IN FRANCE
Jean GUYARD
Louis GUYARD
Jeane GUYARD
Francoise GUYARD
Jean BIENVENU
1661 -
BORN: 1661
Catherine BIENVENU
1663
BORN: 19 AUGUST 1663
Christian Soulard is a descendant through Catherine, and a distant Cousin of mine.
Geneveva
CHARON DIT LAFERRIERE
1679 - 1708
BORN: 7 DECEMBER 1679
IN QUEBEC
MARRIED: 1701 IN CANADA
(family moved to Detroit before 1704)
DIED: 14 AUGUST 1708
IN DETROIT
Francis
BIENVENU DIT DELISLE
1666 - 1751
BORN: 19 SEPTEMBER 1666
IN PARISH OF
ST PIERRE LE VIEUX,
LA ROCHELLE, FRANCE
DIED: 29 SEPTEMBER 1751
IN DETROIT
Mary Ann LEMOINE
(LEMOYNE)
1685 - 1754
BORN: 5 APRIL 1685 IN LACHINE
MARRIED: 20 AUGUST 1708
IN MONTREAL
DIED: 6 SEPTEMBER 1754
IN DETROIT
continued on chart 2
continued on chart 2

FAMILY CHART NO. 2 - Descendants of Francis (Francois) Bienvenu 'dit' Delisle

Francis **BIENVENU DIT DELISLE**
1666 - 1751
BORN: 19 SEPTEMBER 1666
DIED: 29 SEPTEMBER 1751 IN DETROIT

Geneveva Chron dit **LAFERRIERE**
1679 - 1708
BORN: 7 DECEMBER 1679 IN QUEBEC
MARRIED: 1701 IN CANADA
DIED:14 AUGUST 1708 IN DETROIT

Alexis **BIENVENU DIT DELISLE**
1701 - 1763
BORN: 1701 IN
SOUTH WEST COAST OF DETROIT
DIED: 13 OCTOBER 1763 IN DETROIT

Mary Joseph **BOURON**
1718 -1758
MARRIED: 17 JANUARY 1739/40
IN DETROIT
DIED: 30 MAY 1758 IN DETROIT

Raphael **DELISLE**
1703 -
BORN: 1703

Joseph **DELISLE**
1703/04 -
BORN: 5 MARCH 1703/1704

Mary **DELISLE**
1705 -
BORN: 8 DECEMBER 1705

Alexis
BIENVENU DIT DELISLE
1740 -1787
BORN: 25 NOVEMBER
1740 IN DETROIT
DIED: 12 NOVEMBER 1787
IN DETROIT

Mary Ann **CAMPAU**
1745 -
BORN: 7 OCTOBER 1745 IN DETROIT
MARRIED: 26 MAY 1763 IN DETROIT
DIED: IN DETROIT
(Descendant of Leonard Campau and Francis Mauger - and their son Stephen (Etienne) Campau. Born: 1638, La Rochelle Died: 1721, Montreal, Canada)

Joseph **DELISLE**
1742 -
BORN:
7 APRIL 1742

John Baptist **DELISLE**
1743 -
BORN:
13 APRIL 1743

Mark **DELISLE**
1744 -
BORN:
30 MARCH 1744

Charles **DELISLE**
1745 -
BORN:
14 SEPTEMBER 1745

Mary **DELISLE**
1746 -
BORN:
31 DECEMBER 1746

Alexis **DELISLE**
1764 -
BORN:
13 FEBRUARY
1764

John Bapist **DELISLE**
1765 -
BORN:
2 OCTOBER
1765

Alexis **DELISLE**
1767 -
BORN:
30 JANUARY
1767

Joseph **DELISLE**
1769 -
BORN:
3 JANUARY
1769

Isidore **DELISLE**
1771 -
BORN:
3 JUNE 1771

Henry **DELISLE**
1773 -
BORN:
6 JULY 1773

Louis **DELISLE**
1775 -
BORN:
7 OCTOBER
1775

Bienvenu **DELISLE**
1776 -
BORN:
5 DECEMBER 1776
IN SOUTH WEST
COAST
OF DETROIT
DIED: IN DETROIT

Monique **LIVERNOIS**
1788 - 1849
BORN: 5 APRIL 1788
IN DETROIT
MARRIED: 25 DECEMBER 1817
IN DETROIT
DIED: 9 FEBRUARY 1849
IN ST FRANCIS XAVIER ECORCE

Mary Louisa **DELISLE**
1779 -
BORN:
11 OCTOBER
1779

Monica **DELISLE**
1781 -
BORN:
5 APRIL 1781

Basil **DELISLE**
1783 -
BORN:
13 OCTOBER
1783

FAMILY CHART NO. 3 – Descendants of Francis (Francois) Bienvenu 'dit' Delisle

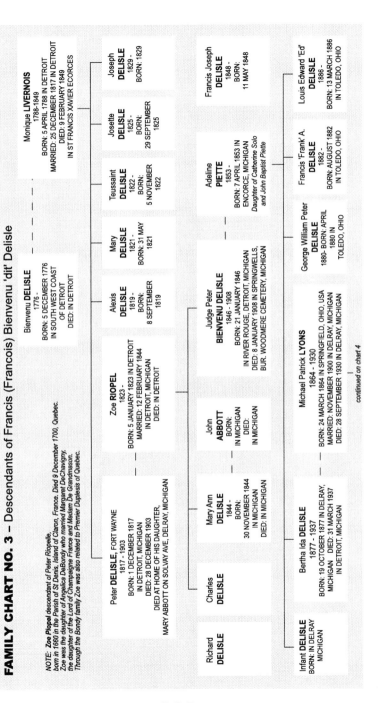

*NOTE: **Zoe Piopel** descendant of Peter Riopelle,*
born in 1660 in the Parish of St Denis, Island of Claron, France. Died 9 December 1700, Quebec.
Zoe was the daughter of Angelica DeBondy who married Margaret DeChavigny,
the daughter of the Lord of Champaigne France and Madam De Grandmason.
Through the Bondy family Zoe was also related to Premier Duplesis of Quebec.

Bienvenu **DELISLE**
1776 -
BORN: 5 DECEMBER 1776
IN SOUTH WEST COAST
OF DETROIT
DIED: IN DETROIT

— —

Monique **LIVERNOIS**
1788-1849
BORN: 5 APRIL 1788 IN DETROIT
MARRIED: 25 DECEMBER 1817 IN DETROIT
DIED: 9 FEBRUARY 1849
IN ST FRANCIS XAVIER ECORCES

Peter **DELISLE,** FORT WAYNE
1817 - 1903
BORN: 1 DECEMBER 1817
IN DETROIT, MICHIGAN
DIED: 28 DECEMBER 1903
DIED AT HOME OF HIS DAUGHTER,
MARY ABBOTT ON SOLVAY AVE, DELRAY, MICHIGAN

— —

Zoe **RIOPEL**
1823 -
BORN: 5 JANUARY 1823 IN DETROIT
MARRIED: 12 FEBRUARY 1844
IN DETROIT, MICHIGAN
DIED: IN DETROIT

Alexis
DELISLE
1819 -
BORN:
8 SEPTEMBER
1819

Mary
DELISLE
1821 -
BORN: 31 MAY
1821

Teussaint
DELISLE
1822 -
BORN:
5 NOVEMBER
1822

Josette
DELISLE
1825 -
BORN:
29 SEPTEMBER
1825

Joseph
DELISLE
1829 -
BORN: 1829

Richard
DELISLE

Charles
DELISLE

Mary Ann
DELISLE
1844 -
BORN:
30 NOVEMBER 1844
IN MICHIGAN
DIED: IN MICHIGAN

— —

John
ABBOTT
BORN:
IN MICHIGAN
DIED:
IN MICHIGAN

Judge Peter
BIENVENU DELISLE
1846 - 1908
BORN: 21 JANUARY 1846
IN RIVER ROUGE, DETROIT, MICHIGAN
DIED: 8 JANUARY 1908 IN SPRINGWELLS,
BUR. WOODMERE CEMETERY, MICHIGAN

— —

Adeline
PIETTE
1853 -
BORN: 7 APRIL 1853 IN
ENCORCE, MICHIGAN
Daughter of Catherine Solo
and John Baptist Piette

Francis Joseph
DELISLE
1848 -
BORN:
11 MAY 1848

Infant **DELISLE**
BORN: IN DELRAY
MICHIGAN

Bertha Ida **DELISLE**
1877 - 1937
BORN: 19 OCTOBER 1877 IN DELRAY,
MICHIGAN DIED: 31 MARCH 1937
IN DETROIT, MICHIGAN

— —

Michael Patrick **LYONS**
1864 - 1930
BORN: 24 MARCH 1864 IN SPRINGFIELD, OHIO, USA
MARRIED: NOVEMBER 1900 IN DELRAY, MICHIGAN
DIED: 28 SEPTEMBER 1930 IN DELRAY, MICHIGAN

continued on chart 4

George William Peter
DELISLE
1880- BORN: APRIL
1880 IN
TOLEDO, OHIO

Francis 'Frank' A.
DELISLE
1882 -
BORN: AUGUST 1882
IN TOLEDO, OHIO

Louis Edward 'Ed'
DELISLE
1886 -
BORN: 13 MARCH 1886
IN TOLEDO, OHIO

FAMILY CHART NO. 4 - Descendants of Francis (Francois) Bienvenu 'dit' Delisle

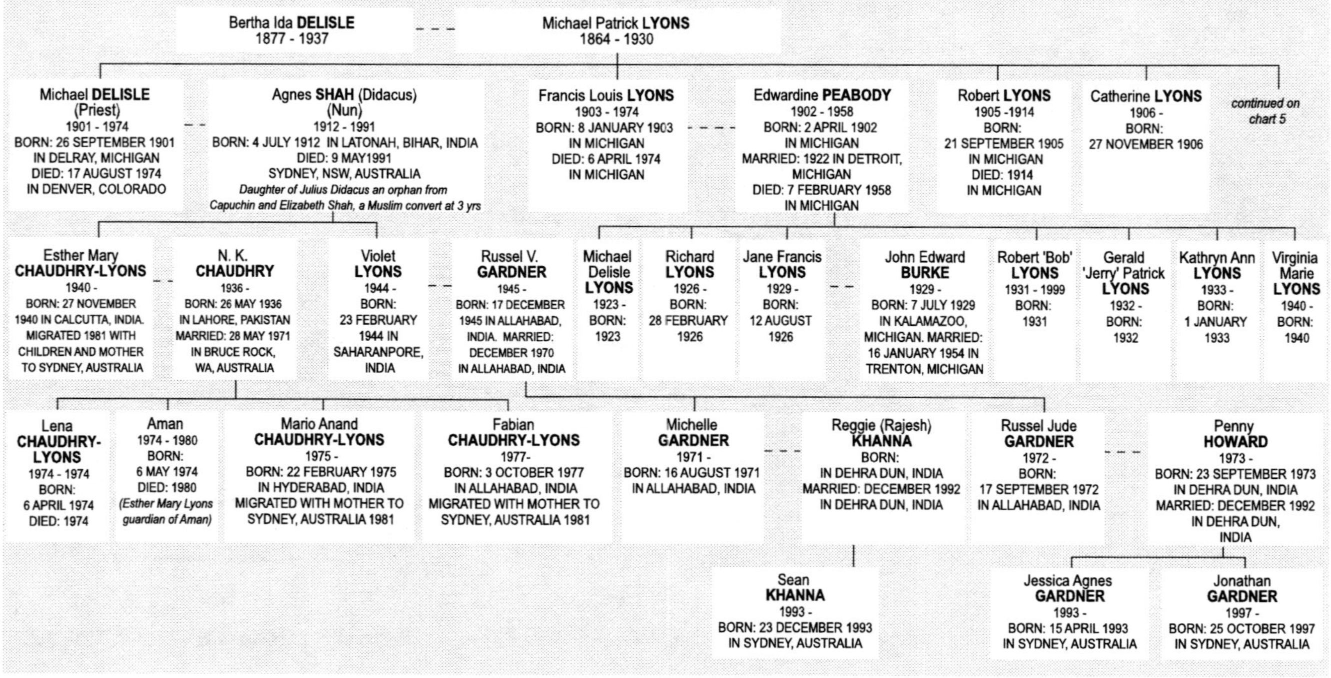
Bertha Ida **DELISLE**
1877 - 1937
Michael Patrick **LYONS**
1864 - 1930
Michael **DELISLE**
(Priest)
1901 - 1974
BORN: 26 SEPTEMBER 1901
IN DELRAY, MICHIGAN
DIED: 17 AUGUST 1974
IN DENVER, COLORADO
Agnes **SHAH** (Didacus)
(Nun)
1912 - 1991
BORN: 4 JULY 1912 IN LATONAH, BIHAR, INDIA
DIED: 9 MAY1991
SYDNEY, NSW, AUSTRALIA
Daughter of Julius Didacus an orphan from
Capuchin and Elizabeth Shah, a Muslim convert at 3 yrs
Francis Louis **LYONS**
1903 - 1974
BORN: 8 JANUARY 1903
IN MICHIGAN
DIED: 6 APRIL 1974
IN MICHIGAN
Edwardine **PEABODY**
1902 - 1958
BORN: 2 APRIL 1902
IN MICHIGAN
MARRIED: 1922 IN DETROIT,
MICHIGAN
DIED: 7 FEBRUARY 1958
IN MICHIGAN
Robert **LYONS**
1905 -1914
BORN:
21 SEPTEMBER 1905
IN MICHIGAN
DIED: 1914
IN MICHIGAN
Catherine **LYONS**
1906 -
BORN:
27 NOVEMBER 1906
continued on
chart 5
Esther Mary
CHAUDHRY-LYONS
1940 -
BORN: 27 NOVEMBER
1940 IN CALCUTTA, INDIA.
MIGRATED 1981 WITH
CHILDREN AND MOTHER
TO SYDNEY, AUSTRALIA
N. K.
CHAUDHRY
1936 -
BORN: 26 MAY 1936
IN LAHORE, PAKISTAN
MARRIED: 28 MAY 1971
IN BRUCE ROCK,
WA, AUSTRALIA
Violet
LYONS
1944 -
BORN:
23 FEBRUARY
1944 IN
SAHARANPORE,
INDIA
Russel V.
GARDNER
1945 -
BORN: 17 DECEMBER
1945 IN ALLAHABAD,
INDIA. MARRIED:
DECEMBER 1970
IN ALLAHABAD, INDIA
Michael
Delisle
LYONS
1923 -
BORN:
1923
Richard
LYONS
1926 -
BORN:
28 FEBRUARY
1926
Jane Francis
LYONS
1929 -
BORN:
12 AUGUST
1926
John Edward
BURKE
1929 -
BORN: 7 JULY 1929
IN KALAMAZOO,
MICHIGAN. MARRIED:
16 JANUARY 1954 IN
TRENTON, MICHIGAN
Robert 'Bob'
LYONS
1931 - 1999
BORN:
1931
Gerald
'Jerry' Patrick
LYONS
1932 -
BORN:
1932
Kathryn Ann
LYONS
1933 -
BORN:
1 JANUARY
1933
Virginia
Marie
LYONS
1940 -
BORN:
1940
Lena
CHAUDHRY-
LYONS
1974 - 1974
BORN:
6 APRIL 1974
DIED: 1974
Aman
1974 - 1980
BORN:
6 MAY 1974
DIED: 1980
(Esther Mary Lyons
guardian of Aman)
Mario Anand
CHAUDHRY-LYONS
1975 -
BORN: 22 FEBRUARY 1975
IN HYDERABAD, INDIA
MIGRATED WITH MOTHER TO
SYDNEY, AUSTRALIA 1981
Fabian
CHAUDHRY-LYONS
1977-
BORN: 3 OCTOBER 1977
IN ALLAHABAD, INDIA
MIGRATED WITH MOTHER TO
SYDNEY, AUSTRALIA 1981
Michelle
GARDNER
1971 -
BORN: 16 AUGUST 1971
IN ALLAHABAD, INDIA
Reggie (Rajesh)
KHANNA
BORN:
IN DEHRA DUN, INDIA
MARRIED: DECEMBER 1992
IN DEHRA DUN, INDIA
Russel Jude
GARDNER
1972 -
BORN:
17 SEPTEMBER 1972
IN ALLAHABAD, INDIA
Penny
HOWARD
1973 -
BORN: 23 SEPTEMBER 1973
IN DEHRA DUN, INDIA
MARRIED: DECEMBER 1992
IN DEHRA DUN,
INDIA
Sean
KHANNA
1993 -
BORN: 23 DECEMBER 1993
IN SYDNEY, AUSTRALIA
Jessica Agnes
GARDNER
1993 -
BORN: 15 APRIL 1993
IN SYDNEY, AUSTRALIA
Jonathan
GARDNER
1997 -
BORN: 25 OCTOBER 1997
IN SYDNEY, AUSTRALIA

FAMILY CHART NO. 5 - Descendants of Francis (Francois) Bienvenu 'dit' Delisle

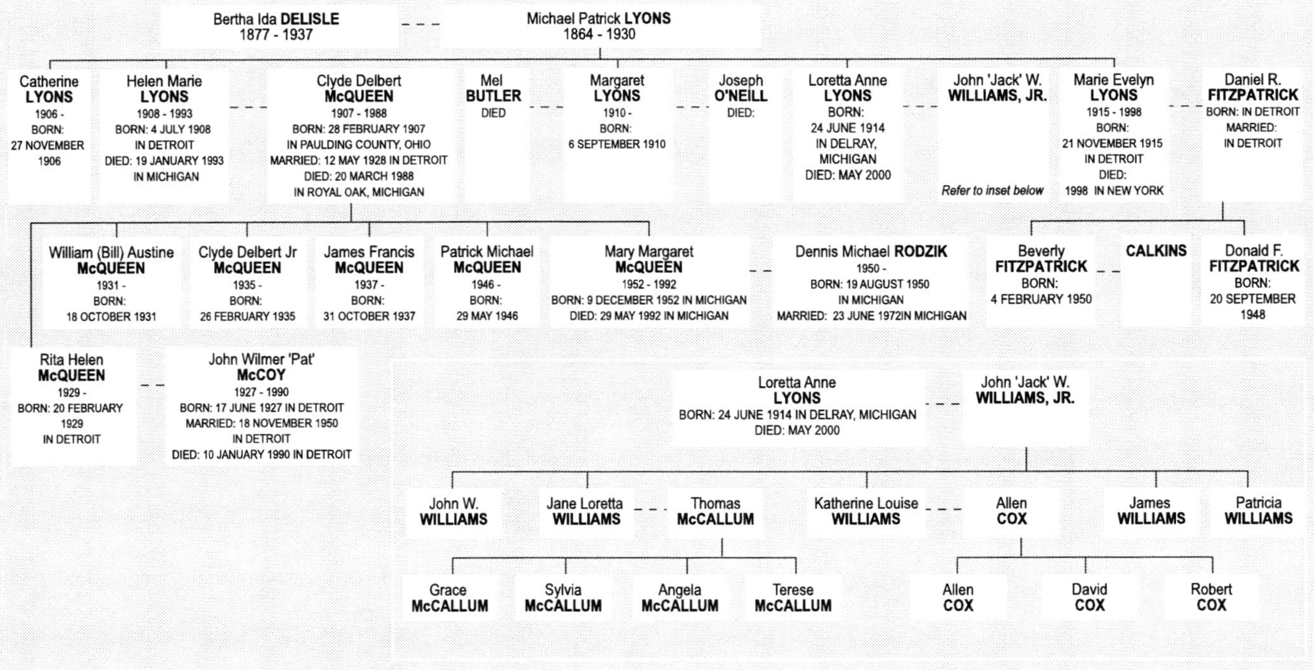

FAMILY CHART NO. 6 – Descendants of Francis (Francois) Bienvenu 'dit' Delisle

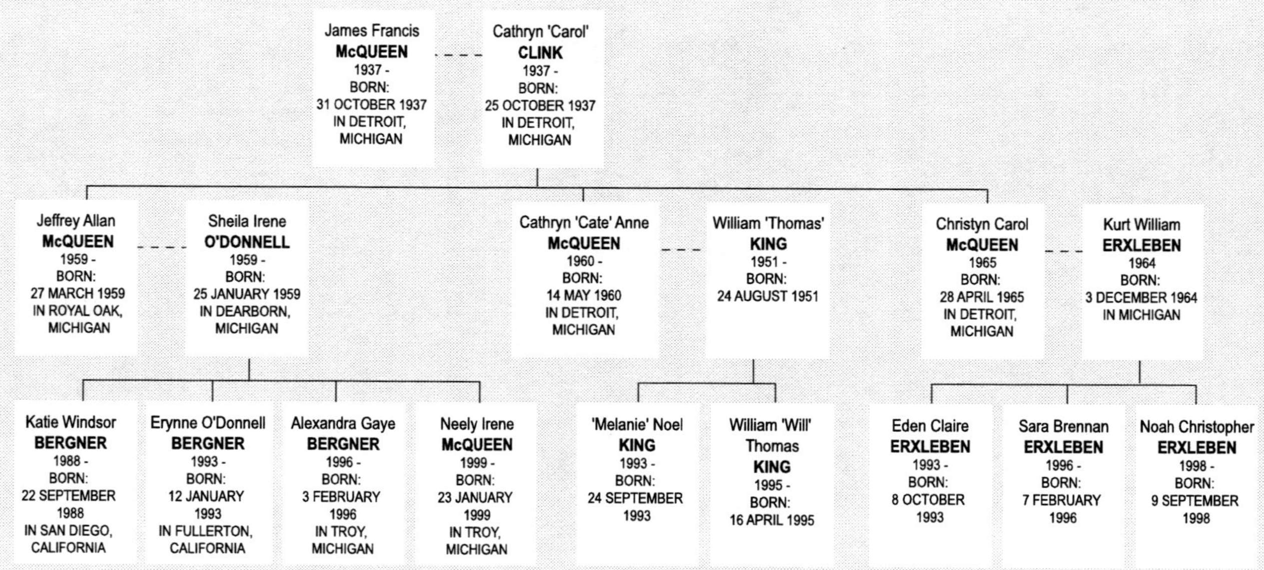

FAMILY CHART NO. 7 – Descendants of 'Unknown' Lyons and Ellen Lyons

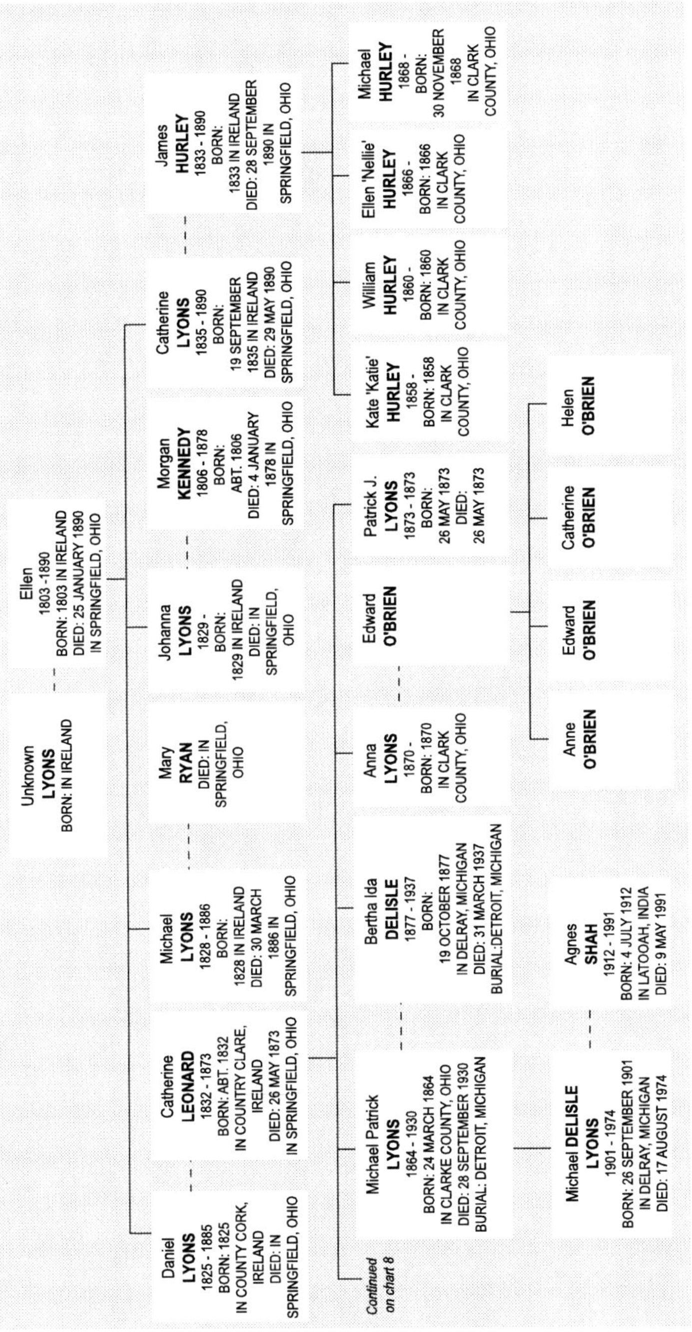
Unknown LYONS BORN: IN IRELAND
Ellen 1803 -1890 BORN: 1803 IN IRELAND DIED: 25 JANUARY 1890 IN SPRINGFIELD, OHIO
Daniel LYONS 1825 - 1885 BORN: 1825 IN COUNTY CORK, IRELAND DIED: IN SPRINGFIELD, OHIO
Catherine LEONARD 1832 - 1873 BORN: ABT. 1832 IN COUNTRY CLARE, IRELAND DIED: 26 MAY 1873 IN SPRINGFIELD, OHIO
Michael LYONS 1828 - 1886 BORN: 1828 IN IRELAND DIED: 30 MARCH 1886 IN SPRINGFIELD, OHIO
Mary RYAN DIED: IN SPRINGFIELD, OHIO
Johanna LYONS 1829 - BORN: 1829 IN IRELAND DIED: IN SPRINGFIELD, OHIO
Morgan KENNEDY 1806 - 1878 BORN: ABT. 1806 DIED: 4 JANUARY 1878 IN SPRINGFIELD, OHIO
Catherine LYONS 1835 - 1890 BORN: 19 SEPTEMBER 1835 IN IRELAND DIED: 29 MAY 1890 SPRINGFIELD, OHIO
James HURLEY 1833 - 1890 BORN: 1833 IN IRELAND DIED: 28 SEPTEMBER 1890 IN SPRINGFIELD, OHIO
Continued on chart 8
Michael Patrick LYONS 1864 - 1930 BORN: 24 MARCH 1864 IN CLARKE COUNTY, OHIO DIED: 28 SEPTEMBER 1930 BURIAL: DETROIT, MICHIGAN
Bertha Ida DELISLE 1877 - 1937 BORN: 19 OCTOBER 1877 IN DELRAY, MICHIGAN DIED: 31 MARCH 1937 BURIAL:DETROIT, MICHIGAN
Anna LYONS 1870 - BORN: 1870 IN CLARK COUNTY, OHIO
Edward O'BRIEN
Patrick J. LYONS 1873 - 1873 BORN: 26 MAY 1873 DIED: 26 MAY 1873
Kate 'Katie' HURLEY 1858 - BORN: 1858 IN CLARK COUNTY, OHIO
William HURLEY 1860 - BORN: 1860 IN CLARK COUNTY, OHIO
Ellen 'Nellie' HURLEY 1866 - BORN: 1866 IN CLARK COUNTY, OHIO
Michael HURLEY 1868 - BORN: 30 NOVEMBER 1868 IN CLARK COUNTY, OHIO
Michael DELISLE LYONS 1901 - 1974 BORN: 26 SEPTEMBER 1901 IN DELRAY, MICHIGAN DIED: 17 AUGUST 1974
Agnes SHAH 1912 - 1991 BORN: 4 JULY 1912 IN LATOOAH, INDIA DIED: 9 MAY 1991
Anne O'BRIEN
Edward O'BRIEN
Catherine O'BRIEN
Helen O'BRIEN

FAMILY CHART NO. 8 – Descendants of Mr Lyons and Ellen Lyons

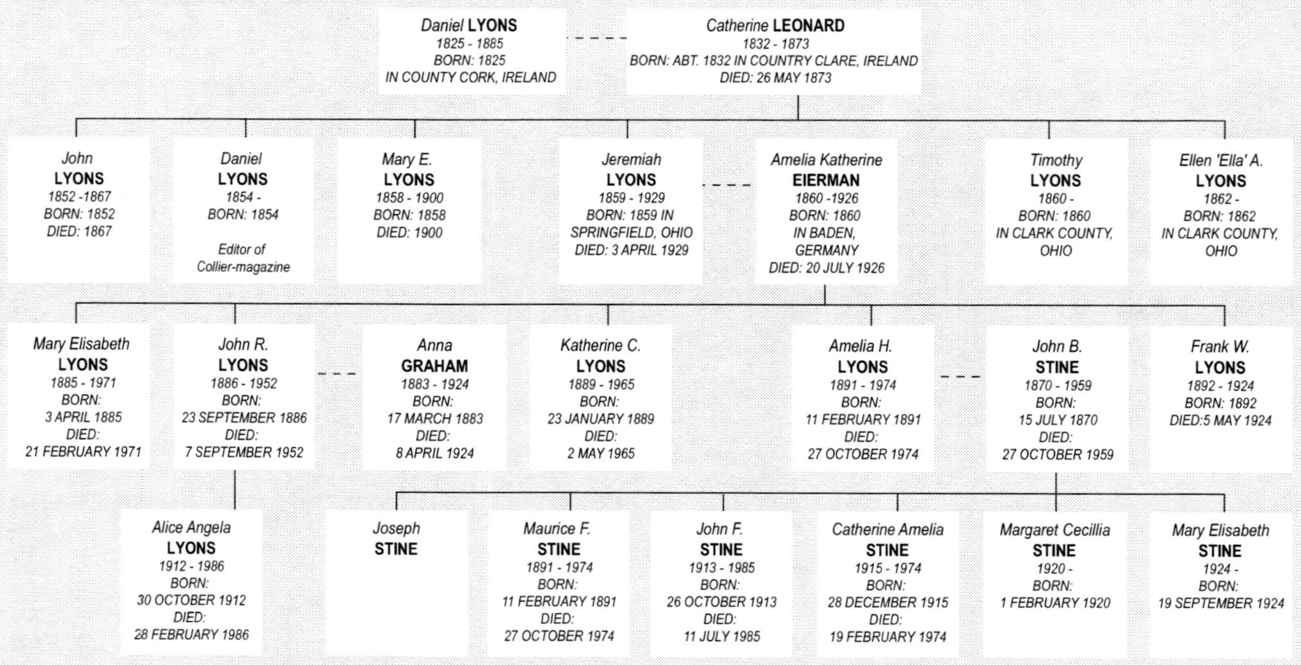
Daniel LYONS
1825 - 1885
BORN: 1825
IN COUNTY CORK, IRELAND
Catherine LEONARD
1832 - 1873
BORN: ABT. 1832 IN COUNTRY CLARE, IRELAND
DIED: 26 MAY 1873
John LYONS
1852 -1867
BORN: 1852
DIED: 1867
Daniel LYONS
1854 -
BORN: 1854
Editor of Collier-magazine
Mary E. LYONS
1858 - 1900
BORN: 1858
DIED: 1900
Jeremiah LYONS
1859 - 1929
BORN: 1859 IN SPRINGFIELD, OHIO
DIED: 3 APRIL 1929
Amelia Katherine EIERMAN
1860 -1926
BORN: 1860 IN BADEN, GERMANY
DIED: 20 JULY 1926
Timothy LYONS
1860 -
BORN: 1860
IN CLARK COUNTY, OHIO
Ellen 'Ella' A. LYONS
1862 -
BORN: 1862
IN CLARK COUNTY, OHIO
Mary Elisabeth LYONS
1885 - 1971
BORN: 3 APRIL 1885
DIED: 21 FEBRUARY 1971
John R. LYONS
1886 - 1952
BORN: 23 SEPTEMBER 1886
DIED: 7 SEPTEMBER 1952
Anna GRAHAM
1883 - 1924
BORN: 17 MARCH 1883
DIED: 8 APRIL 1924
Katherine C. LYONS
1889 - 1965
BORN: 23 JANUARY 1889
DIED: 2 MAY 1965
Amelia H. LYONS
1891 - 1974
BORN: 11 FEBRUARY 1891
DIED: 27 OCTOBER 1974
John B. STINE
1870 - 1959
BORN: 15 JULY 1870
DIED: 27 OCTOBER 1959
Frank W. LYONS
1892 - 1924
BORN: 1892
DIED:5 MAY 1924
Alice Angela LYONS
1912 - 1986
BORN: 30 OCTOBER 1912
DIED: 28 FEBRUARY 1986
Joseph STINE
Maurice F. STINE
1891 - 1974
BORN: 11 FEBRUARY 1891
DIED: 27 OCTOBER 1974
John F. STINE
1913 - 1985
BORN: 26 OCTOBER 1913
DIED: 11 JULY 1985
Catherine Amelia STINE
1915 - 1974
BORN: 28 DECEMBER 1915
DIED: 19 FEBRUARY 1974
Margaret Cecillia STINE
1920 -
BORN: 1 FEBRUARY 1920
Mary Elisabeth STINE
1924 -
BORN: 19 SEPTEMBER 1924

FAMILY CHART NO. 9 – Descendants of Ellen Lyons and Francis (Francois) Bienvenu 'dit' Delisle

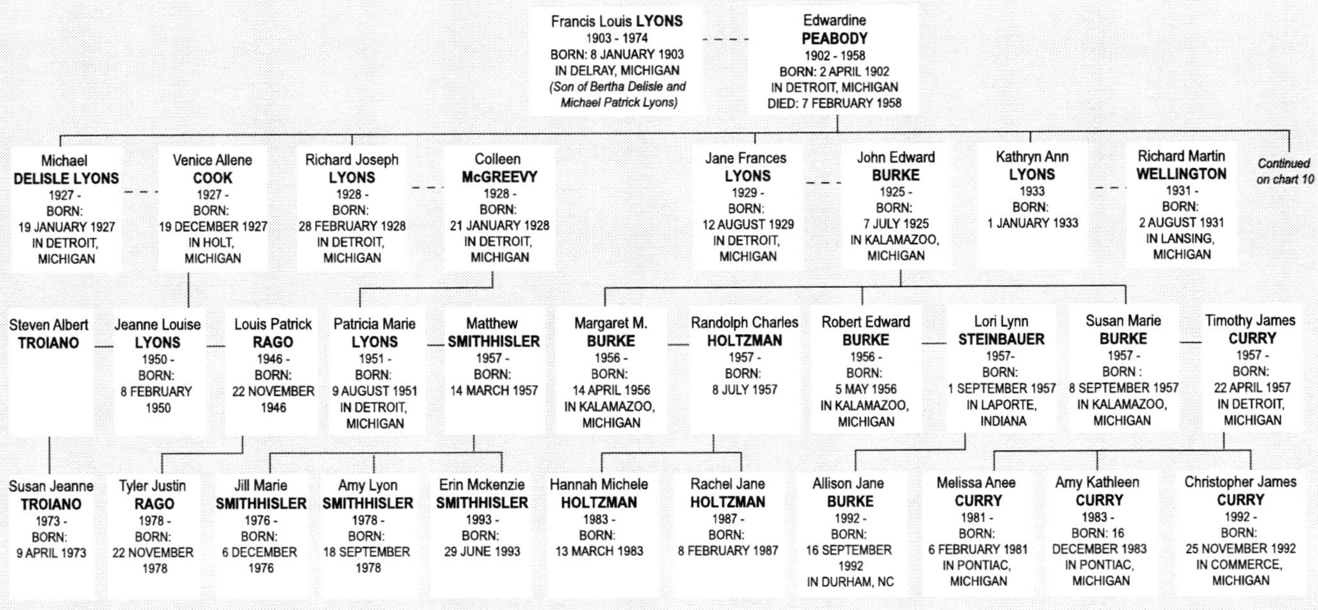

Francis Louis LYONS 1903 - 1974 BORN: 8 JANUARY 1903 IN DELRAY, MICHIGAN (Son of Bertha Delisle and Michael Patrick Lyons)
Edwardine PEABODY 1902 - 1958 BORN: 2 APRIL 1902 IN DETROIT, MICHIGAN DIED: 7 FEBRUARY 1958
Michael DELISLE LYONS 1927 - BORN: 19 JANUARY 1927 IN DETROIT, MICHIGAN
Venice Allene COOK 1927 - BORN: 19 DECEMBER 1927 IN HOLT, MICHIGAN
Richard Joseph LYONS 1928 - BORN: 28 FEBRUARY 1928 IN DETROIT, MICHIGAN
Colleen McGREEVY 1928 - BORN: 21 JANUARY 1928 IN DETROIT, MICHIGAN
Jane Frances LYONS 1929 - BORN: 12 AUGUST 1929 IN DETROIT, MICHIGAN
John Edward BURKE 1925 - BORN: 7 JULY 1925 IN KALAMAZOO, MICHIGAN
Kathryn Ann LYONS 1933 BORN: 1 JANUARY 1933
Richard Martin WELLINGTON 1931 - BORN: 2 AUGUST 1931 IN LANSING, MICHIGAN
Continued on chart 10
Steven Albert TROIANO
Jeanne Louise LYONS 1950 - BORN: 8 FEBRUARY 1950
Louis Patrick RAGO 1946 - BORN: 22 NOVEMBER 1946
Patricia Marie LYONS 1951 - BORN: 9 AUGUST 1951 IN DETROIT, MICHIGAN
Matthew SMITHHISLER 1957 - BORN: 14 MARCH 1957
Margaret M. BURKE 1956 - BORN: 14 APRIL 1956 IN KALAMAZOO, MICHIGAN
Randolph Charles HOLTZMAN 1957 - BORN: 8 JULY 1957
Robert Edward BURKE 1956 - BORN: 5 MAY 1956 IN KALAMAZOO, MICHIGAN
Lori Lynn STEINBAUER 1957- BORN: 1 SEPTEMBER 1957 IN LAPORTE, INDIANA
Susan Marie BURKE 1957 - BORN : 8 SEPTEMBER 1957 IN KALAMAZOO, MICHIGAN
Timothy James CURRY 1957 - BORN: 22 APRIL 1957 IN DETROIT, MICHIGAN
Susan Jeanne TROIANO 1973 - BORN: 9 APRIL 1973
Tyler Justin RAGO 1978 - BORN: 22 NOVEMBER 1978
Jill Marie SMITHHISLER 1976 - BORN: 6 DECEMBER 1976
Amy Lyon SMITHHISLER 1978 - BORN: 18 SEPTEMBER 1978
Erin Mckenzie SMITHHISLER 1993 - BORN: 29 JUNE 1993
Hannah Michele HOLTZMAN 1983 - BORN: 13 MARCH 1983
Rachel Jane HOLTZMAN 1987 - BORN: 8 FEBRUARY 1987
Allison Jane BURKE 1992 - BORN: 16 SEPTEMBER 1992 IN DURHAM, NC
Melissa Anee CURRY 1981 - BORN: 6 FEBRUARY 1981 IN PONTIAC, MICHIGAN
Amy Kathleen CURRY 1983 - BORN: 16 DECEMBER 1983 IN PONTIAC, MICHIGAN
Christopher James CURRY 1992 - BORN: 25 NOVEMBER 1992 IN COMMERCE, MICHIGAN

FAMILY CHART NO. 10 - Descendants of Ellen Lyons and Francis (Francois) Bienvenu 'dit' Delisle

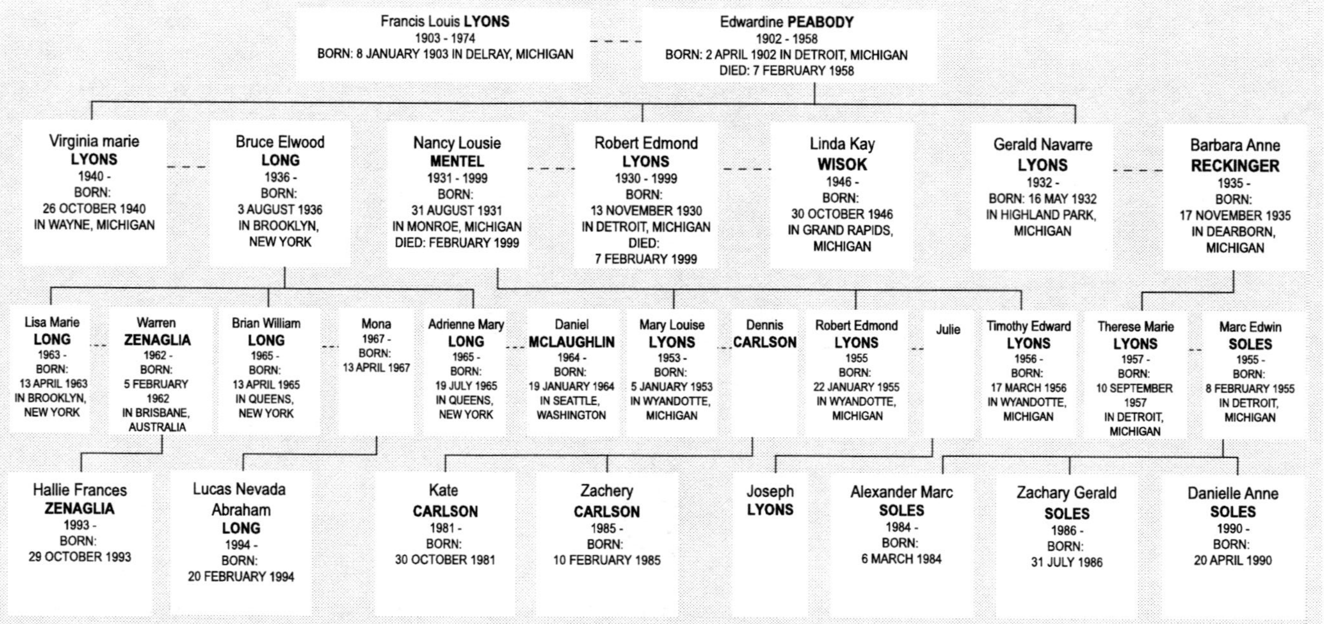
Francis Louis **LYONS**
1903 - 1974
BORN: 8 JANUARY 1903 IN DELRAY, MICHIGAN
Edwardine **PEABODY**
1902 - 1958
BORN: 2 APRIL 1902 IN DETROIT, MICHIGAN
DIED: 7 FEBRUARY 1958
Virginia marie **LYONS** 1940 - BORN: 26 OCTOBER 1940 IN WAYNE, MICHIGAN
Bruce Elwood **LONG** 1936 - BORN: 3 AUGUST 1936 IN BROOKLYN, NEW YORK
Nancy Lousie **MENTEL** 1931 - 1999 BORN: 31 AUGUST 1931 IN MONROE, MICHIGAN DIED: FEBRUARY 1999
Robert Edmond **LYONS** 1930 - 1999 BORN: 13 NOVEMBER 1930 IN DETROIT, MICHIGAN DIED: 7 FEBRUARY 1999
Linda Kay **WISOK** 1946 - BORN: 30 OCTOBER 1946 IN GRAND RAPIDS, MICHIGAN
Gerald Navarre **LYONS** 1932 - BORN: 16 MAY 1932 IN HIGHLAND PARK, MICHIGAN
Barbara Anne **RECKINGER** 1935 - BORN: 17 NOVEMBER 1935 IN DEARBORN, MICHIGAN
Lisa Marie **LONG** 1963 - BORN: 13 APRIL 1963 IN BROOKLYN, NEW YORK
Warren **ZENAGLIA** 1962 - BORN: 5 FEBRUARY 1962 IN BRISBANE, AUSTRALIA
Brian William **LONG** 1965 - BORN: 13 APRIL 1965 IN QUEENS, NEW YORK
Mona 1967 - BORN: 13 APRIL 1967
Adrienne Mary **LONG** 1965 - BORN: 19 JULY 1965 IN QUEENS, NEW YORK
Daniel **MCLAUGHLIN** 1964 - BORN: 19 JANUARY 1964 IN SEATTLE, WASHINGTON
Mary Louise **LYONS** 1953 - BORN: 5 JANUARY 1953 IN WYANDOTTE, MICHIGAN
Dennis **CARLSON**
Robert Edmond **LYONS** 1955 BORN: 22 JANUARY 1955 IN WYANDOTTE, MICHIGAN
Julie
Timothy Edward **LYONS** 1956 - BORN: 17 MARCH 1956 IN WYANDOTTE, MICHIGAN
Therese Marie **LYONS** 1957 - BORN: 10 SEPTEMBER 1957 IN DETROIT, MICHIGAN
Marc Edwin **SOLES** 1955 - BORN: 8 FEBRUARY 1955 IN DETROIT, MICHIGAN
Hallie Frances **ZENAGLIA** 1993 - BORN: 29 OCTOBER 1993
Lucas Nevada Abraham **LONG** 1994 - BORN: 20 FEBRUARY 1994
Kate **CARLSON** 1981 - BORN: 30 OCTOBER 1981
Zachery **CARLSON** 1985 - BORN: 10 FEBRUARY 1985
Joseph **LYONS**
Alexander Marc **SOLES** 1984 - BORN: 6 MARCH 1984
Zachary Gerald **SOLES** 1986 - BORN: 31 JULY 1986
Danielle Anne **SOLES** 1990 - BORN: 20 APRIL 1990